S0-ARL-470

"Life can only be understood backwards;
but it must be lived forwards."
- Søren Kierkegaard

This book is dedicated to my boys.

I have written about my life.
Other characters in this book might well
describe the same events differently,
but this is how it was for me.
- Eileen Dight

Plate Spinner

Eileen Dight

ISBN-13: 978-1463734459

ISBN-10: 146373445X

INTRODUCTION – WHY AM I WRITING MY MEMOIRS?

I shared with a friend the idea of writing a dust jacket before you write the book, which helps one to shape the contents and identify the parameters. I said that I'd made a spoof dust jacket on the computer and given it a title, *Plate Spinner*.

He replied 'I have to say the dust-jacket idea wouldn't work for me. I wouldn't do the victory-lap before the race. For a more measured person it could be inspirational, but for a non-completist like me it's inadvisable. I know of several people whose autobiographies should consist of a dust-jacket only and blank pages in the middle.'

Thinking about dust jackets I asked myself: Who am I writing my memoirs for? I'm writing them so they don't all disappear when I die, because I had some really interesting times, and so that my grandchildren and even great grandchildren will know who I was. I don't even remember the name of my father's mother, who died before I was born. She was always referred to as 'your grandmother' and it's terrible that her name escapes me. In raising my father, she shaped who I am. As my father was born in 1898 and was nearing forty in 1937, I have many Victorian values, although I'm up to date on issues like evolution, divorce, abortion and homosexuality. You adapt as you go along, but the way your parents were raised has a powerful influence on who you are, even when you don't realize it. I wish my grandparents had left some memoirs.

When my father was in his sixties I urged him to write down the stories he told me throughout my childhood. He was a great raconteur and had done a lot in his life (Royal Flying Corps in France in World War I, eight years as a merchant seaman sailing around the world, and he had a mind that always went on enquiring). I loved to hear his anecdotes of the time a rickshaw runner took him down a dark alley near the docks where two men were waiting to rob him. He pulled out his service revolver and they ran off, despite the fact that it wasn't loaded; and how he heard a musician playing a mandolin in Sorrento, and bought the instrument from him, regretting his own lack of expertise; about the time his fellow seaman spotted a barrel of whisky on the dockside and said 'Let's have a drink', pulling out the bung and tossing it away, and how my father fretted about the wasted remains draining into the dock; about the elephant carving he bought in Rangoon (I have it still). He saw a man carving and said he'd buy it if it was ready before his ship sailed, and the man worked all night. He showed me a book of pictures of the aftermath of Vesuvius' eruption that captivated my young imagination.

He told seafaring stories and sang me foreign songs, referring to the wicked women of Marseilles and the thieving natives of Valparaiso. On one occasion with friends he was sloping arms in a bar with a billiard cue and accidentally pierced an oil painting on the wall behind him. 'Please write your stories down so that I don't forget them when you've gone,' I begged him in my teens, but nary a one did he record and now the only fragments remaining are the ones I'll share with you.

So that's why I'm writing my memoirs. I'm in my seventies and my grandchildren range from 16 years to 3. My grandchildren in Australia didn't see me for nearly five years (except on Skype.) They know little of me, and so much of my influence, values, heart and energies have gone into loving and shaping them. It's not enough that my genes will persist (my mitochondria have been cut off, having no daughter): I want them to know *me*. I want their children to know me. Not just that I liked sewing, writing, cooking, could sing in tune, spoke Spanish and French and had a big heart. I want them to know that I was courageous when I travelled alone at twenty to Spain (without a word of Spanish) and spent 16 months there, learning every day, absorbing the Spanish language, customs, music, mores and attitudes. I want them to know that I had a sense of humour, and that I loved to teach and play with children. I want them to know how seriously I take work, how good it is to be creative, how one can adapt to all sorts of upheavals in life with a positive attitude, and overcome surprising setbacks. Why did my two marriages end in divorce? How did our family disperse globally? What shaped their fathers' characters? Where do their values come from?

How will they have a clue if I don't write to them, the unborn ones of the next generation or two? I probably won't live to see the current generation grow up and this is my way of being with them in mind when I'm in spirit. It's not just egoism, I hope. It's the desire to continue tending, loving and encouraging our young. So there will be no blank pages between my book covers. They are there for a purpose.

CONTENTS

1 EARLY DAYS

My earliest memory is starting to walk. I must have been about 12 months old. We were on the front lawn at Mottingham Gardens. I know this is not a false memory because I see the scene clearly from my own body. When I told my Mother about it in later years she had no recollection of it.

I am sitting on the grass. My Mother is a small distance ahead of me and my Father is somewhere to the left. I stand up and take a step, another, and another and suddenly my Mother screams and shouts. She must have been saying 'Fred! Look! She's walking!' or words to that effect but of course I didn't understand. Her scream startled me and I sat down heavily. Somehow, without the vocabulary, I had the insight, 'ah, this is how it works…' but I didn't try it again for a couple of days.

My brother remembers lying in his pram and looking up at the leaves. In those days it was the practice to put babies out in their prams in all weathers, warmly wrapped. My Mother spoke of brushing the snow off the pram cover. It was good for their lungs, she said. A 'pram' for the benefit of Americans, is a 'stroller' or buggy. We had large perambulators with four big wheels of the sort Prince Charles was pictured in, with strong hood and padded sides. My children had one, but we don't see those now. They went out of style in the seventies.

Memories of my early childhood are cut across by the Second World War. I don't remember my Father's father who died when I was small, but he was reputed to have wept when he saw me with a Mickey Mouse gas mask that was issued to babies. I was two and a half at the outbreak of war. People thought Hitler would immediately start to bomb England and many people were evacuated at the beginning, including me. We lived in south east London, exactly on the flight path between Germany and London. What had been a leafy suburban village ten miles from London's centre became a hazardous flight corridor. My Father decided that Mother should take my brother John (7) and me to North Wales, for safety. He probably took us in his Austin 7 car, unless by train, and installed us in a caravan at Rhyl, with my Mother's sister-in-law Maud and her three daughters. It must have been crowded. I remember seeing Maud and her girls sitting on the other side of the table in the small trailer. Recently I found an account of this time written when I was fifteen. It described how we went to the standpipe in the field for water, carried in a tall enamel pitcher, and how every time my Mother drew water from the standpipe, she sighed. I'm grateful to my fifteen year old self for remembering this, because I do not, and amazed that my two year old self noticed her Mother sighing. I have always been more aware of a person's mood than what they are wearing.

Recently I heard a story from my cousins who shared this experience that surprised me. Twins Pat and Maureen (7) had been left to watch Veronica and me as we paddled on the seashore. Suddenly a large wave knocked us into the surf. The twins managed to catch hold of us and pull us out, kicking and spluttering. All my life I've been afraid of water. My brother pushed me into the public swimming pool to encourage me when I was about eight, but I don't recommend this. I didn't learn to swim until I was 41. Veronica shares my fear and never learned to swim, despite taking lessons as an adult. I'm the only person I know who watches filmed underwater scenes and gasps for breath.

As summer ended my Mother, brother and I moved into a farmhouse as paying guests. The scent of wood smoke evokes this scene and I have loved it all my life: I picture the farmyard, with outbuildings around a midden, with troughs for cows to drink water, and a path that sloped up to the road beside the farm where a shed served as a tiny shop. In the cowshed there was a ladder and the farmer's son Johnny, not much older than me, took me up there one day. We were in the loft, looking down between slats on the backs of the cows, steam rising from them, when somebody closed the huge barn door and we were trapped. It was some time before they found us but I don't remember feeling anxious. *I* knew where I was.

The farmer's son showed me how to whack the cows with a stick to make them move. At first I was frightened, but soon discovered that the most a cow would do when I whacked its hind leg, was turn slowly around to stare at me. Then it would amble forward, towards the water trough. Once I fell in. We had the run of the yard and must have got very muddy. My Mother kept me in the kitchen one day and stood me on the draining board to watch through the window a bull that had 'gone mad' and gored a farm worker. The bull was pulled with ropes, kicking and bellowing in protest, up a ramp into a lorry. It was exciting.

In that sink the drain hole was so large that teaspoons were regularly lost. There was an infestation of mice in the farmhouse. My Mother claimed she had killed several with the flick of a wet tea cloth, but she was prone to exaggeration. I remember lying in bed with her asleep and feeling the tickle of a mouse on the top of my head, but being so tired I brushed it away and went to sleep.

My parents must have suffered from their separation. They were a loving couple and the fear that my Father was in peril if Hitler attacked England, must have been dreadful. Fred was lonely, living for months without his family and working in central London as an engineer surveyor. By 1939 he was 41. He came to visit us, on the train. I had a fluffy beige woollen coat with brown woven leather buttons, I called it my teddy bear coat, and I felt proud of it while waiting on the platform. I was the first to spot him in the crowd, ran forward, and he picked me up. Suddenly I felt shy. I don't remember what we did during that weekend until he took us to a pantomime. During the show he left us without saying goodbye. I was aware of him leaving but so engrossed in the show, I let it pass. How must he and my Mother have felt?

Margaret used to write to him. She used a fountain pen. One day she sent me on my first shopping expedition. By now I must have been just three. Go to the shop, she said, and buy me a bottle of ink. I felt thrilled. I set off with pennies in my hand and walked up the path to the shop in the shed. It had a sloping display board in front with all the things that were for sale. I said I would like a bottle of ink please. The woman said I'm sorry dear, I haven't got any ink. In that case, I said, I'll have a tin of sardines. My Mother laughed when I came back with sardines, but I was determined to make a purchase. And I loved sardines.

My brother was at school. The teacher insisted that he learn Welsh. Impossible, I've tried since to learn Welsh and it doesn't relate to any language I know. It has mutations and word stems that might have come from outer space. The teacher hit my brother on the head with a ruler when he could not sing the folk song Ar Hyd y Nos (All Through the Night) in Welsh. (Perhaps she was taking revenge on him for the way English teachers made Welsh children don a dunce's cap a century before, when they spoke Welsh in class.) It must have been distressing for him, an intelligent and sensitive child. Being only 3 most of the experience went over my head because I felt secure with my Mother.

While alone Fred slept under the stairs for safety. One night a bomb dropped in our garden only 15 ft. from the house, and my Father slept through it. When he got up in the morning he was surprised to find neighbours looking at the crater. Eventually my parents decided that they would rather take their chances together, than endure more separation, and my Father took us back to London.

In the garden he constructed an air raid shelter. He dug down a foot or two, installed an Anderson shelter with earth over the top and turf so it looked like a small hill. (The outline is still there today, with flowers all over it.) I played in it as a child but we never used it as a shelter. Instead we bought a sturdy cast iron table and base called a Morrison shelter, erected in the sitting room. Whenever the sirens sounded we dived underneath; it had a mattress and blankets so we could sleep if it was night time.

My Father acquired one of these Morrison shelters for some friends, who lived about five minutes' walk away. It saved their lives. When their house took a direct hit the shelter stopped the rubble from crushing them. There was terrible dust and destruction of course. They brought their three children to our house. They thought the baby was dead. He was covered in plaster and soot. My Mother put him in the sink and washed him and he recovered. Their house was not rebuilt until after the war.

Later in the war when we saw the first 'Buzz Bomb', a rocket with its tail on fire, we thought it was a damaged plane and that any minute the pilot would bail out; we didn't know they were unmanned and designed to crash when the fuel ran out. The sound of their engines was a deep, aggressive drone. If you heard a rocket's engine cut out you counted seconds, and if it was more than about five seconds you were all right. It would fall on someone else. These came by the dozen. The people who died often did not hear the engine stop as it glided silently to earth. One day my Mother had to turn off the pan of eggs and bacon for lunch three times, for air raids. She laughed (to reassure us?) as we dived yet again under the shelter without lunch. She was a remarkably resilient and good humoured woman.

When I was six the raids came thick and fast. My parents were distressed that I cried with anxiety. They discussed the possibility of my Mother taking us to stay with relatives in Wigan, north of England. I was so thrilled at the prospect that I cried even more, in order to visit my cousins. My brother stayed in London. By then he was eleven.

On this occasion my Father drove us to Lancashire, passing through Luton the day after it had been bombed. I saw chaos and destruction, fire engine hoses and rubble everywhere. My Mother and I spent a week or so with my Father's niece Peggy and her children, Brian, Wendy and Graham. At the end of their road was a camp for Italian prisoners of war. They used to talk to us over the hedge with a barbed wire fence. They loved to talk to children. I suppose they had their own in Italy. I imagine their life was tolerable, away from the fighting, sitting out the war with three meals a day and no pressure. In any case, they seemed cheerful.

Before the war, when I was two, I had eaten bananas. I remembered how delicious they were. After hostilities commenced bananas were no longer imported. We had neither the money for such frivolities nor the cargo space in ships that brought us essentials. I recall standing in the green grocer's one day, seeing a bunch on the shelf. 'Ooh, bananas!' I cried, and everybody laughed. They were plaster ones, a Fife advert. I was keenly disappointed. The first time we bought bananas after the war I hid the skin for a week in a brown paper bag under the what-not, so I could go and smell it whenever I wanted.

When the news was read on the radio I had to be quiet. My Father would follow the fortunes of the Eighth and Red Armies, towards the end of the war. My Mother's brothers John, Dick, Dennis and Con were in Italy and at some point met up. (Jim and Bill were too old). My Grandmother cried so much for her boys, she went blind. As a mother now of sons I understand her anguish. She recovered some vision later with an operation (she had cataracts and glaucoma). Only Dennis was injured, suffering bomb blast on a beach in Italy. He had to learn to walk and talk again. They all returned safely after the war.

I was eight years old, swinging around a lamp post near my house, playing with neighbours' children. 'The war has ended!' said one of them. 'Thank goodness for that,' I thought, 'now I won't have to be quiet while the news is on.' I thought the news would stop now that the war had ended.

I was less frightened by the bombs than you would suppose. I had total confidence that my parents would not let them drop on me. Their loving devotion provided me with a truly secure childhood. The rest of my life has not matched up to that confidence, but I was lucky to have it then. The values my parents passed on to me are the same ones I have tried to pass on to my sons.

2 THINGS WERE DIFFERENT THEN

I was born before sliced bread and supermarkets were invented. Things have changed a lot since 1937. We lived in a modern three bedroom semi (duplex) in Mottingham village, south east London on the border of Kent, later swallowed by suburbia.

When eggs were largely unobtainable, Fred kept four Rhode Island Red chickens in a henhouse in our garden which he built while I watched. He painted it with black creosote; the smell of creosote forever after evoking this scene. The chickens were named Goldie, Feather-eater, Scraggy-neck and Evil-eye. Aged three, I spent hours observing chickens, the way they moved and clucked, drank from a trough, beaks pointed upwards as they swallowed, squawking, slowly strutting: cackling with triumph when they laid an egg.

We bought groceries by the ounce, in twists of brown paper, strictly rationed and marked off in a book of coupons for each person. Sugar was spooned out of a large sack into a small paper cone. We got four ounces of butter per family of four one week, eight ounces the next, alternating weeks of deprivation. Our meals were often sandwiches. Margarine in those days tasted disgusting. It was made from whale fat, pale and tainted. Mummy mixed it with the butter to make it taste better. It made the butter taste worse. She sawed slices off a white loaf and occasionally she would cut herself. The only cheese available was Cheddar; my Father called it 'mouse-trap cheese'. Rationing continued until 1951.

I laid the table in the dining-cum-living room. The rectangular wooden table was covered by a red plush cloth with fringes, and spread with a white cotton tablecloth at meal times. In my head I recited the list: 'bread, butter, sugar, milk, knives, forks, plates, cups, saucers…' which reminds me that tea was always served with a meal, but I never drank it. To this day I hate the taste or even the smell of tea. My Mother chided me when I put a bottle of milk on the table one day, insisting it be served in a jug. I recall standing beside that table, about age 3, not quite tall enough to see over the top. My Father said affectionately, 'You're no good for anything, are you?' and I replied, 'I'm good for eating, Daddy.' How he laughed, and how I loved my Dad.

I started school aged four. The classroom windows were covered with criss-crossed sticky brown paper strips to minimize bomb blast. The windows at home, some blown out four times, had similar reinforcement.

We had our own pegs in the cloakroom at school on which we hung our coats and shoe-bags with plimsolls (tennis shoes) in case our feet got wet. The toilet blocks were separate from the school and sometimes we had to dash through the rain.

Everybody had blackout curtains to avoid creating targets for the Nazi bombers we could hear above us in the night on their way to central London. They sometimes dropped their bombs on us as they fled the anti-aircraft guns and searchlights that swept the sky in hot pursuit. One of these heavy guns (nicknamed 'Big Bertha') was stationed in the school grounds opposite. We heard them booming. In the large garden of the big Victorian house next door a barrage balloon was tethered to discourage low flying enemies, presumably to protect the battery.

One of many nights when the sirens wailed and we got out of bed to huddle under the shelter in the front room my brother John knotted his tie as he walked down the stairs, half asleep. It didn't strike him as odd to be so formal, but my Mother laughed.

We listened avidly to the radio. My Father never missed the news but I liked listening to a singer called Issy Bonn, (Let Me Call You Sweetheart), imagining him shrunk to the size of a pea so that he could walk inside the wires into our large wooden boxed wireless. I don't know how I thought the orchestras arrived. Later I followed 'Dick Barton, Special Agent,' with my ear close to the speaker turned low, while my Father wrote his reports. I can still hum the thrilling signature music to that.

We had no telephone, no fridge, no washing machine, and dryers and TVs had not been invented. My father mended our shoes on a cobbler's lathe. He would cut pieces of leather to shape and nail them on. One time he added studs to my sturdy, laced, unflattering brown shoes to prolong their life, because shoes were scarce in the war. I was mortified as my studs clanked on the concrete pavement. When our saucepans wore out my Father mended them with rivets.

A team of men came to remove the metal chain links between neighbours' gardens for scrap iron for the war effort. I watched them from the front lawn.

One day I stood on the bridge over the railway near Mottingham station, watching the steam train approach, its copious clouds briefly interrupted while passing under the bridge, resuming its sulphurous belch as it pulled into the platform. Doors slammed, the whistle blew and off it chugged again. (As the carriages went over the rails there was a tattoo sounding 'da-da-da-dum, da-da-da-dum', that you don't hear on modern trains.) I can still hear, smell and taste steam trains, pictured in my mind's eye. They sounded purposeful.

Once I was sent to an old cobbler who lived in the village, working from a tiny shed in his back garden with tacks between his lips and a genial smile as he hammered. He asked me if I knew how many days there are in a month? When I said I didn't, he taught me the rhyme 'Thirty days hath September, April, June and November. All the rest have thirty one, excepting February once in four, when February has just one day more.' This happened while I waited for him to mend my shoes. I never fail to remember him when I use that rhyme.

At the dentist's the drills were robust and slow. We had no anaesthetic for our fillings. Oh, the relief when high-speed drills were invented in my teens and moreover, you could ask for an injection. But those dentists (and lack of candy) saved our teeth and I was over seventy before my first extraction.

My tonsils were removed when I was seven. There were no relaxing drugs to give one the sense of trust and euphoria that accompanies modern surgery. I had to climb onto the operating table, lie down and watch as they put a mask over my face exuding foul tasting gas I fought to avoid, before it overcame me. It was the only time during the war that I was given ice cream and jelly to eat, in the hospital. Ice cream was generally unobtainable.

My Father maintained his own car and as his chief helper, I watched him replace the brake pads and grease the wheels. He demonstrated the clutch and gear system so I would understand its function. (Later he would teach me to drive, double de-clutching.) Small orange Bakelite arms lifted from the sides to indicate turning right or left, but Fred added hand signals to be certain. This meant driving with the windows open and there was no heater in the car. The windscreen could be opened outwards like a window; the car had a retractable roof to let in sunshine on good days. It was started with a winding handle. It had the power of seven horses. There was not a lot to go wrong on an Austin 7.

It was a luxury to own a car during the war. If your journey wasn't necessary, you were obliged to leave the car at home for lack of petrol. A family car supported on bricks to save the tyres was a common sight for the duration. Most people had to walk, bike or take buses.

Our car seated four and had no boot or trunk, but there was a flap on the back which could be lowered with a hinge to accommodate a suitcase and strap. Because my Father was in a reserved occupation (more useful to the state as an engineer than as a soldier) and needed to drive to the London factories he inspected, we always had (strictly rationed) petrol. In spring he would occasionally drive us into the country to the bluebell woods. I recall the vivid blue carpet of flowers amid the trees, and their fragrant, heady perfume. You don't 'pick' bluebells, you pull, and their white stems slip out. In late summer on a Sunday (Fred worked a six day week) we would occasionally tour Kent, looking for mushrooms. They grow naturally where horses have been. The white buttons gleamed in the green sward and tasted divine, fried in butter that evening. Wild mushrooms bear little resemblance to the cultivated fungi. They look similar but the flavour of natural ones is beyond imagining. Those were happy outings. My parents were always good natured and kind to us, and to each other. I thought the whole world was harmonious like that. It was many years before I learned it wasn't.

On several summer holidays after the war we toured the Cotswold region in Oxfordshire for two weeks at a time in the Austin 7. On rare occasions it made its top speed of sixty miles an hour when a wide straight road coincided with a jaunty mood. Mostly we drove at 30. My Father had bought the car new in 1939, and for the first two days of every holiday I was sick from the petrol fumes, until I became accustomed. We drove from one beautiful Cotswold village to the next, staying 'bed and breakfast' wherever we stopped. Distinctive local honey-coloured dry stone walls divided small fields in beautiful countryside. We lunched picnic-style, by the roadside, brewing tea on a small methylated spirit stove. My Father would take a nap under a hedge while we sat patiently. Sometimes he would hire a rowing boat and take me on the river. He taught me to row. My brother John would rather read his book. A highlight of those tours was exploring cemeteries beside ancient churches, hundreds of years old, reading the inscriptions on tombstones and speculating about the people named thereon. Some of the headstones had amusing epitaphs. Others were poignant, recording deaths of young mothers and babies. Contrast such a holiday with Disneyland today. I would still prefer the Cotswolds.

Children were far less entertained in those days. When my Mother snoozed in her chair (that stands in my bedroom today), I sat patiently waiting for her to wake up, watching the flames from the fire, listening to their hiss and flicker, smelling the coal. I was sometimes bored, but never moved or woke her. We had hardly any toys or books at all. My grandchildren in contrast play computer games or watch children's TV if I don't play with them. They have battery operated and electronic toys, jigsaw puzzles, I-pods and the Wii. Yet they are more easily bored than I ever was.

I recall lying on my back on the grass, watching white clouds scudding across the blue sky. Their speed is amazing on a windy day. In the same grass I watched busy ants and the red ones stung me. An owl sat hooting at dusk on top of the radio aerial in the garden, and red squirrels (almost extinct in England now) played in the trees. Flocks of sparrows (also now diminished), thrushes, blackbirds and occasional robins hopped in the garden. A robin will perch on your paused spade as you hold it, looking for tasty worms. We transplanted a suckling apple tree from my aunt's orchard and later enjoyed its unusual sweetness, which now I recognize as 'golden delicious'. My Mother planted marigolds and salvias. I set a packet of aubrietia seeds in a wooden tray which later filled the front border and flowered for many years. Every spring there were daffodils and tulips.

Early in the war a small bomb fell in the side garden, and my father took the opportunity to make a vegetable plot in the ruined lawn. He planted potatoes and I helped him harvest these gold nuggets from the brown earth. New potatoes with salt and butter are fit for a king. Our neighbour made blackcurrant cuttings and we established ten prolific bushes. Margaret made jam from the fruit without a recipe (or water); so solid, a knife would stand upright in it. Lettuces and radishes we grew in rows and Fred allowed me to pick them at an age when I was so small, he could walk me around with my feet on his, holding my hands and laughing. He always wore a waistcoat over his shirt, and when he hugged me my long hair tangled on the buttons. He would tenderly unwind it.

Casual clothes in those days meant overalls or an apron. My Father even went to the beach wearing his working suit and brown trilby hat. Our clothes were limited in number, without style, washed by hand with hard soap (detergents not yet invented), pegged on the line to dry and laboriously ironed. When the New Look came in after the war, my Mother bought a brown woollen dress with long skirt and fitted bodice. The look was 'New' because material was rationed and in short supply during the war, so skirts were short. Later I would remodel this dress and wear the skirt to work.

At fifteen, desperate for new clothes but lacking money, I started to make my own clothes and continued until I was past forty. I could make a new dress for pennies as material was cheap. At school in domestic science sewing lessons, we learned to make a blouse with its darts, gathered sleeves and button holes, perhaps the most practical lesson I ever had. We used sewing machines with winding handles. At home I used my Mother's treadle Singer. I was in my late thirties before I bought an electric sewing machine.

At seventeen I bought my first pair of jeans. My parents said, 'You're not going out in public in those, are you?' Photographs of those days show people in most unflattering gear. Hair was usually frizzed with a cheap home perm until it grew out. Nobody had heard of designer labels.

One of the most worrying prospects for a girl like me was the fear of becoming an old maid. Unmarried women had no status, no money, no love and no children. More than anything, I wanted children. If you were not married in my day by the age of 25, you were officially 'on the shelf'. This was a terrible tyranny, which I 'm relieved today is not an issue. I was 22 when one of our neighbours said chattily, cattily, 'And why did you never marry?'

We were also led to believe that girls do not need further education. My Mother said, 'You don't need to worry about school work, you're a girl and you'll get married and have a family.' My Father encouraged my schooling, and would have let me go to university if I'd wanted. My brother said helpfully, 'You should make her go!' (He was reading History at Kings.) But 95% of the teachers in my grammar school were unmarried and I was afraid that education would make me unmarriageable. That's another canard we never hear today. I did eventually graduate, aged 46, proud to add BSc (Econ) to my name.

There was a lot of hypocrisy in those days, especially about relationships. The word 'illegitimate' was muttered like a curse word. People sat in church and judged their neighbours. A few pregnant girls were sent away for months and their babies adopted in secret, or put in an orphanage. Some unmarried mothers were tragically put in mental hospitals and became institutionalized. Hypocrisy is definitely in shorter supply than it was fifty years ago.

We saved for everything we wanted. Credit cards had not been invented. When my Father discovered that at age 21 I had bought a radio on the 'never-never', with three monthly instalments, he went to the shop and paid for it, and I then had to pay him.

I don't think of them as the Good Old Days. Society was less dangerous in terms of muggings, drugs, STDs, scams and terrorists, but we had other hazards, notably shrapnel in the street, incendiary bombs which we sometimes managed to put out with a bucket of sand and water, posters showing Nazi booby traps although I never found one, conscription and the perennial tragedy of war, dead servicemen and civilians. For years after the war one could see London houses split vertically by bombs, with fireplaces, wallpaper and room features exposed like dolls' houses. It took years to rebuild parts of London.

Distances seemed longer, communications slower. Life was less affluent on every level. We had no central heating. My Mother's shins were mottled red from the living room coal fire, while her back froze away from it. But the post was reliable. Letters were delivered next morning for a penny stamp, everywhere in Britain. They were just different times, in some ways pleasanter, but in many ways deprived, compared to life today.

[I was amazed, when proof-checking this book, to discover recordings of Issy Bonn on YouTube, singing his melodious songs in the thirties.]

3 STARTING SCHOOL

It's 1941 and I'm four years old. I'm excited because I'm going to school for the first time. Mummy told me I'll enjoy it and meet other children. I'm wearing my red coat, feeling smart. I'm ready well before it's time to leave. I walk up and down the hallway, impatient to be off.

At the school gate Mummy is talking to another woman whose daughter is also called Eileen, starting school today. We walk into the building and hang our coats and shoe-bags on hooks in the cloakroom. There are gas wall lights. I reach up to touch a filament to feel its texture and am dismayed when it crumbles.

We're taught to raise our hands and ask, 'Please Miss, can I go to the lav?' This sounds crude to me. Mummy tells me to say 'May I be excused?' Miss always says yes, even during lessons.

We have small black slates with wooden frames and white chalk. I'm proud to have my own. We learn to do sums on them, add and take-away, and write letters and later words. My first teacher is Miss Boyteau with blonde hair, who smiles, and another is Miss Miller. She is strict but not unkind. Her hair is short. She is thin and not happy. We gradually learn to read, sounding the letters and stringing them together until we know what the words say. Soon I can read 'The cat sat on the mat'.

One of the girls in my class, Helen, knows a lot more than me. She tells me that my doll did not come from Father Christmas. I protest 'No, really, I got a stocking with presents from Father Christmas.' 'There's no such person, it's your parents who put it there.' I am deeply disappointed. I don't tell Mummy or Daddy because I'm afraid that will stop the presents. It's my first great disillusion.

The only picture on the wall is a drawing of a booby trap allegedly dropped by Germans to blow up when people touch them, so we are warned not to. It looks interesting and complicated when I study it, but I make a mental note to leave it well alone if I find one. The most I ever find is pieces of shrapnel in the roadway on my way to school. Most kids have some of that. One of the boys wants the piece I have and offers to swap it, but this is the first I've heard of swapping, and I'm suspicious. I keep my shrapnel.

Walking alone to school at age 7, I get as far as the hardware shop where my father once bought a bucket, when the air raid siren sounds, a familiar rising and falling wail. I run on to school because it's nearer. We can hear planes overhead as we huddle in the air raid shelter. In there it is dark and musty, lined with benches, and the teachers have us singing to keep our spirits up. It works. I like singing. I become engrossed in the music and am only slightly distracted by the sound of bombs dropping.

One day we have a sale of work for 'Waifs and Strays' and for sixpence we can take a lucky dip for a surprise in a packet. It's exciting. I dip my hands into the sawdust and rummage, feeling the lumpy packets. I select a large one, with disappointing contents (a glass necklace). Somebody tells me that 'good things come in small packages', and they choose a small one, which is definitely better than mine. Forever after I will remember this lesson. I think about watches and diamonds.

I'm reading at six and thrilled by the world of books. My brother pushes my old pram to the library every week to carry home his books. He often requests obscure ones (he is described as a 'book worm'). He takes me to the library too. The librarian tests my reading to be sure I can read. I read to her easily, and am given a library ticket. Books for children are in the far left corner, and over the next few years I will read most of them, including all of Biggles and Warrells, all of Arthur Ransome's Swallows and Amazons stories, The Secret Garden, I Capture the Castle, Treasure Island, Anne of Green Gables, Pollyanna, a book about an actress in repertory theatre named Carol, and Sue Barton Rural Nurse. I decide I'm going to be a nurse when I grow up. As soon as I can read I think about becoming a writer.

Every week I get a copy of *Sunny Stories*, mostly written by Enid Blyton. It costs two-pence. I read it cover to cover. (It will be years before Miss Blyton is labelled 'politically incorrect, middle class and a chauvinist'.) It's where I first meet Noddy and Big Ears. There is a story about a boy with hiccups, and today I still quote 'He's got the hee-cups' to my grandson. Another story is about 'eating humble pie', from which I learn a valuable lifelong lesson, that it is easier to apologize than to prolong a stand-off. My brother considers my taste needs improving and cancels *Sunny Stories* at the paper shop, substituting *The Children's Newspaper*. I object, and to my relief our Mother reverses his decision. John is the object of my unqualified admiration. School friends say 'You are always talking about your brother!' He refers to me as his 'blister'.

In my last term at primary school, aged 7, I'm appointed conductor of the school orchestra (percussion and combs with tissue paper). I can still remember the tune, standing on a wooden chair, signalling each section when to come in, conducting to a beat of four, hands up, down, across, out and up again. There is a maypole and I long to dance around it but am told 'No, you are too busy conducting'.

One day there's a new fashion. Several children wear sandals. It sparks a yearning in me for a pair in red or blue. I beg for them, but Mummy says they are dangerous - they leave the toes exposed and I might get hurt. Daddy agrees. It's a risk I'm prepared to take, but I don't get them. I still have lace-up shoes with metal studs.

There are only a few children who stand out in memory now. Valerie smells because she regularly wets her pants. Nobody wants to sit on the wooden chair after her. She is permanently troubled and pinched-looking and never smiles. I don't talk to her either.

John Inkpen is an attractive character, with a shock of curly hair, freckles and a mischievous face. He is full of fun, and seems to like me because he always plays nearby and looks at me. When we play kiss chase in the playground he always chases me. He is the first boy I like, but I leave that school at age seven and never see him again.

Eileen T. is always somewhere around, although never a close friend. We will keep in touch all our lives. She emigrates in her twenties to Massachusetts and becomes a well-known judge and scorer at equestrian events. I play at Eileen's house often; she lives near me and has a green tricycle (which I covet) and they have a refrigerator, which we do not. Her mother gives us glasses of orange squash (another luxury) with ice cubes, so I go there often. This must be after the war, when we are eight. Eileen is mad about horses and spends her pocket money on a bun for the baker's horse although in later years she denies this. But I remember clearly because there is no way I would share my bun with a horse, even if I had a bun, which I don't. Her parents are freer with money than mine. Her father is a nice man. After the war he's a steward on passenger ships.

My father must have noticed I use a lot of toilet paper, because one day he tells me that I should take only three or four sheets of paper, fold each in half and use it carefully; otherwise it might block the toilet. During the war the only toilet paper we have is newspaper cut into squares, threaded on string with an upholstery needle. Toilet paper is unobtainable, like ice cream, candy, tooth paste, imported fruit and other inessentials. (We're told you can clean teeth with soot, although we never try it.) Every last resource is dedicated to the war effort. To this day I still fold three or four paper sheets in half and think of my beloved father. (Recently I taught my grandsons in Virginia to do this, thinking fondly of my Father.) One day when I'm about nine, my mother is waiting to be served in a chemist shop and I'm standing beside her. A man in front of us asks for toilet paper. The assistant asks, 'Which brand would you like, sir?' and he says without hesitation, 'The best quality'. My mother turns to me, grins and whispers 'He's got a lot of respect for his bottom,' and I, a prude, am ashamed of her, tutting, till she stops.

My Mother often meets me after school and every time I see her, my heart lifts. I feel the flutter in my chest. She is so pretty and I'm so proud. She smiles a lot and talks to everyone. She often wears an emerald green dress that sets off her shiny blond hair. She colours it with peroxide in a saucer which she sets on the mantle-piece before the mirror and dips in cotton wool which she dabs on her hair. My Father says, 'I wish you wouldn't do that, Chick.' He always calls her Chick, although her name is Margaret. She laughs and carries on until many years later, after he has died; her hair is grey all over when she stops.

My parents often put their arms around each other for a cuddle. They include me in their hugs. My brother is too independent for such nonsense, although he likes to wrestle with our Father. All my childhood I believe that I'm the best thing that ever happened to my parents, and it gives me confidence.

I went back to see my first school in Mottingham, with Andre a few years ago. The original Victorian building is obscured by ugly later additions front and back, taking up the asphalt playground. The trees where we played mob are cut down. It's still a primary school, seventy years later.

We looked inside the library too, which has hardly changed.

4 THE GRAMOPHONE

There was a tiny green and gold tin box with a hinged lid, less than half the size of a box of matches. It contained many brass gramophone needles, each of which could only be used once, held in place by a screw adjustment. The turntable was housed inside a polished wooden box with bevelled lid, and a handle protruded from the side with which to wind it. Every record required winding in advance, and if it was a little long, the speed dropped and the notes with it, so one had to wind it again to finish the song before it ground to a halt.

I was a willing handle-winder. The box stood on a low table, just the right height for me to read the label 'His Master's Voice'. I must have been about six to read the words with such a sense of triumph. In the picture a dog sat beside the trumpet of a gramophone, on a green background. I asked my Father what he was doing and he explained. I imagined the dog listening.

The records were made before vinyl was invented. Perhaps they were made of Bakelite. We were repeatedly told 'Be careful, they are valuable.' We handled them with reverence.

There were about twenty records at most, mainly songs. My Father's taste included Gilbert and Sullivan, 'Three Little Maids from School are We' from the Mikado. 'The Floral Dance' was on one side of a record and 'A Wandering Minstrel, I' on the other. There were arias by Caruso, and airs from Puccini's Madame Butterfly. There was one record for me and I sang along: 'Polly Put the Kettle On', and 'Hey Diddle, Diddle' on the reverse. Daddy always smiled when I sang.

I can still sing some of those songs. There were not many to learn. As I got older I listened repeatedly until I had written down the words and learned them by heart. Every time we heard Caruso's rich tenor voice singing in Italian my parents revered its quality.

In my early teens my brother listened to classical music on the radio and taught me to distinguish between Mozart, Bach, Beethoven, Handel and Haydn. 'Who composed this, Eileen?' He could not tolerate, and tried to suppress, my taste for popular music, which of course made me keener.

Years later I came naturally to appreciate classical music. My early resistance in part fostered by my brother, dissipated. The ear he helped to train listened. Now I heard the shape of movements, the orchestration, musicality, invention and wit of the composer. I respond to the intelligence and dignity of music and am seduced by melody. I still do not appreciate dissonant chords in modern or jazz music. Some of my favourite pieces are Requiems (Mozart, Faure). I was exhilarated when I discovered Monteverdi.

For my twenty-first birthday my parents bought me an electric record player with a bright red case and automatic arm to lower a small number of records in turn onto the turntable. I bought 'Mr Wonderful' on a 45 rpm disk, 'Rock Around the Clock', *'Domani'* and *'Que Sera Sera'.* I bought Nat King Cole's long player including 'Get your Kicks on Route 66.' (I didn't know where Route 66 was, or that I would one day drive on it.) I sat with my boyfriend on my parents' living room sofa listening to West Side Story night after night. I can still sing every word. 'Hey, Officer Krupsky, you're really a square…'. And 'Maria, I just met a girl named Maria…' One day I accidentally dropped a pair of scissors on the record while it was playing, and forever after the needle stuck at the point, 'I feel pretty'.

My father died in 1965 and his records remained un-played. The player and the record box collected dust under the stairs for thirty years, in later years under my stairs, moving many times. My Mother died in 1995 and my brother said he wanted the records. When I opened the box the valuable records were beginning to crumble, no doubt unplayable.

Today my grandchildren have I-pods (one each) onto which they download thousands of songs from the internet and enjoy them on tiny earpieces. I don't know how they choose from thousands. I bet they don't know all the words. If they want to share the music they play it on the computer or email it to their friends, with a forward click. I wonder how they will experience music sixty years from now. Humming 'A wandering minstrel, I' today, I realize I'm straight out of the Ark.

5 MISS CATO

I was in Miss Cato's class at the Catholic school for two years from the age of eight. There were 43 pupils in the class aged 7 to 10. Most of the teachers were nuns. Miss Cato had thick grey hair in a pudding basin haircut, ruddy cheeks, a stocky body in its forties, brogues and fat legs in lisle stockings. She wore tweed suits and woollen jumpers. She kept good discipline and was not afraid of anyone. She didn't try to be popular and did not smile a lot, but she was just and reasonable and we knew where we stood. One couldn't describe her as kind, but she was not unpleasant to the children and she was fully in control.

She gave us a solid grounding in reading, writing and arithmetic. She taught us our tables with a long pointer to the blackboard as we chanted in unison. She taught the whole class at once, which is remarkable considering age range and numbers. No small work groups for us. Talking was not allowed in class. We sat at desks in rows, and wrote with pencils. Miss Cato wrote words and numbers on the blackboard with chalk, which we had to copy. She was hot on spelling. I give her credit for my early ability to spell.

At playtime we were given milk in third-pint glass bottles and urged to save the silver foil caps for recycling, although it wasn't called that then. It was 1945 and everything was rationed. We had quite good cooked school dinners.

Occasionally Miss Cato would allow a little light relief on a Friday afternoon when we were invited to sing or say a poem in front of the class. I always offered to sing. It was my earliest opportunity to gain confidence before an audience.

Miss Cato would sometimes urge us to 'use a little elbow grease'. Sad to say, I never understood this direction. I wondered what elbow grease was, and where could you buy it? I imagined a small round shallow tin of it, like my Mother's floor polish, and I was mystified about its purpose.

The youngest boy, the only seven year old in our class, was called Patrick. He had a cheeky smile and was often in trouble for his ebullient nature, but I was amazed when Miss Cato smiled at Patrick's naughtiness. Years later I named a son after that mischievous small boy.

In retrospect Miss Cato was probably a lonely spinster, unfair of face and prematurely stout. But she had a purpose and we were the beneficiaries. When I later chided my teenage sons for their poor spelling they would say 'It doesn't matter, Mum, this is History homework, not English,' and I would recall Miss Cato's face and her determination to instil correctness.

6 FRED NAYLOR

My Father, Frederick Naylor, was born in 1898 to English parents living in Ditton, Widnes, Lancashire. During the Industrial Revolution rural people in Britain moved about in search of jobs, but Fred's families had probably lived there for generations. His father was a railway engineer and his grandfather was the village blacksmith. Fred attended the local school and his school books showed that at ten he spelled perfectly in copperplate handwriting. At fourteen he left school and was apprenticed to be a fitter. His best friend, Peter Marsh, took the same path. In 1915 Fred declared himself to be two years older than seventeen, and joined the British Forces. He didn't tell his Mother in advance. Her dismay can only be imagined. If she had realized that he would never come home again to live in Lancashire, it would have been even harder. Early in her marriage his mother had taken in washing to supplement their income, but later she became a woman who rested every afternoon and came downstairs for tea in a black dress with white lace collar. Her son would bring her mementoes from his sailing trips around the world, like a Japanese what-not, a fine Chinese porcelain tea set and a woodcarving from Rangoon. When she died she was laid out in the parlour for friends to visit. An old neighbour came, doffed his cap and said respectfully, 'Goodneet, Mrs.'

My Grandfather in later years was appointed Relieving Officer by the Board of Guardians. He was the first person in the district to own a car. He personally distributed the modest support of a few shillings to buy shoes for children who were unshod, or food for hungry families. I don't know if this was a paid or honorary appointment, but when he retired he was presented with a handsome air rifle engraved with his name and the appreciation of the Board of Guardians. As a child I became a crack shot, shooting match boxes for target practice in the back garden. To my brother's regret and mine, my Mother gave this relic to a passing rag-and-bone man after my Father's death. I suppose she thought she had no further use for it.

At seventeen my Father was posted to France in the Royal Flying Corps, maintaining the first biplanes of the future Royal Air Force. He was entirely green, for the first time away from home and from an essentially rural background. He asked in his first camp, civilly, 'Sergeant, where do we sleep?' and the man barked, 'Anywhere!' He slept that night on the floor with his head resting on a fireplace fender.

(The first airplane flew in 1903, and the first bombing raid was by a single Italian pilot over Libya with a small suitcase of round bombs and a spare one in his pocket, in 1911. The word 'bomber' had not yet been invented.)

Airplane mechanic in World War One was a safer job than fighting in the trenches, but occasionally Fred was sent to retrieve a crashed engine across enemy lines. One evening he was about to set out on such a trip when he was told to go on guard duty. 'But I'm going to pick up a wreck' he said, and the officer barked 'Obey the last order!' Fred went on guard duty; his friend took his place, and was killed that night. On that thread hung not only his life, but the lives of all our family that followed.

He told me that once a pilot described a strange noise in his engine and Fred said 'Take me up to let me listen to it.' When Fred stepped out of the cockpit and onto the wing of the biplane to hear better, the pilot was horrified and shouted 'Get back in, you fool!'

Fred was there when the Red Baron crashed in an airfield, after being shot down by the British. As they pulled him out of the wreckage Fred noted his strong hair and healthy features, and thought how sad that such a vital young man was dead. He had photo frames made from both ends of a polished wooden propeller, which rested on the mantelpiece at home with photos of my parents.

In 1918 Fred arrived at the small Belgian village of Clermont, near Charleroi. A flat field nearby served as a landing ground. The liberating forces were warmly welcomed by the villagers. He rigged up the first electric light to shine in that village, using an army lorry as generator. He formed a friendship with the people with whom he billeted, Laurence and Alexander Niset, who later became the district electricians. He went back to see them in the 1920's. I am still in touch today, 93 years later, with their daughter Emerance (born like me, in the thirties).

In 1945 when the villagers of Clermont wanted to let young men in the Resistance know that they could soon come out of hiding in the woods they sent a message that 'Frederique is coming down the road' and this was understood by the locals. He was legendary in the village.

In all my life I have never experienced a warmer welcome than we received in 1946 on our first visit, when I was nine. They served us seven course meals every evening, digging their best wine, covered in cobwebs, out of the underground cache where it was hidden during the Nazi occupation. In WWII Laurence had been obliged to sip 18 cups of coffee every morning before the Germans billeted with her would drink it. On that visit my Father was the only French speaker in our family. He taught me to say *'Donnez moi une tasse de thé, avec sucre s'il vous plaît,'* without either of us recalling that I didn't drink tea. I played shops with the children in the attic, where they kept a grain store, learning my first words of French.

I was fifteen when we went again. As we walked around the village, talking to everyone we passed, I said to my Father 'I could never live here.' 'Why is that?' he asked. 'Because all that ever happens here is you get born, you grow up, you get married, you have children and you die.' He smiled. 'That is all that ever happens anywhere', he said.

Fred's war experience deeply affected him and forever after he realized his good fortune to have survived. After the war he went to see the film 'All Quiet on The Western Front', but half an hour into it he had to leave the cinema in tears.

Richard and I took the boys to Clermont in our camping van in 1978. Laurence was still alive. She spoke fondly of Frederique and gave me the silver RFC wings brooch my father had given her sixty years before. I wept.

Fred was full of anecdotes and I loved these vignettes. One day as a youth he was sitting on a bench in the sunshine when an old man sitting next to him said, 'Art married, lad?' 'No.' 'Thee doan't,' said the old man, with feeling: six words that spoke a volume.

Today my father would be 113. He died in January 1965. Of his grandchildren he saw only my Peter and James, my brother's only child. Eventually he would have six grandsons and fourteen great-grandchildren.

He would be astonished at the way those offspring have gone into orbit, living in four different continents. He was the first to wander, of course. After the War he couldn't settle in Lancashire, and joined the Merchant Navy. For seven years he sailed around the world while studying for his Chief's Ticket to qualify as first engineer. He married Margaret and they settled in southeast London, where they lived until he died. My parents' preferred holidays were in Paris. He enjoyed travel and entertained us with stories of Valparaiso, Rangoon, the Red Sea ('the hottest place on earth' he said), the Far East and so on. He told stories of people and scenes he saw on his travels. I was an avid listener. He had a world view, which was unusual in those days. His time in France and Belgium during the First World War had given him a taste for other cultures, French and wine, at a time when his peers drank only beer. He studied French all his life; his vocabulary was beyond my brother's at 18, doing university entrance exams. He was entirely self-educated. When he died the reading matter beside his bed was in French: *Moliere* and *Guy de Maupassant*.

He had a philosophical turn of mind. He once posed the question to me over a glass of beer in my twenties: how is it that we replace every cell in our bodies every seven years, and yet we retain our memories? He had the driest sense of humour; people seldom knew when he was joking because he kept a straight face. But his core stance was serious. He had strong principles, had been brought up a Wesleyan and his sense of honesty and straight dealing was absolute. He was conscientious in his work. Testing boilers for weaknesses with a hammer, he was half deafened by the blows. He used a typewriter and two fingers to fill in his daily reports. One day he was moving a pile of coal into a new bunker he had built from the old Morrison shelter, after the war. My mother, helping him, threw a piece of coal which hit his index finger, causing an injury so severe, forever afterwards he typed with that finger sticking up.

He deplored any show of pretentiousness, and pricked the bubble of pomposity. I told him that a friend's father wore leather driving gloves, and he said 'You tell him I can drive without them.' He never claimed to be anything but working class, although he voted Conservative, had a car, a salary, a mortgage and savings. He was sensitive and tuned in to a small girl who loved and trusted him completely. At night as I lay in bed he always came to say goodnight, and listened if I had concerns. I think he came to put my worries to bed. He never laughed at me for being over sensitive. I remember asking him when I was about eight, and had been told at school that we must love everybody equally (Catholic rhetoric), 'Does it matter if I love you more than Mummy?' 'No.' 'Does it matter if I love you more than a black man?' 'No, it's alright', he reassured me, completely serious and understanding. I weep now as I write, reliving the loss I felt at losing such an understanding father. He was an act impossible to follow.

He told me that as a boy, he knew every clump of grass in his village. (If he knew that his part of Lancashire is Cheshire now, he would turn in his grave.) He used to take the farmer's dog ratting. The dog would go down the sewer with Fred's encouragement. They would come back happy but filthy and Farmer Williams could not understand it. He would chuckle as he told me this. Fred had a strong sense of mischief as a boy. He described how he tied the door knockers together on adjacent house doors in a terrace and knocked on both doors simultaneously; he watched the fun as both housewives tugged to open their doors. He filled a tea packet with sand, left it in the road, and watched from behind a hedge as a passer-by spotted it, looked around, then picked it up and put it in her basket. He used to say 'We made our own fun.'

Fred was one of six children, by far the most intelligent and enterprising of them, although I didn't know his sister Emily, who died young; she was a nurse. Her daughter Peggy was Wendy's mother. I was interested to learn from Wendy (who lives in Perth, Australia now) that her grandmother Emily enjoyed sewing patchwork. Fred's brother Bill could play half a dozen musical instruments and sing tunefully. My Father's only musical talent was to play the mandolin. He would fetch it when I asked, and play the tunes he and my Mother used to sing: Home on the Range, Because I Love You, With Someone Like You, Rosemarie. His singing range was one octave but my Mother and I could sing two, and in good tune. His head shook as he sang, and I teased him.

Fred's sister Alice married Bert and lived in a two-up, two-down terrace house like the ones in Coronation Street, within walking distance of their childhood home. She rode an upright bicycle until her seventies. She had a loud voice and bulky figure, and Bert was a quiet little man who left no impression beyond that. We called on them one day and she gave us our first taste of instant coffee, but using only half a teaspoon per cup, we were not convinced.

There was also a sister called Jessie, but all I remember of her is her policeman husband.

Daddy's brother Ernie was a painter and decorator. His wife and baby had died in childbirth before I was born and he was a lonely man with a sharp sense of humour and beautiful piercing eyes like my Father's (and like Patrick's son Harry). He boarded with a spinster cousin and her ageing parents in a terrace house. He married the cousin (Aunty Alice Marsh) late in life, when he retired. I was intrigued when her lingering, arguing parents eventually died in their nineties, within months of each other, asking 'What did they die of, what got them in the end?' and my parents laughed. I was reminded only this week when teaching Jake to peel a hard-boiled egg, of Aunty Alice's trick to insert the handle of a teaspoon under the cracked shell. Uncle Ernie always teased me. It was his idea of fun (not always mine). One day when I was about three we were eating winkles with bread and butter for our tea, and I called for 'Pins, pins!' and forever after he called me 'Pins'. He never failed to send me a pound for birthdays and Christmas (a generous amount in those days). Sometimes he came to London for the Rugby match at Wembley when Widnes was in the finals. He chided me playfully one day, 'You talk like a halfpenny book,' which annoyed me, but I loved him really. After the war he introduced us to the new emulsion paint, and showed us the first paint roller. He died the same week as my Father, mercifully both in ignorance of each other's death.

Fred's sister Floss was intelligent but limited by her narrow environment. She married a nice man with a big smile, Sam Booth, who drove a lorry and was not as sharp as she was, but had a more cheerful outlook. They had one son called Arthur who played a trumpet in a marching band. They bought a three bedroom semi a couple of streets from where she was born, and never went anywhere. She was a discontented woman who suffered migraines; I think she would have flourished with a little education. The others never progressed from the workers' cottages they lived in and they all had modest occupations. My Father respected my grandfather's intellect and there must have been intelligent genes in the family, because my brother was academically and professionally successful, as author and managing director of two publishing companies.

Fred's best friend Peter Marsh joined the RFC with Fred. Fred's officer was the son of the owner of Bibby Line Shipping. At his suggestion they joined the Merchant Navy after the War. Fred was engaged to Peter's sister Gertie Marsh (a school teacher) for years, but she tired of waiting for him to finish his exams, away at sea for months at a time, and married a local garage owner. Fred was devastated.

Peter and Fred later worked for the same Vulcan Insurance company as engineer surveyors in the North and South of England respectively, until they retired. Peter met Eileen Higgins while in port at Tilbury, Essex, and married her. He took Fred to meet Eileen's family and eventually Fred married her younger sister Margaret. He was 32 and she was ten years younger. He used to tell me 'I thought I'd missed the bus and that I'd never get married'.

(My Mother's sister Eileen died aged 27 from peritonitis. My parents, just married, looked after her baby Paddy for some months until her father Peter could take care of her again.)

My father was totally dedicated to his family. He hated his work - it was dirty and soulless, he should have been a teacher, but it paid well and he was employed when many in the nineteen thirties were not. He never passed his work frustrations on to us. He took pleasure in us, and my parents' devotion afforded me a lasting sense of security and self-worth.

Gardening with my Father was one of the highlights of my childhood. I felt excitement as we dug potatoes from his vegetable patch: new white tubers emerging from the earth like nuggets of gold. I can smell the earth he rubbed from them. We boiled them with mint and ate them with butter. We grew lettuce and radishes, tomatoes, blackcurrants, leeks and Brussels sprouts. We kept chickens for their eggs when food was rationed. In all these activities I was his small shadow. (My brother's head was always in a book.) I held Fred's tools, standing beside him as he worked at his bench. Today I see his hands in my sons. Some of the tools he made as an apprentice fitter reside today in a toolbox in Arizona: measuring callipers, devices for making screw threads, and so on. His hammer, pliers and bradawls are still in use.

Fred was frugal by training and inclination. He never threw away an item he could mend. He left enough money to buy a thousand saucepans, but I recall him mending holes in them with rivets, and replacing lost lid handles with homemade metal ones. My Father made lampshades which my Mother covered - notably a wooden chandelier with four pink shaded lamps. The wire hoops were shaped around saucepans. All evening he worked with metal frame in one hand, soldering iron in the other. He heated the iron in my Mother's gas cooker flame and with both hands occupied, cooled it by spitting on the sizzling solder. It was a laborious process. One evening he rested the finished lampshade frame on his armchair while he went to brew some tea. On his return, mug in hand, he sat on the frame and flattened it. His face was a picture that made us laugh for years afterwards, whenever we recalled it.

In 1939 he bought a new Austin 7. He was accustomed to changing cars every two years for a new one, but during the war new cars were unobtainable. Resources were channelled into armaments. He ordered a new car after the war, was on a waiting list for two years, and when it became available he decided to keep the old one a little longer. He maintained it himself. The car lasted until he died in 1965, when my Mother gave it to his colleague's student son. We couldn't watch it go, it held so much of his presence. Fred would never have understood conspicuous consumption. Having no desire to impress anyone, and no respect for anyone who sought to impress, modesty came naturally.

In later years Fred was afflicted by lumbago and migraines. He suffered from depression after early retirement at sixty, with high blood pressure. I think the medication in those days had that effect. Otherwise he had a good constitution. He was six feet tall and never ran to fat. His blond hair had turned white by the time I was born. He set a standard of loving care that I never found thereafter. Seeing him with our Mother, I thought all marriages were happy. He would be sad that I have twice divorced, but he would be sadder still if I had stayed in those marriages.

He was nearly forty when I was born and my youngest children, the twins, were born when I was 33, so there was a long generation bridge from Victorian to Elizabethan times. It echoes today, as my grandsons Connor and Jake in America say please and thank you conscientiously. My Mother had a strong in-put, and her mother too.

John Paul in Arizona read an account I wrote of Fred's life, and said that driving his second hand car to work, he now realizes where his own frugality comes from. His peers all drive expensive new cars on credit; he has money in the bank and owns his seven year old car outright. In England Peter skilfully keeps bees (an interest inherited from his father) and grows vegetables in his allotment. His honey and homemade preserves win prizes at the Village Fete. In Dublin Patrick went to sleep feeling lucky after he found a fifty Euro note sticking out of the ATM machine one evening, but in the morning inheriting my father's honesty, he telephoned the bank to transfer fifty Euros from his account to the previous customer's. In Australia his grandson Mark, a lawyer, reads and writes poetry and enjoys Shakespeare, a book always beside his bed. In Virginia his grandson Andre makes wooden bird boxes, cultivates his garden and tenderly cares for his family.

I wonder, if Fred could see his family now, what would he think? Many of his values are exemplified in our lives. How I wish he could see my children and grandchildren. I recall him crawling on the floor with Peter riding on his back. It was the Christmas before he died of a brain haemorrhage at the age of 67 when Peter was 21 months. He chuckled indulgently at the little fellow. He would be pleased to see his grandsons establishing homes and nurturing their families. His influence on the way they live is vastly more than they imagine. Although they never knew him, he was there, influencing the way I brought them up, and he is here now in their genes and in our values.

Recently I came across this quotation from the Talmud: 'When you teach your son, you are teaching your son's son.' The same goes for daughters.

Hamlet said 'The evil that man does lives after him, the good is oft interred with his bones.' Fred Naylor never did anyone a bad turn, and the good he did lives on.

7 THANK GOD FOR EDUCATION

My Mother Margaret (Maggie Higgins) used to say, 'One day I was beating the mat hung over the garden gate, and I thought 'Is this all there is?' This vignette encapsulated her sense of deprivation. I think that's the cry of a woman who suffered from lack of education. Her teachers were nuns who themselves were ignorant, whose most memorable lesson was silencing the class, dropping a pin which they were all supposed to hear, and saying 'Forever and ever your soul will burn in hell if you don't go to Mass on Sundays.'

Margaret left school shortly before her fourteenth birthday, going to work in her aunt's boarding house where she made the beds, scrubbed the floors and emptied the chamber pots. For this she was paid 2s.6d a week, most of which she sent home (she was the fourth of nine children). Her aunt complained because she used too much water when she scrubbed the floor. My Mother was an exemplary and energetic cleaner.

Later Margaret worked in Jurgens margarine factory. When she married my Father she thought herself fortunate never to have to work again. She had two children and kept the house immaculate, dusting and polishing every day. She planted flowers in the garden. She took craft classes in basketwork. She did voluntary nursing at fifty to counteract her empty nest. After my father died when she was 57, she worked as a nurse in an old people's home, caring for the residents, handing out the medicines, becoming the proprietor's right hand woman. My father had left her a pension. She didn't need to work, but she relished the activity, was energetic and took her role seriously. I think she would have made a good business woman.

For seventeen years she called almost daily on an old lady, Miss Rastin, to do her shopping. Before that she took out Aunty Rastin's niece in a wheelchair. Mary was in her twenties when we met her in the park, wheelchair bound after a traumatic experience when her house was bombed during the war. After Mary died my Mother continued to keep a friendly eye on Aunty Rastin. After she died her appreciative nephew, Charles Craft, sent flowers to my Mother every Christmas, until she died.

Despite her lack of education, my Mother was a resourceful lateral thinker. When the sheets on my washing line threatened to drag on the grass, she found a strong branch, lopped off its twigs and used it as a prop. Again and again I noticed her solutions for small problems that flummoxed my more conventional approach. Her school reports had dubbed her 'Intelligent with a lazy brain'. But my Mother was not lazy. All her life she worked with vigour and generosity. She didn't need a gym to keep her fit. Without her I'd have foundered, when I had the last three babies in sixteen months. For over twenty years she was an unfailing strength and support to me and my family, a second mother to my children. And she kept my home, as well as hers, immaculate.

What seemed problematic to me, she dismissed with 'Let's try it this way.' She saw through pretentious people. She was unimpressed by consumerism. Ready to work hard at any task within her range, she threw herself into the breach. She laughed at pomposity. She seldom complained. She was buoyant, resilient and willing. She had an irreverent sense of humour. Her good nature constantly sustained me. I respected her opinion.

She was a good influence on the children, insisting on politeness, training them to wait at the curb on a walk until she caught up with them, soothing their worries and comforting them. She played cards in parody with the twins, slapping the cards on the table before they had any idea of a system. She could always relate to a child's level.

But she lacked the ability to develop her own interests. She lived largely through me and my children. She absorbed without question the advice from her Mother, 'The secret of happiness is to forget you exist. Live for others.' This was a couple of eras before the 1970s roused women everywhere to expect something more. But at that time putting yourself last was a pragmatic response to a difficult situation.

After grammar school, and technical school where I studied practical subjects to my liking, I was in my forties when I went to university. The study of international politics teaches one about the way the world functions politically.

Along the way I learned French and then Spanish, which opened up more worlds than I had thought possible: social contacts, culture, music, cooking. Learning languages was a huge enrichment to my life, still of benefit today as I interpret at the Free Clinic in Virginia, participating in a medical setting without any formal knowledge of medicine. I enjoy assisting nurses taking health histories of patients and their families. We reassure and educate patients newly aware of diabetes, or counsel ones suffering from anxiety about their health. Without Spanish interpreters there would be no communication between doctor and patient.

Education has enabled me to work at a wide variety of jobs: I've been a secretary in London and Madrid, an interpreter at trade fairs, a ground hostess at Heathrow, PA to a writer in Mallorca, worked in a realtor's office, a property developer's, manufacturers and wholesalers. I was an editor in a publishing company, fundraiser in a charity, marketing manager in a language school, ran my own business export agency, interpreted in a range of industries; wrote magazine articles, managed tourist apartments in London, and bought and sold property in England, France and the United States.

New technologies which would have bemused my Mother have made the world my oyster. Communication is instantaneous through the internet. Search engines make everything accessible. Desk top publishing opened another world to me, design and digital photography that previously only publishers and journalists could handle after long apprenticeships to develop their skills.

Information has exploded exponentially. If my Mother needed advice she sought it from a doctor or a priest. Her reliance on both was greater than either could realistically deliver. The scope for confusion was particularly noticeable in the case of priests who were often uneducated, but my Mother's engendered respect for Father O'Brien or Father Murphy often left her open to misinformation on an impressive scale. Without objectivity she was sometimes challenged to distinguish between wisdom and ignorance.

My generation looked things up in books. We were taught to question, and use a library. We had dictionaries and encyclopaedia. None of this could compete with the speed or the scope of the internet, which instantly delivers information and solutions in abundance to your home computer. When my son was diagnosed with petit mal I was able to find within minutes advice on every aspect of the condition, and contact societies supporting epileptics. Support groups exist in every category. The speed with which the internet has accumulated and disseminates information is astonishing. And to think most of it was not widely available until only ten years ago.

Every morning my first action is to switch on the computer on my way to the coffee machine. I have instant access to family news, friends, weather reports, newspapers on line and breaking news. I can listen to BBC radio programmes live and recorded, or watch videos on YouTube. It's as if my living room had picture windows on the world.

THANK GOD FOR EDUCATION

Today John Paul telephoned from Arizona, said "go to Ustream-dot-tv on the computer and type in my name." Seconds later he was live on my screen, cooking with a friend in his kitchen, making buttered chicken curry. Then I clicked on a video recording of his son's birthday celebration in a restaurant, captured on his mobile phone webcam. We can all be broadcasters now.

Through internet we have access to information, advice, poetry, history, maps, recipes, diagnoses and blogs. Word processors enable us to cut, copy, paste, rearrange, spell check, word count, and upload. Remember hand-written drafts with crossings out, arrows, carbon copies, errors? They're history.

With these tools I can say, hand on heart, that I am never bored. When children say 'I'm bored', I want to shake them. You can read? Write? Play computer games? Listen to I-pods? Watch videos? Surf the net? Research anything under the sun? You have your own DS, laptops, musical instruments, sports equipment, kayaks, Wiis, mobile phones, books, puzzles and television. How dare you say 'I'm bored'! That's an admission of something deeply lacking inside of you. And there are millions of children with more pressing problems: hunger, sickness, lack of shelter, abused, orphaned, their very survival threatened, lacking education or prospects. And you are *bored?*

My Mother thought, quite reasonably, 'Is this all there is?' For her, that was all there was. She read magazines, but not books. Her education did not teach her to use a library. Or network. Her religion didn't encourage her to think for herself. Society frowned on women who wanted something more than domesticity.

Thank God for education!

8 MY IRISH BACKGROUND

I don't know much about my Irish background, beyond the flavour of it. My Mother claimed she was wholly Irish, and genetically, she was right. But she and both her parents too were born in England. Her grandparents on both sides had emigrated before their children were born. My maternal grandmother, Helen Tobin (also known as Nelly), was born in 1878. Probably her parents were children of the famine when they came to England. She spoke of Bandon, County Cork. Her husband was William Higgins.

All my Mother's siblings are dead now, and their personal history is lost. It's sad how family history is quickly forgotten in families that are not rooted in one parish, or have no tradition of record keeping. I recall my grandmother speaking bitterly about 'the dirty Orangemen' – in other words, the Protestants, and their despicable ways. She once said to me 'My grandfather was a land steward, and they burned his house down in front of him.' I was struck by this phrase, and know no more about the incident than this one sentence. What was a 'land steward'? Did he have any status? I know that the English landlords did everything to encourage the peasant farmers to move off their land so they could enlarge and consolidate their holdings. I have read how they razed houses to the ground in the late nineteenth century to drive farm labourers away. The people grew potatoes on their patches which gave no profit to the owners. The English brought in Scottish workers more competent to tend the land, thus compounding the fissure and resentment between Catholics and Protestants that foisted the Troubles on subsequent generations, including my own.

I recall Bernadette Devlin aged 21, making speeches in the 1960s when Peter was a baby, stirring the population to redress the unfair political balance between Protestants and Catholics in the North of Ireland, where the Protestants were still the oppressors and the Catholics suffered from discrimination in jobs and political influence. There followed nearly forty years of terrorism, restaurant bombs, knee capping by one side or the other, murders, mayhem, bigotry, bombs at London stations, Docklands and even in Ealing, where I lived in the 1990s. The Catholic Church did little to calm the dispute, often sympathizing with the IRA (Irish Republican Army). American descendants of Irish émigrés sent money that paid for IRA armaments. But more Catholics died at the hands of other Catholics than from Protestant murder, due to factions within the IRA and the criminal activity that flourished in that environment.

All this had its origins in unfair treatment by the English of the Irish, who have long folk memories. My grandmother never set foot in Ireland, and my mother only visited twice, but their social memories were fiercely nationalist in character. I suppose if people have nothing of worldly goods, and are dispossessed of even the turf huts they live in, despair may last for generations. Consider that the average farm worker survived on 8 pounds of potatoes a day (and little else), and that the potato crop failure removed their life support. While their hungry bellies were griping, the English suggested recipes for making soup with the slime of rotten potatoes, while sitting down to elaborate dinners served by their Irish servants. The hungry cried and moaned in agony at the gate and thousands died amidst English indifference. Imagining this perhaps you will catch the whiff of resentment that grew into a wind of change, first causing mass emigration to England and the United States in search of survival or a better life, and ultimately to the Peace Settlement in the late 1990s.

Helen Tobin as a young woman was in love with a young man who had tuberculosis. She waited and waited for him to recover, but finally he died. She was 26 when, sitting in church at Mass, she heard her name called in banns with William Higgins. This was news to her. Her father had arranged the match with his pal William, 'a sculling champion'. They probably belonged to the same boat club, if it was sufficiently organized to be called a club. My great grandfather thought well of the match, but my grandmother was not so sure. I think it's fair to say that it was not a great love story. Little was said but undercurrents of resentment continued to surface in family anecdotes long after he died of cancer in his fifties.

I know nothing of Helen's background, but I observed that she borrowed books from the library and read them, that she insisted on politeness, a tradition that has come down to my own grandchildren; that some of her children were intelligent, most notably John who was a union representative, a town councillor and wrote plays. Her grandchildren benefited from the education that was denied to her own.

My Granddad doted on his daughters, of whom he had three, and six sons whom perhaps he saw more as rivals. He would introduce his friends to his 'beautiful daughters', stroking my Mother's golden hair. She was fond of him, but also ambivalent. He was a drinker, if you can call a man a drinker who saved his thirst until the weekend pay packet enabled him to drink enough beer to come home feisty. My Mother recalled him once pulling the tablecloth off the table when drunk, spilling the tea plates to the floor. His oldest son Bill (who emigrated to Australia) once told his mother when he was a boy, 'Never mind Mum, when I grow up I'll kill him.' But there is no suggestion that my grandfather was heavy handed with his family. He was good natured, faithful, he went to church and worked all his life to support them.

William worked as a docker at Tilbury (as did his sons, later). It was hard but well paid work. He was a physically hearty man who loved to eat oysters. His wife always gave him the best food because he was the breadwinner and needed to sustain hard work. When she was pregnant at 42 with her ninth and last child (Cornelius De Valera Higgins, known as 'Con'), she used to send my Mother to the fish and chip shop to buy the batter that fell into the fat from the fish, because it was cheap and she was hungry.

On Saturdays they would buy 14 loaves of bread to last the week. My Mother spoke of 'twelve shillings a week' but I don't know if that was housekeeping money or his wages. It's impossible for us to appreciate anyway, not knowing the price of things. Suffice it to say that there was no spare money for luxuries. Nevertheless my Mother said her prayers at night with gratitude that she was born into this family, and that they were so happy. Her siblings were indeed a cheerful group, as I can recall. They were always joking, laughing, singing and enjoyed being together. They were not serious or anxious like my Father's family. All but Bill and two sisters (my Mother Margaret and her older sister Eileen) stayed in their neighbourhood, and when my Mother and I went to visit they joined us at my grandmother's house and sang songs while my Mother played the piano, which she vamped very well. I loved to go there! It was a jolly atmosphere. We would stay the night every few weeks, travelling by train, ferry across the Thames and bus to Nana's house.

Bill, the eldest, worked on a ship that sailed from Tilbury Docks to Australia. Returning late to the harbour in Sydney he found the boat had sailed and he was stranded. He told me this when I met him nearly fifty years later, but the family version was that Bill had 'jumped ship' as if intending to settle in Australia. When my grandmother realized from his letter that he was not coming home, 'she went to bed for a fortnight and when she got up her hair had turned grey'. She was a possessive mother, and a loving one. Her grief was inconsolable. It must be remembered though, that in those days when a person went to Australia they were seldom seen again; in fact, Bill didn't return until he was seventy, when she was long dead.

Eileen was the second child. She became a nurse and worked for a while at Hanwell mental hospital, west London. She enjoyed the work and befriended the patients, but such hospitals were difficult places in those days, before the advent of psychiatric drugs. One of the patients, disappointed that she had not brought the sweets he'd asked her for, wrestled her to the ground. She was rescued by other staff, but soon after she left because she was physically slight and it was too dangerous.

Jim, Veronica's father, came next. He was like the patriarch of the family when I was a child. A lovely man, good natured, generous, responsible and loving, he never failed to give pocket money to his nephews and nieces when they met him. He bought clothes for his mother, and handed out money to anyone in the family who needed it. He was a teller at the docks and worked on commission, so was well paid. But like his brothers he lived in a council house and his needs were modest. None of them drove cars, took foreign holidays or had expensive tastes at any level.

My Mother Margaret (Maggie to her family) was the fourth child. She was blessed with a serene and happy nature.

Dick, John, Kit, Dennis and Con followed. They were all educated by nuns. They all left school at 14. Between the nine of them they produced only 14 children (of whom 11 were girls).

Dick, John, Dennis and Con all had to fight in World War II. John was a PT instructor. He also boxed. There is a silver cup awarded to him for winning a boxing tournament. He was so fit, I recall him walking into the room on his hands when I was visiting Nana, just to make me laugh. He had red hair, freckles, a deep voice and a hearty chuckle. I once asked him to read me 'Doctor Doolittle' and he did so, but at such breakneck speed, I couldn't follow the words. Meanwhile his brothers were helpless with laughter. I was disappointed, but it makes me laugh now. Most of my Mother's brothers and her sister Kit died in their forties of cancer, and Con was only 39 when he died of leukaemia.

It's hardly surprising that given such deprivation, my grandmother was a poor cook, and my mother was no better. No tradition of eating well or interest in cooking existed in our family until I discovered food at 17, while staying with our Belgian friends on holiday. When my family was growing up I always cooked an evening meal. My Mother (to whom cooking was a burden) used to say 'Give them bread and jam. It was good enough for us.'

My Nana was a sweet woman, very like my Mother, who loved her family and nurtured their souls. I think I come from a long line of fond mothers. She died in 1954 aged 76, when I was 17, many months after a stroke. I was sad. I loved her. She was an important presence in my childhood. I only remember once sitting on my grandfather's lap when I was tiny (I think he died when I was two). He had white whiskers. I grew up thinking that was what God looked like. His children all loved him but I'm not sure whether his wife did.

The only thing I know about sleeping arrangements in my Mother's house as a child, was from an anecdote about her 8 year old cousin visiting, who was an only child. He was settled to sleep between my Mother and two of her sisters, who slept head to toe in a big bed, and he commented, 'Don't you sleep funny in your house?'

Another little anecdote: When my Nana was in labour and told her husband to go fetch the midwife, it was the middle of the night. She heard the donkey protesting about being woken in the night to pull the cart, and her husband consoling him, "Poor old Andrew, come on now." She thought he was tenderer toward the donkey than he was to her.

Once when I was about ten I slept with her in her double bed. She snored all night. In the morning she said 'I didn't sleep a wink,' and I laughed. But now I sometimes think I haven't slept, my mind is lucid even as I sleep, and I think I'm awake until I wake myself up, snoring. It's an old person's thing.

Another memory: Sitting by my Nana, stroking her soft forearm with its many wrinkles, saying 'Oh Nana, isn't your skin old?' and she was offended. I didn't mean to upset her. My skin is like that now. Jake recently asked me 'What are those things?' (wrinkles and skin tags on my neck), and I smiled and said 'That's just my neck getting old.' He said, not for the first time, 'Granny, I don't want you to die.' And I don't want him to worry.

Patrick once remarked (at Andre's graduation) that every time he sees me I look more like his Nana (my Mother). Well now, when I look in the mirror, I see my Nana too.

9 A STOMACH WITH ATTITUDE

My Mother always said that I cried for the first eighteen months of life. My Father said he would give the first place in heaven to the person who invented dummies. They once drove back twenty miles in the car to pick up a missing pacifier from Nana's house. They couldn't face a night without it.

My Mother also said that as a baby I had green motions in my diaper. Nobody knew the significance. Today we know this signifies hunger. I have only once seen a green motion: in my grandson's diaper after he had been sick for two weeks, not eating and unable to keep milk down.

Another clue is that I was exclusively breast fed until a year old, but my Mother only functioned on one side. These facts convince me that I was hungry for the first year. Both my brother and I have had a lifelong preoccupation with the arrival of the next meal.

In those days an influential authority on child care asserted that children should not be picked up unless to feed or change, and that feeds should be every four hours to the minute. It was hard for my Mother to hear me cry before the allotted span. She yearned to pick me up, but she and a whole generation of mothers believed the expert knew better than they did. I have a stomach like a clock and that man has a lot to answer for.

My Mother was not much interested in food, growing up as the fourth of nine children. It must be remembered that in England food took low priority in those days. My first spark of interest in cooking was kindled by my Nana who was also a poor cook. Aged six I watched her add milk and butter to mashed potatoes. I told my Mother about this trick and she took it up, but she seldom consulted a cookery book, never planned a meal, and was often heard to say at 5 o'clock when our stomachs were already rumbling, 'I'm just walking to the village to get something for supper.' The only things she kept in stock were bread, milk, eggs, cheese and 'a nice tin of baked beans'. I've avoided Heinz Beans ever since. It didn't help that there was rationing, and we didn't possess a refrigerator.

In the 1920s as an engineer on merchant ships for seven years, travelling the world and eating well, my Father spoke fondly of the pink sauce they had with fish on the ship (it must have been a prawn sauce). If he cooked (he was limited to eggs and bacon and fried cheese) he did it with care, basting the egg with a tablespoon scooping up the bacon fat, and the bacon was always cooked just right. But that was the extent of his cooking. They had their gender roles and stuck to them. He didn't want her to go out to work and she didn't expect him to cook.

We had salads with bottled salad cream. I was in my late teens before I discovered vinaigrette with olive oil. My Mother made bread occasionally, without salt because my Father's blood pressure was dangerously high. It tasted like cake, yeasty and delicious, but I missed the salt. Meanwhile they used lard in the chip pan and for pastry and fried bread. We ate eggs and dairy food every day of our lives. Fred had hardening of the arteries and died at 67 and all my family have inherited high cholesterol levels. I've been taking four times the basic dose of statins daily for years.

We spent good money on food: roast beef, steak, boiled ham, fish, vegetables and fruit. But I didn't know that beef came juicy, or that steak was worth eating until I was nearly adult. My Mother fried it till it was dry and tough, or roasted topside beef until it was shrunk and grey. But she made good pea and ham soup and delicious beef stew. Whenever she asked me 'What would you like to eat this evening?' I would answer 'beef casserole and sprouts' because she did that to perfection. My Father grew the sprouts in our garden. When I left home to be married my Mother joked that the family butcher was in despair at the loss of my business.

The only pasta we knew growing up was tinned spaghetti or macaroni cheese, but that was the culture in the forties and fifties. I was seventeen when I discovered spaghetti bolognaise with dried spaghetti two feet long, sold in a blue wrapper and imported from Italy.

At seventeen I went to stay with friends in Belgium, in the family with whom Fred was billeted in 1918. The two old widowed grand-mothers spent their days preparing a meal for the family, vying with each other to produce delicious dishes. Suddenly I discovered food. There wasn't much to do in the village so I watched them cook and we talked about recipes. For breakfast they had French bread, cottage cheese and strawberry jam, with bowls of milky coffee. They taught me a new recipe they had just learned: cheese soup. It's made with chives and milk and grated cheese, and it's delicious. I still make it occasionally. They rubbed the salad bowl with cut garlic before adding fresh lettuce from the garden, a finely chopped hard-boiled egg and vinaigrette. They grilled steaks just enough.

Their roast pork contained knife-point pockets with tucked-in garlic slivers. The butter was fresh unsalted and there was always wine. The Belgians are the world's best cooks, better than the French in my experience.

When I went to live in Spain I experienced a whole new cuisine, more robust than the Belgian: olive oil instead of butter, a great variety of fish and seafood flown daily to Madrid from the Spanish fishing ports, tomatoes, chorizo, paella: the Mediterranean diet. At first I deprecated meat and fish in the same rice dish, but I got used to it. In Spain the cooking was strictly to recipe and style. The only difference between paella in a duchess's house (where I started my working days) and a worker's kitchen, was quality of the ingredients. You would find chunks of chicken and pork in the former and chicken's feet in the latter. I thought the foot was a mistake, but my landlady picked it up and sucked the juice from its claws as she stood there, with a toothy grin. When she cooked sheep's brains for once in my life I asked for a boiled egg instead. 'I'll have a boiled egg' is an escape route my children always had as I introduced them to a vast range of dishes. None of them was ever made to eat something they didn't like. Nowadays they will eat almost anything.

I learned from my Mother how to make cakes. She followed recipes for that, and they were good. She baked my wedding cake and I've baked 'Mummy's Fruit Cake' every Christmas and family wedding since. I still have her edition of Mrs Beaton's cookery book to which she seldom referred; not surprising when you read directions like 'Take a dozen pheasants' as a preamble to the method. These recipes were designed for downstairs cooks and upstairs diners.

While single my social life was far more important than cooking, although I developed a few tasty dishes. When I got married I could cook meat curry, spaghetti bolognaise and corned beef hash. By the fourth night I'd run out of ideas, so I cooked something different every night for three months from a growing collection of cookery books, not once repeating myself, at the end of which I felt I could cook.

One of the bonuses of being married was that I suddenly found myself in charge of the menu. I only cooked dishes that appealed to me. As a result, the pounds started to accumulate and I haven't been slim since my mid-thirties, when I weighed 40 pounds less than I do today. I don't know many good cooks who are slim and those who are must be constitutionally slender. I store every calorie I don't use and would have made a good Bush Woman.

When Richard took a job as a farm manager of a thousand acres, along with a Georgian farmhouse we acquired a kitchen garden with rows of raspberries and other soft fruits. He grew vegetables in abundance. From the first summer of our marriage I made dozens of jars of preserves and chutney and we always had a full store cupboard.

My early fear of hunger has never left me. When hungry I feel deprived and unloved, threatened and bordering on depression. With a full stomach I am totally benign. The stirrings of appetite move me to create the next meal. While raising five hungry boys I never tired of cooking, making pies and roasts, casseroles and risottos, pasta and vegetables galore, homemade bread and yoghurt, soups and crumble puddings. We had ten apple trees in a Victorian garden and I could write a book about cooking with apples. I could write another about ground beef. Despite a thrifty budget, we always ate well, and I found it more congenial to cook with children than to play with them. Today they are all excellent cooks. Our social life revolves around the table.

I catered for two of my sons' weddings and on the last occasion when I was overstretched at the last minute, Peter and Patrick stepped in and cooked for the reception in the hired marquee in our London garden. I simply said 'Bone and stuff a turkey, roast the beef, boil the ham, prepare this list of salads and puddings, and make lasagne for fifty.' They didn't need recipes. What is not in their heads is all in the family cookbook I compiled after thirty years, so that we all had the same hymn sheet. We could produce another volume from the diverse dishes we developed in the last fifteen years. They are adventurous cooks.

My love of cooking will no doubt shorten my life as I'm overweight and unable to go hungry. I'm willing to die sooner if necessary. As I'm enjoying life I struggle to avoid getting heavier, controlling my intake of food and wine more than you would suppose. I was once buying diet tonic and the shop assistant asked me 'Does that work?' I said 'Oh my goodness yes, you should see me if I didn't put diet tonic in my gin….'

My doctor in England discussed weight and emotions with me, and agreed that the feeling of depression when I'm hungry was more threatening to me than the extra weight. I'm convinced these reactions stem from the same source as the green motions. My attitude to food is emotional. Whatever privations I may suffer as I grow older, I believe that as long as I have a good digestive system and a full set of teeth, life will be worth living.

10 GRAMMAR SCHOOL

Education opens windows, exercises the brain, fosters ambition, directs our studies, develops our interests and equips us to explore what's of interest to us. I am grateful for the schooling I received due to 'passing the scholarship' at age 11.

I discovered my strengths and weaknesses early in life. I was good at French in Grammar School, best in the class at conversation. My natural urge to communicate fostered my language development. I was good at English, gymnastics, history, geography, biology (at least on the lower slopes of the subject), but at mathematics I discovered a mental block with numbers. I learned by heart my tables (no calculators in those days); I found algebra and fractions challenging and at sixteen got to the stage where geometry became opaque. I was fine up to the point of Pythagoras' theorem. I could add, subtract, multiply and divide - well, up to a point; the decimal point. This sent me into a flurry of apprehension like walking on a cliff top in fog, afraid to put a foot wrong. Even in my fifties, when I read gas and electric meters for our letting apartments, I was never sure where the decimal point belonged, whether they owed one pound ninety or nineteen pounds. I had to rely on my gut feeling. My guts are quite reliable when it comes to the larger picture concerning my money. I think 'I've got a bit here, and a bit there, and so much invested in so-and-so, and altogether that makes...' (and I'm seldom more than a few thousand out). I've never been in debt, due to careful budgeting. But gut feelings are useless in a maths lesson.

In primary school when they posed the question, 'If it takes so long for a gallon of water to drain from a bath, how long will it take to empty...', and I would think 'If I ever need to know, I'll take the plug out and use a stop watch.' In all my life I've never needed to make that calculation.

Another problem is that I take things literally. I tend to be pedantic. In a mock 'O' level paper in Biology at school, the question was posed, 'Describe an experiment to calculate the volume of air in a laboratory.' What they should have asked was 'Describe an experiment in a laboratory to calculate the volume of air.' I could have told them about dropping a glass stopper into a graded measuring jug and reading the new level.

Instead, I started 'First close all the doors and windows….' I didn't get a mark for this. This incident made me nervous of misinterpretation.

My worst subject was Latin. How can one learn a dead language that cannot be spoken, with word endings varying according to, who is doing what and when to whom? I learned declensions by rote, but couldn't deploy them. Latin homework regularly reduced me to tears of frustration. My brother tried at first to explain it to me, but was understandably irritated by my tears; after a bit he declined to help. I was bottom of the class. My teacher said later that I was the only girl she ever met in her long career, who asked 'When can I give up Latin?' before the end of the first term. It was inflicted on me for three years (as Welsh would be later, on my boys in Wales where only two subjects were compulsory: Religious Education and Welsh.) At my school Latin was an essential subject to gain university entrance. I recall elation one term when my mark rose from 29 to 31%. My failure was not for want of trying.

Later I would learn enough Spanish in six weeks to find my way around Madrid on the Metro, order meals, tell the taxi driver where to go and to answer the phone to would-be beaux. I learned rapidly, and fifty years later I'm still a fluent interpreter. Spanish would have been a better use of my efforts than Latin.

The top five per cent of the school population in those days could earn entrance by examination to a Grammar School, the best education available outside private schools. The bulk of the population went to 'Secondary Modern' or specialist 'Technical' Schools where they learned useful skills like shorthand and typing. Some schools were like holding pens where youngsters stayed till they were fifteen, then found unskilled work. This was before Comprehensive schools were invented to give better opportunities to the wider population. My brother got a free scholarship to a Public School (private in America) which was usually beyond the means of all but the wealthy. At eighteen he earned a State Scholarship to University to read History. All our education was free, subject to examinations passed.

In those days one took Ordinary and Advanced level exams at 16 and 18. 'O' level passes in eight subjects would ensure one a promising occupation. 'A' levels gained in three to four subjects would take one on to University. A university degree was a guarantee of employment for life. It isn't now, when around 40% take some form of higher education, and jobs are scarce.

There were 530 pupils at Chislehurst & Sidcup County Grammar School in a modern brick building set in many acres of grounds, at Beaverwood Road, Chislehurst. We had good facilities like laboratories, a gym and tennis courts. I was fortunate to have a good group of friends throughout my years at Grammar school: Pamela Merson (with whom I'm still in touch), Anne Bryce, Anne Briddes, Anne Brown and later Diane Robertson were my closest friends. We used to walk around the school, arms linked, talking and joking, during lunch hour and break. When I joked they used to say 'Oh Eileen, you are funny!' and I basked in their appreciation. They were nice girls, not one of them was catty and they were all bright. I wish I knew where they all are now. Changing one's name on getting married makes it difficult to trace old friends, especially from another continent.

I was in the school choir and my friends all liked to act. One of their performances was Macbeth. Pamela was Lady Macbeth, Anne Bryce was Macbeth and Anne Brown was Banquo. I was impressed by their ability to learn whole plays. As I was on my own when they were rehearsing I once took a part in The Importance of Being Ernest. I was Doctor Chasuble, a deplorable performance which convinced me for life to avoid acting. I didn't feel like an actor, I was Eileen Naylor standing on a stage, struggling to remember the words and feeling like an idiot. Years later I admired Mark acting at Hills Road, LAMDA and fringe theatre. He has skills that are totally beyond me. He said he liked being somebody else when he acted, but I could only be myself. I like public speaking, but the source has to be genuine.

I liked to sing. I can still sing most of 'Nymphs and Shepherds', and 'Hiawatha's Wedding Feast'. We had an excellent choir mistress who lifted our performance to a higher level when I was in the fifth form. One Saturday we met up with half a dozen senior choirs from local schools at the largest school in the district, to sing songs communally learned in our separate choirs. A young man came to be our conductor. He had an ability to stretch and improve our performance which was exhilarating. I have never enjoyed singing so much. It gives me goose pimples to remember that thrilling experience. The young man was 26 years old. His name was Colin Davis (later knighted) who became Britain's most distinguished Conductor, now in his eighties.

At age fourteen I suffered a back injury that would plague me all my life. I was quite athletic, being good at high-jump, the first in my class to climb the rope to the gym ceiling, doing handstands off the horse apparatus to the floor, and back-bends. During an exciting game of 'pirates' when one person was pursued by all the others, leaping around the apparatus, I was 'he' and in an attempt to avoid being tagged I grasped the bar at chest height and swung backwards underneath to pass quickly. I felt my back shift and fell to the floor. I could barely get up and crawl to the bench. I sat there shaking until the end of the lesson. I could barely walk and was in extreme pain. The teacher showed little interest. It was the last day of term and next day my parents and I went to Wales on a caravan holiday near Rhyl.

I was in constant pain, could not get comfortable, and could only walk a little way. I sat in the caravan and my parents were deeply concerned. When we got back to London they took me to see a bone specialist, Mr Levay, at Eltham Cottage Hospital. During the next two years I had 40 X-rays on the lumber region of my spine in a series of appointments, but no manipulation. 'Don't go to a chiropractor' he warned us, 'they are quacks.' I was put in plaster of Paris from above the breasts to my hips for three months. The only effect was to reduce my girth slightly from the friction. For several months I took eight Codeines a day prescribed by the specialist. Today that would not be allowed as Codeines can be addictive, but fortunately it did not happen to me, and gradually I decreased the dose as the pain diminished slightly in my late teens.

The summer I was sixteen Mr Levay suggested I should have bone surgery. They would take a bone graft from my hip to join the dislocated vertebrae, and I would have to lie in a hospital bed for four months while the graft grew into the spine. I was told I would be stiff afterwards, but it should strengthen the back. Meanwhile I was studying for 'O' Level exams, standing up to do my homework as it was less painful than sitting down. The prospect of exams followed by surgery was depressing, especially when a friend told me in conversation 'Oh, I wouldn't let them operate. A friend of mine did that and she was paralysed from the waist down afterwards.'

My Father sought a second opinion and paid for me to see a Harley Street specialist, who said that my skeleton had not finished growing and he advised me to wait until I was 21 before having an operation. I was in constant pain for several years and never could bend forwards to wash my hair, after the injury. My parents helped me put my socks on. My Father said he wished he could suffer the pain to spare me.

Although in the 'A' form at the Grammar School (above B and C), my inability to get to grips with Latin was enough to deny me entry to University. But there were other fields I could have entered. I just didn't know about them. We thought of education in terms of subjects: English, History, Geography degrees etc. Nobody suggested journalism, medicine, architecture or publishing. These careers were mainly perceived as male territory, although one girl in my class became a dentist. I was interested in nursing, but my back injury made that impossible; they said I would be unable to lift patients. Careers advice was limited to a half hour interview with the head mistress. She asked me what I wanted to do and I had no idea. I just wanted to leave school at sixteen. She tried to persuade me to stay on, but I was tired of it. I wanted to be out in the world. I didn't have any interest in the secretarial course Miss Huxstep suggested. The first I knew of my enrolment was a letter from Sidcup Technical School for Girls during the summer holidays, with a list of school uniform items I would need to buy. I was ambivalent but by the end of six weeks off school, had no better ideas, so I turned up as bidden.

In the Sidcup Technical School's sixth form I found I was good at shorthand and typing, that I flourished in practical subjects and enjoyed cooking classes. I was top of the class. I left school at seventeen in 1954 with certificates for 120 words per minute shorthand, 60 wpm typing and the rudiments of keeping accounts. I still touch-type like the wind. It's an essential tool in my Communication box. It has been useful all my life. I found these skills and my languages would allow me to work anywhere in the world, at any time, and I've never been out of work when I wanted it. More than ever now I'm grateful for my ability to touch type, as writing and desk top publishing on the computer have become my preferred occupations.

I took a job in a typing pool at 5 pounds a week. I thought about working for a local newspaper to learn journalism, but that only paid 3 pounds 10 shillings a week. Given that the first years of training were usually spent listing mourners at funerals and describing council meetings, I doubted I had the patience to be a cub reporter. But I should have tried it because that would have been a good career for me.

I also wish I had studied Psychology, but that was beyond my Freudian dreams in those days.

Looking back on the sixty years exactly since I injured my back, I can report that it did not stop me doing most of the things I wanted to in life. I could never play sports or go skating, ride a horse or play tennis, but I managed to have babies, to dance and to travel. Only a few times have I been totally incapacitated, and they passed. The bones the specialist wanted to join by surgery have fused naturally since the disk disintegrated. I have two curvatures of the spine, looking like a sideways S shape on an X-ray, so I'm lucky that I ended up still going in the right direction. I've lost two inches and most of my flexibility, and haven't been able to get in and out of a bath for at least ten years, but I have a lovely shower in my bathroom, I swim twice a week at a gym and there's far less pain since the bones joined together. Not a bad result after such a bad beginning. I'm so lucky I wasn't born into a family of potato pickers.

11 COINCIDENCE: THE CLOCK STRUCK TWELVE

One beautiful summer morning in 1954 when I was seventeen, I decided to visit my grandmother by myself. This was quite an undertaking as she lived on the other side of the River Thames, a two hour journey I normally made with my Mother by train, ferry boat and a bus ride. This time I was going to find my way by Green Line Bus, a long distance, rural network a little like the American Greyhound. I had all day to explore this new route and the beautiful weather made it an inviting adventure. I could not know it would be the only time in my life I would ever travel by Green Line.

Half way there, on a whim, I decided to leave the bus, alighting on the crest of a hill in farmland mainly planted with wheat and fruit trees and dotted with sheep in pastures. It is a famous beauty spot near the town of Routham in Kent. I left the bus stop on the main road and walked at a right angle, down a verdant lane beside an orchard, passing no one.

The birds were singing and there were hundreds of wild flowers growing naturally in the hedgerows. Those were the days before they were decimated by spraying. I picked a variety of flowers as I walked about a mile until I had a small bouquet. I realized they would soon wilt, and at that point reached a small country church with an ancient graveyard, so I thought whimsically to place the flowers on one of the graves.

I walked through the old gate, reading the inscriptions on half a dozen graves until I found one that belonged to a young sailor who had drowned at sea, aged 17, like me. I was full of compassion for his precipitate early death, denying him the beautiful world I now stood in. My foot stumbled against a small vase lying in the long grass beside his unkempt plot, and I put the flowers into it, bending to arrange the tribute on his grave. I imagined his mother's anguish and prayed for the repose of his soul.

At this exact moment the church bell chimed midday. As it slowly tolled, I read the date of this young man's death and discovered it was this very day, one hundred years ago, in July 1854. I felt goose bumps on my arms at this remarkable coincidence, and I feel them every time I recall that scene.

I retraced my steps to the bus stop, in need of human company, and completed the journey to my grandmother's house. I wish I had made a note of his name and the exact date. I could never find that church again, but I'll never forget that remarkable coincidence.

12 MY FIRST JOB: 1954-57

Walking to catch the bus to school in the mornings, I often met Mr G K Johnson walking the other way. His chauffeur would wait for him a mile away at the other end of Mottingham Lane, as he took his exercise at the start of the day. He was a gracious old gentleman who stopped to smile and chat with everyone he met. He took an avuncular interest in me (he had no children of his own) and when he heard I was soon to leave school with secretarial training, he offered to introduce me to the company where he was a director, in British Insulated Calendar's Construction Company, BICC.

He took me to lunch at Bush House (from whence the BBC still radio broadcasts to the world). In the restaurant he offered me my first cigarette (I didn't take it). It was a strange experience for me to eat in a fancy restaurant and I'm sure it amused him to treat a naïve seventeen year old. He was always correct.

The upshot of my interview in BICC Leicester Square was a job in the typing pool starting at five pounds per week. This was good for a beginner. My train fares to work cost one pound a week, I gave my Mother one pound fifty for my keep, and the rest was mine. I didn't earn enough to pay income tax. As I only had one dress (which I had been wearing at weekends for two years, and had been second hand when I got it) apart from school uniform, my first purchase was a green sweater and a skirt, and I added to my wardrobe as fast as I could to disguise its limitations.

I saved to buy my Mother an ironing board for three pounds (she had never before had one. She used a gas iron on a folded sheet on the metal kitchen cabinet). Another early present for her was *Good Housekeeping's Cookery Book*, which I still have today and occasionally refer to. I often spent two shillings on a bunch of anemones for her on Friday evenings. It felt good to be financially independent and generous.

In the typing pool about twenty young women sat in rows of five with a desk and typewriter each, and went to take dictation from the men who produced overhead electrical lines all over Britain and parts of the British Empire (when we still had one). At first I mostly worked for the

Estimating Department on the same floor. Mrs W, a florid, lusty, good looking woman in her mid-forties with died black hair, glasses and bright red lipstick, presided over her 'girls' like a madam. She sat at a desk facing us, and if two girls spoke more than a couple of words to each other, she would tell them to be quiet and get on with it. She flirted with all the men who came into our office, ogling them with merry eyes, and spoke dismissively about Archie, her feeble husband who languished at home. Most of the men were probably terrified of her. She reminded me of the kind of insect that eats her partner after mating. For that species, *coitus interruptus* takes on a whole new meaning.

In the Estimating Department about thirty men sat in rows just like we did, turning their heads at every girl who entered, but most of them were married. Terry B was the exception. He was 24, not tall, had an unusual face to put it kindly, but he was witty and his banter greatly amused me. Before long we were meeting after work, having a drink, an occasional meal or seeing a film. He was a keen ballroom dancer of the type one sees on television dancing in professional competitions. I danced on a far inferior plane, which he tolerated. He was one of the funniest men I ever met, but after a while our relationship fizzled out. Later he dated Sheila, one of my colleagues, and it was several months before we discovered he had been married all along. It was a shock for me, and for Sheila.

Other characters I recall from this era were Edna, the Teddy Girl from east London, who murmured her words with an air of pert confidence. She was popular but I wasn't sure why. Irish Mary regaled us with belly laughs and stories about her Tom, whom she eventually married (I liked her). Val was engaged to a Cypriot who knocked her about a bit, until it became too painful even for this masochist. Connie, a pretty girl with a bit of class (she wore cashmere twin sets and pearls) had her heart set on finding a husband among the company Trainees, who were destined for higher things. She aimed at the top prospect, John Kemp, a 6 foot 4 hunk Michael Aspell lookalike, for whom every woman in the company sighed. He was tall and handsome, poised and confident and too canny to settle for a girl from the typing pool. Connie married another trainee, who was more accessible. During these three years I was dating Australians, Spaniards, Middle Europeans and miscellaneous exotics from other lands who were naturally more appealing to me than the local lads.

One day I was asked to serve coffee to the board of directors around their boardroom table. I was so nervous my hand shook as I passed the cups, rattling in their saucers. It would be many years before I had the confidence to deal with guys like that on my own level, when I was Director of Export Connect.

After three months in the typing pool I was promoted as secretary to one of the directors, CK. This was a dizzy achievement for a seventeen year old. But I soon realized he was no pleasure to work for. My ego was stroked by having my own office next to his, with my name on a metal plate on the door. They asked me what kind of dictating machine I would like. I said 'An Adler' because it was the only one I could name, and they bought me one so large, it took up half my desk. It was enlightening to hear my own voice recorded on it, which up till then I had not heard. I think everyone should listen to themselves and learn to modulate.

I took dictation, typed reports and letters and cut those awful stencils that we repaired with something like nail varnish when we mistyped a character. This was before the invention of photocopiers. The typewriter was mechanical, built like a tank, and every line was carriage-returned with a left hand flourish. We had to make up to four carbon copies and if we made a mistake, erase all five layers or start again. We could never have imagined a word processor.

My boss came in each morning without greeting. He barked orders at me and scared me half to death, and in the afternoons he was often the worse for a wet lunch. He would grunt rather than speak and I never, ever saw him smile. I stuck it for perhaps three months till I went to the personnel department to hand in my notice. Why are you leaving, they asked? 'Because I cannot stand working for Mr. K a moment longer.' 'You don't need to leave because of that,' they said, 'we know he's difficult, we can accommodate you somewhere else.' For the next three years I worked for the four engineers who designed the overhead lines. They were Ken O'Dell (a nice married man with two small children who once invited me home for supper to meet his wife), Philip Dey, an Indian married to a Welsh woman, who read my palm and accurately foretold my future. John Kemp, the aforesaid trainee and Andre Drutskoy who was 38, single, a stateless Russian who had escaped to Italy as an infant wrapped in a shawl, travelling in a cart, during the Russian Revolution. He was one of the nicest and most cultured people I have met in my life. My youngest son is named for him. I was a little sweet on Andre but he was 18 years older and he was always correct.

My other colleagues were Doris, the office manager and secretary to the head of department (she was elegant, beautiful and about thirty) and Maggie (who was unwilling to admit her age, but probably forty), with a dry sense of humour that I treasured. I could not understand why Doris was not married when she was so attractive. After I left the firm and Maggie was visiting me in Madrid, she told me that Doris had been having an affair for years with a senior manager, who was in his fifties and had no intention of leaving his wife. It was common in those days for young women to waste their best years on such selfish men.

Today there is a celebrated series on American TV, 'Mad Men' which won the prize for the best drama series two years running. It's about a firm of Madison Avenue advertising executives in 1960. It captures well the culture and chauvinism of the offices I worked in, in London. We young women were sex objects and proud to be so. We didn't know any better. We were patronized without objecting. The men were self-seeking and often dismissive towards women, but I was extremely fortunate in 'my men' as I termed them, who treated me always with respect and enjoyed our interaction. I think they saw me as a younger sister and I was happy working there until I reached the age of twenty, which my parents had insisted was the earliest I could start to travel.

Suddenly I was free to see the world and I handed in my notice. Called in to the boss's office on the last day I found the whole department waiting to present me with a travelling alarm clock and to wish me happy travelling.

Andre came to Madrid on holiday with Ken from the design office, while I was there and looked me up. We had a wonderful evening, in the company of my friend Heinz. We took a taxi ride to Segovia and ate roast sucking pig in a lovely restaurant near the ancient aqueduct. On the way home we all sang a Spanish classical guitar theme which I can still hum but not identify, and between Heinz and Andre in the back of the taxi, I held hands with both. Apart from one visit to the office in 1958, I never saw any of them again. Today Andre would be 91. Andre wrote me long afterwards that he had married an Englishwoman. I hoped she knew how lucky she was.

Philip Dey's predictions from reading my palm were, that I would have six sons, two husbands, and be increasingly successful as a writer, but not until well after forty. Counting Bill's son Justin as my step-son, I did have six sons, which at the time I dismissed as ridiculous. I did have two husbands. I'm still working on the success as a writer prediction, but that has always been my ambition. He also said I would be 'rheumatic in old age, and live to be 93', so I'm pacing myself.

13 1956 - MEETING MARIANO

Within half a mile of my home there was a large Victorian house at 43 West Park, Mottingham, let out to students by the room. The house next door was similarly let by the owner, Mrs. Rankin. She was a keen artist and spent her days oil painting in her living room, mostly forest scenes with dramatic trees and strong colours. Her pictures were quite good.

The rooms were shabby and cheaply furnished. The carpets were worn and grubby. Foreign maids kept house rather carelessly. (I saw there my first dish washer. I couldn't imagine what kind of machine would take in cups and saucers and wash without smashing them, until I saw how they were stacked.) Their Sunday lunch was invariably spaghetti with tomato sauce from a tin. But the house was full of lively, happy students from all over the world, who created a wonderful spirit and social environment.

I had noticed these students and wanted to meet them for several months. One day, walking home from the village, I saw three of them starting to walk into the back footpath that would eventually take them to the other end of the lane, near my house. So I started at my end of the lane, and when I met them, spoke to the tallest, who later I would learn was Lars, asking 'Have you seen my dog?' They asked me what he looked like, and I described the dog living next door to me, a golden retriever named Tarzan. 'I think it is not easy to lose so large a dog,' said Lars, smiling. We abandoned the search for the 'lost' dog and chatted as we walked back to my house. They invited me to a party at their house that evening. Thenceforth I was welcome any time I set foot within those doors.

There were students of every colour, speaking many languages, from all over the world (about forty in all). We were all colour blind. I was the only local English girl who came to visit. I remember Chu Chad from Siam (now Thailand), Talib from Singapore, Pepe, Graham and Charlie from British Guiana, Trini (Jean) from Trinidad, Lars and Barbara from Sweden, Jacqueline and Francoise from France, Joshi from India, Sui-Sim from China, Ilkka (Finland), David (Wales), Bob (Bolton), Boa (a Seikh from Africa) Ted (Malaya), Mariano (Spain), Hans (Germany), Jose (Canary Islands), Burt, Ramsamooj, and others from Turkey, Syria, Iraq, and I don't recall where else. There was a large back room containing a billiard table and a few upright chairs. They had only to put on a 45 rpm record like Little Richard's Great Balls of Fire, or Bill Hayley's Rock Around the Clock, or various calypsos, some of which I learned, and we had an instant party! There was never any alcohol. There was no warm up stage, just music and high spirits, creating their immediate impact.

The Calypsos were saucy. Here's one I remember:

> Now listen here, just recently,
> a girl decide to make a baby for me.
> But when the baby come, she white as snow,
> the reason why I wanted to know.
> I ask her mother and she say,
> the girl been drinking milk of magnesia every day.
>
> That's why I ain't payin', I ain't payin',
> put me in jail the way I like but I ain't payin'.
> She tried to put the blame on me,
> but every woman got a right to mind she baby.

One evening there was a new student, Mariano. He was extremely handsome. He looked like Rossano Brazzi, but with a firmer mouth. He was elegant. He held his cigarette finely, he didn't smile a lot. He had a deep voice. He was reserved, but seemed to be enjoying the company.

During the evening they put on Spanish music, for some reason urging me to dance flamenco. Now that was ridiculous, because I had only glimpsed it in films (we still had no TV at home). But they stood me on a chair with an artificial rose between my teeth. Hey, I was eighteen, and having fun. Hands in the air, I stamped my feet a little and laughed. Mariano, who up to then had said little (he hardly spoke English), said 'You say 'nada!' and look down.' 'Nada!' I said obediently. It means 'nothing', and I think that's what you get when you ogle a flamenco dancer.

I asked him where he came from. Madrid, he said. To my shame I didn't know what country that was in, so I still didn't know he was Spanish until a few sentences later. He asked for my phone number and I gave him my office number (we didn't have a phone at home). The next afternoon he called me. Eileen? Yes? How are you? Fine. Will you meet me? Yes. What time? Five o'clock. Where are you? BICC. Leicester Square. OK. See you. That was the level of his English at that time. Mariano had come to England for six months after gaining his Economics degree, to learn English. I became his teacher. Every night he waited for me at 5 o'clock, after a day spent reading in the British Museum while I had been at work.

We fell in love. When his six months were up he was unable to go home for political reasons. A student friend of his had been arrested during a demonstration in Madrid with a letter in his pocket from Mariano. (General Franco, only half way through his term as *Generalissimo* with twenty years to go, was firmly in control.) I was delighted that Mariano's visit was extended for three months. But the sad day came when he had to go home and we spent our last evening together. We walked around the vicinity of Charing Cross until finally we parted. He stood at the bottom of the stairs as I walked up to the station. At the top I turned and sadly waved. I thought I would never see him again. I was not to know that he would still figure prominently in my life in later years. He was the reason I subsequently learned Spanish instead of Italian. He would eventually become Governor of the Bank of Spain and help me to make my first business contacts.

Of the few students I heard news of in later years, Charlie from BG married the English maid from the boarding house and had ten children in what became Guyana after independence from the British. Ilkka became the Mayor of Helsinki. Chu Chad, violinist, became leader of the Military Band in Thailand. Jean, the most popular girl in the house, never married. David (who once took me to a Tchaikowski concert at the Festival Hall) owned a hotel in the seventies on the seafront in Aberystwyth which I discovered by chance when I walked into his bar along the road from where we lived. In an extraordinary coincidence, Mrs. Rankin who sold up and retired to Aberystwyth, lived a few doors away from him, also on the seafront, and I met her there too. Bob (who had asked me to marry him) eventually became a Minister of the Church of Scotland. I feel sure all those former students fondly remember the buoyant, carefree days they spent at West Park in the fifties.

1956 was also the Year of Suez.

When Colonel Nasser, president of Egypt, decided to nationalize the Suez Canal which belonged to the British, the outcome was a coordinated attack on the Egyptians by Israel, Britain, and France. The Suez Canal, built in the nineteenth century by the French and Egyptians and later sold to Britain, provided a vital channel between the Mediterranean and the Red Sea, thus dramatically shortening the journey of shipping on its way to the Far East and Australia, avoiding the need to pass around South Africa.

The Americans disapproved of this attack on Egypt. It was election year and they opposed the Europeans. They put economic pressure on Britain, which caused the British to abandon the fight. America always disapproved of British 'colonialism', while practising its own version without a qualm.

In Whitehall, London, there was a huge demonstration against the war. The British were divided on this issue and the demonstration was violent. The majority opposed the war. The police were out in force, with batons. Mariano, keen to observe history happening, left me beside a government building in Whitehall and told me not to move, while he went to investigate. He was gone for half an hour and I was terrified by the noise of shouting and pushing all around me. I didn't dare to move and wondered what would happen if he did not come back, but eventually he did. It's the only time I've been in a noisy political demonstration, and once is enough. It's not for the faint hearted.

Later I would talk about this with my tutor at university, who had also been there as a young man, and remembered people throwing marbles under the hooves of the mounted police horses, to trip them. My fellow students had not even been born in 1956.

14 1957 - THE BEST YEAR OF MY LIFE

From the many foreign friends I had in my teens, I caught the travel bug. Australian, Canadian, South African, Continental friends had made me geographically restless. The Australians in particular were intrepid travellers, exploring Europe during their year in the UK. The English only went to Australia as emigrants, (one could emigrate with an assisted passage for ten pounds in those days). Australian wages were higher, so it was easier for them to earn money to travel, than it was for us.

At seventeen my Mother had urged her parents to let her go to France as nanny to a French family in Paris, recruited by her local priest. She had to cry for days before they gave in. Sadly, it was a bad experience because they expected her not only to look after their little boy, but do all the housework and the cooking. I'm sure she was a capable nanny and her cleaning was exemplary, but I don't know how they ate her food. On the first night they gave her a raw chicken and told her to prepare dinner. I don't think she had ever cooked anything in her life. She saw little of Paris (or Sevres, where they had a country home) although she spent a night in Claridges Hotel in London on her way to Paris. Her chief memories were of polishing the floor with pads on her feet, and being poked in the ribs with the collecting plate by an usher at Mass who did not appreciate that she had no money.

My Father had also demonstrated his love of travel, so it was hardly surprising that seeing the world was one of my top priorities. I used to walk along Mottingham Lane on my way to school and later to work, thinking 'I hope this street and these lamp posts are not all I shall see of the world.' At seventeen I received my first marriage proposal, and answered 'Oh goodness no, I haven't lived yet.'

My parents insisted that I must be twenty before I travelled anywhere alone. A friend I'd known since the sixth form, Pat Head, planned to hitch hike with me through France and Italy. It wasn't the hazard then that it is today; young people routinely hitched. I even bought a rucksack from a girl from Melbourne. We talked about finding work in Rome and learning

Italian. I saved for months. I was so sure this would happen that I quit my job at BICC a few weeks before my twentieth birthday and Pat and I got jobs at a coffee bar in Sidcup, because we thought it would be fun. (Coffee bars were a new concept in the fifties with their espresso machines and continental atmosphere.) My Father was dismayed that I was wasting my education.

Working in a coffee bar is not fun. For a start, our Italian boss insisted we memorize people's orders from the menu without notes. I never had that sort of memory. Then he insisted after working there for about ten days, that we come in on Sunday and work a ten hour shift. The other girls muttered resentfully, but agreed. I argued that ten hours was too long without a break. He said I don't need girls with 'O' levels, I need girls who do as they are told. So I quit.

One could always find temporary secretarial work by the week through an agency in London, so I signed on with the Alfred Marks Bureau. (Alfred Marks was a well-known character actor who established the agency as a side-line. It became his gold-mine. I saw him once, in Leicester Square. I also saw Ted Ray when he stopped his impressive car to wave me across the road, smiling at me, and I spotted Yuri Gagarin in Tottenham Court Road.)

On the Sunday before Easter, Pat had stayed the night at my house. We had been to a party at West Park the night before. My parents had gone to Mass. I remarked casually that I wished I could be in Spain for Easter, and Pat said 'Well, why don't you?' and in that second, my life seismically shifted. In a way that I would later realize is part of my character, I said 'Alright then, I will.' I've made several big decisions on the spur of the moment, and I can't think of one I have regretted.

Pat could not go with me. She'd spent her money on clothes and having her hair dyed blonde. My clothes were few and worn, but I had saved forty pounds. When my parents came home from church I said 'I'm going to Spain this week!' and by the Wednesday, I was gone. My Mother cried into the flowerbeds, weeding, for two days. I didn't want to upset her, but the world was waiting.

The one way train fare to Madrid was fifteen pounds, for a journey that took 36 hours. I could have flown in 4 hours for thirty pounds, but I thought it something only rich people did. Being on a long distance train was a thrilling prospect in itself.

My Father took me to the station in London and put me and my suitcase on the train. He didn't cry. He kissed me and gave me a traveller's cheque for thirty pounds so I would always have my fare home. Eight months later I gave it back to him. While I lived in Spain he paid my national insurance contributions.

On the train I was exhilarated by the adventure. Chatting to everyone I met, I didn't feel lonely. The train took us to Dover where we boarded the Channel ferry for Calais. A French train took us to Paris. I met a German girl on the train who was heading for Madrid. Ursula had been there the year before, working as a nanny. When we get to the Spanish border, she warned me, don't tell them you are looking for work. They won't let you in. Tell them you are a tourist. It was the most useful advice I heard all year.

In Paris we transferred stations, then found that a rail strike had halted all the trains in France, and we were stranded. France is like that, even today. As a precaution I had changed a couple of pounds into Francs for the journey. Now they came in handy. We met two other British girls on the station. None of them had Francs. We rented two rooms near the station and went to a café to eat. My Francs paid for the rooms, two loaves of bread and a bottle of cheap wine. When you are young and giddy, eating a French baguette from one end with another giddy girl on the other, is Living. In good spirits we splurged one coin in the juke box to play *'Malagueña'*.

Ursula and I slept in a double bed, my wallet and passport under my pillow.

Next day we discovered a sole train running from Paris to the Spanish border at Irun.

At the border I was alarmed by Spanish G*uardia Civil* with holstered revolvers, swarthy complexions and strange hats (sun-guards rolled up behind). My heart beat faster. They examined our faces and our luggage sternly. I said 'tourism' when they asked me. With a sigh of relief we were through. In the Spanish train we found an empty compartment where we could sleep during the journey. I was thrilled by the sound of the train's horn in the night, and even today the freight train hooting in Virginia is evocative and stirring.

Arriving in Madrid I took a taxi, showing the driver Mariano's written address. He lived in a first floor apartment. The maid opened the door. His family were away for the weekend so we ate lunch alone, served by Pilar. She offered me a Spanish omelette on a tray and I didn't know how to serve myself, so Mariano cut me a wedge.

Then Mariano took me by taxi to a pension in the centre of Madrid, in an old building with large mews entrance. My room had tall windows and austere furniture. He left me there. I made a great effort to talk to the concierge, with phrase book in hand. In London I had bought Hugo's Teach Yourself Spanish in three small volumes (I have them still) for five shillings. They were good for learning basic verbs, a few prepositions and sentence structure. But mostly I learned Spanish through conversation. I ordered a bottle of red wine to keep in my room, astonished that it only cost sixpence. It was barely drinkable, like alcoholic vinegar, but I sipped my way through it over the next few days, experiencing independence for the first time. Heady stuff.

Foreign travel is a sensual experience. First impressions of Madrid: the smells, which I couldn't place, whiffs of sweet cake-like odour with an unpleasant undertone. I discovered it was sewage. All Madrid had storm drains instead of sewers. Fish fried in olive oil wafted from restaurants. The sights: girls in beautiful dresses with layers of stiff *broderie anglaise* petticoats that made their waists look tiny, with high heels, beautifully made up. (I never owned one of those petticoats, although they were all the rage. They were not my style.) The main streets were lined by trees, watered daily. There was endless sunshine. After an English winter the sun felt exotic on my skin. The sounds: traffic, tooting horns, blaring radios, loud exuberant conversations in bars, flamenco music, braying donkeys in the early mornings. Cows were tethered in concrete byres between apartment blocks, visible from the street, lowing mournfully. Milk had to be fresh: there were no refrigerators in the apartments.

Taste: Olive oil, garlic, tomatoes, fresh fish, rice dishes, chicken, grilled lamb, steaks and salads. The food in Spain is traditional, hugely varied, and the same dishes occur in every household, varied by the quality of ingredients. Paella in a rich man's house contains meat and seafood. In the pension where I lived it contained chicken's wings and feet. The restaurants without exception served good food, and it was cheap for a person who had changed pounds to pesetas. Butter was rarely used and always rancid. (Why does it taste like soap? I asked in my innocence.) Wine was served in a carafe at every meal except breakfast. In the bars where I took coffee and *churros* (extruded loops of deep fried donut), men often drank brandy with their breakfast coffee, toast and grilled tomato.

Ursula took me to the agency recruiting nannies for rich families. I was placed with the Duchess of Escalona, who lived with her husband, four children and nine servants on an entire penthouse floor. There were no houses in Madrid, only apartments. I discovered they belonged to the Domecq family that owned most of Ibiza and the entire Domecq Wine enterprise. She had two baby boys and two girls aged 3 and 4. I was to look after the girls, from 10 in the morning until they went to bed. We had a siesta after lunch at 2. Dinner was served at 10 pm. It was a difficult adjustment. With meals so late, I was always hungry. There was *manchego* cheese with honey from their Ibizan estates. I ate lunch with the children. A maid served me dinner alone in my room.

The chauffeur was told to drive the girls and me to the scrubland outside Madrid for fresh air. There was nothing there but sand and small hills. He sat in the car smoking, while I played with the girls. I had dressed them in underclothes including flannel bodices with buttons (we used to call them liberty vests), dresses with puffed sleeves, over-coats and felt hats, with long socks and shoes. It was April, it seemed hot to me (I wore a dress) but the Duchess insisted. I took off their hats and coats and woollen gloves and encouraged them to run around. I hoped it would make them tired, and give me a break. When we got home for lunch at 2, the Duchess was delighted that suddenly they had appetites in place of sour faces. Whatever you are doing it is wonderful, she said. I didn't mention taking off their coats and hats, or tipping sand out of their shoes before we got back in the car.

I was supposed to teach those little girls English. I taught them 'Water please' at the table, and 'Good morning, please and thank you.' In reply they taught me to count to a hundred, recite the alphabet in Spanish, and name a few colours: invaluable lessons.

The only time I was allowed out was Sunday afternoon. I was lucky. Maids only got one afternoon out a month, and they worked till midnight. Mariano and I went to a bar to talk over coffee. We thought it unsatisfactory that I had so little freedom. The next day I spoke to the Duchess, who was a very nice woman. She had told me, 'Don't get married too young. Once you are married it's a baby every year and it's very tiring.' I said I had no intention of having all the babies that came my way. I told her I am very sorry, I have not come all this way to be confined to the house six and a half days a week. I need more free time. I will have to leave. She was upset, but probably not surprised. We parted on good terms. Later I would recruit a nanny for her through an advert in a London newspaper which had only one reply. I had misgivings about the nanny I sent, but she was all I could find. (English girls seldom went to Spain in those days.) I would love to know how long that lasted. Many years later I read in the press that the little girl aged 4 with whom I had romped in the sand hills, had married Spain's richest nobleman, the Duke of Alba. What a happy coincidence that the heirs to two great families fell in love.

Another memory from that time: The Duchess told me she knew that in England we did not eat meat on Fridays, but in centuries past the Spaniards had helped the Pope in one of his battles, and as a reward Spaniards are exempt from that privation. I said That's OK by me, whatever you wish. She added, I asked the priest for your dispensation and he sold it to me for 25 pesetas. Oh, I said, I wish you had not done that. I don't approve of paying for indulgencies. Either something is right or wrong, one cannot buy forgiveness. For me that was an early nail in the coffin of the Catholic Church.

I left the Duchess's pent house suite and took a room in a pension near the Retiro Park on Menendez Pelayo. Understanding between me and the landlady was minimal. The next morning I set out to look for work. Walking a block along Menendez Pelayo, I knocked on the door of an attractive building with the name 'Comar' over the door. The man who opened it smiled and said 'Good morning!'

'I'm an English secretary, looking for work,' I said. 'Come in, come in!' he said, opening wide the door. 'Our English secretary is leaving this week. We are delighted to meet you!' We were in a beautiful salon with a small stage, little tables and gilt chairs.

Comar was a fashion house for American tourists. Four Spanish models showed a range of suits and dresses and two Austrian dress designers adapted them for clients, or designed new outfits. The guests were served sherry as they watched the collection. The prices were modest for wealthy Americans. Behind the showroom half a dozen girls sat at looms, weaving woollen cloth for the suits, singing as they pushed the shuttles back and forth. It was picturesque and irresistible to the clients, who, sipping sherry, ordered more than they came for. They were usually in town on tour for three days. In that time the outfits were measured, cut and fitted before they departed, and shipped by airmail on completion. It was my job to handle all the correspondence.

There were 17 different nationalities in the shop. The hat makers were Rumanian, the handbag and shoe maker Bulgarian, the interpreters mainly Dutch. The owner was a Hungarian Jew, Charles F, who had stubby fingers in several pies. He dabbled in real estate and provided reconstituted milk to the American forces in Spain. There was an American military air force base near Madrid.

Mrs F had been a night club hostess in Hungary. Charles met her there and married her and brought her to Madrid where they lived in a sumptuous apartment and had two small children. I upset her unintentionally. I didn't mean to offend her. She was showing the girls in the shop her enormous diamond engagement ring and I said innocently, 'My girlfriend in London said 'I'd like a diamond that big, I wouldn't care how vulgar it looked!' She gulped and forever afterwards made catty remarks when I met her, about my figure.

Temple Fielding, travel writer, promoted Comar in his *Fielding's Guide to Europe*, described by the publishers as the 'tourist's travel bible'. He recommended hotels, shops and attractions all over Europe and his readers followed faithfully in his tracks. His wife Nancy Fielding had also put Comar in her separate *Shopping Guide*.

Mr. F's nephew Herman was the nominal manager, but often absent, so it was Mr. Albert (French, born in Egypt) who managed the business. He was the one who welcomed me when I first arrived. We shared an air-conditioned office. He was a nice man, had a French wife and mother in law. One Sunday they took me in their car to visit Toledo.

Being blonde and free to go out in the evenings without a chaperone (unlike nice young Spanish women), I had my pick of all the young men I met. Every evening half a dozen would ring me and I'd wait for the one who wanted to take me to dinner, or dance, or talk, depending on my mood. I never had it so good, before or since.

An American ventriloquist and singer, Mitch, came to visit Mr F, and took me out for a drink. We saw each other two or three times a week before he went back to America a month later. One evening in a nightclub he sang 'I love you so, sonny boy' for a free supper. He left a neck tie with me and asked me to return it to a friend of his.

Heinz Putzenbacher called at my office around 7 to pick up the tie. I was delighted when this tall, blonde, athletic man resembling the film star Anthony Steele, walked in. Heinz and I would spend the next three months enjoying convivial evenings around Old Madrid, drinking *copas* and talking till the early hours of the morning. He was engaged to a Spanish girl from Almeria who was staying with his mother in Austria, learning to be a good Austrian wife before their wedding in September. If he had not had a fiancée, I'd perhaps have married him. He was the best company I'd ever kept. He introduced me to so much of Spain that was inaccessible with my lack of Spanish (although growing all the time). He was well read, travelled, amusing, good natured and musical.

Heinz was thirty, had been living in Spain for six years, spoke Spanish, Italian, French, German and English. He warned me not to attempt to learn Italian as it would corrupt my Spanish. At the end of the summer he had a job lined up as a hotel manager in Ibiza.

Soon after I'd arrived in Spain a girl had taken me to see a film about bull fighting. I found it disgusting. The blood and violence alarmed me. I hated to see the bull pushing its horns into the picador's horse's heavy woven armour. I expressed distaste and dismissed bull fighting as barbaric. This is a common English reaction.

Heinz was an *aficionado*. He had followed bullfighting all around Spain and was knowledgeable about the spectacle. Over glasses of wine in the evenings (a halfpenny a glass) he talked about it, describing the sequences, kindling my curiosity. When my Mother arrived in Madrid six weeks after I did, her visit coincided with a bullfight in a country town where Heinz's friend living in the same pension, was fighting. Heinz told me there was a bus leaving Madrid for the bullring at Colmenar Viejo, a small country town, and he might see us there. He expected to suspend our evenings out during my Mother's visit.

She and I took the bus and sure enough, in that tiny town, encountered Heinz. We lunched together, eating lamb chops and salad and drinking enough red wine to take the edge off our apprehension at the scene to come. Heinz explained as the musicians played their traditional trumpet themes and six toreadors ambled into the ring: 'Notice how they are out of step, despite the martial music. They never walk in time.'

The men were beautifully dressed in 'suits of lights', pastel shades of silk with heavily embroidered jackets, matadors' hats, pumps and stockings, carrying swords and capes. They were followed by the *peónes*, assistants who distract the bull when the toreador is under threat, the *banderilleros*, men with barbed sticks, and *picadores* on horseback with long lances. The function of the *banderillas* (darts) and lances is to weaken the bull's muscle behind his neck, to lower his head as he charges at the cape, making that area accessible for the toreador to thrust his sword between the vertebrae.

The ring was cleared, the toreador stood alone with his sword and cape, and the gate opened to let the first bull charge into the ring. Heinz explained how the first few passes between bullfighter and assistant are designed to study whether the bull hooks to the right or the left with his horns, if he runs straight, smoothly or dashes, and whether he takes up a particular spot in the ring which he makes his territory, and is at his most dangerous.

Heinz was concerned for his friend who fought the second bull. He's lost his nerve, said Heinz. He has a wife and children and he'd like to give it up but needs to support them. To our dismay his friend was gored in the groin, staggering back to his feet to kill the bull before collapsing and being carried out on a stretcher for surgery. Every bullring is equipped with an operating theatre attended by a doctor. He recovered some weeks later but I don't know if he fought again.

We travelled back to Madrid in the bus together. Every evening Heinz took me and my Mother drinking in Old Madrid. She had a wonderful time. Our feet could hardly feel the stone stairway as we walked up to our third floor pension after midnight, as the elevator was noisy. Elevators in old apartments were OK for ascending, but not safe to descend as they were prone to plunge. We were advised to keep off balconies too. Occasionally a balcony on an old building would fall under the weight of occupants and crash to the street below.

In the early mornings we heard donkeys braying. I never saw one but they woke me at six when they came with carts to collect the trash. Water trucks drove by daily to fill the reservoirs around the trees. The streets were noisy with hooting traffic. The dry heat was extreme. For the first time I noticed the oxygen that trees give off when you stand under them, their shade essential. There was air conditioning in shops and offices, but not in apartments.

At night a *sereno* patrolled every street, a man with a staff and keys who was there to open the gate to each apartment block after dark, protecting the inhabitants. Arriving at one's door, one clapped hands noisily to summon him. It was customary to tip him 5 pesetas.

I'd encouraged my Mother to visit me, to see my surroundings and lifestyle, and she was reassured. She had travelled all alone by train for 36 hours through France and Spain, knowing only English, and arrived looking fresh and exhilarated by the experience. In 1957 she was 49. We had a ball.

Being away from home for the first time was liberating. Being sought by young men for my company was good for my ego. Learning Spanish rapidly, a dozen new words a day, I gained confidence. I made an effort to get the tenses right. I didn't want to say 'Last night not possible come,' I wanted to say 'I would have come if I could'. I loved the music, food, ambience, customs and the gregarious nature of *madrileños.*

Heinz and I went to the bullfight every Sunday until he left. Besides the usual six bulls being fought by three toreadors, we saw *rejoneadores* (bullfighters on horseback) a demonstration of equestrian skill and bravery, and once I witnessed Domingo Ortega fight on foot. By then he was getting old, perhaps 60. He dominated the bulls with slow grace and an authority that was breath-taking. It was a privilege to see his mastery.

Bullfighting is a magnificent spectacle and I missed it for years after I left Spain. I read the Madrid bullfight reports in the press, improving my literary skills.

During the evenings Heinz and I talked endlessly. It was an education. All the memories I have of Heinz are positive, apart from the pang of parting. He wrote in a book of Garcia Lorca's poems (I have it still), 'D*e un amigo platónico, Heinz.*' He said I was the only platonic girlfriend he ever had. It was hard to let him go.

I changed pensions several times, and spent a month with Mariano's family when he was away working in the Canary Islands for the Bank of Spain. He was too modest to tell me that he'd gone to reorganize their economic system. His sister Mari-Tere told me. Tere was the oldest, then Mariano, with two younger sisters, Mari-Cruz and Ana, 18. Tere and I spoke French for the first couple of months until my Spanish improved. I liked her enormously. She had never worked and longed to do so. She had to overcome her father's reluctance to be allowed to work (at age 30) in a travel agency where her French was useful. Eventually Mari-Tere married a French count. Mari-Cruz married Eloy (whom I particularly liked), a diplomat, who would later be Spanish ambassador in Vienna (they had eight children) and Ana married Enrique. I loved that family. Mariano's mother Emilia and his father treated me like a daughter.

My recurring eight months cycle urged me to go home in the November. I was ill for a week before I left. The Asian 'Flu epidemic of 1957 swept the world. I was still feeling ill on the train as it left Madrid, bound for the French border near Irun. I was the only person in the carriage, until a man came and sat opposite to engage me in conversation. He asked questions about what I'd been doing in Spain, where I'd been, who I knew etc. Fortunately I was cautious and vague (I didn't have a work permit) and said I'd been on extended holiday. He asked me what I thought of the political situation in Spain. Every person to whom I'd posed that question clammed up immediately. Franco's secret police were everywhere. Sometimes even family members didn't know their brother's affiliations. During the Civil War it was common for brothers to fight on both sides. There was an underlying, realistic paranoia.

My suspicion was confirmed when the ticket collector came to punch my ticket, and the man in my compartment merely lifted his lapel and flashed a badge. He left me alone just before we arrived at Irun.

As the train crossed the border slowly, I stood looking out of the corridor window, weeping softly as I said goodbye to Spain, which had become a lifelong love of mine. A Spaniard working by the track looked up and said softly, *'Ya te vas?'* (Are you going already?). *'Si,'* I nodded, and felt the empathy between us.

On the other side of the border a French railway worker looked up at me and whistled. I shut the window in disgust.

I sensed that I would always return to Spain, although I couldn't know how soon or how often. A gap without visits would pass between 1960 and 1982. But I lost count of the times I went to Spain in the five years I was running Export Connect. Madrid is still my favourite city. And 1957 was the best year of my life.

15 EARLS COURT, 1958. RUPI

This is the hardest part to write about; I have not attempted it before. It includes the only major disagreement with my parents in my life. I was attempting to achieve independence and they were resisting. It's the reason I later said to my sons, 'Whenever you want to go, you can leave, and if it doesn't work out, you can come home and try again. Home is a jumping off place.' I wish I had had that freedom.

Living in a pension in Madrid had given me a sense of freedom that I relished. I wanted to live in town in my own place. I found a room in Earls Court on the top of five floors (no lift), with breakfast included for 3 pounds a week. It was really half a large room, divided years before, in an old terrace house. The servants must have lived on the top floor. It was long and narrow, with a single bed, a wash basin and a gas ring on the floor. In retrospect that was a terrible hazard, but it was routine then.

I loved it! It was ten minutes on the underground from wherever I was working in the west end. (Mottingham was an hour's commute.) Earls Court was full of foreign students and I knew it from the days when Margaret Arnold from the typing pool lived there. I'd gone home with her to parties where I met Australians, South Africans and so on. This shabby room with dull painted walls, a scruffy mat and lino, a metered gas fire and a single window overlooking Penywern Road, was my domain. I happily cooked on the gas ring while sitting on the bed. When friends came to eat and I didn't have enough dishes, we drank soup out of small glass milk bottles, and felt Bohemian.

In the mornings we went to the basement where we were served a good cooked breakfast. The tenants chatted freely. I met an Indian from Mombasa in Kenya, called Rasik Ruparelia, Rupi to his friends. He was 22 and rented the room next to mine. Sometimes when I cooked a meal others were delighted to join me. My limited cooking skills were more developed than theirs. I produced a pasta dish with bolognese and cheese sauce which was popular.

One day we all went to the coast near Brighton, to a beach house owned by one of the students' uncle. It was a working party. They scrubbed and painted while I cooked lunch for a dozen hungry people: corned beef hash. Somebody had brought half a bottle of gin but no tonic. It tasted horrible with the juice from a tin of peaches. We drank very little in those days. It was a jolly party and on the way home in two cars, we paused in a traffic jam alongside a car full of nurses. The boys flirted with them and invited them to a party that evening. Some of the girls came and one of them fell in love with an Englishman in our party. About eighteen months later I spotted this couple pushing a pram, in a London street as I passed in a car. Such is the gossamer thread of chance which brings people together and new lives into the world.

Rupi and I quickly fell in love. He was a sweet man, with a tender nature and we were totally happy in each other's company. He was studying at a London college. His father owned a factory in Mombasa and his extended family lived in a compound which is traditional in Hindu families. His mother wore saris and worshipped Hindu gods. They must have been good people to have such a lovely son.

Every evening I would return from work and run up over a hundred stairs to the top of the house. Rupi was always waiting for me. He would cook lamb or chicken curry with half a dozen tubs of spices he kept. Hindus do not eat beef. Or I would make something English. We had music. In anticipation of my twenty-first birthday my parents had bought me a record player. My favourite record was Nat King Cole's long player, 'It was only a paper moon,' and other classics, which we played so often, we knew every note. I had a Perry Como record too. Rupi used to sing 'Catch a falling star and put it in your pocket, save it for a rainy day…' He had a good voice. Rupi had Indian music on 45 rpm discs and I grew to love these strange melodies. Sometimes he sang Indian songs to me, translating the romantic lyrics. We talked a lot about his culture.

I don't think anyone else I was in love with, ever loved me as much as Rupi did. The feeling of closeness and mutual attraction was overwhelming.

My Mother missed me, living away from home, and asked me to go home at weekends. To begin with I went every weekend, which was hard for me because lots of our social activities peaked at the weekend, like friends' parties. I began to skip weekends at home but never two weeks running. My Father who seldom put pressure on me, did so then, saying 'Try to come home. Your Mother misses you.' I felt torn. I would sit in church with them thinking of all that I was missing in London.

When I told them I had a nice Indian boyfriend, they became deeply anxious and questioned me at length. I assured them that he looked after me, that he was in no way a threat to my happiness, but they were not convinced. At the very least he was a threat to theirs.

Rupi asked me to marry him. I gave this serious consideration, but my misgivings were deep. Firstly, I thought about our children who would be Anglo-Indian; in those days it was harder to be of mixed race than it is now. I thought about living in Africa (he came from Mombasa in Kenya), where Rupi joked that although we'd live in the family compound, on evenings when his family were all out he would cook for me, saying 'Beef tonight, sweetie.' He always called me Sweetie. I didn't like the idea of living with his family, although he assured me they were wonderfully loving and inclusive, and that his mother had written to him, in response to his revelation that he was in love with an English girl and considering marriage, 'If you love her, we shall too.'

One day we passed a couple in the street, an Indian man and an English woman, pushing a pram with a beautiful baby in it. 'He looks a nice baby' said Rupi, 'not too dark.' I thought it sad that he was wishing his baby to be paler, for my sake.

Although we had all the freedom and opportunity, we did not sleep together. I still felt it was important to wait until I was married and Rupi respected that. I am convinced that in time we would have come to the conclusion that the gulf in our cultures was prohibitive.

On the eve of my twenty-first birthday, my parents came to the house while I was at work, packed my belongings, paid my bill, and waited for me in my room. When I came home and found them and saw the room stripped of my belongings, I was distraught. I told them that Rupi was in the next room, that I wanted them to meet him, that he was a good man and they would like him, but they absolutely refused to meet him. They insisted that I accompany them home, and my father picked up my suitcase. I had no chance to say goodbye to anyone. The record player was already packed in my Father's car. They had fixed it all.

I cannot express how angry I felt to be taken home in this fashion, above all as I was turning twenty-one, the supposed age of adulthood and independence. The next day I left my hair in curlers and wouldn't eat. The neighbours came in to have a drink to celebrate my birthday and Eric chided me for the curlers. You should make more effort, he said. I don't feel like celebrating, I said, I'm supposed to be independent at twenty-one, and I'm not.

Rupi and I continued to meet after work, but I had to go home in the evenings. My father suddenly imposed a ten o'clock curfew, which I thought ridiculous after my days of freedom in Madrid when I was regularly out till 2 a.m. I must have been churlish, but I was always polite to my parents.

My Mother, who was menopausal at that stage, was agitated at my continuing friendship with Rupi. One day she became hysterical until she collapsed on the floor and I thought she was dying. I was terrified. I begged her to be calm, promised I would not see him again, if only she would not die. She rallied, and I felt stuck with the promise I had made. I telephoned him and told him what had happened, and that we could not meet again. We were both truly miserable.

The next day I emerged from the office where I worked, and there was Rupi. We hugged each other and went to drink a cup of coffee in a bar nearby. We talked about it and agreed we should not meet again. He came with me in the underground train to Charing Cross. We held hands and saw our miserable faces reflected in the carriage windows.

He was there again next day, and we continued to meet. But I felt torn between him and my parents, and could not lie to them. It was a sad and stressful time. Rupi was so distressed, he failed his exams.

I decided to go back to Spain, to get away from all of them. So my return to Spain in the summer of 1958 was very different in tone to my first adventure. I was escaping rather than exploring.

Rupi and I exchanged a few letters while I was in Mallorca. He sent me a coral necklace. I tried to put him out of my mind. Even so, when I got back to England after eight months and went with the students to a party where I hoped to see him again, wearing the red mohair stole (I have it still) that he'd given me for my 21st birthday, I was deeply disappointed to learn from a mutual friend that he had sailed for Mombasa the week before. I never saw him again.

In 1979, 21 years later, I was a mature student at Aberystwyth's University of Wales, when I met a pretty Indian girl in my international politics group. I asked her where she came from. Mombasa. 'Ah, I knew a lovely young man from Mombasa when I was young. His name was Rasik Ruparelia,' I said.

'I know him! He's my girlfriend's father!' He now owned a camera shop in Mombasa, had a son and a daughter who was a model. (I had heard from our mutual friend when we were young, that he had an arranged marriage.) 'Tell him, when you see him, Hallo from Eileen,' I said, 'that I have nothing but good memories, and that I have five sons.' After the

Christmas break she told me she'd passed on the message, and Rupi said, 'Tell Eileen to come to Mombasa for a holiday.'

I didn't dare. We were both married, and had seven children between us, but I feared that the magic might still be there.

16 TEMPLE AND NANCY FIELDING, TRAVEL WRITERS

Most of our clients at Comar fashion house in Madrid came through *Fielding's Guide to Europe.* Temple Fielding had a folksy style of writing which was entirely fresh in those days. He confidently assessed what would attract American tourists in the way of hotels, restaurants, shopping and general information. Americans came to Europe in droves in the fifties, dollar rich and privileged in contrast to Europeans who were barely recovered from the privations of war. Fielding's guide, described by Americans as 'the travel bible', dispensed quirky gems such as 'Ask Pablo, the head concierge at the Ritz, and tell him I sent you.' The hotels, shops and nightclubs he led them to, gained by his recommendations. To his credit, he did not take kick-backs, which he underlined in each year's edition. He was popular and famous and he always paid his own bills.

He described Comar in the 1959 edition as 'a knockout', a 'howling success'... 'looks like a motion picture set, a sizable factory' (weaving woollen cloth) 'to the rear, a Dior tailor, a celebrated French hat maker named Zoe and more than 150 workers'. He mentioned '3-day delivery if sorely pressed, but try to give these good people enough Grade A Cream of Human Kindness to allow 4 or five.'

Time Magazine in April '58 described his book 'The No. 1 Travel Guide' used by 700,000 voyaging Americans headed for the 'dizziest, busiest merry-go-round in European travel history' carrying a stowaway – Temple Hornaday Fielding' and 'A modern Baedeker whom more people swear by than at,' adding that 'Fielding's personal, pithy and frank approach would make old Herr Baedeker blush'.

Having failed to settle down in London in 1958 I wrote to friend Fernando, son of the head of IBM in Spain, that I would take up his father's kind offer of a job any time I wanted to return to Madrid. I started work there in the summer of '58. I was bored at IBM, copy typing Spanish manual texts about computers, so when I dropped by at Comar to see my old friends at the end of the first week, I was interested to hear, 'Eileen, Nancy Fielding is in town, interviewing for a secretary to Temple Fielding and she wants to meet you.' So goodbye IBM and two days later hallo Mallorca (one of Spain's Balearic Islands in the Mediterranean) where the Fieldings lived in a villa overlooking the bay of Formentor. I was exhilarated by my first flight in an aeroplane, and a ride in Temple's shiny black convertible Cadillac. Formentor is one of the world's most stunningly beautiful bays with a natural cove and a few small verdant volcanic hills emerging from the blue Mediterranean. I was happily installed in my rooftop office in their villa before my parents got the letter saying that I was no longer in Madrid.

The island of Mallorca was largely rural with small towns dotted around the coastline at natural inlets with sandy beaches and trees. The hills were wooded and the narrow roads folded on themselves, transcending the mountains of the interior. The Fieldings' villa with its long terrace overlooked the bay. Cacti grew in the scrubby garden and the sky was nearly always blue. Mrs Fielding was a pleasant woman and we got on well, playing Scrabble many evenings throughout the winter of '58 with a 5 peseta bet, so evenly matched that the same 5 peseta note went back and forth all winter, kept in a small jar on her bedroom mantelpiece. She was kind and light hearted and I liked her.

It wasn't entirely easy living as their secretary. I had my own large airy bedroom and en suite bathroom, but little independence. I had no transport and there were few opportunities to socialize, although I became friendly with some of the staff at the hotel where I collected the mail. I wasn't at the bosses' lofty level, and I wasn't on the servants' level either, so I ate alone, my dinner cooked by Catalina and served by the housekeeper, Francesca. Francesca's husband Martín was the butler/handy man about the house. He and his wife were genuine, likable people whom I came to love. Francesca had never been to school, so could not write, but Martín had a few years' schooling till age 11 and was literate. They were both capable, intelligent, dignified and admirable people in my estimation, who being from a modest rural background, were held back only by lack of education.

I soon found that Temple Fielding, larger than life, full of bonhomie, sharp as a claw, attractive to famous people and hugely celebrated, was an egoist with great presence. He was already famous in America. He would later be showered with honours and titles, visited by royalty, and featured on the cover of *Time* magazine in 1969. In my day he impressed friends like Art Buchwald. Cat Brown (Admiral of the Sixth Fleet), the owners of the Danish newspaper 'Extrabladet', and a department store in Copenhagen (Illums Bolighus). Writers, musicians and celebrities galore all came to visit them.

I had only been there a few days and was sitting in his office, taking dictation, when he said, 'Eileen, you need never worry about me chasing you around the desk, that's not my style.' I was astonished, not having considered even the remotest possibility that he might. He was 45 and I was 21. How do you answer that? 'Thank you very much'? I just looked at him in stunned silence. His intentions were without doubt honourable. Besides, he was happily married. Some of his guests, however, needed my firm resistance.

Nancy had been his literary agent when Temple came back from the war. He had made a name for himself writing articles for the American forces. He'd been a psychology major, was swept up in a war in which he flourished, with his big personality. He was sent by the military to seek collaboration on behalf of the Americans with Marshall Tito of Yugoslavia. He had met Tito in a cave and had a photograph among the many on his study wall to prove it.

When Nancy took a fancy to Temple I think that was his lucky day. She was devoted to him It was her idea to write a travel guide to Europe. They soon married and the Guide became their life's work and income. Later Nancy compiled a Shopping Guide.

They lived on a scale I had never witnessed. The servants and I got board and keep, and I was paid 3000 pesetas a month, then worth about $50. At that time Temple told me proudly that the Guide was bringing in $300 a week. Fifty years ago that was a lot of money.

I learned a lot from the Fieldings. I learned how to set an elegant table and entertain with confidence. I learned from Nancy to keep a record every time I entertained so that I'd never give a guest the same dish twice; I still maintain that. Not to drink too much when others are in their cups. I learned that famous and successful people generally have intriguing personalities and considerable sparkle. We had frequent celebrity visitors who came to enjoy Temple's lavish company from many countries, mostly from America.

I was not encouraged to call them by their first names, and Mr and Mrs seemed too formal. The Fieldings asked me to address them instead as 'Mam and Pap' as their previous secretary had. I tried, but it stuck in my throat. I didn't see them as parents, so I mostly avoided calling them anything.

In that balmy climate (apart from a few chilly months in winter) after a long day's work we relaxed on the terrace where Bougainvillea bloomed in huge pots. Every evening, whether or not they had visitors, the

Fieldings would drink three tumblers of whisky with ice and soda. If they had no visitors they would often retire to bed around 6 p.m. and after their highballs the servants would serve them dinner in their wide bed under a mosquito net, with trays on their laps. They were very compatible. In the ten years they'd lived there Temple never learned Spanish and Nancy spoke pigeon Spanish without reference to grammar or accent. '*Señor gusta sopa*,' she would say to Francesca in broad American, meaning he'd like soup.

The Fieldings had a thirteen year old son Dodge, who was educated at a boarding school in Copenhagen and flew home (unaccompanied) for the holidays. Dodge was tremendous fun. He and I would walk down to the hotel every afternoon to collect the post, and as we walked he'd re-enact whole films he'd seen, for my entertainment. He made me laugh. He told jokes like: Two people sitting in an aeroplane, looking out the window: 'Look at those people down there, don't they look like ants?'.... 'They *are* ants, we haven't taken off yet.' In addition to English, Dodge spoke fluent Danish, Spanish and Mallorquín. He took after his mother, being physically slight. Dodge was funny and smart, affectionate and such good company. During the summer he had a small enterprise, selling bags of fresh peanuts from a tray to holidaymakers on the sandy beach below. The tourists thought he was a local. Nancy adored him, but confided to me that Temple was so needy of her attention, she sent Dodge away to leave Temple more space. She admitted she put Temple first. I disapproved in silence.

At Christmas we were excited when Dodge came home for the holidays. He and Martín went out in the woods with a saw and came back dragging a huge pine Christmas tree through a foot of snow. Nancy and I hollered and whooped from the terrace to encourage them. I pinned up coloured sheets of paper with their Christmas cards by the thousand stapled all over, which looked festive. Temple had designed their card which I addressed to the hundreds of people on their mailing list. It consisted of a funny message in his handwriting, summarizing the highlights of their year, which he decorated with round faces with upturned smiles, or downturned mouths to denote dismay. With hindsight, he may have been the inventor of emoticons.

We sat by the log fire and opened our presents. The Fieldings were generous and my best present was a pretty blue negligee and matching nightgown. Dodge's glee in Christmas lifted all our spirits. Catalina cooked a turkey feast and we all felt cheerful. When Dodge went back to school in Denmark after Christmas, Nancy, Francesca, Martin and I were all sad.

Two villas and a hotel were the only buildings in the bay of Formentor in those days. The only other visible building amongst the mostly fir trees lining the slopes down to the sea, was Whitney Straight's villa, just visible in the distance. I never met Whitney Straight, novelist, magazine proprietor and art collector, although I once met his nephews by the hotel pool. They bought me *'cuba libre'* – Bacardi with coca cola. The hotel beach stretched from below our villa to the hotel a mile away, with its straw umbrellas and narrow sandy shore. I could hear distant shouts of holiday makers on the beach from my office desk where I sat toiling.

One day in the hotel gift shop I met an English woman shopping for a bikini. She was friendly, blonde and pretty and asked me if I thought it flattering to wear. And was I staying at the hotel? I said no, I was Temple Fielding's secretary. Oh my goodness, she said, her husband would love to meet the Fieldings! Well, I knew better than to offer invitations on their behalf, even when she told me her husband was Stanley Black, the band leader. I said I would mention it to the Fieldings. When they heard I'd met Stanley Black's wife they sent me back to the hotel, a mile away, with a pressing invitation for drinks. (By design there was no telephone, to protect their privacy at the expense of my legs.) When they arrived, Stanley's LP was playing 'I left my heart in San Francisco' on the terrace. Temple was a fan. Stanley and his wife were really nice and his orchestra sounded wonderful in that setting.

The Fieldings told me that one time they had entertained the man who wrote the song 'Three Coins in A Fountain' and his wife at the villa. As they drove back to Palma they had crashed in the car and the wife was killed. They still felt bad about that.

I nearly always joined their entertaining sessions. I didn't speak unless spoken to. I had an instinct for these things. But they would sometimes include me in the conversation. When reference came up to the death threat Temple had received from an aggrieved tour guide he had slated in his book, 'Eileen,' Temple would say, casually, 'See if you can find that death threat in the records' and as this happened half a dozen times in as many months, I kept that crudely written threat permanently to hand in my office. The guide would have been mortified to know how Temple relished his death threat.

One day a woman visiting from California mentioned a book that was popular at that time, *The World of Suzie Wong*. As it happened, I was half way through reading it. The Fieldings insisted I give it to the visitor to take away with her. I felt bereft as I handed over the engrossing novel, and the visitor, sensing my feelings, later posted it back to me with a thank you note. I really appreciated the considerate people I met.

Art Buchwald and Temple carried on a very funny correspondence, which I much enjoyed. I never met him, but felt sorry when I heard years later he had died. I felt the world was poorer without his wit.

At one stage five prominent Danes arrived to spend a few days with Temple. I was warned it was a man's scene and I was considerately moved to the hotel for the duration. We put a 'Gone Fishing' sign at the gate to prohibit visitors. The guests brought with them a whole kilo of Beluga caviar – it filled a large serving bowl. The men sat on the sunny terrace in bathing trunks and took off their watches. They drank, ate and slept at irregular hours so that night became day and vice versa. *'Skol!'* It was a mercy to be staying in the hotel. Even so, one of them knocked on my hotel door and it took all my determination and firmness to get rid of him.

Later, Al Read, a prominent British comedian, came to stay for a month, during which time Nancy had to go to Madrid to have her gall bladder removed, and Al came with us. I had long listened to and admired his half hour radio sketches. Al's sense of humour appealed to me. It was opaque to Americans, so he could subtly pull their leg and make me laugh at the same time. He was far more polished than one would suppose, than his radio persona. They also thought him funny, but we laughed at different aspects of Al's jokes. How I had missed the British sense of humour over the preceding months. Al was a tonic.

We stayed in the Palace Hotel in Madrid for a month, a five star treat that had its limitations for me as I could not see my friends; I was expected to be available all day and every day to the Fieldings. It was nice to have fresh flowers and fruit in my suite from the management, but I would rather have had a breath of fresh air, and after three weeks without emerging from the building, Fernando telephoned me close to midnight (I'd worked till 11.30) as I was about to go to bed and we agreed to have a drink in the hotel bar. When I got back to my room an hour later I found a note on my bed from Temple chiding me sharply for leaving. They had tried to call me at midnight for some task, and I could not be found. The note was reproachful and wounding, to the effect that, 'If you want this job you'll be available when you're called.' I didn't sleep well at all that night. I felt hurt by their unkind tone after months of devoted attention. I'd had only alternate Sunday afternoons free for eight months, unless my presence was needed then too. I had no predictable time off to meet friends. Once in Mallorca Francesca had been sent to wake me at midnight to go and take dictation, which they scrapped the next day; it had been about something they were discussing over drinks. I felt more and more like a servant.

Back in the villa, one morning we woke up and the Sixth Fleet was anchored in the bay. It was an impressive sight: half a dozen American warships and flags all over. Admiral Cat Brown had come to look up his old friend Temple. Naturally Temple was delighted.

The Admiral and a few officers arrived for lunch on the terrace. Among them were three young officers who were there to fetch and carry, like me. They were friendly, and I enjoyed their company. They were dashing in their white uniforms and officers' caps trimmed with black and gold.

Soon after, Temple left on a working trip, leaving Nancy to recover from her operation, cared for by the three servants and me. I had plenty to occupy me. On my arrival there had been 3,000 unanswered letters following their ten months absence on an extended tour researching the current edition of the Guide, and I had been steadily responding to these with individual answers over the preceding eight months, in addition to my other work.

A couple of weeks after the Admiral's visit, on a Sunday afternoon the three young officers hired mopeds and drove across the island to see me, without notice. (The fleet was now anchored near Palma; they were patrolling the Mediterranean at the time.) Unfortunately, near to the villa one of them had fallen off the moped and seriously gouged his chin and knee. He was bleeding profusely and had such a deep gash on his handsome chin that he is probably still scarred today. I called Francesca to help me clean him up and put a dressing on his face. He was trembling, weak and deathly pale. His friends said 'How can we get him back to Palma? There is no way we are getting back on those mopeds.'

Martin walked down to fetch the hire car and its driver from the hotel. Nancy meanwhile, was having a late siesta. The officers asked me to go with them in the car to interpret and help negotiate with the moped company, and hire a boat back to their ship. I knocked softly on Nancy's door to ask her permission, even though it was Sunday and technically my afternoon off, but as she didn't answer I took a chance and said I would go with them. They had after all been the Fieldings' guests.

We drove to Palma, and had an omelette in a café while I interpreted and struck a deal for them with the moped owner. They didn't have enough money for the boatman, so I loaned them about thirty dollars and they promised to send it to me when they got back to the fleet. I saw them off, then Miguel drove me home, by which time it was about ten o'clock in the evening and the house was in darkness.

On my pillow was a note from Nancy which said 'You don't really want this job, do you? You went off like a bitch in heat. See me in the morning.' She was not normally so rude. I was appalled. It took me less than a minute to respond mentally, 'No, I don't want this job. I am not treated with the courtesy I deserve.' Until then I had no intention of leaving. The next morning, to her astonishment, I told her that I could no longer work where I was not respected, and that I would not return from the trip to London scheduled for a few days later, my first holiday in their employment. Nancy was taken aback and tried to persuade me to stay, but it's not in my nature to take two insults meekly; one might be excused, but two is a pattern. The day before I left I finished off the last of the 3,000 unanswered letters, leaving their affairs in the best state I could.

Temple had written in the text for the 59/60 edition, 'Nancy is my right hand and Eileen is my left.' He hurriedly deleted this before publication, and perhaps he thought I had deserted them. Maybe Nancy forgot to tell him what she had written in her note to me. I met Nancy and Dodge when they visited London a few months later, and they were friendly, but Temple never gave me the reference Nancy had promised and I never heard from them again.

I was replaced by a married couple who stayed for many years.

I wept when I left Francesca and Martin, and Bullet the dog, who had all become very dear to me indeed. We exchanged Christmas cards every year with loving messages, until they died. I did see them once more. I was in Mallorca in 1989 with a client on business, and on a whim took a taxi across the island on the Sunday afternoon to see if I could find them in *Pollensa*, their home village. I knocked on their door, watched by the taxi driver with interest. I did not know the man who opened the door. Martin, who thirty years before had a shock of black curly hair had gone bald and shrunk, but fortunately he recognized me. 'Eileen!' he shouted, taking my arm, pulling me inside, calling 'Francesca! It's Eileen!' and she came out to meet me, still entirely recognizable (her hair had been grey at 34), hardly changed at all, hugging and kissing me and making me feel like their prodigal daughter. I reminded them that I used to say in 1959, thirty years before, 'One day I will come and call at your door, "Francesca!" And this is the day!' We sat and talked for a couple of hours, catching up on the news while Francesca stroked my hand and gazed at me. Their house was a witness to Francesca's beautiful presentation and housekeeping skills.

A few years after I had left the island, their long hoped-for pregnancy had resulted in a son (Francesca was then in her late thirties). I had included them in my prayers and asked many times for them to be so blessed. Martiniti was educated and wrote me in excellent English on behalf of his parents, and although I never met him, I spoke to him on the telephone when I was in Barcelona with clients, sadly too busy to meet him. He was married with two children.

Francesca and Martin told me that the Fieldings had died in their sixties (they had been 45 when I knew them). Nancy had lived a year longer but languished without her beloved Temple. They looked after her till the end. Martin arranged her funeral. Their son Dodge came for the interment. What a sad outcome for such lusty-living people.

Living with Nancy and Temple Fielding in their heady environment was an education in worldliness and style. I'll never forget the unrivalled beauty of the Bay of Formentor.

The naval officer once wrote to me, but never repaid my loan.

17 AQUI ES LA GLORIA

In 1960 I had a third opportunity to visit Spain. I had lived in Madrid for most of 1957, 1958-59 in Mallorca, and now I was being invited for a six weeks stay in Estremadura, a province I had never visited, in the far west of Spain.

Two young men rented an apartment in the house next door to our house in Mottingham: Augustin from Siruela de Badajoz and John from America. Augustin said he was engaged to John's sister and wanted to take her to visit his family, but in Spain that was impossible without a chaperone and he invited me to be the chaperone. That made good sense, from my knowledge of Spain which at that stage was only half way through the forty years presidency of Generalissimo Franco, still in the dark ages in comparison to other European countries. They still ploughed the fields with oxen while we had modern tractors. Nice girls were not allowed out without a chaperone, even when engaged, and had to be home before dinner in the evening. They were not supposed to kiss until they were married and it was illegal for anyone to kiss in public – the police would arrest you on the spot. In cinemas every kiss was censored, which made a film like Picnic which I saw in Spanish, even more erotic when the censor cut the film just before the clinches, and the audience sighed.

Being arrested was a serious prospect. You did not want to see the inside of a Spanish prison, where conditions were foul, and you were not always fed. You were seldom charged, let alone tried. They would only let you out when they felt like it in Franco's Spain, and sometimes they didn't. As a result the public behaved itself impeccably. It was a repressed society in every sense.

Augustin and I set off, 36 hours by train from London to Madrid. We slept on the comfortable padded leather compartment benches along with other travellers. I loved these long train journeys.

Lying awake with my eyes closed at 6 in the morning I heard Augustin softly singing a flamenco song (a reminder of the Arabic influence still strong in Spain today), and I stifled a giggle. He was singing 'I am going to make a rosary of your teeth' and while he contemplated his beloved's sacred teeth in place, I pictured them extracted and hanging on a string. He didn't appreciate my mirth.

I was puzzled when Augustin announced just as we were pulling into Madrid's Atocha railway station: 'My fiancée will not be here, she had to go back to America suddenly, but you can still come to my village.' I wondered how he had received this news (no mobile phones in 1960) and it's a measure of my naiveté that I smelled a whiff of curiosity at that stage rather than a rat.

During a two day stopover in Madrid I stayed with Mariano's mother Emilia who told me 'Come back if you are not happy there.' I was planning to visit friends in Lisbon after that. She warned me that conditions might be deprived in the province and to prepare myself for primitive plumbing. In fact there was no plumbing: Estremadura was the back of bloody beyond.

On the way Augustin told me that the week before a girl from the village had been taken ill with polio and gone to hospital. This was alarming news indeed. Polio was highly contagious, usually water borne. In 1960 we all knew people who had been killed or crippled by polio – Dr. Salk had yet to produce his vaccine.

After the train we took an ancient bus crammed with peasants who had never seen a foreigner before, laden with live chickens, bundles of clothes, food and cheeses.(It is the region where *Manchego* cheese is made from sheep's milk.) It took two hours over bumpy roads (the bus had no springs), and it was a relief to arrive at *Siruela de Badajoz.*

A great crowd came to meet us. Augustin introduced me to his mother, looking older than I expected, prematurely aged by her shabby black dress, hair pulled back in a bun, no make-up and the strong sun. Every married country woman wore a black dress from the day she gave up her single status until she was buried. I was 22, with blonde hair and colourful dresses - an exotic bird indeed.

Augustin's mother shook my hand and called me '*Señora'*, a mark of respect as I was only *señorita*. We walked past the village well, down the narrow street with its open drainage channel in the middle, towards their house. Out of politeness I said 'Your village is very beautiful' to which she replied *'Si, señora, aqui es la gloria'* (Yes ma'am, this is heaven). I realized then that she had never been anywhere else. Stuck for conversation I admired some trees and she said 'Have you not seen trees before?' 'It's a beautiful day, the sun is lovely,' I said inanely; and she replied 'Do you not see the sun in England?' I gave up.

Augustin (in his mid-twenties) did not smoke in front of his father (who smoked like a chimney), out of respect. I would learn that only one 'foreigner' had been seen in the village before, a girl who was born there and went to live in France. When she returned for a visit she wore pants and smoked, so was labelled a '*sin vergüenza*' – a shameless one. I endeavoured to avoid this epithet.

Although they had one of the better houses in the village, it was still whitewashed, single storey, low ceilinged, dark within, almost windowless and the cooking was done on a pile of twigs lit on the earth floor in the living room, like a small indoor bonfire. The smoke went out through a hole in the roof. Mercifully there were stools to sit on, but there was no table and the food was served in one large earthenware dish set on a stool between us into which everyone dipped their own spoon. I asked for my own dish and they gave me one, laughing. About seven of us sat around (the family was out in full to welcome the prodigal son who hadn't been home for three years). Nobody mentioned the fiancée. It slowly dawned on me that I was there to conceal the fact that Augustin was probably gay and John was his partner. The fiancée didn't exist. I was the supposed 'love interest', or rather the smokescreen: so much for the essential chaperone.

I discovered that the well was the sole source of water in the village, and that this family was richer than many, having a donkey to fetch the water in scuffed leather panniers. So, there was no running water in the house, no bathroom or lavatory, no drinkable water, given the polio threat. Their substitute for a restroom was a pile of ordure 4 ft. high in the barn next to the house which stank to high heaven, and the donkey tethered nearby brayed and honked as only donkeys can, every time I added to the pile.

Now I was seriously alarmed. I could not drink the water and the alternatives were beer or wine. In the house only wine was offered and I sipped a glass, but didn't finish it when the old grandfather who looked as if he shaved once a month whether he needed it or not, told me proudly, 'I trod the grapes with my own feet.'

I asked for an appointment with the hairdresser and they laughed. There wasn't one. The women simply pulled their black hair back in a bun and accumulated grease. They were highly entertained when I asked for a bowl of water to wash my hair, and gave me a piece of washing soap in place of shampoo. The enamel bowl was set in the tiny inner courtyard on a low stool. I kneeled on the weedy earth, watched by the family and half a dozen chickens. I had to shoo the chickens from the water which was cold and soapy, and no second bowl to rinse with. I began to feel wretched.

They had given me a bedroom in a neighbour's house (presumably out of decency, not to be under the same roof as Augustin) and the only light was a 6 watt bulb. There was a single bed and a kitchen chair. My smart black dress made of crepe with silky lining, was heavy and slipped off the chair onto the floor. When I picked it up it was smothered in dust and detritus which must have taken years to accumulate, invisible in a windowless room's dim light. It took ten minutes to brush off the fluff with my hand.

The food was surprisingly delicious – a rich stew with pork or lamb and vegetables, and chunks of bread. They made Manchego cheese in the village and proudly showed me how they shaped it with their hands into plaited rope moulds and left it on store room shelves to mature over months.

Predictably, within two days I had gastro-enteritis and misgivings in equal measure. The intervals between the donkey's honking shortened.

Augustin and I went to a bar for a beer; without that I might have suffered dehydration. Beer is not a patch on water when you're thirsty. Now I was desperately planning my escape from the village. I feared that six weeks in that environment might kill me. How to leave without insulting them? Fortunately the next day was my 23rd birthday and I knew my parents would send me a birthday card. So I sat waiting for the post to arrive, with a scenario prepared in my head.

I opened the envelope, looked at my birthday card briefly and shoved it back inside. 'Oh my god, my Father has had a heart attack! I have to go home at once!' There was consternation and Augustin asked to see the letter, which I of course refused. I could tell he was suspicious, but he arranged a car to come and take me to the train stop where I could board the Lisbon train. Lisbon was much nearer than Madrid and I said I would get a flight from there. Again the village came out to see me off, tears flowing. I had hardly stopped crying since I'd opened the mail, tears of weakness and genuine relief.

Although I was still throwing up all the way to the border, the happy refrain kept going through my head 'This is a lovely way, to spend a birthday'. I found a hotel room in Badajoz on the border, took a very long, deep bath and next day continued by train to Lisbon to stay in my English friends' luxury apartment. Never take a bathroom for granted.

I enjoyed a couple of weeks in Lisbon, and a couple more with Emilia in Madrid on the way home. In the train from Portugal I met and travelled with two handsome young German guys who told me how to make brandy and drew the diagram of a still in my notebook. I was thrilled to have the recipe for brandy until I found that it's illegal to make your own spirits.

I didn't go back to Spain for 22 years because I was married with five children and we couldn't afford the fares.

When I returned to Spain with the family in a Toyota camper in 1982 I noticed two huge changes: Men no longer looked at me as if I was Goldie Hawn and they were in with a chance, and in place of oxen they now had combine harvesters.

18 GROUND HOSTESS

Of the many jobs I had between the ages 17 to 25, the one I disliked most was working at Heathrow Airport as a ground hostess in 1960. Perversely it was the hardest job I had to land. 534 people applied for two positions as summer staff with Trans Canada Airlines (now Air Canada). The other girl was Polish and we both got in on the strength of our languages.

Working for an airline was considered a glamorous occupation by those who hadn't tried it. We wore uniforms designed by Hardy Amies (the couturier who also dressed the Queen) and they were smart: best quality navy serge suits made to measure, with crisp white blouses. We had perky hats and court shoes and sashayed between the TCA desk and the transit lounge. We worked shift hours to meet the planes that arrived in the early morning, requiring a 5 a.m. start, or in the late afternoon. On early days we were collected by taxi from our digs near the airport. On other days we had to take the bus. Passengers would stare admiringly and ask, where are you flying to today? with envy and admiration. I would adjust my shoulder bag and either smile or come clean with the news that I never went anywhere.

Airline passengers were treated like royalty. They wore their best clothes and for one day they felt important. They required recognition of their specialness. Some would be pleasant and friendly but others would be rude and demanding. Often the men would try to grope the girls, especially as we loaded them onto the transit bus to London after a boozy flight, when they could hardly stand.

Equally tedious was the fact that all the men working at Heathrow seemed to be doing it for the uniform. How they admired themselves as they strolled along the concourse pretending to be pilots. I realize now that many of them were probably gay. At the time I wondered what had happened to my usual appeal when no one asked me out. My social life at Heathrow was non-existent.

I rented a bedroom in a private house belonging to a building worker and his feisty wife, who had a little terraced house in Twickenham.

Another of the hostesses who had a room there told me of the vacancy. Had I known her better I would never have taken it. She was petite, poised, pretty, pert, smart and insufferably smug. She also had an affected Canadian accent. She had a peaches and cream complexion and soft blond curls. She ironed her blouses with a level of expertise I had never seen before (or since), pressing the revere to perfection. They looked like new blouses every time. Beside her I felt clumsy and a bit scruffy. She took every opportunity to make me feel more-so. I cannot iron a blouse today without remembering Patricia.

I did not warm to the landlady, she was shallow, sharp and forty-something, a collector of small plaster ornaments and she had a yappy Scottie dog called 'Richard'. 'He has a lion's heart' she used to joke as she cradled him. I sensed her jealousy of these two young women. Her husband, an Irish bricky, had fallen off a ladder two years earlier and was still unable to work. He was quite likeable and suffered his bossy wife with a kind of dumb insolence. One evening I needed to bath and wash my hair before I went to bed at 8 p.m. because I had a 5 a.m. start (leaving the house at 4.15). The hubby was in the bath and the wife shouted through the door 'Come on out, Eileen needs to take a bath and wash her hair!' Half an hour later she shouted at him again. No response. I think he was asleep. This went on for nearly two hours before he finally emerged from the steamy room (only one bathroom of course in a terrace house) with an air of resentment you could bottle. It was inconvenient as I was late to bed and the water was lukewarm, but I thought it was funny.

She cooked the same thing every week on set days. Wednesdays were liver, bacon and onions. I had never enjoyed liver before because my Mother used to fry it with mashed potatoes, and I could not stand liver without the bacon flavour to balance its sweetness. The fried onions were delicious. Her ingredients were always cheap but she was a good traditional cook. No complaints there.

One night I went early to bed, very tired. It was summer and the sun was shining. I set my alarm clock for 8 o'clock, forgetting that it was only now 7 p.m. I fell asleep and next thing, the alarm bell was ringing and I was up, washed and half dressed in my uniform before I realized it was the same evening. Bother. How my landlady laughed.

She introduced me to a neighbour living opposite. He was forty, worked for Hoover, had a pretty wife and two young children. They spent their holidays on the Costa somewhere and he was keen to learn Spanish. He offered to pay me for lessons but I said I didn't feel qualified so I'd do it for nothing. I saw him three or four times and found him often tired and easily distracted. It was difficult to engage his attention. Finally I put down the book we were following and said, Listen, *escucha*, I am going to tell you something interesting - *voy a contarte algo interesante*. He sat up. *Fijate* - imagine, - *estas en un club de noche con una chica guapisima* – you're in a nightclub with a beautiful girl. His eyes widened. *El salón esta en obscuridad* - the salon is darkness.' I was telling him in Spanish and in English to be sure he would understand, and then I eased off the English, like letting go the saddle when teaching a child to ride a bike. 'La chica es encantadora - te mira con sus ojos grandes. *Te sientes muy animado. Toma su mano y ella no resiste. Guitarras suena la musica, empiezan a baillar, estan enamorados y feliz como nunca antes.*' (This translates as The girl is enchanting – she regards you with her big eyes. You are excited. You take her hand and she doesn't resist. Guitars play, you start to dance, you are in love and happy as never before.) I had his attention and he appeared to follow the message in detail, then his wife came in with some coffee and the lesson faded abruptly. But it taught me a lesson: first capture your audience's attention.

[In Cambridge, years later, I was employed by a language school to coach a teenager who needed to pass a Spanish exam to get into university. I asked him to describe his girlfriend, and for homework I told him to prepare a joke to tell me in the next lesson.]

At work Patricia cultivated Danuta, (the Polish girl) with warmth that emphasized the coldness with which she treated me. I liked Danuta: she did not contribute to this rivalry. Danuta became popular and I was generally ignored, except by Erica, the woman who had engaged us, an attractive forty year old top executive. She was nice. She lived in Richmond and once invited me to the cinema and afterwards to her flat for a snack, but that was the only sociable occasion with any of my colleagues.

The work was quite hard and often irritating. Once there was a plane, having problems with its windscreen wipers, grounded at Shannon, causing a delay of many hours and provoking the wrath of people waiting at Heathrow to meet their friends. One could be on duty for hours on end without a break. I recall eating a chocolate bar sitting on a public loo one afternoon because I'd had nothing to eat since the previous day and couldn't take a break from the check-in desk. We had to keep our cool while angry members of the public vented their spleen on us. 'I'll never travel this airline again!' was a common threat which left us unmoved, because they had probably never flown with us, or anyone else.

People who needed extra help would be met off the plane by a specified hostess. A woman with children for example would either hand you the baby or more often, her hand luggage, and you would struggle through customs with her. This was extremely difficult for me as my back then was a great deal worse than it is today. I often returned home in pain.

One day I spotted the name of a former sixth form friend on an incoming roster. I made a point of meeting Mavis. She had her wedding dress hanging over her arm.

A permanent position arose and Danuta and I were both invited to apply for it. All the other hostesses (and a few beautiful young male hosts) seemed to side with her. She's welcome to it, I thought, and did not apply. After a day or two Erica asked me in private for my application. I said something vague and left it. Next day again she said 'Eileen, we really want your application.' I said 'I'm not applying because I don't want the job.' 'Why not?' she asked, astonished. 'Because I have never been so unhappy in a job before,' I replied. I explained how I felt excluded by my co-workers, and how hard it had been to make friends. She tried to persuade me, but I would not be budged.

There was a very hot day and a delayed flight. I was deputed to sit in the transit lounge with an important passenger. I don't remember why she was important. We sat beneath a whirling ceiling fan which gave a cooling draft, and chatted pleasantly for an hour or so. When I got up I found my back locked, the way it would in Spain years later when I sat out on a breezy hot night when we were camping. There was nothing to be done but quit the job in this disabled state. I had only been there a couple of months, not even long enough to have a picture taken in my uniform.

My landlady was kind to accompany me on the journey to Mottingham. I was in pain and could barely walk. I never went back to Heathrow until I was flying to Spain as Director of Export Connect, when I recognized the former single terminal building (now Terminal Two) as I walked along the concourse, this time without the sashay.

19 MEETING RICHARD

There was nothing serendipitous about meeting Richard Dight. Our mothers engineered it. While I was working in Mallorca my Mother wrote that she had loaned my rucksack to Richard, after hearing from his mother that he was going on an expedition to Iceland. I was pleased to think the rucksack was travelling. I had bought it from an Australian girl for a pound. I knew Richard and his brother John by sight, but didn't know which was which.

I recall standing beside his sister Anne's pram when she was about six months old, with Richard standing on the other side. I was then five and he was two years older. Our mothers used to chat when they met by chance, and I recall being bored but thinking, at least there is a baby to look at.

Back in London in late 1961 Richard's sister Anne came to see me. She said there would be a dance at her brother's college, and would I like to go with her to that? Richard and Anne arrived to pick me up for the dance at Wye College. As soon as we got there Richard asked me to dance, but then spotted a friend and left me in the middle of the dance floor, to go off with him. I felt humiliated. All alone in a setting where everyone else is greeting each other with enthusiasm, being ignored made me uncomfortable. After a second dance when the same thing happened, I retreated to the cloakroom and sat waiting for the dance to end. Richard drove us home and I told my mother, He is so rude! I will never go out with him again.

It's fortunate that I changed my mind, or the world would have fewer little Dights in it. When Richard came home at Christmas he was buoyant, thinking 'Now I have a potential girlfriend in Mottingham'. It happened that, that very afternoon I had been at an office Christmas party, and had a few drinks, so when Richard phoned to ask me out I thought, Why not? Now I'll drop him and see how *he* likes it.

But we liked each other, so nobody got dumped. He was very attractive, good looking, presentable, educated and from the same background as me. He went to the same school as my brother, came from a stable family. He had a career I respected. We very quickly became close. On Boxing Day he proposed to me, and I accepted! This was unprecedented in both our lives, to do something so sudden and reckless. Both cautious by nature, it was the one time we threw caution to the winds. We were in love! On a subsequent visit home (he was working in Dorchester) he took me to a jeweller in Oxford Street and bought an engagement ring, which we then showed to his parents, without having mentioned our intention to get married. His father commented , 'You know what they say Richard, marry in haste, repent at leisure.' Twelve weeks after he proposed, we were married in the Catholic Church I'd attended since I was born.

After the wedding, twenty guests sat down to lunch at the Bull Hotel in Chislehurst in an elegant upstairs dining room. I took off my veil because it stopped me turning left and right to talk to people. Richard's mother Mop (so named in tandem with Pop, his father) had helped me make my wedding dress of white brocade with a woven satin design, from five yards of material which Anne bought for me at cost, from Courtaulds where she was working. The dress cost me 5 pounds and had a shaped waist, heart neckline, long sleeves and pleats at the back, giving fullness. I was pleased with it.

My Mother made the fruitcake, Mop added marzipan and iced it to the smooth layer, and had it finished by a friend who did cake decorating classes. My bouquet was of freesias which smelled divine.

It was a happy day. After lunch we all drove back to our house in Mottingham where my Mother served tea and cakes, and soon afterwards I changed into the green suit I had bought for my honeymoon, and Richard and I drove off in his Morris Minor Traveller.

He didn't tell me where we would go on honeymoon. He said it was a secret. We drove to Amersham in the Chilterns for the first night in an old coaching inn. We were self-conscious, spent a long time gathering the confetti from our clothes and luggage and hiding it between the floor boards. We ate in the restaurant, the first time I'd eaten beef stroganoff. In April it was cold in the unheated rooms. But we were excited about being together, and married.

The next night we stopped in Burford, in the Cotswolds, where I'd stayed with my parents on holiday as a child. Those were the two nights Richard had booked, intending to spend a week travelling back to Dorchester, but I said 'Let's just go to the apartment' (which I hadn't seen), so we were at home by the Wednesday, having married on the Monday. The apartment was lovely, a two bedroom attic suite at the top of a house on the high street, next to Thomas Hardy's statue at the crossroads.

We were powerfully attracted to each other. There was a sense of goodwill and pulling together which lasted for some years. That first casual summer was our happiest together, before we became parents. Richard was 27 and had only had one girlfriend, when he was at college.

I had had more boyfriends than I could remember, let alone count. I was good and ready to put all my energies and devotion into our marriage, hoping to live happily ever after. The future looked rosy to us both.

I loved everything about being married. I loved the companionship and daily cuddles, the plans we made for the future, gathering items to make our home, learning about each other in detail. I loved the feeling of security now I had a husband. Richard was reliable and steady. He budgeted carefully to be sure our money stretched. He was affectionate and I loved the feel of his arms around me. When we went out it was good to be a couple. He in turn felt the warmth of my love. He said I was the first person he had met in his entire life who approved of him. His parents hadn't made him feel secure the way mine had. He was good looking and had presence. I was proud of him. He had a job in which his advice was valued. He was enthusiastic and knowledgeable about farming. He had hobbies he liked to share, like fishing. He read a lot. I felt secure emotionally and economically, with him in control. I loved it that he was interested in gardening. When we started to decorate Hill Farm House he used a paint roller for the first time, and said 'Now I know how easy it is to paint, I can tackle anything.' I wielded a paint brush and together we chose the colours. We had similar taste in furniture and fittings. We could look in a shop window and both pick out the same item we liked. He smelled good. He was strong and talented with his hands. He could do woodwork, change plugs, and use tools of all kinds. He tackled many different jobs around the house. We were politically on the same page. Although he was not religious at all, he didn't mind that I went to Mass. He never tried to influence me in that way, and I didn't try to influence him either.

We were compatible in the evenings, enjoying a quiet read or a stroll together. We both liked the countryside. We were keen on making a nice home. He knew something about wine and enjoyed good food. He enjoyed my cooking and encouraged me. We slept peacefully, feeling secure. We laughed at different jokes sometimes, but we both had a sense of humour. He thought Morecambe and Wise were hilarious, but I would merely smile. Different things made me laugh. He hardly ever read novels and when we read the same one, and discussed it afterwards, it was as if we had read different books because we had perceived different aspects. We liked doing crosswords together. We played Scrabble. I thought this compatibility would last forever.

Eleven months after we were married I gave birth to Peter. Maternity Services in those days left much to be desired. We were both shattered by the experience. The trauma I suffered in Nottingham's Peel Street Hospital and my subsequent breakdown put an abrupt end to the first, happiest year of our marriage.

20 A TRAUMATIC EXPERIENCE

This is how I wish it had happened:

It is 1963. My husband sits beside me, holding my hand and giving me sips of water. He is encouraging me in the latter stages of labour with our first child. It's painful, but I can manage, with medication. I breathe deeply and I am excited. This is the most creative thing I have ever done. With the help of a familiar midwife and one last push, Peter is born. A moment later he cries lustily. He is wrapped in a blanket and given to us. My husband and I look at him in delight and wonder. I will never forget this moment.

This is how it really happened:

I am two weeks overdue and weary as hell. My G.P. has told me he does not want me induced. His exact words: 'My friend induced his wife and she perished'. From a small cottage hospital in Newark I have been transferred by ambulance to a bigger one in Nottingham. I don't know where I am and I don't know anybody. I'm surgically induced in the bed within half an hour of arrival. Immediately pains start to jab and slice and they get stronger very fast. I gasp. What was the point of teaching us relaxation in prenatal classes? How to relax while in agony? I wish I was not alone. I'm in a ward full of women I don't know, who can't talk because they are attached to tubes. Is it supposed to hurt like this? I'm terrified. Instead of going with the flow I gasp, brace myself with each contraction, making it worse.

A nurse stops for thirty seconds beside my bed and listens to the baby's heart with a metal trumpet pressed against my belly. 'Can you give me some aspirin?' I ask. She laughs, 'Aspirin won't help. Relax, you'll be hours yet.' Oh dear God, I hope not.

After five hours of labour she comes with the trumpet for the third time. She goes away and comes back with a doctor and a trolley. 'We are going to help you now', she says, 'because the baby is distressed'. I'm pulled roughly onto a trolley, wheeled fast along a corridor where two young mothers are in labour on other trolleys. I will spare the details of stirrups, scalpel, forceps, these unexpected and shocking indignities. Suddenly the baby is born with a whoosh. The agony stops almost immediately. They tell me it's a boy. 'That's Peter' I say, introducing him politely. The Indian lady doctor who delivered him complains to her colleagues about the mess I've made of her sari. They commiserate with her, ignoring me. I do not see the baby, presumably because the women in the corridor take precedence. I am stitched, washed, put back into my bloody nightdress and sent back to the ward.

My husband arrives after work, just as I am back in bed. 'Oh Richard, it was terrible, I could never do that again.' 'Oh, you'll get over it', he says, like a last contraction.

It is two days before I am strong enough to find and put on clean night ware. Meals come and go but are left on a table too far for me to reach and I am too bruised and demoralized to complain. Peter is forty eight hours old the first time I see him. He is thrust at me and I am told 'Ten minutes each side' and left alone. He is ravenous. In twenty minutes he destroys my ability to feed him, despite milk in abundance. My breasts are like bricks, the nipples bleed. My sense of failure is compounded. He is pale-faced with a black eye and bruises from the forceps. His forehead is squashed and he's ugly. He is nothing to do with me. This is the worst possible start for Peter.

At home I do my best to look after him but it's exhausting and nothing like the joy I had anticipated. Richard is also overwhelmed by the difficulty of it all. In a few days depression hits me like a sledgehammer wielded by a psychopath. I am shocked for weeks by the brutality of the experience and cannot sleep for three months without sleeping pills. The first tranquilizers I'm given (Largactil) provoke an allergic response: the whole of my body is covered in a rash.

When Peter is three weeks old I'm in a mental hospital, praying to die. 'Take me now, God. Please.' I am ashamed and alarmed to be a mental patient. The breast abscess bursts but there are no dressings in a mental hospital. When I am refused a dressing, I ask to speak to the matron. I am quietly reminded that in this hospital people who make trouble are put in a lock-up ward. I have heard those patients screaming above our heads, in the night. Eventually they produce a roll of woollen material which itches, and a pad, and leave me to it with a safety pin, to dress myself.

I try to sleep in a ward of thirty women but I'm awake before every dawn chorus despite sedation. Our days are spent doing chores. Three times a day we polish the shining floors with bumpers. We lay tables, clear away, wash up. But vacuum cleaning is voluntary and I volunteer, to disperse my restlessness. Somebody comments 'You can see who is used to keeping a clean house, can't you?' This is the only moment of humour for me because I'm normally a reluctant cleaner. Some nurses and one ward cleaner address me by my surname, without respect, ordering me to do things. Others address me, to my relief, as 'Mrs Dight', and speak kindly. We are all required to attend a dance, no exceptions, mixing with male mental patients from another ward. I shudder at the prospect. My body feels as if it has been sick at both ends since childbirth. The nurses insist, but when Richard comes he tells them to excuse me. They are resentful, but they obey him.

Three times a week patients are subjected to electric shock therapy. Richard and I are asked to sign a paper allowing this to happen to me. We are in a quandary. All the patients are terrified of 'the treatment', I've seen how their memories are battered afterwards. But we are both devastated by my black depression, and we sign. Mercifully I do not become a candidate. We are given pills but nobody listens to us.

Richard visits every night after work. While he goes to talk to the nurse I bury my face in his duffel coat, smelling and treasuring him for his constant support. We have only been married a year. His evening appearances are like anchors to a dangling mountaineer. This is a dreadful experience for a couple at any age. He is my rock. Other women are envious of Richard's daily presence; many wait a week or longer between visits. After 11 days my Mother arrives and takes me home, the day I am scheduled to scrub the toilet floors on my knees. That's a paragraph, but I could write a book.

Peter is twenty years old before I stop feeling sick on his birthday. Now he's in his forties, tall, bearded, handsome and I love him. He has four younger brothers. Having the second baby was the bravest thing I have done in my entire life. It shouldn't happen to a dog.

[At the time the doctors described it as post natal depression and 'hormone shock', but now I think I also had PTSD. The expression Post Traumatic Stress Disorder had not yet been invented. I had flashbacks for years afterwards.]

21 THE FIRST TEN YEARS: THE BOYS ARE BORN

We were married on April 2 1962. The first ten years of our marriage were generally happy. It started out well, in our flat in Dorchester overlooking the high street. Richard was an Agricultural Adviser with the Ministry of Agriculture; his district was the New Forest. Every day he visited farmers to give them free advice on the best way to manage their farms, choose and rotate crops, and diagnose problems.

There was a leather jacket infestation in 1962 and he was the first to recognize it. Farmers were mystified by the crop failure. Grubs ate the leaves, devastating the plants, and he found the grubs. He was always good at diagnosis, logical in his analysis. He was a good lecturer too, as I realized the first time he showed me his Iceland slides, before we were married. He loved his work and MAFF (Ministry of Agriculture, Fisheries and Food) provided their services free, so the farmers fully appreciated his visits. Later ADAS took over from MAFF and charges were introduced, which provoked tensions with some farmers. Richard was not so happy at work after that.

The owner of our two bedroom attic apartment on the third floor in Dorchester was a dentist in his sixties; he and his wife gave us a spider plant, the original parent of those passed down through the family and still with us 49 years later.

In Dorchester I took a job as secretary in an estate agent's office. It was good experience and I enjoyed it.

We had wonderful evenings that first summer of our marriage. The Dorset coast was not far away and about three times a week we drove down to go fishing on Chesil Beach, a bank of pebbles spanning miles of sea front with an inlet of water and sea grass behind. Richard had a beach caster and bought a super fishing reel so he could cast a long way out. He taught me to cast too. We caught mostly mackerel. We could see them shoaling in smooth water, rippled with jumping fish, attracting the attention of gulls. The sun was always going down before we drove home. It was a very happy time.

The only heating in the flat was a wall gas heater, so we sat with a blanket over our knees on cold evenings. A new James Bond novel we'd requested came into the library. We read it aloud to each other. One day in exuberance Richard leaned out of the window in the roof line, three floors up, and yelled to the sky 'I've got a wife!'. I became so engrossed in him, I once caught my reflection in the bathroom mirror and thought 'My goodness, you're still here.' My Father told me that if you're not happy when you are first married, you will never be, and he was right. One evening Richard was late arriving home. Normally he came back around 5.30 but I was still watching the high street out of the window for his car at 7 pm. I was in a panic, thinking he might have had an accident (he was inclined to look at crops and fields as he was driving, the way Andre today looks for ground hogs and deer) and sometimes his swerves alarmed me. I was hugely relieved when he arrived home, saying he'd been caught up in conversation by a farmer. We had no phone in those days.

Shortly after we married I got a kidney infection and the doctor was so concerned, he came three times in one day to visit me. I was delirious with fever. But what I remember most clearly was the pleasure I felt in seeing 'Mrs. Dight' printed on my medicine bottles. My joy at being married to Richard was immense.

We had only been married twelve weeks when I suspected I might be pregnant, despite precautions, and I was excited about this. Richard was very quiet. It was insensitive of me to be so thrilled when he showed so little enthusiasm. I went to see the doctor and leaving his surgery, Richard happened to be passing in his car on the high street. I waved and smiled and gave him the 'thumbs up' sign and his face dropped. It was too early in our relationship to be distracted by a baby. He was a father before he had properly become a husband. It set him off on the wrong foot with the children. My joy in their existence only emphasized his dismay. It was some time before I realized how tough this was on Richard. When I voiced this thought to a friend one day he said 'I never knew you realized that.' The problem was, we didn't talk about such things. Richard was not a talker. On our honeymoon he said that there was nothing under the sun that had not already been discussed by someone, somewhere, and there was no point in us discussing anything. This shut down the communication we should have developed as a couple. We never argued. And nothing was resolved. If I attempted to talk about things he simply walked out of the room. Communication and sometimes even argument are oxygen to a relationship.

At this stage Richard was invited to work for Boots Experimental Farms as Farm Manager. The director of Boots responsible for the agricultural division was an old friend of Richard's boss in the Ministry, who recommended Richard. I advised him to work out the rest of his two year probationary period with the Ministry in case he ever wanted to return, so we didn't move to Thurgarton near Nottingham in the Midlands, until the end of the summer.

We moved house in a Mini, with a roof-rack carrying an armchair Mrs P. (Anne's mother in law, she and Bill had recently married) had given us. We had two deckchairs from my parents and sat on these for months before we bought a sofa. My father bought us a washing machine (twin tub, automatics had not yet been invented) to save my back. We hired a TV for five shillings a week. It was black and white and the frame slipped, so people often had no heads. But on that set we watched Cassius Clay win his first professional fight live, sitting on our deckchairs at six o'clock in the morning.

With the job came Hill Farm House, a beautiful five bed roomed Georgian farmhouse in Thurgarton, which we absolutely loved. It was set in spacious gardens, with a haha in front (a ditch beyond the lawn), affording an uninterrupted, sweeping view over pastures down to the distant laboratories and offices beyond the trees. To the side was a vegetable garden, behind a curved brick wall, and beyond that a copse, with a curving drive to the farm road lined by trees and thousands of snowdrops which bloomed just before Peter was born the following spring. We decorated the kitchen cream with light blue cupboards (it had been beige and green and the transformation was stunning). We bought a second hand table and bentwood chairs for the kitchen for shillings. I covered the table top with yellow Fablon and painted the furniture white. Richard chose tawny red emulsion to paint the dining room walls, with white arched windows to the recessed cupboards. It was beautiful. I've wanted a room that colour ever since, but never had a room that lent itself to this.

The cowman who lived in a cottage nearby came in twice a day to stoke the enormous boiler in the cellar. Coal was delivered by the truck load and shovelled down a manhole. The rent cost us the low sum of 12 pounds a month – rent and heating included. It was the big freeze of 1963 with snow on the ground for months, but we were never cold.

I stopped work as I was pregnant and life was affordable. I relished the role of housekeeper, developed my cooking skills and took up various crafts. I made all our lampshades, buying frames and wrapping them with raffia. We lived as frugally as possible. I always had a meal ready when Richard came in from work. He tackled the garden with enthusiasm (as he always did), planting vegetables alongside the raspberries. Peter was born in March 1963.

Carrying Peter in my arms through the flag-stoned hall between dining and sitting rooms he uttered his first clear word, 'Dark'. I occasionally say 'dark', in the tone he used, but I don't suppose anyone realizes why.

One day Peter was sitting in his high chair, aged 14 months, when I made coffee for a neighbour who was visiting. He leaned over suddenly from his high chair, grabbing the coffee and pulling it over himself, screaming as it burned his upper arm. I pulled his sleeve up and ran his arm under the cold tap instinctively. I was appalled to see his delicate skin peeling as I watched. For a couple of days he was in such pain, he cried incessantly. The only thing that stopped him was riding in the car because he was soothed by the movement and noise of the engine. I drove him around the farm in the Mini for hours, to quieten him. For six weeks I took him daily to the doctor to change his dressings. He was left with a terrible scar which slid up his arm as he grew.

In the garden there were five rows of raspberry bushes. The first summer we picked the fruit and I made pounds of raspberry jam. I even made some jelly, sieving out the pips, for my Father who had a dental plate. Behind the house was a milking parlour and every afternoon I took the white enamel quar can with wire handle to be filled by the cowman. We drank it still warm, and never suffered from lack of sterilization. It was full cream and delicious. We didn't possess a fridge. In warm weather I stood the milk in a deep bowl of cold water in the pantry.

A butcher came by van three times a week from Southwell, the small town five miles away (home of Southwell Races) where we did our shopping. My housekeeping allowance was four pounds a week and we spent one pound of it on meat. For that we had a 3 lbs. sirloin of beef on Sundays, minced beef and liver or lamb chops during the week. I learned to cook mince a dozen ways, as it was cheap and tasty, with Richard's home grown carrots, potatoes and green beans. One day I was wrestling with a clothes line, pegging sheets with some difficulty in a high wind, when a woman stopped her car at the gate to ask for directions and commented, 'I don't know how you live up here, so isolated.' I replied 'But I love it! I don't want to live anywhere else!' Boots's three experimental farms together covered a thousand acres. I dreamed nostalgically about that house for years afterwards.

Mrs Williams (wife to the director) lived at Magadales Farm along the road from Hill Farm. She was kind. She had a pretty daughter Caroline, in her early teens. Mrs Williams gave me advice about recipes and child care. Twice she looked after Peter while I went shopping. He was tiring to take out because he was energetic and reckless. I put him in blue leather reins for safety, and he would swing his full weight on them, and grab shop items at his level, which was exhausting. When one day I whizzed around the shops without him, and returned to Mrs Williams after an hour, I couldn't believe how tiny he was, he loomed so large in my consciousness.

After my bad experience with his birth I was afraid to have another baby, but one day Richard said 'Peter can't be an only child. It's time to have another baby.' Richard was two years younger than his brother John; I suppose that influenced his sense of timing. To me it was as frightening as jumping off a cliff, the bravest thing I ever did. We conceived John Paul the very first month.

One night around midnight Richard and I were asleep in Thurgarton when the dog (a golden Labrador named Rufus) suddenly woke us up with frantic barking. Cursing, I went to the top of the stairs to see what bothered him. He slept on an old armchair in the back hall. Looking down the stairs at him, he was looking up with a look of alarm in his eyes. I shushed him, told him to settle down, and went back to sleep.

The telephone woke us at 7 the next morning. Richard went downstairs to answer it, coming back to the bedroom with a grave expression, saying 'Oh Darling,' as he looked at me. I said 'What is it?' 'Your Father,' he said. 'Is he dead?' 'Yes.' He did his best to comfort me as I wept. Fred had suddenly collapsed and died of a brain haemorrage the night before, around midnight. Suddenly the significance of the dog's barking struck us. I imagine that if there was any way my Father could check on me as he left this life, he would have done just that.

Grief stricken, I packed a small bag and Richard drove me and Peter to the station. On the train to London I fell asleep with him in my arms, tightly held despite sleep. Richard's father met us at the station and drove us back to Mottingham. My brother was with my Mother. It was the only time he ever hugged me. In the days that followed my Mother and I were in a daze. I was four and a half months pregnant. This was my salvation because in comparison to the fear I felt at the approaching birth, my grief at losing my beloved Father was manageable.

Churchill died on the day my Father was buried. The nation's sadness seemed fitting. My Mother and I didn't go to the funeral. She could not possibly face it, and I was glad of the excuse to stay at home with her. He was buried in Chislehurst cemetery, Beaverwood Road, next to my old grammar school. It was years before Richard and his brother drove me there one day to see if we could identify his resting place, but we couldn't.

One great comfort to me was that my relationship with my Father was so close and so loving, I had no regrets. I missed him for months and years afterwards, but I always felt things were good between us.

I went to London to have John Paul, having lost confidence in the Nottingham Hospital and local doctors. I stayed with my Mother for a month before the baby was born (he was two weeks late). My Father having died half way through my pregnancy and my Mother being in a state of shock and grief, it was Richard's parents who drove me to Woolwich hospital to give birth. Mop's parting words were 'I'm glad I'm not the one giving birth today.'

In the labour room all alone during John Paul's birth, I felt my Father's presence powerfully. I counted the window panes as I measured the seconds of the contractions, breathing deeply, and I believed that he was there, helping me. I didn't panic. I practised the psycho prophylaxis technique I had learned from a library book, and controlled my fears the best I could. I have never felt my Dad so close to me since, but I believed then that he was watching over me.

Again I was left alone in labour, in the delivery room. When I suddenly felt the baby about to be born I shouted for help, and a passing nurse walked into the room and caught him as he arrived with a whoosh. Without her timely arrival he could have fallen off the delivery table, as she pointed out to a fellow nurse. No woman should ever be left alone in labour, in my opinion. I would sit with a total stranger, to avoid that experience on anyone's behalf.

After three years living in Thurgarton, Richard tired of the job where any mistakes were blamed on him, but his boss took the credit for his achievements. We went back to the Ministry where he stayed for the remainder of his career. He was assigned to Winchester in Hampshire, a beautiful historic town.

We had two days to find a house to buy in Winchester, having left the two children with my Mother and Mop. We looked at all that was available in the district at a price we could afford, and chose a semi- detached house (duplex) that we never liked much, but it fitted our budget. It cost 4,150 pounds; the mortgage cost 25 pounds a month. Completion of the purchase only took two weeks. We moved to Winchester when John Paul was six weeks old. The house was on a development at Weeke, five miles from Winchester. It had three small bedrooms and a bathroom upstairs, a kitchen diner and living room downstairs. A feature we liked was the coal fired boiler in the kitchen which heated the water. The garden sloped steeply up the hill behind, with a flat area by the house where the children could play. The address was 49 Teg Down Meads. We had saved 20% deposit while living in Thurgarton. In 1965 Richard earned 1,400 pounds a year, up from 850 p.a. as a probationer with the Ministry.

Richard was fired with enthusiasm for improving the world's agriculture. He sought an overseas posting and I fully supported this exciting prospect. He was short listed for a post in St Helena in the Atlantic off the west coast of Africa and we read every book we could find about it. It was a great disappointment to us when the other candidate got the job.

Soon after we moved to Winchester, while John Paul was a baby, Richard was invited to go to Rhodesia on a three year contract. He was granted permission from the Ministry to do this on secondment. A Peugeot car was bought for us, and a house arranged for us to rent. We let our house to a military family. We bought new suitcases and I started to make clothes suitable for a hot climate and pool side activities, but UDI (Unilateral Declaration of Independence) had recently been declared by Prime Minister Ian Smith, and at the last moment the Rhodesians stipulated that our contract should be permanent, not just for three years. We decided not to cut ties with the Ministry in case the life style and the job in Rhodesia didn't work out to our liking. That was the nearest we came to working abroad. Soon overseas postings disappeared along with the Commonwealth.

We had a group of half a dozen of my friends and their husbands, who invited each other every month for parties and pot luck. I'd made friends through taking Peter to play at a mother-and-baby club. It was a pleasant scene. Julian was born at home with only Richard and a midwife present, the easiest birth. I was delighted to have this bonus baby when John Paul was four and soon to start school.

Julian was seven months old when despite an intrauterine device, I conceived again. Richard was moved to Wales by the Ministry. We moved house to Cardiff when Julian was thirteen months old, just before Christmas. We had a four bedroom house built on a new estate at Radyr. Each time the Ministry moved us (every five or six years) we had no say in the location, but they paid all our moving fees, and an allowance towards the increased cost of the next house, so it paid to move, and each time our house was bigger and better.

We packed our moving van in Winchester (where my Mother had bought the house next door after my Father died, selling her London house) and left Julian with her while we went to oversee the furniture delivery next day. When the van was already packed we received a phone call from our solicitor to say that the builders in Cardiff had not received the payment cheque from the Halifax. Neither had the Halifax given the house its final inspection to release the funds. We drove to Cardiff anyway, checked into a hotel, and next morning arrived in the Halifax office asking them to expedite the payment. Peter and John Paul were 7 and 5 and I was six months pregnant. The Halifax official was unmoved. When he told me to sit down while he discussed it with my husband, Richard said 'You may as well include my wife because she has made all the arrangements. She knows more about it than I do.'

Meanwhile, the van was waiting outside 5 Bryn Castell and we could see welcome cards left on the mat inside by the postman, but the builders would not give us the key. The removal men said 'If you haven't got access by 1 o'clock we're taking the furniture back to Winchester.' Our solicitor telephoned the builders and assured them the money was on its way, pleading with them to let us in. Finally after reassurance from the Halifax, they gave us a front door key in the afternoon, but retained the key to the back door until everything was settled a couple of days later. If you have moved house with three small boys just before Christmas, when you were six months pregnant, you may understand how wearing this was.

We liked that house very well. It had four bedrooms, a large sitting room (20 ft. x 12), kitchen, dining room, cloakroom cum laundry and upstairs bathroom. It was the biggest design of half a dozen available on the estate, with picture windows and a commanding view of the valley with Castell Coch on the opposite side. The builders laid turf on the front lawn in the early spring. Richard eventually laid a paved patio behind and there was a steep slope down, only fit to grow fruit bushes. It was in a cul-de-sac with flat road where the boys could ride their bicycles safely. The builders had plastered the walls only the week before we moved in, and painted it to our choice of pastel colours, warning us that 300 gallons of water would have to evaporate before the house was dry, so we should not put down carpets. It was December and we had central heating, but the walls dripped water all winter and I was forever mopping the window sills. By the Spring we could install fitted carpets and we chose green. It looked beautiful.

In anticipation of the house move I had packed a tea chest full of wrapped Christmas gifts for the children, months before. We put up a tree and stacked the presents around it, with a few more from relations. Julian crawled around the tree pulling off all the labels, so we opened them laughing, not knowing who they were for, or from. My thank you letters afterwards were necessarily vague.

I could not walk, being heavily pregnant and prone to backache, and my Mother looked after us all. Four weeks before the baby was due I went for a routine check-up at the hospital where they said 'You are rather large. We should do an X-ray, perhaps it's twins.' I had been told before I might be having twins with Peter and Julian, so I dismissed this. But when they showed me the X-ray picture, there were two little babies sitting side by side. I wish I had kept that picture. They looked amazing. It was a few minutes later that I realized they were both in breech position, heads at the top. I had arrived at the hospital alone, collected by a touring ambulance, and was so shocked, I felt I couldn't wait for the return journey; I telephoned Richard at work and asked him to pick me up. 'Oh Richard,' I said, 'It's twins.' There was dismayed silence at the other end. He arrived and drove me home. We didn't tell my Mother. We thought she had enough to think about with three little ones. Julian was only fifteen months, toddling, going to her for every need. I would say 'I wish he'd call me Mama,' but he rightly recognized that I was pretty useless, and pursued 'Nana'. What would we have done without her?

That evening I started to have practice contractions. I was uncomfortable and they had told me at the hospital, come in any time. So Richard took me in and they settled me in bed. I had hardly been able to eat for weeks, my stomach had so little room, and I was so tired. I slept most of the day and all night. I passed ten days in that state of rest before they decided to induce the twins, who were getting rather large.

Richard came to the hospital to be with me, but in the event they sent him out of the delivery room (they thought this too upsetting for a husband). There were seven doctors or attendants of one sort or another. (Medical trainees are required to attend the birth of a certain number of twins before qualifying.) They had warned me that I might have stirrups and forceps. A young male medical student who was wiping my brow throughout the last hour told me next day, I kept saying 'Don't leave me alone.' When the doctor said 'Is it all right if we put a needle in your hand, Mrs Dight?' I said 'Do whatever you like, just don't leave me alone.' They thought it was funny.

In those days one received Pethedine for the pain and sometimes oxygen. Epidurals had not been invented. Caesareans were rare and only done in an emergency.

Patrick was born feet first. 'I can see the foot, there's another' said the doctor, and he arrived quite quickly. He turned Andre while inside the womb, the better to deliver him, but I don't know why, because Andre was born bottom first. The miracle is, the twins' birth was the only time I didn't have an episiotomy. Julian's birth had been so recent, I was still elastic. So I healed quicker from the twins than from the others. I had also lost weight in the later stages, so I was ten stones after they were born (back to my weight when married, 140 lbs.). Patrick was 5lb. 14 ounces and Andre was 5lb. 8 oz. Patrick's legs were blue for a few days, as was Andre's bottom, but only Patrick needed to be in an incubator for 48 hours. They were concerned about his breathing. He was all right by three days old.

Richard had gone the week before they were born to buy more Baby-grow suits and nappies, which my Mother thought unnecessary. She didn't know until they were born that there was a second baby. We took them home when they were two weeks old, me holding one in each arm in the front seat, without a seat belt (they didn't exist in 1971). We borrowed a second cot from a neighbour and my Mother later bought me a twin buggy.

When Richard returned from the hospital and told my Mother 'Nana, you have twins, two more little boys,' she said she saw stars and hurriedly sat down. What a trouper. She never let us down.

22 A MATTER OF FAITH

During those first ten years of marriage I gradually lost my Catholic faith. I tried to hold on to it, I didn't want to lose the comfort and lifestyle of certainty and faith with which I'd been raised. But it slipped through my reluctant fingers.

I was about 14 when, on holiday in Cornwall, we heard on the radio that the Pope had declared the bodily assumption of St Mary into Heaven. Henceforth it was a doctrine all Catholics were required to believe. My family all agreed that this was an inappropriate directive. It wasn't that we denied it. We simply thought it irrelevant, un-provable and an unnecessary strain on our credulity.

At 16 I recall discussing with Klaus the dogma of Papal Infallibility. I pointed out that the Pope is only human, and that past popes had often been immoral and corrupt. How did that sit with infallibility? Klaus said that he's only infallible in terms of Catholic edicts.

In Spain aged 20 I objected to the sale of an indulgence for 25 pesetas, permitting me to eat meat on Fridays as all Spaniards are, because of the help they gave to a past pope in one of his power battles.

The Inquisition has always struck me as the most indefensible episode in history.

Early in my marriage I watched a TV documentary on South America where peasants living in a mud floored hut, with only two stools and a cooking pot to their name, were interviewed about their lives. The woman said (I understood her Spanish), 'We had twelve children, but God is good because four of them died.' This struck me like a blow.

Around the time we got married the Pope issued his Encyclical about birth control, effectively preventing it. Catholics were not supposed to use any unnatural method to avoid pregnancy. They could play ducks and drakes with withdrawal, or abstain altogether, or use the rhythm method which was notoriously unreliable. No condoms, no pills and certainly no abortions. I would not opt for abortion unless raped, but the Church also forbade it in the case of rape, incest and health concerns. I recall the preteen Irish girl impregnated by her father, who was refused an abortion by the Church and even prevented from going to England for the purpose.

I always practised birth control except by pills, because in those days the doses were high and women often died of resultant thrombosis.

Just before I had John Paul I went to confession and told the priest that I used birth control but did not consider it a sin. When he chided me, I said I had only been married three years and was about to give birth to my second child. I also mentioned the intermittent breakdown. I thought it was irresponsible not to control my fertility. When I told him that my menstrual cycle varied from 3 weeks to 3 months he said that I could take the birth control pill to regulate my periods. I told him that seemed hypocritical to me. He lost patience and said 'If you don't agree with the Church, why don't you get out of it?' I went home and cried all weekend at the sense of abandonment I felt. Richard was sympathetic and did his best to comfort me.

There were many Catholic priests who sympathized with their parishioners and did not insist on following the Encyclical. I felt they were in an impossible situation. I think their understanding permitted many Catholics to stay in the Church, while others left.

In Spain I witnessed plaster saints dressed in jewels paid for by impecunious peasants. The Vatican and Catholic cathedrals are examples of conspicuous consumption, while peasants live on bread and olives.

I liked the ritual, the Latin Mass, the form of worship. I liked the feeling of community and universal membership. I believed the nuns who told me how lucky I was to have been born in the One True Faith. I felt the morality of the Church was strong and virtuous. I appreciated the commitment Catholics had to attending services. I wanted to bring my children up in a strong faith, with conviction. All this made it very hard to let it go. All the boys were baptised Catholic, Peter made his First Communion at age 7, but by the time the twins were born a year later I had lost my faith. I sat in Mass only once after their birth, with uncontrollable tears running down my face, and knew I couldn't do it any longer.

In subsequent years we learned about unmarried pregnant Irish girls routinely incarcerated in convents, their babies taken for adoption, while they were used as free labour in laundries, unable to escape. We heard about child abuse by Catholic priests in Ireland, America and elsewhere. It gradually emerged that paedophilia within the Church was endemic. For decades this was known by bishops who merely moved the exposed paedophile priests to new parishes, where they resumed their activities. They were not unfrocked; their crimes were hidden with the bishops' collusion. Hundreds of thousands of children's lives were damaged by sexual abuse. Millions of dollars and other currencies were paid out in compensation decades later, church collections being rerouted to compensation for abuse. The current Pope Benedict Ratzinger was at that time head of the department in the Vatican dealing with this hot potato. Whether he told Pope John Paul we do not know, but I hope the Pope did not know as he is now in the process of beatification and sainthood.

I know that many good priests and good Catholics are untainted by any of this, but it was too much for me.

Missing my faith, I looked elsewhere. I tried the Church of England and found it too middle class and establishment in tone. I went to the Methodist church a few times (my Father had been a Wesleyan, which became Methodist) and found good people, good ethics, and women reading the lessons too, but the rhetoric and language of the hymns bothered me. Singing along with the congregation that I was 'lowlier than a worm', the worm turned. I am *not* a worm, I thought, I am doing my best....

Around 1980 I consulted the first of three marriage guidance counsellors (a Quaker), hoping to improve our marriage. I told him about my religious dilemma and he gave me a tiny booklet entitled 'Advices and Queries'. It contained the essence of Quaker thought. I was struck by the fact that Quaker thought could be expressed so simply and succinctly. There was not a word in the book that I would disagree with. I discovered that Quakers (generally assumed to be narrow minded and old fashioned) are in truth inclusive, have surprisingly open minds, and no imposed convictions. I went to the Meeting the following week.

Over the next twenty years I sporadically attended meetings in Aberystwyth, Cambridge, Ealing and Huntingdon, sitting on the fence about becoming a Quaker until I decided one day that I needed to commit to a body that would one day handle my demise. Before I moved to Virginia I became a Quaker.

I don't think the only path to God is through Christianity. Jews, Buddhists, Hindus, Muslims, every belief system is travelling in the same direction, seeking the same God or Spiritual Being.

There is a lovely story about an early Quaker meeting in the State of New York in 1775 when the Iroquois were fighting for the British. Friends were meeting on Sunday morning when an Iroquois war party approached. Four braves came through the door, ready for battle, followed by their chief. He sensed the Spirit that filled the room, and that the Friends were peaceful, devout individuals. The warriors sat and joined the Friends in worship. Later the chief and his warriors joined the Friends for lunch and they spoke about the incident through a translator. The natives were surprised to learn that Friends worshiped the Great Spirit in silence, as they did. The chief left a white feather and an arrow as a signal that the building and those who inhabited it were peaceful, and should be left alone. It is hard to imagine two more disparate religious groups than pacifist Quakers and Indian warriors, yet they worship essentially the same Holy Spirit.

In many ways Humanism appeals to me. I admire people who do the right thing without a censor standing over them. I can't picture God, the nearest I come is to a Spiritual Force in unimaginable form. The world seems to me too wonderful, and man too spiritual, to be merely a planet with us animals on it, destined to die within a few decades, and all our endeavours, trials, sufferings, triumphs, works, relationships and love, snuffed out when we stop breathing. I believe in spirits although I've never seen one. I have no psychic faculty whatever. I've slipped in and out of belief in God and the hereafter, often in the same day. Although reincarnation seemed unlikely to me, in recent years it has been gaining credence through forty years of academic investigation and verification by an academic department at the University of Virginia.

Mother Theresa slipped in and out of belief all her life, but she continued to devote herself to the poor and suffering, with or without God. That makes her even more saintly, in my estimation.

When I read about scientists who believe in God despite their dedication to scientific proof, I am excited. Einstein was not an atheist.

Recently two books have been published that argue for and against there being a God:

> *Why We Believe in Gods* by J. Andrew Thomson (who does not believe), and
>
> *Irreducible Minds* by Edward Kelly, who maintains there is more than the brain can fathom.

I intend to read them both.

23 HARVESTING THE FRUITS

Harvesting the fruits of the earth is one of life's most satisfying experiences. As a small child my Father let me pick up the potatoes he grew, like golden nuggets in the dark earth. Boiled with a sprig of mint, with knobs of butter, they tasted divine. He planted lettuces, radishes and sprouts too. He let my tiny hands sprinkle the seeds. My heart was joyful at the activity and his loving company.

In his Austin 7 we hunted for wild mushrooms in the fields of Kent. I could spot white buttons in the lush green grass fifty yards away. They grow in fields where horses have lived. My Mother fried these mushrooms gently in butter, added flour and a little milk. They tasted nothing like the commercial ones – they were food for the gods.

I've always made use of all the fruits and vegetables that came our way, making jam from the fruits and chutney from the vegetables, unless they were suitable for freezing. We had a freezer sooner than most people in England because we grew vegetables, and also practised frugal catering. There was a wholesale outlet rather like Costco, for which one had to own a business, to shop there. We had an old fashioned printing press, with treadle control and a metal plate with rolled-on ink that kissed the type we set laboriously by hand. I invented 'Gala Catering' at our address, so we could print a letterhead and pretend to be a catering company. Every month we bought a 7 lb. block of cheddar cheese, kept ready in the fridge for hungry boys. We bought everything in bulk, including 30 lb. sacks of bread flour. I bought dried soup mixes in large boxes. The boys liked 'Angel Delight', an instant pudding mix. Semolina, custard powder and rice came in 7 lb. bags. 3 lb. bags of mixed fruit became cakes.

In Winchester a French boy stayed with us for a month one summer. Jean-Luc was a forester's son from Haute Savoie. We took him to the New Forest and walking between the trees his eyes were darting everywhere. Finally he said 'Ah!' picking up yellow trumpet-like fungi: chanterelles. They looked poisonous to us but he assured us they were a delicacy. 'People pay a lot of money to buy these in France,' he said. At his suggestion we fried them gently in butter and they were indeed tasty. We only found about half a pound of chanterelles at a time in the New Forest. They grow in leaf mould under beech trees. Years later Peter would spot a carpet of them growing in woods beside the road in central Wales when we were staying in the cottage by the stream. We gathered a large basket full in fifteen minutes. Locals who saw them warned us they would kill us, but we took them home and ate them.

The Ministry of Agriculture sampled dried milk from dairy farms and threw away the samples. With dried milk I perfected the art of making 3 pints of yoghurt at a time, in a large saucepan left in the airing cupboard in winter, or the glasshouse in summer, which I mixed by the bowl with a spoonful of grape jelly. The grapes came from Mop's neighbour in Somerset.

Sometimes we were given surplus fruit by neighbours. In Aberystwyth we had ten apple trees which made pies, crumbles, sauces and chutney. Even dried apricots can be used to make jam in the absence of fresh fruit. In my kitchen cupboards dozens of jars rested with a variety of preserves. One day a cupboard fell off the wall in Aberystwyth from the weight, and 40 lbs. of laboriously made chutney smashed on the quarry tiled floor.

If you have room in a vegetable patch don't fail to grow broad beans whose pods are also delicious eaten whole, when tiny. Purple sprouting broccoli and tomatoes will grace your plates for months.

In a Ministry of Agriculture booklet about preserving, I recorded every pound of jam, marmalade, jelly and chutney I made. I have it still, splattered and stained but still a mine of information. Only since I came to Virginia have I ceased to record my preserving activities.

Every January I bought a case of Seville oranges, yielding 90 lbs. of marmalade to last all year. In the absence of bitter Seville oranges I now make lemon marmalade. John Paul has three lemon trees in his Arizona garden; he posted a box of lemons to me last winter.

I froze the excess green beans we grew, sprouts, herbs and rhubarb. Take note that freezing ratatouille isn't worth it. It turns to mush. You need to know what freezes well and what doesn't.

I was so enthusiastic about freezer cabinets, I was offered a job by a butcher in Winchester to sell freezers, when I was working with Welcome Wagon. I would make two pies and freeze one for later, similarly two casseroles. If you liquidize a dinner with vegetables and gravy for a baby, you can freeze it in yoghurt tubs for subsequent meals. Pizzas happily freeze, as do loaves. We bought ten loaves a week and froze half of them to keep them fresh.

Runner beans grow in a tiny space if you give them sticks to climb. We had a neighbour in Radyr who grew them successfully in the 6 inch space between their house and the concrete drive.

In Girton I planted my own first vegetable patch with lettuces and spinach, and spent an hour each evening watering them with a can during a hosepipe ban. It was therapeutic.

In later years I planted a herb garden everywhere I lived. We had always had mint and sage. Now I added rosemary, oregano, thyme and parsley. Garlic is another easy crop, dividing one bulb into a dozen sets. In France I learned to strew handfuls of fresh herbs over baked meat and vegetables. In Virginia my tiny front garden border is devoted to herbs. Always plant them near the entrance door.

Some of my happiest afternoons have been spent picking blackberries in the wild. A few blackberries turn an apple pie into something special. I've planted rhubarb everywhere I lived. The boys loved rhubarb crumble and today I like it stewed in orange juice with apples. Rhubarb and oranges make excellent jams and chutneys. You can add ginger too.

I planted a few flowers in my time, but herbs and vegetables are always more satisfying to me, when I harvest the fruit.

24 CAR ACCIDENT

In 1970, one sunny, icy morning my friend's husband was killed in a car accident. He was a school teacher and with three others, had been driving to work when a truck coming the other way skidded, crossed the road and smashed into the teachers' car. They were all killed instantly including a pregnant teacher. My friend had four children aged two to ten.

Jenny and her family had just moved to a bigger house from the one she had near me. Her former neighbour told me about Jenny's husband being killed that morning. I went immediately to Jenny's house. She was sitting, frozen with shock. A policeman had come to the house to tell her there had been an accident, and although they had no news of her husband's condition, she should call a relative to be with her. When the relative arrived, they informed Jenny that her husband was dead.

Over the ensuing months, whenever I met her, I was the one who wept. She was still numb. There was one fortunate aspect: the month before, having moved house, her husband had taken out life insurance. When the second monthly payment was due she told him, 'Let's not pay it,' because they were short of cash, but he had insisted. Because of that she had the house, the car and a lump sum that took away her immediate money worries.

One afternoon when the twins were eight weeks old, Richard was at work and there was a knock on my door. Three of his colleagues stood on the step. 'Come in!' I said smiling, 'Richard's not home yet.' His boss told me they had come to let me know that Richard had been in a car accident. How is he? I wanted to know, but they told me they couldn't say. He was in the emergency room and they had no knowledge of his condition. 'We've been advised to ring the hospital in an hour,' they said. The memory of my friend being told this while help was lined up for her froze my blood.

I sat on the stairs. Peter, aged eight, sat beside me and asked quietly, 'Is Daddy dead?' 'I don't think so,' I said, unable to answer otherwise. In an hour we phoned from a neighbour's house, to be told that Richard had two broken ribs, a cut on his chin and a gash on his knee. Otherwise he was

OK. The relief was indescribable. The next day our neighbour Ted drove me to the hospital an hour away, to collect him.

Richard had been on his way home along a newly designated motorway at the top of the Valley. Suddenly the car in front of him had rear white lights shining. He couldn't understand, and although he braked hastily, he ran into the back of the other car. The driver of the car in front had missed his exit on the motorway, suddenly realized and started to reverse. It was the first time Richard had seen reversing lights, which had just been issued on new cars. Although the driver in front had acted illegally in reversing on a motorway, Richard being the driver behind was charged with careless driving.

Richard was brought up by his father always to do the right thing, to maintain his dignity, not to draw attention to himself, to be in the right, and so on. Such a rigid discipline is a heavy burden to carry. Richard was devastated by the careless driving charge. In the hospital when visited by the police he followed the Ministry of Agriculture's guidelines and refused to speak to the police. If he had explained his situation he would perhaps have avoided the careless driving charge, which hung over Richard like Damocles' sword all that summer.

We soon discovered that because of the move and failing to change our address with the insurance company, our mortgage had not been covered at the time of the accident. Moreover, the only life insurance Richard had was for one thousand pounds, unless it was an accident, when it doubled to two thousand. He had taken this out when we were first married. It would barely have paid for a funeral.

At home Richard tried to regain his composure after the crash. His wounds were not deep, but painful enough, especially his broken ribs. He sat trying to relax by watching the family of blue-tits living in the box he had made and fixed on the fence among the blackberry bushes. My Mother and I meanwhile struggled to deal with the twins' three hourly feeds (because they were small), Julian toddling, Peter being reluctant to go to school and showing signs of stress (and who could blame him), and John Paul aged six, his usual sunny self. By the time I had fed and changed the twins for bed soon after 6, got Julian to bed by 7 and the others bathed and bedded soon after, I was exhausted. I often swayed with fatigue as I changed the babies' nappies in their bedroom on the changing table. Even when fit, Richard did not lend a hand with any of this. When I watch my sons now helping their wives, changing and feeding babies, reading them stories, hugging them tenderly, I am immensely grateful for their involvement and understanding.

Richard was so shaken by the crash, he was given tranquilizers for the only time in his life. I was so relieved that he had survived, I became euphoric. I was given tranquilizers too. My euphoria had to be suppressed. I was elated and doctors find this just as alarming as depression. For a while the two of us enjoyed walks together while my mother watched the children, both of us feeling the relief of medication.

I took the two older boys out for a walk one day, with Julian in the pushchair, playing a game with them that I'd once experienced with girl guides when I was a child. We walked through the woods, leaving sticks on the path arranged like arrows and marking trees with chalk, so we could find our way home. In my heightened sense I felt this would be constructive to the boys, to be given a skill to enhance their sense of security. Whether they experienced it thus I cannot say, but we had a happy time together and I returned from this exercise feeling I had accessed their age level of communication.

When the careless driving charge came to court there were three magistrates. One of them Richard recognized as a farmer to whom he'd given advice. His solicitor later told him the farmer had spoken up for him. I felt the other driver who had been reversing when he shouldn't, should have been sanctioned, but Richard was the one on trial. Richard's relief at being found 'not guilty' was unbounded

Soon after this Richard became involved with a woman in his office, who invited him and a couple of other people to her house to listen to records in the evenings after work. He would come home late from an evening enthusing about the music, visibly refreshed. One night as we were preparing to go to sleep he said he had something to tell me, and he didn't know how to let me know because it was going to upset me. I had absolutely no idea what was coming, but feared he might be ill. Finally, he blurted out, 'I think I'm in love with a woman in my office.' I said 'Oh thank God, I thought you were going to tell me you had cancer!' He was elated at my reaction, said 'Oh I feel so much better now I've told you, I can go to sleep in peace,' and he turned over and went to sleep. I lay awake all night thinking, if he leaves me, I cannot pay the mortgage, where will we live? How will I feed the boys? What will happen to us? How can I go to work with five children under eight, three of them under two? My peace of mind was permanently destroyed at one blow.

He started to service the car of the girl from the office. She came to pick it up one day and I invited her in for coffee. I let her see the children in the sitting room. The twins crawled around the floor, picking up bits of fluff from the new carpet, stuffing it in their mouths, and I was forever taking it from them. The others were playing quietly, but the extent of Richard's family would have been evident to a blind woman. After that I think she pulled away from Richard, to my relief. But the pattern had been set for him to look for occasional companionship from other women, and for me to worry myself sick about how I would cope if he left. I confided my anxieties to one friend, who also had three small children under six. She was sympathetic but there seemed to be nothing we could do to assuage my fears. The fabric of our marriage had begun to tear, and it would get worse as time went by.

I asked Richard to take out an insurance policy to help us if anything happened to him and he refused. I said 'How would we manage without you?' He said 'You're a strong girl, you'd get a job.' It was a far cry from the security I felt when first married.

Many years later I wrote a piece which I included in the *Dight Times* as an insert. It was heartfelt advice never to take one's partner's love for granted. I wanted to sound a timely warning to my sons and their wives. It's called *Cherish Them*. I'll include that next.

25 CHERISH THEM

Couples often start out with a deep reserve of good will, like a well of sweet water. It isn't difficult to fill at first when the water table provides half the contents and that's topped up with mutual attraction, anticipation and optimism. When you get thirsty along the way you can both drink deeply from this inspiring reservoir. Sometimes you may take more than your share because there's plenty and a loving partner will not begrudge you. However, never suppose that the well will not run dry.

If a couple loses balance, what starts as a demanding use by one person of your mutual reserves, can become unreasonable, greedy, perhaps unforgivable. Every put-down, barbed comment or selfish act makes one love the other less. Be careful. When somebody erodes one's patience, generosity and respect, the well runs dry faster than you can believe. Once spent, good will is irretrievable. Affection goes first, then tolerance, then all respect.

It's much better to concentrate on making one's partner happy than oneself, in small but important ways. If couples cooperate they can get through anything (think of those coping with sick children). A partner does not need expensive presents, grand gestures, declarations. A partner needs a kind response, a private smile, appreciation and respect. None of these have price tags.

If your partner is more giving than you, be less demanding before you lose it all. If you are the partner whose patience is most stretched, assert yourself. Take your share of responsibility for keeping the balance.

When everyday stresses erode your patience, take the long view. Picture your relationship in thirty years when you are retired, still together, enjoying companionship and the fruits of your joint efforts, and work towards that. Count your blessings: your partner and children should be top of the list. If your blessings are people, cherish them.

26 WELCOME WAGON

In 1970 when Julian was six months old I went to London for a week while my Mother watched the boys, and took a course in working for Welcome Wagon. I stayed with my mother in law and went to London by train every day for the training.

I had a friend doing this work in Winchester and thought I could do better. Welcome Wagon is an American organization which had come to Britain some years before. The English director was a woman with six children. She epitomized the expression 'If you want something done, ask a busy woman'.

The Welcome Wagon hostess would visit people who had just moved into the area, wearing a hat to make her look a little special, and carrying a basket full of gifts from local businesses. She would welcome the lady of the house to the area, tell her about local schools and churches, where to buy things, find the library etc. and answer any questions. In the process she introduced gifts (a record cleaning cloth from the electrical shop, a comb from a hairdresser with a leaflet about the sponsor). In the course of conversation the hostess quizzed the homeowner for information. She had to ascertain the make of car, the size of home, the number of people in the family, and so on for commercial use.

Each family visit was recorded for the sponsors in a weekly report by the hostess. These sponsors paid so much for each visit. I had to send a second report to Welcome Wagon's office, which billed the sponsors and paid the hostess. The more visits the hostess made, the more money she was paid. The obvious room for growth was to gain more sponsors.

We were trained how to approach potential sponsors and sell them the idea. None of the hostesses in my training group relished this aspect, although they were comfortable with the idea of chatting to housewives.

My friend was glad to hand over to me her three sponsors as she had found it a lot of effort for little return. We were paid less than two shillings per person per call. As I could only make about nine calls a week (in three evenings), my income was severely limited. My Mother looked after Julian after 7 pm in the evening when the older two were in bed. She was then living next door to us. She gave Julian his bottle, changed his nappy and put him to bed.

I set about recruiting new sponsors. I worked my way up and down Winchester High Street during the day time, making presentations in every shop. It took me about three weeks to sign up ten new sponsors. One sponsor dropped out. Now I was being paid by twelve sponsors per visit. I found that I soon got bored with making the house calls, but I enjoyed addressing the businesses.

I told Welcome Wagon 'I've made thirty presentations but I've only signed up ten.' They said 'That's amazing! The usual rate is only ten per cent.' I saved all the money I earned, which later paid for carpets in our new house in Wales.

One of my sponsors was a butcher who also sold freezers. After telling him how much I valued my freezer, he offered me commission to sell freezers on his behalf, but I just didn't have time. I could only work between 7 and 9 pm in the evenings, when the boys were in bed and I could use our car.

One of the companies I signed up as sponsor was Rumbelows electrical goods, one of 300 branches all over the country. On the strength of my approach, Rumbelows signed on every Welcome Wagon hostess in England, but the head office took all the commission. I got a lot of kudos for that but I'd have preferred five pounds.

I had to quit when I was several months pregnant and moving to Wales. Welcome Wagon was disappointed.

When the twins were about three months old I got a letter from the London office asking if I would open up Wales to Welcome Wagon. 'You won't be making the calls' they said, 'just recruiting and training the hostesses, and we'll pay you a salary.' I said 'I'm sorry but I've just had twins and there's no way I can fit in a job too!' But it was nice to be asked.

As in every job I had, I learned something. When I set up my business sixteen years later, taking British companies to Spain as director of Export Connect, I had to make presentations to potential clients and persuade them to pay me for the service, but instead of two shillings a time for house calls, eventually I charged 6,000 pounds plus all expenses paid for a week in Spain, for introductions to potential distributors or joint venture partners. The principle was the same.

27 TONI VOLCANI: THE WOMAN WHO CHANGED MY LIFE

I was 34 in 1971 and living in Cardiff, Wales, when my mother brought her neighbour to meet me. It was a most unlikely meeting. Toni Volcani and her husband Ben were on a nine months sabbatical from the Scripps Institute in California. It was my great good fortune that they rented the house next door to my Mother. Toni was then in her late fifties.

When Toni walked into my sitting room there were five little boys under the age of 9 and the twins were still crawling. I had so little time to read or go out or do anything but look after my family, but I could talk to Toni while I did it. We instantly became friends. She was so interesting and interested in all about her. Toni would take a bus up the Valley and sit in a miners' café to absorb local colour. She didn't like the sanitized life - she was drawn to the Latin countries rather than the clean ones of northern Europe. She was not a woman who shops in Kohls, she would rather rummage in a market.

I saw her often during the coming months - we talked about everything under the sun, and especially people. Toni had worked seven years at the Carl Rogers Institute in San Diego, an early proponent of encounter group work. She introduced me to reading about psychology and all kinds of social studies. She was warm, humorous, compassionate, enquiring, colourful and iconoclastic. She was full of expressions that amused me 'Oh, heavens to Betsy, happy as a clam, out in the boondocks,' and so on. At the time we were switching our political allegiance to the Liberal Party. I told her that until then we had always voted Conservative. Her 'Oh, really?' converted me in two words for a lifetime. I have never voted Conservative since. She told me about a scrape her son had got into that had caused them great alarm. 'And did you tell him afterwards, don't do that again?' I asked. 'Oh, what would be the point?' she said, 'He'd never want to do *that* again.' She had received a postcard from him announcing that he and his friend who were then in Germany on holiday, had decided to make a raft and sail down the Rhine. Were you worried? I asked. 'Oh no, by then they would either have sailed or sunk,' she said, philosophically. I was constantly surprised by her answers.

Modesty was her strong suit. I knew that Toni had been a journalist in Israel, a jazz singer in New York, a writer and so on, but I didn't know much detail. She came with Ben to supper before they went back to the States and Richard was telling them about a book we had read the year before: 'Do you know Steinbeck's *The Sea of Cortez*?' he asked. ' Oh yes, said Toni, I edited it.' How many people would have neglected to mention during nine months of conversation that they were Steinbeck's editor for many years?

Toni told me she walked out on her first husband together with her two year old daughter in a buggy, and on the front in southern California, she started chatting to a man who turned out to be John Steinbeck. He was living and writing there, and had a friend called Doc (who features in 'Cannery Row'). Steinbeck invited Toni and her daughter Kay to shelter that night with him and subsequently to work for him as his assistant and editor, and soon Toni moved to live with Doc. She stayed there until her daughter, who had a brain tumour, died aged ten. Toni then left and went to live and work in New York.

Toni had met Ben, a marine biologist, when he visited Doc in his laboratory. Ben had come from Israel, where he'd been raised (born in Estonia, I think). The Volcani Institute in Israel was named after Ben's father, an agricultural scientist. When Ben came to America he had an introduction from Ben Gurion to meet Einstein, and he told a wonderful story about visiting Einstein and talking with him in his study, speculating about the number of birds that were in the forest visible from Einstein's house. He did a quick calculation on a piece of paper and told Ben the result, then tossed it into the waste paper bin. Ben regretted leaving it there. Ben was a natural raconteur and a charismatic character. I loved him too. He would talk to anybody and hear their life story within minutes. Ben was working at the Tenovus Cancer Research institute in Cardiff during his sabbatical.

It was Ben Gurion, the prime minister of Israel, who had invented their son Yanon's singular name. Toni and Ben went to live in Israel early in their marriage and Yanon spoke Hebrew, but when they returned to America when Yanon was about eight Toni told me he forgot it all within weeks.

I was bereft when they went home to the States. I told Toni 'I feel as if I'm being unfaithful, but I wish I could go with you.' She said 'I guess that's kind of safe.' I never met anyone more understanding in my life. We corresponded throughout the years at intervals. I kept all her letters and she kept mine. We explored so many themes in those pages. While I was limited by my responsibilities and lack of money, Toni could think and travel freely. Her lack of arrogance, her humour, her perception and intuition shone beams of light into my shaded world. Her insight and grasp of political issues illuminated current events. Her dismissal of small minded people was a tonic. Only once did I display a talent Toni lacked. She had a skirt that needed hemming and I tacked it as we chatted. Toni said that since childhood when she was forced to sew until her pricked fingers bled, she had been unable to sew. In every other aspect I learned from Toni.

Every Christmas until they grew up Toni and Ben sent gifts to the children. That was more than their relatives did. Five children are overwhelming to most people, but Toni knew that every individual needs recognition. She knew every child and his personality. She taught me the importance of choosing gifts specifically to reflect the character of the recipient. They made a special connection with John Paul, my second son, who was seven then; today JP is forty five and has a teenage son named Ben.

Every time they came to Europe in the following years, Toni came to see me, even when we lived in west Wales, a five hour journey from London by train. On that visit Ben joined us after a couple of days. He went up to the University by himself and walked along a corridor in the science department. A lecturer stopped him and asked who he was. 'I'm Ben Volcani,' he answered. '*The* Ben Volcani?' 'Yes.' The lecturer called a colleague and they talked happily. I said to Ben 'Telephone them and invite them to dinner.' Ben did so and Richard and I sat quietly enjoying their conversation over roast beef at our dining table. Ben was overjoyed at this connection.

Each meeting was a joy, and the highlight of my year.

Of all the things Toni taught me, the most important was: it's OK to say 'No.'

She also urged me 'not to take crap from anyone'. I had married in 1962 and the times had taught me to defer to my husband, to adapt and support and live for others. I had been brought up to be good, accommodating and selfless. I'd been taught nothing about asserting my own interests, or even identifying them. The women's movement didn't come to Britain until the early seventies. I joined a class on The Changing Role of Women in 1973, after which Richard used to say, 'You were a good wife until you went to that class.' As things got increasingly uncomfortable in my marriage, Toni uniquely urged me to consider what *I* wanted. It wasn't easy.

In 1979 my brother, who had visited Toni and Ben during his trips to the States on business, urged me to go and see them for a holiday, as I had been ill (following John Paul's breakdown) and needed a change of scene. In the two weeks I spent in La Jolla with Toni and Ben, I decided that my life had to change radically because I was heartily sick of it. I saw people happily living and conversing without any of the strains I felt heaped upon my shoulders. I had become so used to Richard's impatience and criticism, I'd lost the joy of living. I read Yanon's well- thumbed book about Scripts and how people are programmed to live a certain way. I recognized myself as a pleaser, and the limitations placed on my development. As a child I was told 'You don't have to be clever, you're a girl.' My Mother told me repeatedly what her mother had told her: 'The secret of happiness is to forget you exist.' I had done that, and was in peril. Toni counselled me during that holiday. It took another seven years and graduation from university to achieve my independence, but I did it. Without Toni I would never have had the courage, or permission, to choose my own life.

Toni died a couple of years ago. I had last seen her when Bill and I visited her in La Jolla in 2001, and met Yanon for the first time. On his wall was a photograph of a woman so beautiful, I asked if she was a film star. He told me 'That was Toni when she was young.' Yanon, a psychiatrist specializing in helping young people, was just as charming and attractive as Toni had led me to believe. Yanon, married to a TV news presenter, with one son, had built a magnificent Spanish style home near the beach in La Jolla. He was still a surfer, and would run down to the beach often to surf. Toni moved into his home in the last few years, physically frail, but mentally strong.

Yanon emailed me one day to say that Toni was failing, and if I wanted to talk to her I should telephone that day. I did so, but she had just passed away. I told Yanon, 'It doesn't matter. Toni and I had said everything we needed to. She knew how much I loved her.' It makes me weep still, to think how much I miss her. I loved her more than anybody in the world beyond my immediate family.

An extract from Toni's obituary in the *San Diego Union-Tribune* described her thus: 'Mrs Volcani, a professional writer and editor known for her profound appreciation of life, died April 6 at Cloisters of La Jolla. She was 95. As much as anything Mrs Volcani's legacy is tied to the men in her life: her father, Theodore Solomons, who helped discover and define the John Muir Trail; her one-time boss, author John Steinbeck; and her second husband, renowned microbiologist Ben Volcani.'

My brother used to say that when Toni and Ben came to see me, it was like flamingos alighting on a duck pond. But Toni made me feel like a flamingo.

28 BACK TO WORK - ROSIE'S

In Radyr used to watch the woman who lived opposite, who had two girls in primary school, driving off to work in the mornings, and how I envied her. I longed to be back in the grownup world. I was fortunate that Richard could support us but I still missed work. As they were growing up I gave some thought to what I would do when they were all in school.

We moved to Aberystwyth when the twins were five in September 1976. (I have a lovely memory of moving-in day, when the twins and Julian (aged 5 and 6) found an old bird's nest in the garden and they approached birds offering the nest, saying 'Here birdie, birdie'.)

My Mother and I spent the first ten months decorating the Victorian house, built in 1896. It had been neglected for years. There were three floors, with five bedrooms and two huge sitting rooms. (It had been converted to a school at one time. Glen Rosa and the adjacent house had been built by two nieces of Cecil Rhodes.) Our builders knocked two rooms into one large kitchen and Richard fitted new units and a dishwasher.

That summer (1977) we had visitors: My brother and his family, Toni and Ben, and Klaus from Germany all came to stay. At the end of the summer I was ready to get 'back to work'.

As I enjoyed cooking so much I was interested in the idea of running my own restaurant. It was a big project and not one that I could undertake immediately, so I decided to get some experience. When I heard that Rosemary Birkenshaw was planning to open a restaurant in her own home, and looking for a partner to work with her, I arranged to be introduced. Immediately we struck up an enthusiastic partnership.

The restaurant was to be in her own dining room. She and Keith, an anaesthetist at the hospital, and their two young daughters, lived in a beautiful Victorian house in town. She was a Cordon Bleu trained cook and Keith was extremely competent in woodwork and other skills. They converted their dining room into a restaurant seating 24 people. Rosemary and I made seat covers, tablecloths and napkins in royal blue.

Keith made a handsome bar under the stairs with pretty lighting. It was a most attractive scene. I went with Rosemary to the court to acquire a liquor licence. In addition to sharing the planning of menus, buying produce, cooking, serving at tables and clearing up, I was to do the accounts.

The food was excellent – Rosemary was a talented and experienced caterer. I learned a lot from her. When she wondered what to call her restaurant I suggested 'Rosie's' and Keith made a sign to hang by the gate.

We charged a flat rate of 6 pounds per head for a five course dinner, including the canapés. There was a choice of three main courses and as many desserts. It was a bargain. . Although I was doing the books, helping plan the menus, buy the ingredients, cook in the mornings, set the tables, if I wasn't actually there to act as waitress, I didn't get paid the one pound a head. On nights when Rosie had less than half capacity, I wasn't needed. The restaurant was only open three nights a week.

It didn't make economic sense to work at this rate, but it was valuable experience. I learned management techniques, new recipes, accountancy discipline, but what I learned most of all was, I didn't want to run a restaurant. It is a huge amount of work, labour intensive, often unappreciated especially when customers drink too much, and the hours are antisocial. They suited me as the children then aged 6 to 14, put themselves to bed at night. I saved every penny. In eighteen months I earned 250 pounds. If you think you want to run a business, always gain experience first in someone else's enterprise.

There were few good restaurants in Aberystwyth. Rosie's was the best of them. We attracted the more discerning diners, and a few who had more money than taste. I have in mind three couples who owned local businesses and came to dine every month. I recall two snippets of their conversation: one of the women saying 'Oh, I love Paris! You can get pissed as you like and nobody knows you!' and on another occasion, 'The Bistro by the pier is good. They serve typically Welsh food, like quiche.'

Sometimes guests argued with Rosemary that she had not used a classic sauce with a dish, which was irritating. The sauce was good, it didn't need a pedigree. We served gooseberry sauce with roast pork, for example, because they were available from my garden, and tasty. Innovative should cost extra, not attract criticism. Despite the diners who were difficult, or liked to display their knowledge, Rosie's got into the *Good Food Guide* in our second year.

One memorable evening some musicians from a concert at the university were brought to dine. I was particularly pleased to serve Barry Took, the distinguished horn player whom I'd heard play in concerts with the Cardiff Symphony Orchestra.

Keith was an organist who had constructed an organ in his music room, and their daughters played the violin. They were a talented family altogether.

During the 18 months I worked with Rosie, John Paul had a nervous breakdown.

29 FAMILY BREAKDOWN

In the spring of 1978 twelve year old John Paul had a nervous breakdown, which to me proves the theory that it is often the sanest, most balanced person in a troubled family who is so affected.

John Paul was an easy, sunny baby and I dubbed him 'the next pope', long before Pope John Paul was so named. He was undemanding, contented, bubbly and loving. His nature was benign. Always responsive to affection, he asked for little more than to exist in his small space and observe the world.

As a baby I pretended to ignore John Paul because two year old Peter was jealous and jumped on my back when I tried to give John Paul his bottle, so I learned to prop the bottle on a folded diaper and keep a casual eye on him while he fed himself. As he developed, at six every morning he stood in his cot and called me; he was ready for the day.

Growing up he could be mischievous, but was never unkind. He laughed easily, enjoyed life and was keenly intuitive. When he was four I was pushing him in a buggy along the road on a blustery day and he said 'I wish those trees would stop moving about so much. They make it so windy.'

When he was ten he said 'Mummy, why don't you divorce Daddy and marry somebody who likes children?'

Richard was totally committed to supporting the family, but he was overwhelmed by having five sons. He shouldered the financial burden but enjoyed none of the fun of interacting with them. He didn't play with them, or read them stories. He didn't bath them or even say hallo when he came home from work. He ignored them as far as possible, or shouted at them in exasperation. We lived in a very tense atmosphere.

In his defence, I would point out that Richard did not have an easy role model for a father. Although his Mother was nice (I was fond of her), his father was haughty. He consistently employed the technique of putting the other person down in order to make himself feel better. He expected obedience and had little sense of humour. When Richard was small he only once challenged his father, who had sent him to Sunday school before he'd eaten his dessert after lunch. When he came home Richard asked for his dessert and was told, 'You have to wait until supper time now,' which outraged Richard to the point of punching his father, and he was punished for it. I think it was the only time he openly rebelled.

When we bought a new Mini car soon after our marriage and went to show it off to our parents, my father sat inside and admired all its features. Richard's father ignored it, and when Richard drew his attention to it parked on their drive he looked out of the window and said, 'Yes Richard, it's a nice toy, but you're too old for toys.' He didn't step outside to see it. At that time he didn't even possess a car. He wouldn't have been seen dead in an Austin 7.

When Peter was not yet reading at seven, and self- conscious about it, Pop told him 'At your age, my boy, I was reading to improve myself.' Whenever we went to stay with them, or they visited us, Richard's patience with his father would wear thin by the second day, but he invariably controlled his irritation. His father would alter our thermostat, and make critical comments. He did not do praise.

Pop was serious when he reminded his sons at the dinner table, 'Pass the Port to the left, my boy,' for which the origin was the necessity to keep one's fencing arm free to do battle.

When they came to eat with us we would always buy a bottle of wine, and Pop acted as connoisseur, sniffing the cork and sipping judgmentally. As it was barely a notch above plonk it didn't deserve this level of attention. I recall once saying 'I do hope you like it, because it's the only bottle we've got.' I often bordered on irreverence because the absurdity struck me so forcibly, and it didn't endear me to him.

On the occasion of their fiftieth wedding celebration Peter in his teens decided he'd rather go to the Stonehenge Festival. Thereafter Peter did not receive his customary one pound gift at Christmas and his name was left off the card.

Rather than showing approval towards his sons, Pop presided like a judge. He was softer with his daughter Anne. It is hardly surprising I suppose that Richard didn't know how to relate to his own children. I pointed out to him how little he enjoyed his upbringing, and now he was in danger of repeating the pattern, but he said '*I* had to put up with it, and so can they.'

Nana was so proud of the boys. She and I shared our delight in them. When the twins were two Richard's parents came to visit. Nana had knitted them white sweaters. With their flawless complexions, Pat's dark, shiny hair with hazel eyes and Andre's blonde curls and blue eyes, they were striking looking. Nana said to Mop proudly, 'What do you think of them?' and without hesitation their other grandmother replied: 'She should have had an abortion.'

It's no wonder that Richard didn't feel like a loved child. Richard was never pompous. In fact he was modest. He was interesting and could contribute something about most topics without putting himself forward. He had a great many good qualities. He was reliable, honest, conscientious, intelligent, slow to judge, analytical and professional. This made it all the harder to bear that he was irascible and impatient towards the children, creating tensions in the house that made us all walk on egg shells for years.

This situation took its toll on the whole family. In the spring of 1978 when Peter and John Paul were 15 and 12, we decided to take them to Holland in the VW for a week's holiday, staying with Richard's Dutch relations. We left the three little ones in my Mother's care. The fact that we burdened my Mother aged 70 with two seven year olds and one of eight for a week, illustrates both our desperation for a change of scene, and her generosity.

The holiday was a great success. We stayed in the Inn at Bergen op Zoom where Richard's mother was born, and aged 17, met and married her English cable-laying husband who was working in Holland. She was beautiful. He whisked her away without a word of English and they settled in Mottingham, in suburban London. He was ten years older and naturally the dominant partner.

The Inn was large and successful, with frequent coach loads of travellers stopping by for meals and drinks. All our meals were taken in the restaurant where we chatted with family and friends as best we could in Dutch. Richard's spirits soared in this entertaining atmosphere and we all relished the reappearance of the happy man I had married. John Paul did not remember him that cheerful, and his spirits soared too. But on the journey home when the boys were enjoying a fit of giggles in the car, Richard snapped to silence them as he drove, and hit them when they couldn't stop laughing. Suddenly the curtain of misery descended on us all again, and when we got out of the car at home to my Mother's cheerful welcome, John Paul burst into inconsolable tears.

The next day they returned to school. Although he was still crying and agitated, I drove John Paul to school in the hope that it would distract him. After an hour I was called to pick him up as he couldn't stop the tears. Thereafter for three months John Paul would cry for about three hours every day. At first he refused to take off the clothes he had worn on holiday. I supposed he was trying to hold on to the memory of the happy holiday. We cajoled and argued, but after a few days we forcibly removed them and put him struggling into a warm bath. He slept badly, woke early and resumed his keening. I recognized that he was depressed, and took him to the doctor. Nonsense, Mrs Dight, said the GP, children don't get depressed. It must be something physical. We'll run some tests.

They checked his urine, blood, X-rayed his lungs and so on. After a few days the doctor admitted that John Paul was depressed. I was frantic. Depression and I are old enemies and I wouldn't wish it on my worst foe, let alone my lovely son.

I took John Paul for long walks and tried to talk him out of his depression. It was useless. What a person needs in that state is a quiet companion who simply listens, barely speaks. In my desire to help, I probably made it worse.

John Paul said he was afraid to grow up. He didn't know what sort of man he wanted to be but he didn't want to be like Daddy. He was going to kill himself before his thirteenth birthday in June. When a family member is psychologically disturbed, it throws the whole family out of kilter. It was like poking an ants' nest with a sharp stick, watching the ants run chaotically around, trying to save the eggs.

After a bit Julian said 'I think I've got what John Paul's got.' Julian refused to have his hair cut. When his hair grew too long I said 'You must have it cut, you don't look like a loved child,' and he said 'I don't *feel* like a loved child.' He was eight.

This situation went on for three months. I decided to take all the children out of school one day, for a picnic. They needed some light relief. I drove them to nearby woods and we walked along a path in beautiful dappled sunshine, enjoying the fresh air, forest fragrance and peace. Suddenly John Paul found a baby rabbit beside the path, all alone. He emerged from his torpor, concerned for the tiny animal, wondering where its mother was and how he could help it. I was relieved by this change of mood and hopeful for his improvement.

The days passed in a haze of anxiety and exhaustion. One day John Paul was in the house but when I went to check on him, I couldn't find him. We lived in a huge Victorian pile on three floors. I checked his attic bedroom, the floor below, the bathrooms, the kitchen, playroom, living rooms. I ran around the garden calling his name, set his brothers to search for him. Probably only about twenty minutes of searching elapsed, before he emerged from the cupboard under the eaves in his bedroom. He hadn't heard us calling him. I had pictured the worst and the relief on finding him unhurt was indescribable. When I read about parents seeking lost children for days, sometimes weeks or months on end, I remember those terrible twenty minutes and my heart goes out to them.

At this stage I wrote to my brother. 'Here is the state of the family: Mum is her usual supportive self, Richard is a rock, Julian thinks he's got what JP has, Peter is helpful....and so on.' I listed seven people. I thought, but there are eight of us. Who is the eighth one? I went over them again, ticking them off on my fingers, but still I could only remember seven. It was on the third attempt that I realized I had left out myself.

When John Paul had again expressed his fear of growing up, Richard overheard me assuring him, 'You will be a lovely man, John Paul'. 'Are you mad?' Richard asked me unkindly.

John Paul was taken into the children's ward of the local hospital for a few days. The paediatrician was kind. He had children in the same school as mine. I confided I was anxious that the strain of the situation would make me ill too. 'Nonsense, Eileen,' he said, 'You're as tough as old boots.' But a week later I was in the county mental hospital. I had become exhausted by three months of his crying, missing a whole term at school, worrying, trying to cope with the other children's unease, and seeing no improvement in John Paul. We were preparing to go on holiday in the cottage by the stream. I had slept badly throughout those months and finally could hardly sleep at all. I went to bed at noon and asked Richard to call the doctor to give me something to help me sleep and cope.

When the doctor came I was dismayed to hear Richard say on the landing outside my bedroom, 'My wife has a history of mental illness.' Fifteen years previously I had suffered a breakdown after Peter's difficult birth, and then had been euphoric after the car crash, relieved that Richard was not dead. Did that constitute 'a history of mental illness' ? Years later I would be diagnosed as bipolar, prone at long intervals to a bout of depression or mania, depending on which stresses provoked the mood swing. It never happened without provocation. Richard was always good at diagnosis, but I felt betrayed.

The doctor prescribed three kinds of pills to take immediately. He said 'If you have not slept by 5 o'clock this afternoon we are going to take you to hospital.' That afternoon I felt as I imagine one might on an LSD trip, with jumbled thoughts streaming. The deadline of 'Sleep by 5 p.m.' was an added pressure. When the doctor returned and Richard made it clear that he was prepared to commit me if I didn't go willingly, I complied. It is difficult to get out of a mental hospital once you have been committed. All your autonomy disappears at the stroke of a pen.

Richard was smiling as I got into the ambulance with a social worker to be driven 60 miles to Carmarthen mental hospital. Perhaps it was with relief. My Mother stepped in as always, to take care of the boys.

Within half an hour of my telling the admitting doctor that I was allergic to Largactil, she made a mistake and injected me with 100 mgs of it. Next morning I got out of bed and fainted, breaking my leg. I fainted twice more before I crawled back to bed. Now my situation hit a new low: in a mental hospital with a broken leg in plaster to the hip, with crutches, worrying about my son's upcoming birthday and his threat to kill himself. In addition, I lost all confidence in the hospital when I discovered their mistake after a few days of taking Largactil pills, and refused to take more medication. It was about a week before Richard came to visit, and discovered my broken leg and the drug mix-up. He had taken the children to the cottage for a break and was completely incommunicado, although he passed a telephone box every time he went to buy groceries. It must have been hard for him caring for all the boys, with John Paul still deeply disturbed, but I think during the week he should have telephoned to ask about my progress.

At first the hospital admitted their mistake. The chief administrator came to see me and apologized. He said the admitting doctor was devastated and he hoped I understood. I didn't want to accuse anybody. I thought it an honest mistake. But by the time Richard came to visit they had changed their story. He told me they said I had imagined being allergic, and this was not the case. They didn't say I imagined the Largactil mistake, but this was brushed over.

With crutches and a plaster it was difficult to walk, but after a day or two I managed to walk to the lift, and go down a floor to the wall phone to call my brother. 'Please John, come and get me out of here,' I begged. He was in London and I was in west Wales, but I had no one else to turn to. His reply: 'My dear Eileen, it sounds to me as if you are in the right place.'

I resumed medication after two or three days without it, feeling more wretched than I can describe. After another week or so, they let me go home. I was at my lowest ebb: anxious, depressed, frightened, unsupported, on crutches, frantic about my sick son, responsible for my large family of small boys, unable to cope, suspicious of health authorities and their treatments, and mistrustful of the man on whom we all depended for food and shelter. It's hard to see it at the time, but the Good Thing about the lowest ebb, is that there is nowhere to go but up. One has to rearrange one's priorities, to survive. From then on I made a conscious decision to put myself first in every calculation. In the following years I was often mildly depressed and wearied by the effort, but in retrospect the graph of my recovery showed a relentless upward trend.

The following spring I went on holiday to California to visit Toni. It was my brother's suggestion. He generously offered to pay my fare, but the 250 pounds I had saved at Rosie's restaurant just covered it. While there I saw people living light-hearted lives, discussing interesting topics, not battling with depression and being constantly undermined by their spouses.

Toni and I talked into the night about what I should do, and how I could achieve independence. There was no way I could bear to grow older with a husband who snapped at us continuously. His unfaithfulness was not the main issue for me. He saved his smiles for others and took other women to restaurants saying to me 'There is no point, the cooking is always better at home.' If he had come home from his adventures in a happy mood, I might have settled for that. My biggest concern was his relentless barking at the boys.

One day I heard a window cleaner whistling and I thought, 'I want a husband like *that.*'

On my return from California I did not sleep the night before I left, nor overnight in the plane, and by the time I got home after staying a night with my brother in London, I was exhausted. I was overwhelmed by the need to be separated, and yet the inability to cope without Richard's support. I told Richard immediately that I wanted a separation and he dismissed this. He would not even discuss it again until the Christmas holidays eight months later. He accused me of spoiling Christmas when I raised the issue, but there had not been an earlier opportunity to talk; he was always busy. He said 'Leave if you want to, I'm not going anywhere.' Of course I could not leave the children, and I could hardly take five of them with me, with nowhere to go and no income.

We limped on for seven more years, before I felt strong enough to go it alone.

It is no wonder that with this family background, John Paul had a nervous breakdown. Gradually he began to improve, with the help of tranquilizers for a few weeks.

We took John Paul to see a psychiatrist. I showed his school reports to illustrate how cooperative and able he was, normally. The doctor talked to him and to us. He asked Richard why he spoke in such a small voice when he expressed his anger. Richard lowered his voice even further. 'Do you realize how menacing that sounds?' asked the doctor. To John Paul he said 'You are an intelligent young man. I have no doubt you will soon be better. I'm going to give you some homework. Go home and do something enjoyable.' When we emerged I felt that at last somebody understood and was prepared to help us. But as we walked out the door Richard said, 'Well, that was a complete waste of time.'

When a month passed and I was supposed to take John Paul back to the psychiatrist, I went by myself. I told him 'Thank you for your help, I know you understood. He is back at school, but now I have come to you for advice because I am in turmoil.' He answered 'What would make your life better?'

'If Richard could get the promotion he wants,' I started. 'No,' he said. 'If John Paul could catch up with his lessons…' 'No,' he said, 'If Peter…' 'No. What would make *your* life better?' I couldn't think of anything. 'I'm going to give you some homework,' he said, 'I want you to go home and do something selfish every week.'

I wracked my brains. On reflection I couldn't think of anything, except I liked Cadbury's Milk Chocolate, and if I had some, I always shared it with the family, which left me very little. So I bought a large bar of Cadbury's chocolate, and I told them all, this is Mummy's chocolate, and you can't have any. I was amazed that they didn't argue. It felt wonderful. It came to symbolize my right to keep something back for myself. Over the years I have helped my family all I could, but I still don't share my Cadbury's chocolate.

30 MONEY

Money troubles are often cited as the source of friction between partners. I think it goes much deeper than that. One's attitude to money can be a good indication of character.

Richard and I had only been 'together' twelve weeks when we got married. In fact we were apart most of that time because I lived in London and he was in Dorset, a four hour drive away. We only met at weekends. We didn't go out much so there was no opportunity to discover how important money would become, and I was so ignorant about this I would not have recognized its significance anyway. In my family we were always careful with money, but never mean. It was never perceived as a means of control or bribery. It was there to be managed judiciously and debt was to be avoided at all costs. In 1962 credit cards had not been invented. If you couldn't afford something you simply did without.

The first time I was aware of Richard's tightness with money was about a month after we got married, when we went out with another couple to eat at a restaurant. The two men, who were colleagues, had arranged this. I liked the wife very much. They had three children, and were friendly and open. She told me, 'Don't believe what they tell you about having babies – it's like shelling peas.' Well, it was for her.

We went to a smart restaurant and had a good meal with a bottle of wine. When the bill was laid on the table by the waiter, the two men reached for their wallets. However, Richard was slow on the draw, fumbling in his pockets until the delay became embarrassing and the other guy said 'Let me get this,' and put his money on the table. Richard let him, 'Oh thanks very much.' I was mortified.

When we got home I had to tackle this thorny issue. I reproached Richard for his slowness in producing his wallet, and for letting the other guy pay for our expensive meal, when the understanding from the start had been that we were 'going Dutch'. He was embarrassed. I said 'Tomorrow we must go and buy wine to the equivalent of our share of the bill, and take it to them.' We took three bottles of good wine and gave it to these friends, who were embarrassed too. I never saw them again.

When the boys were grown up, Richard went with two or three of them to the pub a couple of times, let them pay a round each and then, when it was his turn to buy a round, said it was time to go home. It was as if he didn't realize this trait was noticeable.

His family background partly accounts for this approach to money. I was once sitting on a bus with his mother, returning from Eltham to Mottingham, when I opened my purse to pay our fares and she reminded me that I owed her eight pence for a packet of seeds she'd bought me the week before. I wondered if she was serious, and handed over the eight pence, which she put in her purse. She was serious.

Richard was always in control of the budget. He earned the money, which went into his bank account, and he decided how it should be spent. To begin with he gave me four pounds a week in cash for housekeeping, which increased gradually to eight pounds a week ten years later when there were five of us. When the twins were born he increased this to twelve, now paid monthly at my request. I had my account in a different bank, into which I deposited the housekeeping cheque. I had to manage on that money for the month, whether or not it was sufficient, and it often wasn't. The boys' clothes, shoes, dinner money etc. all came out of the housekeeping plus family allowances. If two boys needed a pair of shoes in the same month, it was a crisis. I learned not to ask Richard for it because I would get a lecture but seldom money. My Mother stepped into the breach from her modest pension, and later when she took in students, she helped me even more. I had no reserves at all.

In the early days I recall having to live the last few days of the month on carrots and potatoes from the garden after his parents had stayed with us for a week, and the budget did not stretch. He seldom gave me extra for visitors. I recall his brother remarking, 'What, more peasant food?' when I served spaghetti bolognaise. I didn't have money to buy more than a pound of minced beef to feed nine of us. I didn't tell him that, but I smarted. We enjoyed people coming to stay for the weekend, but it was a strain economically.

Every month Richard put away sixty pounds towards the next car. Even when he had just changed cars, the same rigorous budgeting applied. The twins were a year old before he bought a new car and kept the old VW Beetle so I would no longer be limited to how far I could push a pram with three babies. The twins sat behind the back seat on top of the engine, which in a VW is at the back.

For eight years running we rented one holiday cottage or another for a week in Pembrokeshire, and unfailingly it rained. We all remember 'Dight holiday weather', which didn't improve until we went to France in the camping van, where the sun shone. There was never a washing machine on holiday and I spent the last day cleaning the rented accommodation to leave it in fit state for the next people. I didn't get any holiday money and still had to manage on the housekeeping. One year I spent my last pennies on a packet of cornflour on the Thursday, so I could make cheese sauce and pasta to fill up the boys. Another year I was walking around the Welsh resort of Fishguard with not a penny in my pocket, and Richard would not give me the money to buy a postcard to send to my Mother. The boys didn't even ask for ice cream, which they only ever tasted at home from a supermarket tub.

The boys' pocket money (pennies, to my regret) also came out of the housekeeping. Once I found a five pound note on the floor in a supermarket. I put my foot over it, and bent down to retrieve it. What a thrill! Without hesitation I went to the greengrocers and bought five pounds worth of fruit and vegetables which I brought home in triumph on a wooden tray. We had oranges and grapes for once.

When I went to university, most of my grant was used to repay the loan from my Mother to buy the Toyota Hiace.

The money I earned from Welcome Wagon was spent on carpets for the new house in Radyr.

In Cardiff I worked one half day a week for a man who owned a nightclub, typing his correspondence, and that money was spent on cutlery when we moved to Aberystwyth. We planned to run a guest house in Aberaeron so I bought a dozen sets of steel cutlery, but the surveyor's report was so critical, we bought Glen Rosa instead.

While I worked at Rosie's restaurant I put the money aside as usual. It amounted to 250 pounds over eighteen months. Richard thought me selfish when I spent the money on an air ticket to California.

The worse our relationship became, the more control he exerted through money. I often had to ask twice for the housekeeping, and once on the third request, he wrote the cheque and threw it on the floor in front of me. In silence I bent to pick it up. We depended on him for food and shelter. There was no other choice, with five little boys. I sometimes used to think, 'What a way to make a living'. But it was a powerful incentive to study for a degree to become independent.

One has to sympathise with Richard. He married a young woman to be his life companion and within a year her attention was focused on caring for a baby. Within eight years there were five. He was responsible and conscientious but twins born sixteen months after the third child suddenly propelled the family into barely manageable proportions. His wife's energy and attention were consumed by their needs.

He shouldered the financial burden single-handedly. By his own admission he didn't like children, and this responsibility felt to him like a life sentence. Despite all his planning this was not how he would have chosen to live. If he had entered into the spirit of being a parent, helping with bath time, reading to the children, or even engaging them in conversation, he might have learned to interact and appreciate them. Instead his resentment drained his energy and he failed to recognize the attractions of his family, which were legion. I don't think he ever looked into the eyes of any of his children to see the love and sparkle that filled them, and they were brimming with it.

31 CATCHING THE MOMENT

If there are children in your life you should endeavour to capture for yourself, and posterity, some of the funny, entertaining, touching things they say and do. Parents by definition are busy people, and for every time you record a special moment, a thousand are lost forever. That I didn't do better is one of my greatest regrets. Keep a special notebook and write it down today, or you'll forget it.

In August 73 I recorded Julian asking as we walked across the allotments, 'Mummy, is this Britain?' I told him yes. 'We've got to keep Britain tidy,' he said, quoting an advertising slogan and picking up some litter.

[Julian was christened Julian Mark Alexander Dight. Until he was thirteen when we moved to Cambridge, he was called Julian. During the move he elected to be called Mark in future.]

Peter was ten when he asked, 'Has your voice broken, Mummy?' 'No, only boys' voices break, but surely none of the boys in your class has a broken voice?' 'Well, only Mr Wilson,' he said.

Aged 4 Julian said to Nana, 'You mustn't say "bloody" because that's a swear word, and you mustn't say "Oh God," must you? You can only say that when it's expensive.'

He also said 'When I grow up I'm going to be a lollipop man...or a Soil Scientist.' I asked him which do you think is harder work? Julian: 'I think a lollipop man because he has to hold up that heavy stick so long.'

Aged 6 Patrick was telling me about the harvest thanksgiving assembly at school. 'There was a churchman there, you know – a dicker.'

In school Andre was listening with the rest of his class to the story of the Good Samaritan. The teacher: 'And the Samaritan said, Are you with me?' and Andre called out, 'No, we're with the Woolwich!' (another catch-phrase).

July 1978: Patrick, aged 7, watching a food advert on TV: 'My teeth are getting strong and juicy.'

The same year we were fishing from the rowing boat in the bay and Patrick failed first time to catch anything. Andre caught a mackerel, the first of the season. Pat said 'I have a very sad life. I've never caught a fish.' Next turn out an hour later he caught four pollock at once. (I was reminded of this when his son Harry caught a load of fish in Dingle Bay in 2010.)

Scenes from 1981: 7 April. We've just been to see a speech therapist. The appointment was for the twins although I was mystified by the school's referral. She looked at them and Julian and said, 'Are these all yours? They don't look at all alike.' 'Oh yes, and I've got two more at home,' I said.

First she asked Andre to read a card with three phrases. He giggled at 'Peter and Jane play with the red ball,' because they had just been laughing at a rude joke about playing with balls. Then he had to count to 10, which he did slowly and pedantically. 'And now backwards,' she said, which he did. She flipped through a book of pictures. He interpreted a child's reclining head as 'Bed, well, sleeping child.' When it was Pat's turn he commented, 'Sleeping beauty.'

Pat counted to 10, then he said the days of the week. 'Would you like them backwards?' Not particularly, but the therapist was losing the initiative. 'Sunday, Saturday, Friday' etc. he recited glibly, ' anything else?' Still serious, she said she had picked out his tendency to say his 'Rs' with slight immaturity. I said it hadn't done Roy Jenkins any harm, and his father also had this tendency. They were mostly tongue tied, but only the oldest had had his tongue cut. 'Oh no, we don't do that now, as long as they can lick their top lip, it's all right...We will only do something about it if it worries him.' 'It doesn't worry *me*,' said Pat gleefully, 'I mostly read in silence anyway.' She remained solemn. 'What would you do about it?' I asked, struggling to keep a straight face. 'Oh, exercises,' she said, 'Leave it a couple of years and then come back if he's still doing it.' I made a harassed mental note to keep that in mind for 1983, along with Julian's blood test in three months' time. She asked about the rest of the family, with a look of disbelief. I said, 'In Russia I'd get a medal. Here I just get funny looks.' 'Would you *really* get a medal, Mum?' from Andre. 'Oh yes, I'd be up there beside Breznev on May Day.' She seemed genuinely relieved when we left.

Another scene: Andre asked, Why can't I watch *The Professionals?* 'Because it's not suitable for ten year olds.' 'If you mean it's full of sex and violence, I'm growing up in a world full of sex and violence and I have to learn how to cope with it,' he said. 'I managed to grow up without sex and violence.' Andre: 'Yes, but Mum, you're nearly extinct.' (I was 44.)

Sitting in the Theatre y Werin, mid scene in *The Boyfriend*, Pat turned to me and whispered, 'How do they wind up Big Ben?'

Driving down to Ilminster in September 81 for the Dight 50th wedding anniversary celebrations, Pat told me about a documentary he'd seen on TV about an African Chief who had 100 wives and 600 children. The boys constructed various amusing fantasies around this set-up. Then Pat said, 'Imagine, if he has 100 wives and there are 365 days in a year, each wife only has to do it 3 and a half times a year.' I thought this a precocious speculation for a ten year old, but said nothing. Then he added, 'Fancy, all that washing-up for 700 people!' He also thought post cards and stamps would cost a lot when the chief went on holiday.

There was a family supper for 16 on the Saturday night, before the hotel dinner on the Sunday. In the excitement of the occasion Julian offered to tell his 'monk in a silent order' joke which he'd been telling since he was about five (50 years and no sugar in my tea – I'm leaving. Thank goodness for that, you've been nothing but a chatterbox ever since you arrived...) All the children told jokes amid much laughter. Later Pop said he hoped they wouldn't do that the next evening in the hotel.

We moved into a Victorian house with a scruffy garden and lots of space. That autumn they found a tortoise in the garden and named him 'Flash'. The little ones made a pen to contain him and piled in dry leaves for the tortoise to hibernate. They spent the day offering him lettuce and cucumber to eat. They were surprisingly attentive for so little response. After supper they went out to check on him for the night, but he had escaped. With torches they walked around the garden in the twilight calling 'Flash, Flash' but he had not known them long enough to answer to his name. They never found him, and in bed they worried about him, lost in the dark.

Children are so original. They haven't yet learned to think in clichés. Like learning a language, they sometimes search for parallel words if the first one doesn't come to mind. When Patrick was seven he ate 'toad in the hole' for the first time. (In England that's sausages baked in batter in the oven.) He couldn't remember the name, so he asked 'Can we have frog dumplings?' When Nana's brother, Dennis and Barbara met the little ones from school and took them to the Wimpy Bar, Patrick told me excitedly, 'Uncle Dennis bought us knicker-knocker glories!'

I took them to an amateur production of Joseph's Amazing Technicolour Dreamcoat. It was good and quite absorbing. In the middle of a number Patrick, aged seven, turned to me and whispered 'Mum, how do they clean the gutters on a sky scraper?' I had to admit I was stumped.

When he was four Julian told me 'I think worms must be very clever.' Why is that? 'Michael Walsh tied one in a knot and it undid itself....mind you, he did not tie the knot too tight.'

I read the little ones a story about Paddington Bear, whose hat fell in the river, and he was upset because it was a family heirloom. I knew each boy's precise vocabulary, and they hadn't met this word before. 'An heirloom is something precious handed down within families,' I explained. 'I know!' said Andre, 'like our coats!'

In 1980 when the twins were 9, Patrick took an ice cream tub half full of slugs and snails to school for a nature lesson (our garden was full of them). He edged a pane of glass with Sellotape to display them. When he came home he said the teacher was so pleased with him, he'd given out the slugs to each table and they'd all been able to find the breathing hole. Andre said indignantly, 'Yes. His table had all the best slugs. They had one each. We only got one small one between us. And in the second lesson ours fell asleep!'

Here's an entry for 18 January 1980:

The alarm bell didn't go off, and I woke at 7.45. I got up immediately and shouted to the boys 'I've overslept, get up quickly!' (Richard was away in London). I started to dress. Patrick was sleepy. I heard Andre (8) getting up and talking to him. I said 'Hurry up, boys! This is the day I get locked out if I don't arrive in time,' (Prof. Garnett's 9 a.m. lecture.) After a bit Andre came in, very worried, saying 'Pat won't get up! I told him if Mummy's late she won't be let in, and it all counts towards her degree, and if she doesn't get it we won't move to London, and I won't get my gerbils, and you won't get a better tool set, so get up!' I laughed and said, 'What did he say?' 'He just said "Shut up!" '

My granddaughter Leah was four when she complimented me, in France, 'Your hair looks nice, Granny' (after a trip to the salon). 'Why thank you, Leah.' She continued, 'Yes, because before it was *horrible*.'

Her brother Charlie was four when he told me about his best friend. 'You'll like Dylan, Granny. He's cute.....He hasn't got a dog.' Neither has Charlie. I wondered why he mentioned it. 'He *had* a dog' he said, darkly. 'It was gross. It was old and smelly and it kept licking everyone... It's in heaven now. In fact it's probably licking God right now.'

When Charlie was four and Leah five, they were left in their car seats while their mother ran in with a message for a neighbour. They were parked on the driveway. Charlie got out of his car seat and sat in the driver's place, slipping the car into reverse. When his mother came out she was horrified to see the car was now parked parallel with the curb (he'd slipped the gear out again). Leah said reproachfully, 'Charlie, I *told* you not to drive the car.'

John Paul had an air rifle in his teens. He was going out in the field behind the house with his gun. 'Can I come?' said Julian. 'No! You'll frighten the rabbits.' I said 'Julian is very good at being quiet.' 'Yesterday,' said JP, 'he was shouting "Hallo rabbits, hurry up before he gets you," and singing at the top of his voice.' I laughed. JP was so good natured about it.

They had a teacher at junior school, Mr. L. I thought he was excellent, clearly in command and energetic. He cultivated the parents with charm. But Andre said 'I don't like him. I don't like his eyebrows.' The others didn't like him either. 'He shouts,' was all they would say. I knew what he meant about eyebrows. Lowered eyebrows are threatening. Lifted eyebrows are defensive. (Think Saddam Hussein when captured.) The boys were good at reading expressions.

The three youngest boys were in their late teens before they confided to me their hatred of Mr L. One of them had had a nightmare and shared it with his brothers. Over the years they had all had nightmares about him. 'Mum, he was a bully. He demanded total obedience and if a child was distracted and didn't jump to it immediately he would pick him up and hold him in the air at face level while he shouted at him in front of the whole school. He always picked on the weak ones. I hate him, and if I saw him today I would punch his lights out.' The others concurred. Patrick added, 'He had a cane too, and struck it so hard on the desk it broke in two and half flew across the class room. The boys he liked were all good at sport.'

You don't have to be a political dictator to be a despot. I should have paid better attention to the eyebrows.

Here's a recent anecdote: Connor (aged 7) saw the letters 'JMU' here in Harrisonburg and asked what they meant. I told him that James Madison University is named after an important man who was president 150 years ago. He asked, 'Is he still alive?' No, I said, he's dead now. 'Mommy says that when you die they put you in a box and put it in the ground and then you go to Heaven,' said Connor. 'That's right,' I said, 'and then you have wings and you can fly' (trying to lighten the tone). 'You'll be flying soon, won't you Granny?' said Connor. That's right, I said evenly, and when I have wings I'll fly around looking down and make sure you are safe. 'I don't want you to die, Granny' said Jake (4). And I don't want him to worry. I assured him that I had no plans for that for a long time to come.

The wonders of children are so great that your head cannot hold them. Write it down or suffer the loss.

32 UNIVERSITY 1979-1983

I had only been back from California two days when something happened that changed my life. I was on my way to the bank when on impulse I thought to call in at the University Careers Department to ask for guidance to improve my earning power.

They suggested I take a business course. What would that teach me? I asked. Shorthand, typing, filing, accounting.... I told them I had secretarial experience, I'd done a little accounting, spoke Spanish and French, I'd done all that. They asked me what else I was interested in.

I told them that in Cardiff I'd done two of four years of a social studies course at the University College of Wales, in Social Psychology and Sociology, which I had to leave to move to Aberystwyth. They asked me 'How would you like to do a degree in Sociology? ' I don't have 'A' levels I said, only 'O' levels. They said if my tutor in Cardiff gave me a good reference, I might be acceptable.

They contacted the psychology tutor who gave me a great reference, adding 'This woman has the ability to make things happen.' I had an interview at the college and was offered a place to start that autumn.

Richard said, 'Haven't you got enough to do?' I said I'd get a grant and all fees paid, and I could fit it in with the children's school timetables. So it was agreed I'd go. I was nervous of the hard work, but can never turn down a challenge or an opportunity. Even a third class degree would be better than nothing.

At an interview in our first week with a head of department, surrounded by other students, he looked at my details and said sardonically, 'You have no 'A' levels? But I see you have "other quals." ' Silently I looked him in the eye and thought, 'I'll show you.'

In the first year we took five basic courses: Economic History, Sociology, International Politics, History and one option: I chose Spanish. 'We don't advise you to take a language,' they said. 'If you don't pass all your exams at the end of the first year you can't continue, and more people come unstuck in a language than any other subject.' I told them that Spanish was an easy option for me, the only exam I felt certain to pass.

I found Economic History more interesting than History. International Politics was a bit of a challenge. The subject matter of Sociology interested me, but the language was difficult. We had to be so careful in our use of words, I felt inhibited when writing essays.

In a Sociology seminar with the head of department one day, the topic was religion. 'Why is religion so important to people?' he asked. Nobody responded. 'Why do people all over the world embrace religion?' he persisted. I knew a couple of the students were Catholic and felt uncomfortable on their behalf. Dr Van Velsen asked the question three times until I lost patience and said, 'Perhaps there's something in it.' He exploded with fury. It seemed he was atheist with no tolerance for faith. The answer he sought was, 'People need to make sense of their lives so they invent religion to make it easier.' He ranted and although rattled, I said mildly, 'I thought university was supposed to be a place for debate.' He was still protesting when the seminar came to an end and we filed out. Afterwards a friend who was a lecturer in the Sociology Department told me that he was asking colleagues 'Who is this dreadful Dight woman?' After that I knew I was doomed if I continued with Sociology.

When I'd told Rosemary Birkenshaw I'd been offered a place to read Sociology she said 'Yes well, they are desperate for students up there.' I'm not surprised that the Sociology Department subsequently folded.

So in the second year I chose to major in International Politics because it was the best department in the university. I didn't want to do Strategic Studies which involved knowledge of weapons and modern warfare, so I took joint honours with History. And of course I kept Spanish.

Choosing all the modern periods, from early 19th century on, so that current affairs would be more transparent, I was relieved to leave out the Peloponnesian War but had to do International Institutions (The League of Nations, United Nations, International Court of Justice and so on).

Becoming an undergraduate at any age involves finding your way around a new campus, new faces and unfamiliar timetables. I was 42 and older than some of the lecturers. This didn't bother me. I enjoyed the lectures, the research, writing essays. Even walking purposefully around the buildings with books in my bag felt good. I typed all my essays on a portable Underwood, and turned every assignment in on time. Because I had so many family commitments I worked ahead of schedule, to allow time for a boy off sick from school, or an unexpected workload. Time management is as important as study.

My Mother was my main support. She came every weekday to work in the house while I was out, keeping us tidy and clean and doing the washing. Without her help it would have been chaotic. The dishwasher was essential. I drove the boys to their schools at 9 in the mornings and went on to University until 3 p.m. when I picked them all up and drove us home. They were in junior and high schools, aged 8 to 16 when I started my course.

The boys were my next line of support. They understood that I was doing homework at weekends when I wrote essays. If friends phoned me they would say 'Mummy can't come to the phone right now, she's writing an essay. She'll call you later.' I didn't tell them to say this, it was their own initiative. During the week, by the time I had put in a full day at college and cooked the evening meal, I was too tired to do book work. I'd watch some television with the boys and check they did their homework too.

We rigged up a bell on the top floor, with a string hanging down three floors between the pitch pine staircases, to let them know when it was time to get up. They would wash, dress and come down to get their own breakfast. They could choose cereal or cook themselves a fried egg and toast. They ran their eyes down the check list poster I'd put up in the kitchen: HAVE YOU? Brushed your teeth, combed your hair, cleaned your shoes, got your homework books, sports kit, dinner money? I clearly recall Patrick checking the list, saying 'I haven't combed my hair!' and running off to do it. Putting responsibility onto children to organize their own lives pays dividends. They were all in the car with relevant books, sports gear and dinner money, in time to drive to school. They were never late. I am proud of them.

After years of domesticity, I thoroughly enjoyed the lectures. In some ways I think education is wasted on the young. Going straight from school to university is a continuation of learning, with the added value of being independent of parents. But study can seem tedious to an eighteen year old still feeling like a cog in the education system, lacking life experience.

I had expected to find lively debate among undergraduates, but they seemed a dull lot on the whole. There was a culture of being late with assignments and proud of it. Students boasted how little work they did. Their social lives seemed to revolve around drinking too much beer. But they were pleasant and sometimes invited me to have coffee with them in the canteen.

There was a particular lecturer with admirable style and content. In addition to his academic role at Aberystwyth, Dr. Garnett was an adviser to the United Nations. At the end of one of his early lectures I sat there thinking, 'That was a privilege to listen to'. But two girls in front of me closed their books, one saying to the other, 'God that was boring. Yeah.' They were too ignorant to recognize a brilliant speaker, and had not spent un-stimulating years at a kitchen sink.

The first two years went smoothly. There was so much to read, I only allowed myself one novel a year in the school holidays, when we were camping in France. I chose Jane Austen. During the holidays the boys reverted to needing more emotional support, lifts in the car, more of my attention, but as soon as I went back to college they supported me.

I enjoyed the seminars. Half a dozen students would meet in a lecturer's room to discuss a particular topic. I was less reluctant than most to participate. One lecturer, Ritchie, a bachelor, gave us a reading list for the next seminar. I went to the library to consult the books.

The following week I protested that he had suggested Churchill's Memoirs as a source. When I looked in the library there were several volumes, I said. Could you give us a more realistic reading list for the next seminar? After that, he frequently added to his instructions, 'and for the benefit of Mrs Dight, there is a short volume on so and so'.

On the last day of term I was the only one who turned up to his seminar. So we sat and talked for a bit. When I mentioned that I had five children in school he was shocked. I said 'It wasn't laziness that made me unwilling to read Churchill's Memoirs, it was time management.' I felt the change in his attitude.

I nearly dropped out at the beginning of the third year when Richard and I were discussing divorce. I consulted a solicitor, looked at alternative properties in town to see if I could run a boarding house to support us all. I was so agitated, I became 'high'. My brain raced too fast and it was obvious I could not work in that state. I told my tutor I could not go on. The college authorities were understanding and sent me a letter suggesting I take a year off and come back again. I didn't think I could, but Julian continued to urge me. He had bought a bottle of wine with his own money in France that summer while we camped, and kept it on his chest of drawers in a wine cradle. He said it was for my graduation. He reminded me several times over the months that we would celebrate one day, though I did not believe it. He was 13 and wise beyond his years.

The next autumn I returned to college. During my final year, Richard was working in London, coming home every other weekend. The boys continued to take care of themselves and leave me free to work. And Nana kept us tidy.

Alarmed at first by examinations, I followed Richard's advice, to condense my lectures onto index cards. In the process I became familiar with the themes: Aspects of Foreign Policy, The United Nations, etc. using acronyms to remind myself of key concepts. The components of Foreign Policy are Strategic, Political, Ideological, Economic and Legal: SPIEL. It was like making a sauce, reducing the liquid to its essence, then reconstituting with more liquid. By this means, reworking the cards, I managed to commit the essence to memory. I had sixty cards for International Politics alone. There were nine examinations. In Economic History we were also required to write a 5,000 words essay of our choice, in advance. I researched and wrote mine during the last summer holidays before Finals, to leave myself time. I chose to examine how far Hitler went to war for economic reasons, a question that sparked my curiosity while reading. I was lucky that it was accepted as an appropriate theme.

For three months before finals, I got up at 5 a.m. and studied until 8 o'clock when the boys came down for breakfast. I was at my best early in the morning.

We took our exams in the main hall of the university, at desks in rows with supervisors. Many students had packets of Polo peppermints to suck during the exam. I got myself a packet too: anything to help! I felt on top of my game. The revision was a marathon, but the exams were a walk in the park.

I was conscious at the time that this would be the last big mental push of my life. Every resource I could bring to it was thrown into the enterprise. I wanted to prove to myself the level I could reach, with application. I got a 2.1 degree (with a 1st in Spanish).

The boys were proud of me. Julian and Patrick sent me cards addressed to Eileen Dight, B.Sc. (Econ), which touched me. The boys and my Mother came to my graduation. I felt all their names should have been on the certificate. And finally, we opened Julian's bottle of wine in celebration.

33 MASS OBSERVATION ARCHIVES

In September 1982 (I was 45) I joined the Mass Observation Archives at the University of Sussex, as an Observer. I had responded to a report in the Sunday Times saying I was interested in current affairs and politics and a keen observer of the social scene (having studied social psychology and sociology at university evening classes). I described myself as an undergraduate, 'about to become a single parent after twenty years of marriage, and concerned about lack of employment opportunities for my growing sons'.

Observations were filed anonymously under a number system, and made available for future historians to read contemporary reports about historical issues.

Professor David Pocock replied 'We would be very grateful for your help – not least because of your background and your address – we would like more people in Wales.'

He sent me the Summer Directive for 1982 which asked Observers to write about Public Services, Private Services (repairs, decoration, installations, faulty goods and 'cowboys'). We were asked if this year's Budget had affected us directly and could I tell them how? Under 'Self Portrait' they asked for a typical day's meals on a weekday and a typical main meal on a Sunday, including times.

Here's what I wrote:

Pattern of Family Meals.

Breakfast at around 8 a.m. Everybody has cereal or egg and toast. Bacon became too expensive for breakfast years ago and is only eaten now as a main meal. Coffee or tea.

Lunch: Unless children are at school (school dinners are 60 pence a day each) we lunch at 1 p.m. Example: Salad and bread rolls and cheese, fruit; or homemade soup, or macaroni cheese etc.

Supper: (We do not eat 'tea'.) 5.30 p.m. when husband returns from work we have a cooked meal. Meat and vegetables (e.g. meat pie, or liver, or meatballs, or pasta, or a hot cheese dish (e.g. ratatouille with cheese) or omelette, soufflé, gougère, stuffed pancakes etc. – in other words making cheap meat or modest ingredients go as far as possible, as deliciously as possible. I would prefer to cook more expensive meals, but cannot afford the ingredients. Usually I make a pudding, like apple crumble or gooseberry pie (fruit from garden) and custard, or scones and jam, or an apple.

Sunday lunch: 1 p.m. A joint of meat (usually lamb, hardly ever beef as it is so expensive). e.g. shoulder of lamb, three or four vegetables, onion sauce. Pudding: apple sponge and ice cream, or orange mousse, pastry or profiteroles, pancakes, whatever. Usually we open a bottle of wine on Sundays.

I make a great effort with cooking, being a good cook and enjoying food, and having a family with hearty appetites, but am hampered by a tight budget. I make about one third of the bread we eat and all our buns, cakes, biscuits, yoghurt, soups and sauces. We have a large variety of dishes. We never eat out or have takeaways.

I buy in bulk from the local cash and carry: goods in season, basic ingredients like sacks of potatoes and 7 lb. bags of rice, dried fruit, flour, etc., getting the best price and value. I make all our jams, marmalade, chutney, pickle and home-made wine. I freeze fruit and vegetables when in season and at lowest prices, hardly ever buy convenience foods which are expensive, and contents are sometimes suspect.

Further economies:

I make as many of our clothes as I can. I used to make my sons' trousers, but eventually considered two days' work for one pair of trousers more time-consuming than worth it, all to save about 2 pounds. I make all my clothes except underwear. I even make my husband's safari jackets and occasionally trousers and Viyella shirts, if I can buy the material cheaply enough to justify the effort. I made my husband a grey safari jacket for 3 pounds, indistinguishable from a shop-made one at 30 pounds. Of course it took me several days. When we lived in Cardiff I bought materials from local material factories at the market in Pontypridd, but fabric is so expensive here, I make fewer clothes.

My husband made the children's bedsteads and installed kit-form kitchen units. He used to grow all our vegetables and soft fruits but the garden here is unsuitable for produce.

I do all the inside decorating and my husband paints the outside. This represents a huge saving in money. He also services the two cars, since he took evening classes in car maintenance eight years ago. He doesn't like servicing cars but garage repairs have become prohibitively expensive. Our cars are 5 and 10 years old.

I've just bought school uniforms for our twins to start comprehensive school this term. I bought as little as possible (only one pullover each, for example) in an attempt to keep down the expense, but here is the list of essential items, bought at the cheapest suppliers, for which I had to shop around:

2 pairs shoes 32 pounds

2 jumpers 9 pounds

2 pairs trousers 21 pounds

2 ties 3 pounds

4 pairs socks 3.60

2 rugby shorts 6.50

2 rugby shirts 15 pounds

2 pairs gym shoes 8 pounds

4 shirts 22 pounds

Total 120.10

I also had to replace shirts for two of their older brothers. I bought no blazers (which are regulation) as they are 25 pounds each, which would cost me 100 pounds. No gym shorts or satchels (now 15 pounds each). They use plastic sports bags to carry their books and homemade pencil cases.

I'm annoyed that as all my children take size 6 shoes or over I have to pay VAT for 'adult' sizes. I also had to pay VAT on one of the twin's shirts as he takes size 14.5 neck and although I bought from the school uniform supplier, this is considered adult size. There must be many more children having to pay VAT on larger sizes, than dainty adults buying children's clothes.

As the school leaving age is 16, why do we have to pay full fare on public transport, in cinemas etc., for children at 14?

Periodically I've kept records of every penny I spent over a couple of months, to discover where the money has gone and how I can economize. I have to hand the most recent study, May-July 1979. I kept a complete record of absolutely everything I spent, then broke the expenditure down into the following categories:

May 1979:

Food 67.70

School dinners 20.87

Clothes 29.37

Miscellaneous 30.71

Household 21.30

Stamps 1.15

Petrol 12.00

Total Expenditure in May: 183.10

Income for May: 170.00
(150 pounds housekeeping plus 20 pounds Family Allowances.)

I notice in June my Mother gave me 20 pounds. She usually makes up the difference when I overspend. Although a widow and pensioner she takes in university students, which enables her to help me.

Items which have increased with inflation and others which are stable:

3 lb. bread flour has only gone up 4p since 1979, whereas 24 frozen beef-burgers have gone from 1.05 (one pound five pence) to 2.28. Lamb's liver was 60p, is now 1 pound per lb. Bread was 35.5 pence, is now 49 pence. 24 cans evaporated milk was 5.39 pounds, is 7.08. School dinners were 1.25 per child per week, are now 3 pounds each. Petrol was 1.16, is now 1.72 per gallon. Haircuts for the boys were 50 p each, are now 1.15 each. Stamps were 9 p are now 12.5 pence and 15 pence first class.

My income in the summer of 1979 was 170 pounds per month. Now (1982) it is 250 housekeeping and 84 pounds family allowances. My husband's income was 8,000 p.a., is now 12,000 pounds p.a. As a student I receive 1,250 grant a year.

We encourage our children to go on to further education, and they are all bright enough, but the oldest dropped out of school the Christmas before his 'A' levels. The second son is only taking two 'As' next summer and is doubtful about going to university. He's afraid to commit himself to a particular line of development and then fail to find work after three years of effort. Living in a university town they see many students fail to find work after they graduate, which has radically affected their expectations. They frequently speculate about whether there will be jobs, and if they should train to become plumbers or electricians, to be self-employed. Sociologists would class us as 'middle class' but we have all the expectations without the affluence.

I feel too much of my husband's and my time is spent exercising our ingenuity and effort to make money go further. We never go out for a meal, or to a pub, although we drink wine at home quite often. We have managed a holiday abroad the last five years, but only by camping and doing all our own catering. Before that we were 15 years without a holiday abroad, something I took for granted when I was single.

We used to take *The Times* and *Sunday Times* and discovered it cost over 90 pounds p.a., for which amount we could have a telephone instead. Since then charges for newspapers and telephones have soared. Our telephone, sparingly used, costs around 48 pounds a quarter. I think it's uncivilized to have no daily paper, but it's a necessary economy. We usually buy a Sunday paper. We buy no magazines although I enjoy *Time, Cosmopolitan, Punch* and *The Economist*, (at the library or dentist's). Our minds are constantly exercised in deciding what we can afford and what we must do without, although I'm sure we are better off than most.

We have a modest mortgage on a large Victorian house with five bedrooms and one third acre garden on the edge of Aberystwyth: two cars, gas central heating (which we installed in 1976 but cannot afford to run except in freezing weather). We have an automatic washing machine and tumble drier, dishwasher and various electrical appliances. This takes a lot of drudgery out of housework. Our furniture and carpets are extremely modest (some second hand). We would like to buy paintings, books, more alcohol, clothes, have better holidays, pay someone else to paint the house, service the cars, clean the windows, do repairs. We feel extravagant if we buy a record, and never buy anything ready-made if we can make it cheaper ourselves. We'd like to travel more, eat out, throw away old clothes instead of patching them, give the children more pocket money. The twins (aged 11) get 40p each a week and the 12 year old gets 50p; the oldest two have no pocket money since they got jobs washing up weekends in a hotel. I would like to buy more varied and expensive food, more fruit and less starch to satisfy hungry boys. I'd rather serve a good lamb stew or roast, than the boned breast of lamb with stuffing, or the sausages or home-made pizza we more often eat.

Thank goodness for the public library and for television, an underrated asset as well as a public menace, portraying ideal people living ideal lives in smart clothes, shiny cars and spotless, well-furnished homes, to say nothing of amoral lifestyle, and sex-stereotyping which has much to answer for. However, with selective use I think British television excellent value but I wish they would tone down the violence and stop blunting our sensibilities in relation to man's inhumanity to man.

When we had our drive resurfaced (tarmac) at 450 pounds, or pay for repairs as today on the water heating system (21 pounds) we offer cash. We patched up a leaking roof ourselves through lack of funds (we're waiting apprehensively for the next downpour). We need to replace broken window frames. The record player has broken down but we can't afford to have it mended this month, probably not next month either. When we had a carpenter repair the back door about three years ago we were charged 7 pounds an hour for the labour in addition to materials, and as he lingered most of the day it cost 38 pounds, which seemed a waste of money, but was something we couldn't tackle ourselves.

If we were not both capable people, good with our hands, I cannot imagine how we'd manage. The drudgery of bringing up a large family has defeated my husband and made him morose and irritable. He longs for the time when they are grown up and gone. Consequently I'd prefer to live alone (with the children of course) and manage on even less money, in an attempt to stay cheerful and enjoy the undoubted pleasures in my life. What a good thing a sense of humour is free; a more cheerful and positive attitude helps things smooth over. My expensive boys are also extremely attractive, cheerful, loving and rewarding and I would not be without them for the world.

I hope on graduation to get work, but if not I'll take in students and try for a grant to do a PhD. if my degree is good enough. I'd also like to write, if I can get a commission. I expect the next few years to be very tight financially. But it will be so for a lot of other people too.

I am uneasy about the political future of this country. Although we have been stable for so long, people's expectations have changed, and will they put up with the stringent economy we are heading for? I feel the Thatcher government is misguided in its adherence to monetarism. I also feel they are indifferent to the suffering unemployment has brought to many people. They still believe that the unemployed are feckless and the unions greedy. This is dangerous ignorance. Even if people do not become angry enough to revolt, society is changing radically. My oldest son is so disaffected and cynical. He was for a time a member of a left wing organization until he became disillusioned by them too. He has no sense of contributing to society, or desire to be self-sufficient, as we had at his age. He thinks we are mad to be 'locked in' to a middle class life style with all the effort entailed in supporting it. He may be right. But it's important to me to have a roof over my head that I at least half own, and to send my children to school with appropriate clothes. We tried to bring our children up to fit into the society we knew, but it has changed and we have to adapt. I'm alarmed at the latest cabinet discussion of cutting government expenditure on higher education and the health services. Access to all that for everyone is one of Britain's best features. If they try to make universities available only to those who can afford it and a few of the best brains by scholarship, I shall march and wave a banner too. And how can people on the poverty line afford to pay for medical insurance? If this all makes a conventional middle-aged woman rebellious, what will it do for the young?

It's not all gloomy. I think there is more compassion and less hypocrisy around than when I was young. People didn't worry about the third world then, and they tied themselves up in knots with ridiculous ideas about sexual morality. People are developing a different set of priorities. Many people are adapting more moderate life styles and exploring better values.

Please let me know if there is any area on which you wish me to expand. I think your project of amassing contemporary reports for the perusal of future historians admirable. Having worked on the New Poor Law in 1834, about which details are scanty, I appreciate your putting meat on the bones of history.

34 OUR FIRST IRISH HOLIDAY

By 1982 Richard and I were mostly living separate lives. He was working in London, but I didn't know where he lived so I couldn't call him and he didn't call me. He was staying with a girlfriend. Until he came home one weekend he didn't know that John Paul had been in a car crash, hospitalized overnight. Neither could I reach him when Peter was taken to hospital with emergency appendicitis. Peter was very sick, in hospital for some days. I phoned Richard's office and one of his colleagues told me Richard was on holiday in Holland. Peter was so desperate for a drink after the operation, he drank his mouthwash. I was deeply relieved when he was well enough to come home.

In 1982 Peter left home with a rucksack and hitchhiked through England, staying for a while at Greenham Common, the American airbase where protestors were urging the removal of Cruise Missiles. He remained for some days in solidarity with the women who camped there for months on end, until they told him to leave because it was a women's protest. I was proud of him for lending his energies to this good cause.

That summer I decided to take the four younger boys and my Mother to Ireland on holiday. We had little money but the Hiace camper gave us freedom to travel. With my housekeeping and my Mother's pension, we set off to explore the emerald isle. From Fishguard on the Welsh coast we crossed by ferry to Dublin, driving north east through the midlands of Ireland, calling on two of my friends. Ann lived in Mullingar. I knew her from the Catholic Church in Mottingham. While visiting Irish relations she had met and married John, a local Irish solicitor. They had built a beautiful modern home and had four young children. They made us very welcome.

From there we crossed to the northwest, visiting my friend Liz and her husband in Northern Ireland.

Now we drove south, through Galway and Connemara. I had never seen anywhere more beautiful. The fuchsia hedges were in bloom and the mountains reflected in blue lakes. The west coast was largely uninhabited. We enjoyed two weeks of rare Irish sunshine.

John Paul was seventeen. Six weeks previously I had taught him to drive the Hiace, on an industrial estate near Aberystwyth. I let him drive all over Ireland on largely deserted country roads. He was competent and helpful. He built fires for us at camping sites and pitched the tent for himself and Julian. The twins, Nana and I slept in the van. Everybody helped with the cooking. We were in good spirits.

In Killarney my Mother recognized the street where she had stayed on holiday when she was seventeen. Her sister Eileen had a friend called Shannon, whose brother, Bobby Eager, had proposed to my mother on that holiday, telling her he was going to America to work for a couple of years, and 'will you wait for me, Peg?' It was a loose arrangement. When he returned from America after some years and visited her mother in Tilbury, Margaret opened the door to him, with my brother in her arms. She had married Fred a couple of years before. But she always had a soft spot for Bobby Eager. There was a family snapshot of him with a shock of black curly hair and a ready grin.

In Killarney, with its tourist appeal, and flower baskets hanging from the lamp posts, horse and cart rides were on offer; smartly painted shops and thatched cottages made a pretty scene. When Margaret was young the Eager family ran a small hotel in Killarney high street; she recognized the building, although it was now a liquor store. We went in to buy a bottle of wine. At the check-out a smart young man greeted us with a friendly smile, as did all the people we met in Ireland. I asked him if he had ever heard of a man called Bobby Eager?

Oh sure, he said, he lives ten minutes' walk from here. He gave us the address, and off we went to look for Bobby. We parked the van at the curb and stood beside my Mother as she knocked with trepidation on the front door. A woman opened it. Margaret said, 'Is Bobby in?' as if she had come to play. 'He is,' said the woman, 'and who are you?' 'I'm Maggie Higgins,' said my Mother, reverting to her single name. The woman didn't smile. She stiffened; then said coolly, 'You'd better come in.' She showed us into the parlour.

While we looked around at the neat furniture, pictures, china and photographs, ten minutes went by. We looked at each other in puzzlement. Finally, in walked a man with a shiny face, wearing a clean shirt and suit and a nervous smile. He and Margaret greeted each other with delight. He had no hair and his teeth were obviously false, but there was no doubting his genuine smile. We sat down and they started to reminisce. His wife stayed in the kitchen.

After half an hour I asked him if he and his wife would accompany us in the van to drive around some of the places my Mother had told us so much about. He asked his wife but she refused to come. During the drive he explained to us that his wife was a little jealous.

We drove to the Killarney lakeside. Bobby and Margaret strolled along the shore while the boys and I waited near the van. It was here that he had proposed to her all those years before. There was an obvious connection and fondness between them. It was very touching. Margaret was 74 and Bobby a couple of years older. She was still a good looking woman.

We went to visit his sister Shannon, who didn't remember Maggie, or anything else. She was suffering from dementia. She was unrecognizable, an old lady who had once been vivacious. It was sad to see. She died a few months later, we read in a note from Bobby.

Back at the house his wife gave us tea and biscuits. She was still unsmiling, but she shared with us tartly that she'd been hearing all her life about the wonderful Maggie Higgins, and it was interesting to meet her at last. We said goodbye and thank you, and drove away. Margaret was enchanted by this meeting. I'm glad I took her once more to Ireland; she'd talked about it throughout her life. Her mother, Helen Tobin Higgins, was as fiercely Irish as any patriot, considered herself 100% Irish, but had never visited her ancestral country. Her parents left Bandon in the south during the troubles, and settled in Essex. Nana named her youngest son Cornelius De Valera Higgins, and talked about 'the dirty Orangemen'.

From Killarney we drove down to the south western tip of Ireland, and pitched the tent in a campsite on a cliff with magnificent views of the sea. But that night it rained relentlessly, and flooded the tent. The boys came in to sleep the rest of the night on the floor of the van. Next morning we packed our belongings. It is not easy to fold and store a wet tent. We decided to head home because the forecast promised further heavy rain. We drove to a guest house, enjoying a full Irish breakfast before starting the journey across the south of Ireland to the ferry port in the east, hurrying through Waterford in driving rain, where I'd have liked to visit the glass factory, arriving at the port to find one ship waiting.

'Sorry,' said the attendant, 'there's only one space left in the hold, and you'll never get that big van into the small space.' 'Let me try, please,' I said. I didn't want to wait till the next day with the wet contents of the van, and no money to stay in a hotel. He was dubious to put it politely, but he let me try. In those days there was an advertisement on television for the British School of Motoring, with a pupil named Reginald Molehusband who did an exemplary reverse parking move, to onlookers' applause. 'Do a Reginald Molehusband, Mum!' said the boys. And first time, with only a couple of inches to spare, I backed the van neatly into the space, while the attendant expressed surprise and the boys cheered. It was one of life's small triumphs.

We were tired and the ferry was full. The lounge was packed and noisy. The boys slept on the floor under the tables. The voyage took several hours. When we landed we drove on to Aberystwyth for the comforts of home. John Paul and I spelled each other all the way with the driving. We kept talking to stop the driver falling asleep. We got home at 3 in the morning. It was one of those shared experiences that pulled us even closer as a family.

John Paul was now an experienced, competent driver in the space of a few weeks.

[Bobby Eager died a couple of years after that meeting, and so did Ann. She died suddenly of liver cancer, in her forties, leaving four small children under ten for her husband to bring up alone.]

35 WE MOVE TO CAMBRIDGE

A couple of weeks after I graduated Richard announced that the Ministry was moving him to Cambridge. He had been promoted to Grade 1 as head of their Pesticide Residues department. This was a choice promotion and posting.

The house had been up for sale for the previous two years. The price was set high and Richard refused to reduce it, so the sale stalled. We had been anticipating separation all this time. Richard did not want to separate and made an effort to stop barking at us, which meant he would start, then shut his mouth and look apoplectic instead. That still left tension in the air and I was weary of it. We both saw marriage guidance counsellors (I saw three) and the one he met was helpful to both of us. She said she had equally divided sympathies and she hoped we could reconcile our differences.

Now that I'd graduated I had two choices: look for a job in Aberystwyth, which would pay very little, or move to Cambridge with Richard and try there. We discussed it at length and agreed that we'd give our marriage one last chance, and if it didn't work, we would sell our house and divide the proceeds so that we would both have a home.

Two days after we reduced the price, we had two offers on the house. The one we accepted was from the Dean at my college. I had enjoyed his lectures, and his wife taught at the primary school, so they knew the family. I was more than pleased to pass the house on to them.

Richard and I went to Cambridge to look for our next house, while my Mother looked after the children. She was then 75, yet again stepping into the breach. While Richard was in his new office, I went to several estate agents and the first house I looked at was our choice: an Edwardian semi-detached grey stone house on three floors with five bedrooms, Dutch arched roofline and leaded windows, in Tenison Avenue. It had a small, pretty garden and was within walking distance of Richard's office. There was a living room, small kitchen and study on the ground floor, with cellar below. Its main drawback was the small kitchen, which made it difficult for the boys to cook with me. But the study was just right for Richard.

The people who owned the house didn't want to move for a couple of months. The family buying ours was ready to move within two weeks, so we stored the furniture for six weeks and rented near Cambridge during the summer holidays. We rented a caravan for three weeks in the country, and then an apartment in town. We bought bicycles for the three boys.

On the journey to Cambridge by car Julian (13) announced that he was tired of his name and wanted to change it. He chose to be called by his second name, Mark. The twins obliged immediately, but it took me nearly a year to stop saying J-Mark. I love the name Julian and was sorry he changed it. He was reluctant to move because he'd made friends at school, and Aberystwyth felt like home. It's difficult to move schools at that age. The twins didn't mind so much. Peter had no intention of leaving Aberystwyth. He was already independent. John Paul, who had just left high school, would join us later.

While we were staying in the apartment I got the local paper and went to a couple of interviews. I wanted to work for a charity, because I knew I'd get tired working full time, and wanted to feel that my energies were put to good use. I applied for a job as secretary to the CEO of SOS Children's Villages. Even though I'd done a degree to elevate my prospects above secretarial, I knew it was my best way into an organization. The office manager who interviewed me had herself done a degree as a mature student, and being my age we empathized. I got the job.

Hamish, the CEO, was a nice Australian guy with a background in journalism. He was pleasant to work for, apart from his chain smoking. He wrote the charity magazine, the quarterly SOS Messenger, and this interested me. His health was poor, and soon he had to retire although he was under fifty. They asked me, If you are not Hamish's secretary, what role do you see for yourself in the charity? Immediately I answered, I'd like to develop the sponsorship department and write the magazine. They gave me the roles I asked for.

Within a year I had doubled the number of sponsors of children and SOS Villages. The charity sent me to do a one day course on producing a magazine at *Cosmopolitan* magazine in London. It cost 250 pounds, and was money well spent. It was phenomenally helpful and interesting. While I had relied on text, with a few old photographs thrown in, they taught me that people mostly read the captions, so pictures were more important than the text. I asked our head office in Vienna to send us fresh pictures, and wrote stories around them.

(Incidentally, I subsequently wrote and sold an article to *Cosmopolitan* for 75 pounds. It was about how women over fifty are invisible.)

The charity also sent me to visit a Direct Mail company, where I learned how the literature is targeted, prepared, packaged, and posted to a mailing list. They said that a positive response of 2% is normal. They sold us a thousand names to add to our mailing list. I also learned that including a self-addressed envelope increases the response rate.

At that stage our mailing list held 8,000 names. I bought 8,000 small manila envelopes. Over an entire weekend, Andre and Patrick hand stamped them with the charity's address. One was included in each SOS Messenger. At one stroke, the donations doubled. One reader even sent 1000 pounds donation, and others were encouraged to mention the charity in their Wills.

It was not all triumph. Having read that another charity had spent one million pounds to increase its sponsorship support by 6 million, we spent a thousand pounds of the Charity's money on one advert in a national newspaper. It showed a picture of a tearful child sitting alone in a playpen. The caption was: "Your indifference could be the last straw". The response was so small, it was embarrassing. I learned another lesson: Be positive.

After that disappointment, we had to make our own publicity without a budget.

I learned many aspects of marketing, in the process of fundraising. Two students from Cambridge decided to spend a gap year flying to Calcutta with their bicycles, cycling back 6,000 miles to Cambridge. They raised sponsorship for the Charity by the mile. During the journey I put a couple of bulletins in the Messenger. On their return to Cambridge I arranged a street reception outside our office by Magdalen Bridge, with TV and newspaper coverage. The boys cycled down the road (they had actually come home the night before, unannounced) and arrived at noon to be greeted by balloons, banners, a table and umbrella with a magnum of champagne donated by the nearby off-license. A policeman controlled the traffic. Tim Phillips and his Jumping Jazzmen (with whom my boys were friendly) played rollicking jazz in the street. 'Oh when the saints come marching home' was on television news that night, and next day it was in the local paper.

When we had a heavy snowfall, John Paul made an igloo in our back garden and slept in there all night. I called the local paper and they sent a photographer to capture him getting out of his igloo in the morning to receive a donation for SOS Children's Villages addressed to 'The Igloo, 12 Tenison Avenue'.

I wrote articles about the charity for the local paper, and one in *Woman* magazine. If you can't afford an advert, you can usually place an article about your product in an appropriate magazine. They don't pay you, but you don't pay them either.

I answered all the letters that came to the Charity, no chore for me. I totally supported the aims of the charity. SOS provides homes, mothers, schools and clinics to abandoned children in over a hundred countries. The children are educated to the extent of their abilities and feel part of those families for life. I wish this system could be provided for all needy children.

We launched special appeals in famines and natural disasters. The television journalist Michael Buerk phoned me one day for information, after seeing the work our villages were doing to support the local population in Ethiopia. He showed SOS on the national evening news, dispensing food to famine victims.

The SOS office in Salzburg phoned me to ask if I could get Bonnie Tyler to sing at a concert in Austria to raise funds for SOS. I made contact by a series of phone calls and arranged this. At the time her big hit was 'I'm holding out for a hero'. Her agent said, 'See you at the concert, Eileen,' but unfortunately I was not invited.

Father Jim Dodge who lived near Salzburg had worked for years for the charity. He was then in his seventies, still fit, skiing, sailing and swimming. He was an American, who in his youth had been chaplain to the Von Trapp family of Sound of Music fame. He took Tina (the Charity's fundraiser) and me in his camping van on a tour of eight of the nine SOS Villages in Austria in 1985. The charity had been started by a young doctor, Hermann Gmeiner, when he found children living unprotected in the ruins of bombed buildings in Vienna after the war. He took them to a woman and promised to find money for her to house and feed them. He then asked all his friends to pay a shilling a week towards the keep of the children. Soon there were enough children and supporters to form a small community, and the Villages developed from there. His own mother had died when he was small, but a good stepmother had raised him. From this he concluded that a woman dedicated to a small family will love them like a mother. The Villages typically had ten houses with up to ten children in each family. The men who worked as teachers, janitors, gardeners etc. were trained to be fatherly towards the children.

Seeing the SOS villages functioning in many locations helped us in our fundraising work. As a result of our tour, Tina spoke and I wrote with more conviction. In Vienna I went to the sponsorship office to choose a child to sponsor. I wanted a girl because I lacked a daughter, about four years old so that I could relate to her immediately. I chose one who lived in Chile because I could speak Spanish, and because my Spanish tutor at college had come from Chile, exiled after the coup which killed President Allende. I had no clue then that one day I would meet Jacqueline Suarez in Chile and that she would visit me in England. I sponsored her for twenty years until she was working and independent of the Village at Concepcion where she grew up. We are still in touch on Facebook since she found me there. She has two small boys. After the earthquake with its epicentre near Concepcion devastated the country in 2009, I was able to check on Facebook that Jacqueline and her family were safe.

Lady Mountbatten was patron of SOS Children's Villages UK. I met her at Trustee meetings and once wrote a speech for her. She delivered it verbatim from my notes, with hesitations and emphasis as if she were making it up as she went along. I admired her professionalism.

I also met Lady Khama, first lady of Uganda, when she came to a meeting in London. I was designated to spend the day with her, shopping and having lunch. I remembered her marrying Seretse Khama when we were both young. She had been to school in Eltham, near my birthplace Mottingham. When I met her, her four children were grown up, her husband was dead and her son was chief of the country. After shopping all afternoon we failed to find a hairdresser to have our hair done for the evening meeting, so we washed our hair in her suite in the Strand Palace Hotel. She was pleasant and friendly. She told me she had a stack of her late husband's papers and didn't know what to do with them. I suggested she contact a university which would be glad to archive them.

A new member of staff came to work in the Cambridge office, to keep the accounts. He was a young man in his early twenties, ambitious and charming. To begin with we were four employees on an equal basis. Tina was the chief fundraiser, visiting schools and speaking to groups. Barbara ran the two craft shops by which we raised money, and I did all the correspondence and publicity. We each filled our roles competently. Stewart was an accountant by training. Gradually he took on more initiative and thrust his way into becoming the office manager. He smiled as he described himself as 'the first among equals'. After several months he suddenly sacked me one day, without notice. He said we could use the Austrian Messenger; that my roles could be shared among the others and I was redundant. The Charity gave me a month's salary in lieu of notice and one thousand pounds in compensation. I was devastated. I loved this job. I was committed to the Charity and didn't want to leave. I'd worked there four years and thought it the best job ever. But the trustees were in

London and only peripheral, attending occasional meetings. Stewart had seized control on his own initiative. It was the Friday before I was going on holiday with Carl. I was shattered.

I think Stewart got rid of me because I had contacts with the SOS office in Salzburg. He wanted a free hand to pursue his own interests. I telephoned Dr H in Salzburg to protest about my dismissal, who said he would come to Cambridge to sort it out. But a month later Dr H died suddenly of liver cancer.

A year later, Stewart lost his job for dubious dealings in the charity.

During the week while Carl and I were in the Cotswolds, I telephoned a Cambridge employment agency and started work immediately on my return as a temporary worker while I looked for another job. I found one immediately as marketing officer in a language school, at 20% higher salary. I could still pay the mortgage and the redundancy money paid for the replacement of our cracked front window in the house in Girton. But I would rather have stayed with the charity.

36 THE BITTER END

When we moved to Cambridge it was on the understanding that if our marriage didn't improve, we would split up and buy two houses. After a few months it was clear that it was not going to improve.

However, John Paul decided to spend an extra year in school to improve his 'A' levels, so I waited out that year. I felt I could support three in school by myself, but not more. During that year Richard started feeling odd symptoms and consulted the doctor. He had lost his ability to walk ten miles as he'd routinely done in the past. He got tired quickly and had pins and needles in his legs.

In 1984 I went with him to the hospital to see a specialist. To our dismay he told us that he thought Richard had Multiple Sclerosis. He said there was no way of being certain of this until an autopsy on the brain after death, but his opinion was that MS was likely.

We were devastated. Immediately we began to worry about imminent paralysis, wheelchairs, ramps and incapacity. We wondered if this might happen in six months or longer. Richard insisted that we keep this secret to ourselves. He did not even tell his parents. I would have been grateful for some moral support but we didn't tell a soul.

Richard's first response to me was, 'I want to go out and have as many affairs as possible before it's too late.' I had long since stopped feeling jealous about his affairs. He didn't make a secret of them. I had told him 'If we get divorced, I won't accuse you of adultery.' I wanted to make it easy for him to leave.

He began to improve the garden with a pergola, a pond and new plantings. He talked about putting in ramps for a wheelchair.

Now he was sick it seemed to me I could never leave him. I felt trapped. In an effort to lighten our sorrows I bought air tickets to Greece for Richard's fiftieth birthday so he and I could visit our friend who was a teacher in Athens. We left the boys in my Mother's charge for a week.

On that holiday Richard's spirits lifted. He admired Greece and the lifestyle our friend enjoyed. The climate was warm, the sky blue and the food excellent. The cost of living was low. We spent a day touring three Greek islands in a tourist boat. I had a brainwave. I said 'Richard, if you retire early and come to live in Greece on your pension, and leave me in the house so I can take in lodgers' (we had five bedrooms) 'I think I could manage to look after the family by myself. You could paint here in Greece' (he liked oil painting),' fish, relax and enjoy the warmth. If you want to come home we'll still have the house and if you need looking after, you can always come back to me.' At first he considered this idea favourably, and my spirits soared, thinking that at last we had a solution.

But hours later he switched his decision and became reproachful and angry, saying why should I leave you the house? Why should you get all the assets? I said there need be no division of our property, it would still be jointly owned. He could always count on me to look after him if he became sicker and meanwhile we would both be happier. But he was still upset.

We limped on in this fashion for months. I went to the doctor one day with depression and he asked me, 'What do you do for light relief?' I said 'there isn't any light relief in my life. I work full time, I go home and run the house, and meanwhile my husband is sick and we don't get on.'

John Paul one day was standing beside me on the front doorstep when he said 'Why don't you just leave him?' I said 'John Paul, I can't leave him, he is sick,' and he said, 'Yes, you can.' That evening he got Richard and me together in Richard's study, sat us down and said that we must talk. He told Richard, you are not getting on well together. Neither of you is happy. Why don't you agree to split up and lead the lives you both want to? I don't remember the conversation in detail but I recall being glad that John Paul had taken this initiative in a manner that was friendly to us both.

In bed soon after at 2 a.m. Richard told me that as a member of the MS Society he had discovered MS might be catching, in which case I could get it. He knew a man whose wife had caught it from him. Or it might be hereditary, in which case the boys might get it. I said 'Oh Richard, don't tell me that, every time there is something wrong with the boys I will worry that they have MS!' I asked, didn't it worry him too? He replied that he never worried about anything he could not control.

At six o'clock the next morning I went downstairs, not having slept at all, and started cleaning to keep myself busy. I was quietly weeping as I wielded the vacuum cleaner… anxious for the boys and outraged that he could burden me with this worry. Suddenly I thought I hope I don't have another breakdown. I realized that Richard was pressing my buttons, and

I was reacting as always to the pressure. I stopped in my tracks and thought 'no, I am not going to do this again.'

That evening I went to see the GP on my way home from work. I asked him, 'Is it true that MS can be contagious?' He said not at all, and I asked 'Can it be hereditary?' 'Oh goodness no,' he said, 'who has been telling you this nonsense?' 'My husband.' He said 'Oh dear.' I told the doctor that this was the last straw. Richard had no concern for my state of mind and I was going to leave him.

I asked Andre if I could have his bedroom. He protested, saying he didn't want to share with Patrick, and John Paul said quickly, 'Andre, you can share with me if you like!' Andre was immediately taken with the idea of sharing a room with his older brother. I took over Andre's room that night.

A few days later Richard announced, 'I want a divorce!' I said we didn't need to divorce, just to live separately. He said 'I want a divorce so I can get married again as soon as possible!' I certainly didn't want to get married again. I only saw the next step as peaceful independence. I was worried about how I would cope financially, but I knew that if we didn't have a more peaceful living environment, neither of us would enjoy life.

'If we wait two years we can have a no fault divorce' I suggested. When he said he wouldn't wait two years I said 'OK then, you can divorce me if you like, say the marriage has broken down irrevocably.' I thought this would be less of a strain on him, since he wasn't well, and I was the one that wanted separation most keenly.

But I was dismayed when his solicitor drew up the grounds for divorce. 'She made it clear to the Petitioner that she did not want to remain with the Petitioner and that she wished to dissociate herself from him because of his illness, and did not want to have to look after him or help him....She has given the Petitioner to understand that she feels that his illness is a threat to her future career and life style and the Petitioner finds this hurtful and distressing.' I was so angry, that we had the only full scale row in our lives. I was *not* a woman who refused to look after a sick husband. This had nothing to do with our break-up which had been on the cards for years and was first discussed openly in 1979.

I asked my solicitor what it would cost to fight this interpretation. He told me it would cost at least six thousand pounds. I did not have six thousand pounds, and I dared not spend the money I would get from my share of the house on legal fees. I needed every penny to afford a modest home with a manageable mortgage. I earned one third of Richard's salary.

My solicitor said I would be better off financially swallowing my anger and letting it go. Following my protest the petition was amended somewhat, but if you look in the court records in Cambridge you will find that Richard's solicitor drew a line through the above comments about it not being part of my life style to look after a sick man, but it is still clearly legible.

A year later I was invited to become a magistrate, but declined because I knew that enquiries into my background might expose that shameful accusation.

Richard visited his parents, telling them in one breath, 'I have MS and Eileen is leaving me.' He told me this himself. If he had shared the news of his illness twelve months previously, the connection between the events might have been differently interpreted. Perhaps he held back the news anticipating this convenient excuse. His family understandably judged me for what they saw as betrayal of a sick and innocent man. They knew nothing of what had gone before.

His colleagues and our neighbours also got this impression. He told people that desertion was a common spousal response to MS. I know he could not believe this of me, and I know that he was otherwise an honest man throughout his life. His dumping all the guilt and responsibility on my plate to exonerate himself, still rankles with me 25 years later.

To my relief he never needed a wheelchair. Although the doctor said he didn't need to, he chose to retire at 53. I was glad when he married Carmella. They went to live in Spain in a villa with an acre of garden which he tended assiduously for nearly twenty years. I only wished him happiness. He didn't need ramps, thank goodness. He installed a spiral staircase in their renovated farmhouse. Every Christmas he sent me a card from the Multiple Sclerosis Society, not so much a greeting as a reproach.

With Carmella's participation we kept a good relationship going in the following years for the boys' sake. I included them on the *Dight Times* mailing list and reported their activities too, with pictures of their beautiful garden and any news they sent us, including their holiday snaps and the Christmases they spent with Patrick and family in Ireland, and his sons' final joint visit shortly before he died when they cared for him for a week in Spain and gave Carmella a break.

A few months before he died of cancer in 2008 Richard told Andre that he'd been to see a specialist in Multiple Sclerosis, whose opinion was that Richard's symptoms did not fit the MS profile. It was suspected that

Richard suffered from organophosphate poison, a possibility that had occurred to me, after one of his colleagues suffered ME from sheep dip. He was head of the Ministry's Pesticide Residues department and could have been exposed to these in his work. In any case, I'm glad he opted for early retirement and enjoyed the rest of his life.

With the letters of tribute people sent to Carmella after his death, and photographs contributed by his family, I published a twenty page *Tribute to Richard* which was circulated electronically to all his friends and family. In this way we recorded all the good he had done in his life.

37 WE MOVE TO GIRTON

Once the separation had been agreed upon, it didn't take long to achieve. As agreed years before, we would sell the house so that both of us could afford a home to live in. In the two years since we'd bought it our house had risen in value from 75,000 pounds to 100,000. We put it in an agent's hands.

I found a terrace house near my Mother's that would have been convenient, but before I could secure it someone else put in an offer, and I lost it. There was nothing else affordable within walking distance. Nana was accustomed to walking every day to my house while I was at work, cleaning and generally being helpful. I found a house two miles away, and took her on the bus to visit it so that she could gauge the distance. At the bus stop we waited twenty minutes in a cold wind (it was late autumn); she looked pinched and miserable. I realized this was not a good solution. Cutting off her ability to walk to our house would have drastically diminished her pleasure in life.

So I enquired about a house with a granny annexe, and found one immediately in Girton, half an hour's walk from Cambridge and ten thousand pounds cheaper than houses in town. We put my mother's house on the market too. Together we could afford this larger house at 90,000 pounds with a 6000 pounds mortgage, all I could afford on 8,500 pounds a year salary plus maintenance.

Then Richard decided to buy my Mother's house as it was just right for a single person, having two bedrooms and a tiny back yard, right in the middle of town and within cycling distance of his office. He bought a three wheeler bicycle. He kept the Vauxhall and I kept the Toyota camper.

The day before we moved I made a large beef and vegetable casserole. My Mother said 'What on earth are you doing? All you ever think about is food.' But next day, when the removal men left in the evening, the casserole in its iron pot provided a hearty meal for all of us. It is a cardinal rule for moving, in my book, that the first meal be ready without effort.

The second rule is: make your beds. At some point you are going to collapse exhausted into bed after all that seeking, lifting, sorting and putting away, and a ready bed is vital.

This was the first time we had moved house calmly. There was no tension, no shouting, no orders were given or needed. Each boy was responsible for his own room (the house had six bedrooms) and willingly gave any help requested. We moved on a Friday in December, leaving the whole weekend to sort ourselves out before going back to work and school on Monday. Mark had a school exam on the Friday. He cycled to school from one house, and cycled home to the other. That must have been stressful. The twins had a day off school to help with the move, and John Paul was back from Leicester Poly to lend a hand too. Richard and my Mother had already swapped places weeks before.

On the Saturday, Mark had a burning desire to buy a poster for his bedroom. In previous moves he would have been told to stay around and be helpful, but I recognized his need to organize his own priorities, and I wanted them all to enjoy this transition, so I said 'Go and find one in town, there's a posters place in the shopping precinct' and off he cycled. He came back with Marilyn Monroe.

John Paul and Patrick were busy rewiring broken light flexes. The house was in poor repair. It had previously been owned by an academic and his wife who had neglected it, and before that it was built by a couple who had polio and were both in wheelchairs. There was a derelict therapy pool, 9 metres by 6, in an extension at the back. The lining had long since ripped and disintegrated, and a foot or more of muddy water lay at the bottom. As it had brick walls, large windows and a flat roof, I thought the extension would come in handy for something. There was a sizeable garden and we had an ancient petrol mower with which they took turns to mow the lawn. Peter helped me dig a vegetable patch alongside the extension and planted everlasting spinach. I planted lettuces and radishes, and watered the bed each evening with a watering can. It felt good to gather salad and tend my own garden.

Nana had two small bedrooms, a sitting room and a shower room on the ground floor annexe between house and pool, and shared my kitchen. In 1985 she was 77. Although she was still good at walking, she had long lost interest in cooking, and was glad to share the meals I cooked for the family, which I took her on a tray. She liked to watch television while she ate. I bought her an electric 'log effect' fire which gave a comforting glow and kept her warm in addition to the warm air central heating. Her sitting room was the first room I painted. About 100 yards away there was a newspaper shop where she could buy her cigarettes and sweets.

About a week after we moved in I woke up at two in the morning and suddenly sat bolt upright thinking, 'How am I ever going to cope by myself?' My stomach was in knots. I was deeply uneasy and nervous despite the fact that I felt relief every time I turned the key in the front door coming home from work, knowing that the house was peaceful inside. Every person living there was pulling in the same direction. Whatever cooperation I sought from the boys was willingly forthcoming. My Mother of course had always supported us in every way she could. But as number one in the family for the first time, I felt responsible. My income had drastically diminished. I had always done most of the paperwork, even without a joint account. Richard signed the cheques. He had controlled all the budgeting. Under the divorce settlement I got half the joint money and all the children. The judge said to Richard 'It's most unusual in a family with five children that they should all live with one parent. Don't you want any of them to live with you?' We had agreed on joint custody. He started to speak, then he clammed up. I could see his problem. I answered for him, 'He is willing to maintain them but he doesn't want to live with them.' He remained silent. The judge shook his head and then signed the papers. In lieu of a pension in future I was awarded 10,000 pounds more of our joint assets which I put towards the house.

The day after we moved in, the boiler broke down. It was December and freezing cold. I had to pay for a new boiler, which cost one thousand pounds. That was the margin I had held back from the house purchase for emergencies, and it went in one expense, the first week.

John Paul was in his first term at Leicester Polytechnic and for the first six weekends came home to work in the house. It was February when I walked out with him to see him off (hitchhiking) at six in the morning; I left the front door open, joking that it was warmer out than in. As we stood shivering but smiling, I said 'John Paul, don't come home next weekend. Stay with your friends in college and have some fun.' His answer I have never forgotten: 'Mum, I love coming home, the atmosphere is so wonderful.'

That was why I had gone through divorce. I wanted them to experience living in a relaxed, happy home, before they grew up. John Paul was already twenty, but it was not too late. The others had a few more years to learn how it feels to live in a house where you are not disapproved of daily; where any problems or shortfalls are openly discussed and resolved as reasonably as possible, and where your personality is allowed to blossom.

I was still anxious; I walked along Cambridge streets looking at people, wondering if they felt as worried as I did. Probably all of them did at some point in their lives, but I had felt like that for years.

For several months after we moved to Girton, Richard would appear on Sundays in time for lunch, bringing his washing. He sat down to eat with us when we had friends there for lunch too. Eventually I suggested to Richard that the launderette around the corner from him would be more convenient. He didn't bring his washing again.

Richard sold the Vauxhall and bought himself a used Volvo. After a bit I sold the Toyota Hiace. We had bought it nearly new and kept it seven years. By then John Paul had repainted it with a paintbrush as it was rusting. It still started first time, but it was heavy on petrol and I didn't envisage taking anyone abroad in future by myself. I sold it for 850 pounds and used that for the down payment on a second hand Volvo.

On the twins' fifteenth birthday they held a party in the sitting room. Their friends from school came, they played music on the record player and they were dancing. I went to check on my Mother as I always did in the evenings. She would fall asleep watching TV and I would turn off the set and gently remove her glasses. I found her looking uncomfortable and anxious, saying she had a pain in her chest and arm. Immediately I called a medical team, who took a cardiogram and said she had had a mild heart attack, and that it was safer to leave her at home where she was comfortable, than to remove her to hospital. They gave me instructions on caring for her, and left.

I stayed at home for the next week, caring for her. She stayed in bed, watching TV, and was comfortable. After a week I went back to work and returned each lunch time to give her food and check that she was OK. I was distressed when the doctor told me 'She is old and weak, and could go at any time.' Just when we had her comfortably established living with us, I didn't want to let her go! She was so vital to our family and so much loved. I gave her a fat free diet and she lost a little excess weight. Gradually she recovered, but lost confidence and didn't want to venture out alone after that, beyond walking to the newsagent. Although she was forbidden by the doctor to smoke, occasionally I would find a half smoked cigarette in her room and turned a blind eye to avoid distressing her. She would go into the garage to smoke and we pretended not to notice. In this way she cut her cigarette consumption to a minimum. I expressed concern to the doctor that now she stayed in bed all day, or at most sat in her armchair by the bed since we had moved the TV into her bedroom. He said 'She is comfortable; let her do as she pleases.' She began to show loss of short term memory, and this was another worry.

The following year I asked a neighbour for advice about the swimming pool. He told me to hire a pump to empty out the dirty water, so John Paul took care of that. The next day the water was back again. 'That must be the natural water table,' said the neighbour. 'You need to consult a structural engineer.' I wanted to get rid of the murky water and use the extension, perhaps as a billiard room. The engineer came and advised me to fill the hole with six tons of gravel, then put a layer of ready mixed concrete on top. Then I had the bright idea of making a letting unit, so we could increase our income. Before we could do this, we needed to calculate the costs and increase the mortgage to fund it.

John Paul by then had dropped out of his business course and was back in Cambridge, living with us. Together we priced gravel, two lorry loads of ready mixed concrete, wood floor on top of that, roof repair (it leaked in rain), radiators and rewiring. It came to 6,000 pounds. I asked the Halifax to increase my mortgage (in fact, double the one I had) and they said they would do so, after the work was done. I said 'I can't get the work done without the money,' and they shrugged.

I went to see Barclays Bank manager. I'd had a bank account since I was seven years old, when my Father opened a savings account in my name with Martins Bank, later taken over by Barclays. 'Certainly, Mrs Dight' said the manager, 'Would you like us to take over the mortgage entirely?' Richard and I had had mortgages with the Halifax since 1965, so we had over twenty years of good record. I went back to the Halifax who capitulated when I said that Barclays would handle it. We went ahead – spent 2,000 pounds on the roof repair, bought all the other materials including second hand radiators, and between them the boys equipped the extension to make a flat. Peter came to plumb in the radiators. John Paul did the wiring. A circuit breaker was professionally installed because JP had a history of trial and error which sometimes gave him electric shocks. All the boys wheeled liquid cement in wheelbarrows from front to back through the garage and my Mother's apartment. John Paul installed a shower and Patrick (15) installed the kitchen units (taken out of a previous house and stored in the garage for a rainy day).

I called a plumber to come and start up the heating system, extended from our boiler, in case there were any leaks from Peter's plumbing. Not one drop fell.

All the boys worked without payment, and I rewarded John Paul for his project management and three months hard work by buying him his first car, a very old Renault, for 350 pounds. The work was accomplished exactly on budget.

In the main house the boys eventually took out the shabby, ugly kitchen units and replaced them with handsome new wooden ones. Peter re-grouted the bathroom tiles and installed a shower over the bath.

Now I approached the Visiting Scholars accommodation department at the University and Professor Matti Vikkori from Finland became our first tenant.

Matti taught us all to dance to the music of Beethoven.

38 PHOTO ALBUM

'Grandma Naylor', Fred's Mother, in 1928, aged 61.

Fred in September 1915, in Royal Flying Corp, aged 17.

'Nana Helen Higgins' aged about 70

Fred and Margaret on their honeymoon at Southsea in 1930.

Margaret, John, Mother's sister Kit and Nana Helen Higgins.

Eileen aged 5

Eileen with brother John

John, Eileen, Margaret and Fred in 1946

Eileen aged 17, 20, 50 and 73

20 Mottingham Gardens, London SE9

Eileen was born in the bay window bedroom 1937

5 Bryn Castell, Radyr, Cardiff, South Wales.

Bought 1970 (new) Sold 1976

Glen Rosa, Brynymor Road, Aberystwyth, west Wales

Bought 1976 Sold 1983

12 Tenison Avenue, Cambridge.

Edwardian house originally owned by the College.

Bought 1983 Sold 1985

119 Thornton Road, Girton, Cambridge

Bought 1985 sold 1991

16 Queen Annes Gardens, Ealing

Bought 1991 sold 2003

Beausejour, our cottage in France.
Bought 1997 Sold 2003

The boys and Eileen,

Radyr 1971

'All my own work!'

The boys and Eileen in 1973

Patrick, Mark and Andre in 1974

Andre, John Paul, Patrick and Mark 1976

39 ON HOLIDAY WITH THE TWINS

In 1986 after we got divorced, Richard took the youngest boys on holiday to the Norfolk Broads in a sailing boat. John Paul and Mark were chauffeur punters on the Cam, saving for a trip to Italy. Peter was married and living in Taunton. Late in the summer I decided to take Patrick and Andre away for a few days because I needed a holiday too.

In the *Sunday Times* I saw an advert for three nights B&B plus evening meal in a farmhouse in Cornwall. I think the charge was 12 pounds per person per night. That and the petrol to get us there was all I could afford that summer. I wanted to show the boys the West Country and I hadn't been to Cornwall since I was their age. We set off in the Volvo in good spirits.

On the way we saw signs to a 'Rare Breeds Farm' and of course, with Andre we had to explore it. He was so knowledgeable about animals even at that stage. He was excited. He spotted and named a rare pig that I had never heard of, from fifty yards away. He could name every animal in the collection. All those years he had spent pouring over animal books before he went to sleep were paying off. I was impressed.

When we arrived at the farmhouse we were pleasantly surprised to find it smartly furnished with antiques and presided over by the attractive middle aged farmer's wife. There was a pretty dining room with flowers on each table and velvet furnishings. In English farmhouses one often finds antiques that were new when the family bought them. Alan Clark, a notorious high born snob, once described someone disparagingly as 'The sort of person who bought his own furniture'.

I wondered what sort of meals we would be served, keeping in mind the low price despite the comfort and elegance of the house. The answer was low cost ingredients, but expertly cooked with fresh vegetables, and attractively presented. I admired her style.

In a sitting room where tall windows let in the lovely evening light, half a dozen guests sat relaxing in the evening before dinner, and we joined them. A man with military bearing was there with his daughter, about the same age as the twins (15). He spoke haughtily and with authority, obviously public school educated and probably had a swanky title like 'Squadron Leader'. In case anyone might misjudge him as anything but top drawer, he looked down his nose at the rest of us, with a stern face.

He and his daughter were playing a game of chess; naturally Patrick wandered over, sitting quietly to watch the game. Meanwhile there was a very old dog of great dignity belonging to the farmhouse, a golden retriever who sat languidly or wandered around the room looking at people without bothering anybody. As he stood watching the small group around the chess board the man said to the dog, 'Sit,' in staccato tone. The dog ignored him. 'Sit!' he said with more emphasis. The dog almost yawned. 'Sit!' said the man, his voice rising at the prospect of insubordination. The dog turned away and ambled off to watch another guest.

After the man had defeated his daughter at chess he turned to Patrick. 'Would you like a game?' he said imperiously. 'Oh, yes please,' said Patrick politely, and took the stool the girl had vacated, opposite her father in his armchair. They played quietly, without conversation. I sat half reading a newspaper and half taking in the scene from the other side of the room. At the end of the game Patrick said, 'Thank you very much,' and the man nodded, not offering him another game, and turned back to his daughter. Patrick came and sat next to me on the other side of the lounge.

'Did you enjoy that?' I asked Patrick. He nodded. I said, quietly, 'Who won?' 'I did,' said Patrick. I smiled at him. I said 'He has a natural air of authority, hasn't he?' and Patrick said dryly, 'The dog didn't think so.'

40 CARL KILLINGLEY

I met Carl late in 1986. In those days we weren't on line to look for new friends. 'Singles' magazine was delivered by post to my house every month in a plain wrapper. We were more furtive about looking for a new partner than people would believe today, when one in five couples meet through the internet.

I was 48 when I got divorced. I thought 'What if I never kiss anyone else as long as I live?' I feared that my emotional life as a woman was over. I need not have worried. I soon found that a lot of lonely people in middle age were looking to reconnect. Divorce was increasingly common.

I was 49 when I noticed Carl's advertisement headed "Don't Rush to Judgment". He was 68 and recently widowed. I thought the age difference too great to be of interest, but his description intrigued me. He was a writer and naturalist and had attractive qualities. I wrote to him that I was not interested to meet, but had to say how much I liked his profile.

We corresponded by post. He lived in the Chilterns, an hour's drive from Cambridge. He was looking for a house to downsize and raise some cash. He had the whole of the UK to choose from. When he wrote one day that he had had an offer accepted on a house in mid Wales, I hastened to caution him. 'You will not find a soul mate there. Mid Wales is full of women who wear hats, attend chapel on Sunday, and have narrow minds. The pubs are all closed on Sundays. Try somewhere else.'

He wrote that he'd had a mild heart attack while house hunting. He thought it was indigestion at first. I counselled him to choose a house that was not on a hill, as walking his dog up or down could be difficult. He had a Keeshond of which he was extremely fond. It had won best of breed at Cruft's Dog Show. I added, 'You need to be in a small town, where you have easy access to a doctor, library, post office and supermarket. And if possible, buy a house without stairs.'

This correspondence developed friendship between us long before we met. Eventually we met somewhere half way between our homes, in a car park. His first words on seeing me were, 'You are not an old bag at all!' I had described myself thus, so he would not be disappointed. I was wearing a turquoise suit with cream blouse and red high heels.

Eventually I agreed to visit him at his home and stay the night in his guest room. I found he had a cottage house in fine gardens adjacent to his son's property. His son and daughter in law wanted to move and Carl had decided to be more independent.

Immediately we felt a mutual attraction. He was warm, kind, gentle, considerate, romantic and confident, an appealing combination. Soon we were writing increasingly affectionate letters. For years I'd heard love songs on the radio that went over my head, but suddenly I heard loving music everywhere that made sense. Falling in love when you are 49 is a wonderful experience. It must also be at 68. Suddenly the age difference was less important, although the difference in our physical capacities was marked. When I was with him, I slowed to his pace. When I drove away after a weekend, I felt the surge of youth and energy that I had suppressed during the weekend.

He wrote daily. 'Darling, this is madness. You have just driven away and already I am moved to write to you....' We filled important gaps in each other's lives. He even wrote me poems.

Carl told me we would have such happy times together. We'll have a great summer, he wrote. I couldn't imagine that. I had lived so many years with a heavy heart, I couldn't envisage what he had in mind. We spent happy evenings cooking and listening to music, visited craft fairs in the Chilterns, took picnics into the country, walked the dog in the neighbourhood (it was a revelation to me, how dogs are a common interest between strangers). We waltzed in the kitchen; sat on the sofa listening to his records. He played Carmina Burana, opera and classical songs, making tapes for me to play at home. He sang 'You are my heart's delight'. We shared jokes, told each other anecdotes about our lives and our children. It was a very happy time.

His primary identity was as a naturalist. Going for a walk in the country with Carl was an education. Walking along a country lane, up the side of a field, through a wood, he showed me badger droppings, evidence of animals feeding, making their homes, nesting. I remarked on a noisy bird and he said 'That's an alarm call to warn other birds of a threat.' He had co-written *The Badgers of the World* with Charles Long, published in Springfield, Illinois. He'd walked to a badger set in a wood near his home, in every kind of weather in the dark of every night for a year, to make observations and record data. He was a member of a society supporting badgers in the UK, defending badgers against the charge of transmitting tuberculosis to cattle. He showed me how to spot badger activity from a distance, where chalk was disturbed by their digging.

We would stay some weekends at my house, some at his. The boys accepted our relationship and genuinely liked Carl. He related well to them, having been used to young recruits in the Air Force, where he'd spent most of his career. He disapproved of the fact that in the morning, 'strange young men' were sometimes sleeping on the couch in my living room. These were the boys' friends, who stayed the night after a sociable evening. One of them was a boy who had grown up in an orphanage and now was obliged at 18 to be independent. At times he had been sleeping in a telephone box, and Mark often invited him to sleep over. Another was Syd, John Paul's friend, whose father was a builder who owned race horses and lived in a millionaire's mansion a short drive away. Syd just liked staying with us. Rupert, the twins' closest friend and honorary Dight, would also greet me with a morning smile. They were no trouble. The boys cooked them breakfast. I was happy for them to invite their friends into our home. These tensions were the reason I declined to marry Carl right away, insisting we kept our separate homes. I said I'd marry him when the boys had left home.

Carl decided to buy a house near me. We went house-hunting, finding an ideal house near Stamford in Lincolnshire. Cambridge was too expensive. It was big enough to house me and my Mother when the boys had left home, and had a beautiful garden. His offer was accepted. He sold his house. The week before he was due to move he was in hospital, so I went to pin notes on his furniture for the removal men, telling them where to place each piece in the new house.

Carl had health issues. I noticed one day that he coughed blood into his handkerchief, and insisted he see my GP, who sent him to Papworth hospital for a check-up. They took him in to investigate his lungs, putting a tube down his throat. It was not TB but he had an enlarged lung. I had been encouraging him to give up smoking cheroots.

When I arrived at the hospital to pick him up, some doctors and nurses were assembled in Carl's room. He had suffered a cardiac arrest. He was revived, admitted as an inpatient, and for two weeks I visited him daily. I was with him when he had another heart attack. I called the nurse. I had just told him that seeing shepherd's purse growing in the hedgerows would remind me of him forever.

They came to tell me in the waiting room that Carl had died. About twenty minutes later they took me to see him. He lay there, still and empty. His body was a shell; it no longer contained the man I loved. I sat with him for a minute, then I said Goodbye. The nurse was surprised. I said 'He has gone. He isn't here.' I called John Paul. I didn't feel fit to drive. JP and his friend Tom Hartley arrived to collect me. One drove me home, the other drove my car. I don't remember the journey. This was the first (and only) time I have seen a dead person. At the funeral it was a relief to me when I saw his coffin, to know that he personally was not there. All my boys came to the funeral. I would sense his presence all around me for weeks afterwards.

Carl's demise left a sad hole in my life. But he also left a huge legacy. In ten short months together he restored my self-esteem. He transformed my world from anxiousness into awareness of its beauty. He made me feel so loved, so valued, I knew that if no one else ever loved me again in future, I could live on the sense of self-worth and confidence that he'd given me. What a blessing.

Whenever I think of Carl, and it is often, I say aloud 'Oh Carl, you were lovely.' If he could hear me, I'd be happy. I'll never forget him. I would love him to know how much I value what he did for me in 1987. In my kitchen today in Virginia there is a small vase with shepherd's purse.

A brief account of Carl's wartime experience:

Carl was at an airbase in East Anglia during the war, having joined the RAF in 1936. He flew 62 missions over Germany. The normal number was 30 (if you survived that long). He volunteered for a second term. Originally he was a rear gunner on bombers then he switched to fighters. He said he was tired of being shot at; he wanted to become the hunter.

He described the evening before his first mission over Germany in 1939. The plane was parked at the edge of an airfield. He was sitting in the plane, waiting to take off. He heard young tennis players walking home on the other side of the hedge. On the plane radio he heard the strains of Schiller's Ode to Joy (based on a Beethoven theme). He thought, I am enjoying music by a German composer and I'm about to go and bomb Germany. He wondered if he would return. He was fearful but brave.

When he first entered the house where he was billeted he had the smallest room. Eventually he had the best, as all the others died. Crew members touched him surreptitiously for luck, before a mission. He crashed three times. After the war he would never fly again. He thought he had used up all his luck in the air.

Returning from a bombing raid in Norway, his plane was hit. The pilot told them to bail out. Carl thought 'I can't swim. If I fall in the North Sea

I'm dead anyway,' so he stayed with the plane. He saw something fly past the window and assumed it was the pilot. The plane was in a nosedive. He blacked out. When he came to he was soaring skywards in complete silence. He thought he must be dead, en route to heaven. His hearing had been blocked by the sudden change in altitude during the dive. What he had seen was the canopy fly off when the pilot pushed the 'eject' button. It failed to eject the pilot, who then managed to pull the plane out of its dive and fly back to base, where they crash landed without injury. Carl owed his life to the failure of the eject system.

Another time he was at the gunner's position in the tail; seeing a cable near the floor he stood on it to get a better look at the enemy. (He was not tall.) The plane went lower and lower and landed on a French beach. He couldn't understand why, until the pilot came back (there was no intercom between pilot and rear gunner) and shouted at him, 'You bloody fool, you've been standing on the rudder cable and I lost height, had to land!' Another time they were flying over a German airfield in daylight, being shot at, and Carl saw a man on the ground and shot him with the plane's tracer gun. I asked if it upset him to kill a man personally and he said evasively, 'It was war time.'

Carl joined the Air Force when he was 18 (born 1918), in 1936. His Mother had killed herself when he was 15. He found her with her head in the gas oven. He and his father never spoke about the reason, but he blamed his father, and left home as soon as he could. During the war all the other men had letters from home, but Carl never did. I imagine his youthful isolation. He never returned to see his father. He never told his sons that his mother had killed herself. They learned that from me after he died. And I had guessed it.

Carl was always well dressed, smart and composed. He wore Quorum aftershave. He had strong warm hands. He felt and smelled wonderful.

Post script:

Some of the life changes that can trigger depression when there are two or more at once, include: bereavement, divorce, moving house, redundancy, health issues and so on. A high proportion of the population is vulnerable to depression given sufficient stress. It is even more threatening to a person who is bipolar.

Within eighteen months we moved house, my mother had a heart attack, I got divorced, was made redundant and then Carl died. The fact that I did not become depressed with all these life changes was perhaps because I was now in control of my own life. For the first time I was number one to myself, autonomous, making my own decisions. Although I conceived the notion at that stage, that life was a greasy pole up which I was continuously obliged to climb, and frequently slipped down again, I felt limber, ready to climb back up, and resigned to the effort.

Richard stopped paying maintenance for the boys when they left high school, and for me when he remarried, saying 'I can't afford two wives.' As it was only a hundred pounds a month for me it wasn't worth arguing about. Recently I remarked to John Paul that there was a time when the four boys and I all lived on my small salary of 10,000 pounds a year, or $15,000. I don't know how we did it. Between them today the boys earn well over half a million dollars a year. John Paul said 'Yes, and I was just as happy then as I am now.'

41 MARK'S BIRTHDAY GIFT

When Mark was a student at university he couldn't afford a birthday card, so he sent me this poem:

Opera

Throw all your stagey chandeliers in wheelbarrows and move them north
To celebrate my mother's sewing machine
And her beneath an eighty-watt bulb, pedalling
Iambs on an antique metal footplate
Powering the needle through its regular lines,
Doing her work. To me as a young boy
That was her typewriter, I'd watch
Her hands and feet in unison, or read
Between her calves the wrought-iron letters:
SINGER. Mass-produced polished wood and metal,
It was a powerful instrument. I stared
Hard at its brilliant needle's eye that purred
And shone at night; and then each morning after
I went to work at school, wearing her songs.

-Robert Crawford.

I was touched that Mark remembered my old Singer treadle machine, sewing their clothes. I can never read the last two lines without being moved to tears. It reminds me powerfully how much I loved my boys, and how appreciative they were. Mark's gift was a lasting treasure.

42 JOBS I HAD 1959-1987

I sometimes meet people who worked for one organization throughout their entire career, like my father in law who worked for Standard Cables from start to finish. I lost count of the dozens of companies I've worked for. I didn't have a career; I had a series of disparate occupations.

Originally I planned to be a nurse, but a back injury at fourteen when I dislocated a vertebra put a stop to that. I would have liked to be a midwife. A secretarial course after Grammar school led me to offices in more commercial fields than I can recall. In each job I reorganized the office system, put in a database (index files) and when it was smoothly functioning, I'd become restless. I seemed to have a natural cycle of about eight months between job changes. In those days employers did not promote women, and as a result their female staff either stuck in a rut or moved on. The men got promoted, often beyond their capabilities.

On my return from Mallorca in the summer of '59 I took a temporary job with the Guide Dogs for the Blind Association. Four girls with a driver toured Britain in an articulated vehicle with a Morris Oxford car on the back, inviting passers-by to 'win a car for a shilling' by guessing the number of people who would go to the Motor Show this year, giving the last ten years' results as a guide. We had to give that spiel every time we sold a ticket, and some people would ask us to repeat it. It was a strong fundraiser. We would stay a couple of days at each venue in comfortable guest houses, working seven days a week for three weeks, then take a week off, when I would go home. In the evenings we went to a pub and drank with the driver, Ted, who introduced us all to bitter beer, starting with Flowers Bitter in Stratford on Avon. They were nice colleagues and we had a good time. For the only time in my life I acquired a slight tan, more from the wind than the sun.

In one provincial town (I don't remember where) I noticed that Al Read was playing in a local theatre. 'I know him,' I said. They didn't believe me at first. Then Ted suggested we go to see the show. I telephoned the theatre and asked to speak to Al. He was pleased to hear from me. 'Come and see the show this evening,' he said when I told him I was in town. 'Well, I've got four friends with me,' I said, and he arranged to leave five complimentary tickets at the box office. 'After the show, bring them all round to my dressing room and we'll have a drink,' he said.

At the end of the show he said, 'You've been such a good audience, I'd like you all to come round to my dressing room for a drink.....You'll be lucky,' (his catch phrase). My friends and I did go backstage where he entertained us. It was fun.

I took a job as secretary to an English businessman with a string of menswear shops, who had set up his wife Barbara Taylor as editor of *The London American* newspaper. Sometimes I worked in her office, finding her much more pleasant than her husband. She had worked on *Woman* magazine and I admired her. My Spanish was unexpectedly useful there: I telephoned her Spanish maid to tell her what to cook for dinner. About five years ago I was browsing in an American bookshop and recognized her photograph on a book cover. She had become the novelist Barbara Taylor Bradford. In her biography on the book cover there was no mention of her first husband. I didn't like him either. She is the highest paid woman writer in America.

I worked with a clothing manufacturer (Wendy Dresses), and with an antique dealer in Tottenham Court Road (RB& C) which also had a factory making handsome reproduction furniture they shipped in containers to the USA. The Managing Director sipped a bottle of whisky a day from a crate in his office. Pleasant in the mornings, his mood was slightly volatile in the afternoons.

I worked in the head office of 'Schloer Liqvid Apples' as the dear old founder said in his German accent. The office manager flirtatiously harassed all the women in the office. He tore the blouse of one girl. The girls hated it, but accepted it like the office women in the 60s TV series *Mad Men*. I resigned after two weeks but didn't complain to the boss. Harassment was routine in offices and we were expected to fend for ourselves.

I went to job interviews in the lunch hour out of curiosity, and 'to keep my hand in' as I joked. I was nearly always offered the job. There were so many opportunities, we'd never heard of unemployment. My languages were useful at Trade Fairs at Olympia and Earls Court, where I worked as interpreter. At one stage I cooked for television adverts, which paid in half a day as much as I earned in a week in an office. When making a frozen peas advert (I shelled fresh peas flown in from France that morning, which were bigger and firmer than the frozen ones) I advised the little boy in the ad. who was forking mouthfuls and then beaming, to spit them out on a plate after the first few takes, to his relief. When insufficient steam arose from the bowl to register on the film I suggested they blow cigarette smoke into the pile, through a paper tube. That worked.

In a temporary placement through an agency I was in the Law Courts, taking dictation from lawyers, when one of them encouraged me to spend an hour telling him about bullfighting instead of getting on with our work. The following year he recognized me at Heathrow in my hostess uniform and we had a pleasant exchange. I didn't remember him until he mentioned 'bull fighting'.

My most interesting job during this era was with a property developer's agent. Mr. Wiseburgh was in his sixties, previously wealthy, but for business reasons he had put his clothing factory in his wife's name, and lost it all when they divorced. So he was hustling as a developer's agent to provide for his retirement. Wimpy the builders were looking for 30 suitable sites for Tesco supermarkets. He scoured the country for areas ripe for development. He found green-field sites and approached multiple retailers to take units in a mall, an entirely new idea in England in 1962. I listed from memory every shop in Eltham high street, which he used to put a couple of deals together. He sparked my interest in property. I was delighted to hear later that he made millions on one big deal, and finally retired. I worked there till I married in 1962.

Moving to Dorchester with Richard in the West Country, Thomas Hardy's literary backdrop, I worked in an estate agent's office, until we moved to Thurgarton when I was three months pregnant. Apart from part time work in Welcome Wagon 1970, and Rosie's restaurant in '78, I stayed at home raising five boys until graduating from university in 1983 when the boys were aged 12 to 20 and the oldest had left home.

We moved from Wales to Cambridge where I worked in the charity. I wanted to work where I could make a difference. Writing the newsletter was absorbing. Perhaps I should have been a journalist.

After I left the charity I took on marketing in a Cambridge language school,, in a former stately home so prestigious, it had antique tapestries on the walls and priest holes where Catholics had hidden during the time of Cromwell. The Hume family had owned the house since its inception in the 12th century. The current building was at least 600 years old. It stood in its own beautiful grounds. There was a Great Hall as in all old English country homes, with a huge stone fireplace and a log fire always burning. The fragrance of wood smoke permeated the building. I had a wood panelled office. The School catered mainly for businessmen who needed one-to-one English tuition, and as the Director was Turkish, so were many of our students. It was an interesting job. For a start I reduced their glossy twenty page brochure with fabulous colour photographs of the tapestries and house, to a folding leaflet bearing the details of the courses, dates, prices etc. which could be mailed with every letter. 5,000 were printed at a cost of pennies each. All the lessons I had learned at the charity were applicable to promoting the language school.

One of the perks of the job was a canteen serving excellent lunches, free to staff. There I chatted with two young English teachers, one of whom had worked in Italy where he'd met his Italian wife at the University of Turin. They had designed a course for maritime students as the director knew someone in the Turkish navy. The vocabulary was built around their needs. I told the Director that if he designed a course specifically for bankers, I was confident that I could sell it in Spain. The two young teachers were asked to design the banking curriculum and I sent a telex to Mariano asking for a list of training officers in Spanish banks. Back came a telex three feet long with all the contact details.

I phoned all those training officers and booked two weeks in Spain to visit them. I included Madrid (capital), Barcelona (Spain's second city) and Bilbao in the north (industrial region) in my itinerary. Once again I was off to Spain with my briefcase and smart clothes while Nana looked after the boys. By then she was 78 and in reality, the family looked after her.

In Madrid I stayed with my friend Madeline but in the other cities I was in hotels. I had learned on my first trip that Spaniards would ask where you were staying, and you had no credibility if it was not in a four or five star hotel. As I was going into yet another bank in Bilbao I thought to myself, I could be doing this for any industry, with any client who needed me to make his introductions and presentations. Bingo. I'd identified my niche.

In the language school students for the banking classes started to arrive. David was sent to Italy to repeat the approach I had made in Spain. (Later he and the other teacher would leave the Centre and start their own Language courses in Cambridge as a result of this trip. They also became one of my future clients.) Then a dispute arose with the Director when my six months' probation ended and he required me to sign a contract promising three months' notice if I decided to leave. Two other women in the Centre's offices who had been taken on at the same time, signed under duress. But I objected and said that such a clause would make it impossible for me to change jobs in future, because another company would not wait three months for me. In effect I would be signing away my autonomy. We had a heated discussion about this. The Director put pressure on me, but I held my ground.

Immediately I started to look at other jobs on offer in Cambridge. I found one within a week as editor in a publishing company. It was the same salary. I had always fancied working for a publisher.

I went to the Director and apologized sweetly for my heated exchange with him. He smiled, softened and graciously accepted my apology. Then I said that I was giving him a month's notice forthwith. He said 'Eileen, you are pushing at an open door. I accept your condition of a month's notice.' But I left anyway.

At the publishers, I was hired to edit a Guide to the Top Hundred Hotels in England. The Chairman (and owner) of the company had just paid a million pounds for the publication. He was paying me ten thousand pounds a year to assemble and edit it. I had to gather three photographs from each hotel, the report from the hotel inspectors, commission the copy to describe the hotel, and present the details to the production department as they became available. I attended a weekly meeting with the Chairman and the production department to give them the latest figures on how many hotels had been visited, whether they had yet paid their advertising fees, whether the copy had been written by the freelance writers we employed, present the photos and so on. It was onerous.

Today all that work would be coordinated by computer but then it was written on paper lists stuck on the walls around my tiny office. In addition I had a teenage secretary who couldn't spell and I couldn't yet use a word processor (I used a portable electronic typewriter I'd bought myself). The Chairman was the worst bully I have encountered in my entire working life. Every Friday he goaded and harangued me about the exact figures of the work in progress. I worked harder than I've ever worked. My knees shook when we met, I was so intimidated. The woman who was office manager, whom he treated with respect, recognized his poor man management skills and employed experts to give us all assertiveness training. I think she judged it easier to change our behaviour than his. Every month members of staff left and we all attended New Orleans restaurant for the farewell parties. The staff were young and talented, and very nice to me. Few of them stayed more than six months.

I realized that I was bound for a nervous breakdown if I didn't quit. I gave in my notice and it became my turn for the New Orleans party. For the life of me I couldn't understand why the Chairman did not recognize his rapid turnover in staff was a measure of his disruptive style of management, but he was an Old Etonian and you can't tell them anything.

In his office one day I picked up a text book on Management which had the page turned down to a section describing methods of keeping employees on their toes by criticism and challenge.

For a while after I left, I wrote the copy for the hotel entries, working from home (far easier and more lucrative than my full time salary), until he discovered I was the author and stopped it. After I left they were taken aback to realize the amount of work I did, and three people replaced me.

I was continually thinking about setting up my business to help British companies export to Spain, but my difficulty was having no savings whatsoever. The children needed to eat, the mortgage needed paying, I had to put fuel in the car etc. I reverted to temporary work, being tested yet again for my secretarial skills by a teenager.

If this was character building I should have a diploma to show for it. But everywhere I went I learned new things.

43 EXPORT CONNECT

The first time I went to the University Careers department for advice I was offered a place to do a degree. The second time I was about to graduate, and looking for a job.

The careers adviser asked me what degree I expected to attain? I told him Joint Honours in International Politics and History, with Spanish. He asked me what level? I expect to get a 2.1, I said. In that case, he said, you would be ideally suited to the Diplomatic Service.

Wow! That had never occurred to me. The next question was, 'If I'm in the Diplomatic Service and I have children, would I be entitled to the same benefits as a man?' Oh yes, he replied. My head reeled. My brother in law worked for the British Government in Germany and his daughters were educated at Benenden, Princess Anne's boarding school, at taxpayers' expense. Vistas of possibility opened to me. We talked around the subject. I confided to the careers officer that I was in the process of separating from my husband and looking for a serious career. I asked him, 'What chance do you think I have of getting into the Diplomatic service?' 'Oh, you haven't got a snowball's chance in hell,' he said. 'For a start, they don't recruit anyone over 32.' I was 46.

I was furious. I said 'We've just spent half an hour discussing a career opportunity that doesn't exist! Thanks a lot. I could have spent that time more profitably in the library.' I was still furious at his frivolous attitude half an hour later as I sat in the library reading for an essay. That guy was being paid a good salary to advise students, and he wasn't earning it.

In our Economic History class I heard that Spain was planning to join the European Community. This was 1983. (They joined in 1986.) I mentioned to my Economic History lecturer in conversation that I had some special skills which might make me useful to liaise between the United Kingdom and Spain. He was singularly unimpressed.

When Spain entered the EC I was just moving to Girton, in the process of getting divorced. I wrote a letter to Mariano, my boyfriend of thirty years before. I apologized for bothering him, but said I needed some advice and he was the only economist I knew in Spain. Did he think there would be an opportunity for me to be useful between our two countries? He replied immediately in a hand written letter, 'Come and see me. I will be in South Korea at the International Monetary Fund meeting next week, but I'll be here in Madrid the week after.'

I bought myself a smart Windsmoor suit and matching coat, in black and tan, the first expensive outfits I'd bought in my life. I also bought a black briefcase. My Mother looked after the boys while I took two weeks holiday from my job, and flew to Madrid.

Arriving at the Bank of Spain, where Mariano was the Governor (his signature was on Peseta bank notes), I was shown into a sumptuous reception room with plush furniture and old masters on the walls. There were deep carpets and polished armchairs. I sat waiting in anticipation to meet the man who had captured my heart in 1956. We had both subsequently married and I had a family, but he did not. I was shocked when he appeared with white hair. He was still as handsome, however. I was very glad I'd bought my expensive clothes.

Mariano introduced me to his Chief of Protocol, who was to assist me in anything I asked. I said I was looking for Spanish companies who could use a representative in the UK to do research on their behalf, write letters in English, arrange appointments, place adverts, recruit staff etc. They felt sure I would be useful. I envisaged five clients needing my services about one day a week, who would pay me a basic retainer. (I envisaged 6,000 pounds a year, times 5. At the time I was earning 8,500 a year in the charity.) I wondered about visiting Barcelona, but Mariano said there were enough people who would want to meet me in Madrid.

I don't know how they perceived me, but the introductions they gave to me were lofty, and way beyond my ability to operate. I met the head of Barclays Bank in Spain, who had a pretty seventeen year old interpreter assistant; at that stage few people in Spain spoke English. I knew Barclays had no use for me in England. The chief of the Confederation of Spanish Industries was most courteous and intrigued to know how I knew Mariano, but as he walked me to the elevator he said 'Oh yes, we are already having conversations with the Confederation of British Industries.'

A woman who was on the board of another Spanish bank told me, 'You're going to make a fortune in Spain,' and I believed her. I went home to the boys and said 'We are talking Porsches here!' My English friend Madeline who had married Fernando when we were young – they were now divorced, and he was head of IBM as his father had been before him - introduced me to a lawyer friend who wrote an impressive legal proposal for me to present to Spanish companies. He'd made a few copies, handsomely bound, charging me nothing, in anticipation of future business.

I returned to work at the charity. I mailed out twenty copies of the legal brochure to the companies I'd visited and waited for the response. Absolutely nothing happened. It was hard to believe that my wild optimism had been so misplaced. I realized on reflection that I operated on a 'go-fer' basis, but Mariano's introductions had been at a level way beyond my league. I would also have had more credibility if I'd proposed a higher fee or a percentage. But I needed a monthly income.

After the Charity I worked at the Language School, then the Publishing company, before I set up Export Connect in earnest. I temped while trying to promote my idea through the Cambridge Chamber of Commerce. One of the first offices I was sent to by the Agency was the local Employment Centre. There were counsellors advising small businessmen. I ran past one of them my idea for a business introducing British companies to Spain. He was intrigued, asked pertinent questions, helped me to articulate my thoughts, but told me he didn't suppose it would work. 'Your unique selling point,' he conceded, 'is your connection with the Governor of the Bank of Spain. But personally I wouldn't give it a year.' He told me that the majority of all new businesses fail within the first twelve months.

I offered my help with introductions and interpreting, to Chamber members. They put it in their newsletter and I got my first client, Photosound. It was a provider of video services to large companies. They had started with colour slides for advertisers, and developed into an innovative, vibrant company designing multiscreen video walls, and instant films for conferences. They were dynamic. Tony, the founder and Managing Director, wanted to dip his foot into the Spanish market.

While in Spain on my previous visit I'd picked up a magazine listing the top five hundred companies in Spain. I knew that Spaniards don't reply to letters. So I telephoned the managing directors of a selection of companies to say I was bringing a British company to Spain, offering so-and-so, and asking for an appointment to show them what Photosound had to offer. After about sixty calls I got twenty companies who agreed to see us in a week. I booked the hotels for Tony and myself, and all our flight tickets, and we met on the Sunday afternoon at Heathrow. His company paid all my travel expenses and two thousand pounds for my service. It wasn't as profitable as it sounds because it took me two weeks to set up, and the telephone calls I made from home were at my expense, but it was a start.

It was an exhilarating trip. We travelled first class and stayed in the best hotel in Madrid, met the managing directors of some of the biggest companies in Spain, and hosted a champagne and canapé reception at our hotel. The head of El Corte Ingles (Spain's largest department store chain) told Tony, 'I just had to meet the woman who would telephone me personally to request an interview.' He was not the only one. On the telephone I sound young, and no Spaniard can resist a woman asking for a meeting.

I would go twice more with Tony who suggested a job in his organization, but I really wanted my business to succeed. Initially I called it 'Connect' but my brother said that was too vague and I should put 'Export' in the title, so it became Export Connect. He didn't think I'd succeed either, but no effort on my behalf was too great to get it off the ground. I sometimes worked till midnight. I borrowed Patrick's Amstrad computer for correspondence. It would be some months before I bought a word processor and a fax machine. These items were far costlier in the 80s. The hardest part of the business was finding and convincing the clients. They didn't normally consider Spain as an export market, and having no Spanish they didn't know how to tackle it anyway.

Over the next five years these are some of the British products I helped to launch in Spain:

Video conferencing, enamel frits, gas detection equipment, electrical switchgear, insulation foam, armoured plating, language courses, English flower fragrances, re-bars for pre-stressed concrete, portable lavatories, marquees for corporate hospitality, software for the printing industry, coffee dispensing machines, train lighting systems, and silicon chips.

Here's how Export Connect was described in a 1990 article in *Export Today* magazine:

'When a company decides to go ahead with a Spain project, a meeting is arranged with Export Connect. Eileen Dight gathers an in depth knowledge of the company product range, production capacity and likely market areas. Then she researches the Spanish market, contacting possible buyers and distributors and setting up a productive itinerary.

'A Signpost Spain mission normally lasts five days. The itinerary may include more than one major market centre and twenty or twenty-five appointments. It can be a gruelling round, but the results are encouraging. The five-day period allows the British delegate to meet key people in the Spanish market and build up an information base for decision taking. On their return, Export Connect provides a report with the complete list of contact details (what was discussed, agreements and follow-up plans).

'What sort of detailed industries does a company look for? A guide to pricing structures, selling methods, identification of agents and distributors, trade literature in Spanish, interpreting and translation. The service introduces British delegates to vital contacts, end users, shippers and Spanish financiers and lawyers.'

'Signpost Spain' was the title given to my service by the London Chamber of Commerce, to whom I offered my services for their members. They took a percentage of my fee for introductions. The profit margin was narrow.

One quarter I got a telephone bill for 600 pounds. This resulted from a particular client that was hard to place. I burst into tears. I couldn't pay it. John Paul and Peter (who were then living with me again in Cambridge) each wrote a cheque for 100 pounds to help me out. They didn't earn a lot, and I appreciated this great support when I needed it. Later I took on a telemarketing specialist in Madrid as collaborator, to make the phone calls on my behalf. I paid her 1000 pounds per client. It saved me days of work and huge telephone bills. I had to raise my price.

One day I got a telephone call from the BBC. David Dawson, producer of the *Business Matters* series, wanted to make a programme about exporting to Spain, and wondered if I could give him any pointers? I said 'Why don't you make a documentary about me taking a client to Spain?' He said, 'Have you got a client in mind?' I admitted I hadn't, but give me 48 hours and I probably would. I had talked to the managing director of Blackburn Starling in Nottingham, Mike Gutteridge. They designed and installed switchgear for industry. They were in the process of 'thinking about it'. I telephoned Mike and asked if he was interested to participate in the documentary, and he agreed. A few weeks later we were on our way with a BBC team to make the film. It was a trip we all enjoyed, filmed with a follow-up visit from their new Spanish partner, and a few weeks later 'A Contract in Spain' appeared on television.

The Department of Trade and Industry began to promote a series of seminars on trading in Spain all over the country. They invited me to speak and sometimes paid me. On one occasion I was on the same panel at a conference in the Midlands for engineering companies, with a secretary of state and other dignitaries. I was paid 400 pounds and expenses for that talk, and our speeches were filmed for a documentary that was subsequently circulated to universities and institutions throughout the country. I didn't see that one.

I was given a free stand at a Trade Fair in central London for exporters. John Paul helped me man my stall and we showed the BBC documentary on a TV screen continuously. I gave a speech to about two hundred exporters on that occasion. I enjoyed speaking. I was on top of my subject and grateful for the opportunity to tell people about it.

Export Today magazine published several articles about my service and followed my suggestions for other topics. It was a gradual process.

One day at a seminar I met two men from an investment bank in the City of London. They said 'Eileen, come and see us in our office. We have a proposal for you.' I sat in their plush office with mahogany desks and listened to their offer to raise a 100,000 pounds loan from investors, mortgage my house, take on six staff, open a formal office and really go for it. My business was a winner and I should stop playing at it. I said I'd think about it.

I hadn't left the building before I'd thought and rejected their proposal. At present I had a very small mortgage and my house was my only asset. I could lose it all if the business failed. I preferred to grow organically. I gradually raised my prices.

The routine was exhausting. During the five days we interviewed companies, I was the sole interpreter. I translated the client's presentation, and the Spanish response sentence by sentence, to four companies a day. In the evenings we went out with clients to dinner, and I was still interpreting their conversations while trying to find time for a mouthful between sentences. We were often up till midnight, and sometimes up again at 6 in the morning to fly to the next venue. I had to guide them, hail taxis, get them to appointments on time. While we talked to the Spanish companies, I made notes for the detailed report I would write on my return (which never took less than two full days to compile). The clients were often worn out, but in addition I had to repeat everything in the other language. I recall one Saturday returning from Spain completely exhausted, met in the hall by Peter to whom I said "Bed. Cocoa. Hot water-bottle, quick." He brought the cocoa and I fell asleep immediately.

I lost momentum when I moved to Ealing in west London to be near Bill. For three months while my Mother and I stayed with him and he renovated the fixer-upper I bought in Ealing, I had no office. It was a struggle to establish Export Connect in its new location. In the slump after the Olympics and the Expo '92 boom, the market in Spain changed. This was followed by a recession in the British market too, and efforts to export to Spain diminished.

I met those investment bankers at a seminar a year later and said how glad I was that they had not persuaded me. I'd have lost everything in the business downturn. They had the grace to look embarrassed.

Export Connect was an enterprise I designed to suit myself. It gave me a chance to use my skills and special experience, and make regular trips to my beloved Spain. I kept the family for five years on the fruits of my own efforts. I hadn't foreseen that once launched in Spain, the clients didn't need me, so there was little repeat business. And it wasn't a business I could sell because I was its sole property. If I started another business today I'd be sure to choose a field with repeat business. But I gained an insight into Spanish business throughout the country in a range of industries. From the top people I took to Spain I learned how to think entrepreneurially.

Because of the hand-to-mouth nature of my finances I could never be sure where next month's money was coming from. In July and August it is too hot to do business in Spain. The temperatures are enervating. The men in Spanish offices slow down while their families are at the beach for the summer, and amuse themselves in town in their absence. I cannot stand the heat. Once it was 44 degrees in Madrid in June, too hot to leave the hotel. So each summer I temped in July and August. I sold space in a local advertising sheet, in my lunch hour. If I had earned pro rata for the effort expended, I'd be rich. As it was, we scraped by.

With one client I had a different fee arrangement. They said they couldn't afford the 6000 pounds I was then charging. They approached me after they heard me speak at a DTI conference. They wanted to pick my brains and regretted they couldn't afford my fee. I asked them about their product. It was reinforcing re-bars for pre-stressed concrete. I told them that in the light of the construction boom in Spain their product had huge potential, and that I would do the trip for half the cost, if they agreed to pay me 5% of the first year's sales from the date of the first order, and 2.5% thereafter for the next two years. It was a deal. During our trip we discovered that the method of joining the bars in Spain at that stage was by hooking one bent end of a bar to the next, which made it difficult to reinforce slender structures (as in a bridge). My client's company could cold forge the ends, or use screw-threaded joints.

They saved themselves 3000 pounds on my fees, and it cost them 24,000 pounds in commission. I wish I had done that deal more often. I put the money down on a house and started a phase in property dealing which lasted into retirement.

I wish I had the energy to start again in business. I lack physical strength now. These days most of my energy goes into writing.

44 MEETING BILL

One day I was in London, visiting the Chamber of Commerce, when I picked up *What's On* magazine at the news-stand. This paper shows what's happening in London this week. It had a lonely hearts column as we called it then. Now it's a dating service. In it I saw an advert headed 'Bill is 60, 5ft 5 and the rest is all good.' It was amusing. He described himself as 'iconoclastic' and a 'linguist', obviously a man of education. It invited a message to his voice mail and I left one in Spanish. He was amused that I said 'tengo five feet four' and called me five minutes later. He lived in West London. The upshot was that we met half way in a pub car park and had dinner. He was certainly entertaining.

Bill talked a lot. He was quick witted and well read, fancied himself as a scientist and a lawyer, but in fact he was a property developer. He took great interest in legal matters, relished the opportunity to appear in court and often won his battles. He would have made a good lawyer. He was gifted in mathematics and had a good ear for music. He read the *New Scientist* every week avidly, and might have made a good scientist too. But in languages he excelled. He spoke such good Spanish, he was taken everywhere for Argentinian. He retained the German he learned as a youth, and spoke and wrote very good French.

As a child Bill had experienced poverty. He was one of eight children whose father was out of work for years during the Depression. They lived in a basement flat in Gloucester. His breakfast before he went to school was sometimes hot water poured over stale bread. His growth was therefore stunted, but he was immensely fit. His father dealt in second hand cars and kept chickens.

In his youth Bill refused to do Military Service. It was less to do with loving peace than with his refusal to be exploited by the state. His older brother Ken had been a conscientious objector during the war. He'd spent months in the 'glasshouse' and when he came out and was ordered back to his unit, he said 'I have a rucksack full of seditious literature and will distribute it widely.' They discharged him. Bill just missed the war (born in 1928). When he registered as a C.O. instead of military service he was told to report to the Employment Exchange to take any job on offer. He became a carpenter.

Bill lived in Ealing in a large double fronted brick Victorian house which he'd bought some years earlier with a sitting tenant on the ground floor, who had recently died. Bill had converted the upper floor into four letting units and lived on the income. There were lovely walled gardens front and back.

Bill had recently separated from his partner Chris of seventeen years, and moved into one of the flats upstairs while working on the ground floor renovations.

He was an intriguing character. He was tough and tenacious, had strong opinions about everything, and would argue fiercely at the drop of a hat, especially in the evenings when relaxing with a bottle of wine. A week or two later he might come back with your previous arguments, switching sides. He just enjoyed the cut and thrust of intellectual fencing. He had perfected the art of deflating his opponents with various techniques, such as 'comparisons are odious', which seemed unfair to me. He was very funny. He translated Manet's painting *Déjeuner sur l'Herbe* as 'Lunch is on Herb'.

One of the most difficult aspects of integrating with Bill and his friends (whom I liked a lot), was that they'd spent thirty years rubbing edges off each other, and knew the others' opinions which had become homogenous in the process. Every one of them was self-employed. I came in as a newcomer with fresh opinions which frequently clashed with theirs. I was more conventional, more middle class in outlook. Every topic that came up for discussion they had already resolved between them years before, and however carefully I trod, I often provoked opposition. It was a challenge, but in time I did become a member of their group and I am still fond of and keep in touch with several of them. They are an interesting and likeable bunch. I am particularly fond of Bill's former partner Chris and Ros (who both visited me in Virginia) and Bill's sister, Jean.

The aspect I liked best about Bill was his buoyant *joie de vivre*. He was jolly, upbeat, confident, energetic, and lusty for life. He was a grafter, more hard working than anyone I ever met. In his early twenties he had bought an ancient clapped out lorry and set up as a jobbing builder. He bought old Nissan huts (a whole RAF campsite on one occasion), took them apart, salvaged oak floors, disassembled the fabric of the buildings and rebuilt them as sheds for farmers to house their stock. After the age of 24 he never worked for anyone but himself. He graduated from sheds to buying and fixing up old houses, and he'd made and lost a couple of fortunes. At one point he employed his three brothers, all driving Jaguar cars. He eschewed consumerism. He made his young son a bicycle from bits he picked up at the dump, when he could well afford to buy a new one. He laughed as he told of painting go-faster stripes on the side, while Justin smarted from the indignity. When I met him Bill was scruffily dressed in second hand clothes. He lived in a one room apartment with flowered carpets clashing with garish curtains, a narrow bed and a camp-like kitchen. This was off-set by his entertaining character.

The ground floor sitting room was stacked with timber he planned to use in renovations. The ceiling had two false levels, where he prepared to install a small kitchen in one corner but changed his mind. It was years before I discovered the handsome plaster cornices and sculptured ceiling rose in our sitting room, above the plywood ceilings and prevailed upon him to reveal them. Bill could do every kind of carpentry and plumbing, but by his own admission he lacked any aesthetic sense.

It was hard for Bill and me to reconcile our different backgrounds. I was fairly square and he was – iconoclastic. I would be working hard all week in Cambridge on Export Connect, arriving smartly dressed on a Friday evening from some business meeting, to find him invariably covered in a film of plaster and sawdust. He wore a flat woollen sailor's cap to keep the plaster off his head. With that and his skimpy jeans and sweatshirts from the Oxfam shop, he looked a mess. But after a shower and changing into clean clothes, he was transformed. He was highly entertaining. I was never bored with Bill, although often exasperated. I would be varnishing his new shed in my apron on a Saturday, and off smartly suited to meet a client for a flight to Spain on Sunday.

His first marriage was to Ana Maria from Argentina. They had met and married within weeks, and had one son, who was now 21. Bill had left Ana in their marital home after 17 years when Justin was 8. She lived in the ground floor of another double fronted Victorian house, where Bill had developed and sold the upper two flats. Bill was now preparing a flat for Justin to live in, on his own ground floor.

When Bill and Ana had been married a year, she expressed the desire to visit her family in Argentina. This was in 1957, long before long-haul jet passenger flights. There were cruise ships to Buenos Aires, but Bill had a better idea. He sold his business, bought a Landrover vehicle, shipped it to New York and drove it all the way to Buenos Aires, via the Pan American highway which did not then exist. They drove along dirt tracks, through forests and forded rivers while Bill waded in front to test the depth. Crossing rivers was the only time Ana would drive. I don't know how many thousand miles it is from NY to BA, but it took them six months. By the time they arrived they were broke. One of the aspects I most admired about Bill was his confidence in his ability to make money, and his indifference to the notion of a career, or savings. He thought like a businessman, and could always spot an opportunity. He didn't buy insurance and he didn't trust stocks and shares. Having spent a lifetime managing on a modest fixed budget, afraid to give up one job before finding another, I found his attitude refreshing.

In the mountains of Peru Bill and Ana met two Australian hitch-hikers, (one named Hilton Mace), with whom they shared a ride and the cost of petrol for several hundred miles, then ran out of fuel. Ana and Bill stayed with the Landrover in the middle of nowhere while the two Australians walked off to look for fuel, finding it at a remote mine and returning two days later with a full can, in a jeep.

When he started the journey to Argentina Bill had no Spanish, but by the time they arrived in Argentina he was able to converse with his in-laws. Ana's father was a judge, a Member of Parliament and bon viveur. Her mother was a challenging personality, volatile and vengeful. Ana had clashed with her all her life, and left for England in defiance. Bill and Ana must have been like fire crackers together. He retained a deep affection for her all his life.

He would entertain me with stories of border guards whom feisty Ana offended by calling them *'hijos de putas'* (sons of bitches) and speeding away while the guards aimed their rifles at them. They kept a rifle in the Landrover but only waved it once, in self -defence.

He told of the time they went to a restaurant for steak and Ana, tiring of their unsatisfactory attempts to cook it, strode into the kitchen, took a steak from the chef and slammed it directly onto the hot plate, thereby producing steak the way it should be cooked. He obviously admired her, but eventually he couldn't live with her.

One of the stories Bill told about Ana's father, Enrique (of Welsh descent) concerned a time when he was living apart from his wife in a bachelor flat. Every morning at 5 a.m. a *Sodero* (seller of soda) would circulate around the building, shouting *'Soda, sodero!'*, waking everybody up. Enrique went to the door one morning and told him off in no uncertain terms. The same thing happened the next morning. On the third occasion Enrique opened the door and invited the *sodero* to enter. 'Wait here' he said, and the *sodero* waited patiently in the hall. Enrique returned with his revolver and pointed it at him. *'Y ahora, te voy a matar'* he said menacingly, 'and now I'm going to kill you.' The soda seller quaked and knelt and told Enrique that he had children, begging for his life. Enrique let him go with the promise that his one chance of living had been taken. He did not return. Bill and I rocked with laughter as he told this story. He had a wealth of amusing anecdotes. Between our 120 or so combined years of living, we were never short of conversation.

Bill and Chris, his former partner of seventeen years, had recently amicably parted company. Their friendship endures to this day. Because we were so incongruous as a couple, with different back-grounds, attitudes and aspirations, I did not take him seriously as a 'prospect' until we had been seeing each other for a year. Then I thought 'I've had a very good year, I wouldn't have missed it,' and from then on I felt committed. Soon after that Bill suggested I sell my house in Cambridge and move to London, so that we could be together more often. I was spending the weekends with him. I still had my Mother and the boys at home (Peter had moved in with us following his divorce). It was a great upheaval, of benefit only to me, but the boys cooperated. I sold the house in Cambridge and bought a fixer-upper in Ealing which Bill promised to renovate. It was a 1930 'Tudor' style semi-detached house with garden, four bedrooms, in a prestigious suburban cul-de- sac. Squatters had abused it for years. On first sight I said 'I can't live here! It smells, it's filthy and beyond redemption.' The garden was so overgrown. Stone walls around the sunken lawn were indistinguishable from hay field. A derelict garage which had slipped sideways added to its air of neglected ruin. Bill insisted that it was the only scruffy house in a smart street, soundly built, with acres of allotments behind so the air was fresh and birds sang. It was half a mile from Ealing Common. He promised it would be beautiful when he'd finished. By then I had confidence in his judgment and he was absolutely right. I sold the Cambridge house at a profit, paid off the mortgage, bought the London one for 120k, spent 20k on renovations and sold it 12 years later for a good sum. Meanwhile it had been let out and provided income for my retirement, while we mostly lived in France. Bill improved my financial security beyond recognition, using my own assets but generously donating his energy and time as he worked on the properties. It's no exaggeration to say he transformed my life.

He also helped me in another enterprise. Andre had left school at 16, thinking he was helping me by taking a job. I was upset that he left a good school which would have got him into university, but it was a *fait accompli* when I returned from a Spanish trip, to find he had taken a job in the laboratory of a flour mill. Later, when he saw his twin and his slightly older brother graduate, he realized his mistake, and sought a place at Writtle College to study Rural Resources. Meanwhile he had a girlfriend in the bank where he was working, and together they had bought a house when he was 20. To attend college in Chelmsford they had to rent out the house because the housing market had dipped and they were now in negative equity. When they failed to find a suitable rental apartment, I bought a house for them which Bill converted into a three room apartment for them on the ground floor, with a separate flat for three people upstairs. Bill supervised subcontractors, and spent several weeks working on it himself. With the income from this and renting my own house, I repaid the loan in four years. Without Bill's input in the work, and his moral support, I wouldn't have dared to do this, or been able to afford it.

Together we improved Bill's apartments, bringing five of them up to high standard with simple colour schemes. I made new curtains for every room, chose plain grey fitted carpets instead of the garish flowery off- cuts originally installed. I bought plain oatmeal coloured bedspreads to replace the purple ones bought years before as a job lot. We took the flowered wallpaper off the walls and painted them magnolia. Bill installed new kitchens with fitted units and microwave ovens, improved the bathrooms with new showers and ceramic fittings, replacing yellow Formica with white tiles.

After Justin bought his own apartment Bill turned the ground floor into our personal apartment. We had a dining room for the first time, installing double glass doors from the hall and French windows to the garden. The day Bill and I first sat down to eat in the new dining room, with my elegant new curtains, a second hand oval mahogany dining table and chairs that I had reupholstered, looking out on the walled garden (now transformed with patio, raised flower beds and fishpond), was the first time I realized that Bill was well off. 'Look at us!' I said, 'Look at that beautiful Victorian garden with fruit trees and raised flower beds in west London!' We laughed. The improvements had been so gradual and piecemeal, but now it had come together.

When my Mother went into a retirement home (her dementia had reached a stage where it was unsafe to leave her unattended) I left my house with two of the boys living there, and moved in with Bill. We were married a few months later. In keeping with his casual style we walked to Ealing Town Hall with two friends as witnesses, and sent out invitations to an 'All you can eat Barbecue' on the following day, at which we announced to our friends, 'We just got married'. Bill roasted a whole lamb on a stake over a fire in the garden, Argentina-style. Ana and Chris were of course among the guests.

To defray the costs of my mother's residential care I let a bedroom in my house. Mark and Patrick were still living there, working locally. Mark said he knew some nurses, he'd ask one to put up a notice in the hospital for a tenant. Kate O'Connor arrived. She took the room that had been my Mother's ground floor sitting room, with sliding patio doors onto the garden. Kate is one of the great blessings in our lives. She came from a remarkable and musical family. When she and Patrick got engaged I said, 'Kate, we need your musical genes,' and she laughed. She married Patrick and they now live happily in Ireland with their four children.

For five years Bill and I ran the apartments together. We redesigned his publicity leaflet. We used my word processor and fax, now that my business had closed. We handled the bookings professionally. I suggested we stop the linen service, buy poly-cotton sheets and get a cleaner to do the laundry. I was happy to answer the phone, show people around the apartments etc. but I never liked cleaning. Bill said 'You will never have to clean again as long as you live' and sometimes today I think wistfully of this promise.

From the originally scruffy flats with no repeat business, our smart apartments featured in the London Tourist Board's starred lists and repeat bookings became routine.

45 ONE DAY DIARY – MARCH 2 1995

The Mass Observation Archives invited contributors to record one day in their lives in detail: 2 March 1995.

'When you write, please pay special attention to what you eat that day. This might include the times and places of your meals, any snacks you might have, what exactly you eat, who prepares it and how, what you feel about it and other thoughts on the subject. Don't neglect the other things in your day, though, just because you are thinking about food.

'Please end the account of your day with a note about: When you wrote up your report, and Whether you made notes first, and Whether it was a typical day for you (if you have "typical" days) and if it wasn't, why it wasn't.'

Here's my day:

6.30. Woke up.

7.45. Got up. Showered and dressed. Put on a load of automatic washing. Drank coffee with muesli, then ironed a shirt for No.3 son (25) who stayed here last night before an early appointment in the City. He will leave his car here.

8.30. Checked garden pond and found a dead goldfish which I scooped out, the fourth to die this winter out of our 14 fish. Fungus infection? Checked greenhouse and opened air vent.

8.45. Sprayed 'Cutless' on recently trimmed shrubs to stop them sprouting, inhaling some which I could still taste an hour later. Perhaps it will stunt my growth.

9.00. Drove son to Ealing Broadway Underground, then called at garden centre to check prices of garden pots.

9.30. Went back to shop where pots are on offer at half price and bought two.

10.00. Set new pots in position in garden with husband's help.

11.00. Stripped 10 sheets from two of our tourist flats, just vacated, and started washing machine. Collected bathmats, shower curtains, blankets and quilts for washing, too. Also sofa bed covers to wash. No cleaner available this morning, and people waiting to move in.

11.30. Started cooking lamb and mushroom filling for cannelloni, and cream caramel for pudding tonight. Drank half a glass of milk.

12.00. Ironed sheets. Listening to Radio 4, From our Own Correspondent, and You and Yours. Answering telephone enquiries from Italy and New York. Also from No. 5 son who is coming to stay tomorrow night. Drank a glass of water.

12.30. Touched up paint work in one of the flats at Bill's request. He is also busy.

1.30. Lunch. Heated home-made celery soup from yesterday for Bill. I had an egg and toast and an apple and piece of mature cheddar. Cup of coffee.

1.45. Put on dishwasher and another load of washing.

2.00. Made béchamel sauce for the pasta. Answered phone. More ironing. Filled cannelloni with cooled stuffing. Listened to Afternoon Play meanwhile, about a woman writer in residence in a women's prison. Interesting.

2.30. Climbed ladder to get spare blankets out of high store. Ironing.

3.30. Made more béchamel sauce to fill up dish. Cleaner arrived (welcome!) to finish cleaning flat which Bill had started. Put blankets on to wash. Emptied dish-washer. Now listening to The Afternoon Shift.

3.45. New tenants arrive. Want telephone installed (Bill will do this), larger TV and a toaster (will not do). Meanwhile he has gone to Kings Cross to buy new mattresses for the sofa bed.

4.00-4.45. I lie down with aching back.

4.45. Make a cup of tea for Bill, coffee for self, and finish laying table.

5.00. Wash salad. Put on P.M. at 5 p.m. Nick Leeson has been arrested at Frankfurt Airport. I'm fascinated how a young man my son's age can ruin a merchant bank. Glad my money is in property. Prepare mixed salad of little gem lettuce, cucumber, red pepper, tomato and spring onions with vinaigrette dressing to add later (virgin olive oil and balsamic vinegar). Prepare garnish for first course (smoked salmon and cottage cheese, cress, radishes, chicory and grated carrot).

5.30. Tidy kitchen.

5.45. Put away ironing board. Prepare black olives, hummus and tortilla chips for drinks before supper.

6.30. Send fax to enquirer. Open Chilean Cabernet Sauvignon Villa Montes to breathe (nice). Sew up clean cushion covers which Bill has put on sofa mattresses: zip has broken.

6.15. Wash, change.

6.45. Turn oven on, pour us both a gin and tonic to revive flagging spirits. No. 3 son arrives in Ealing Broadway and calls to be collected from station (pouring with rain).

7.00. Put Cannelloni in oven, finish salad. Arrange starters. Chat with son before he drives off home in his own car.

7.30. First guest arrives.

7.45. Two more guests arrive. During the evening we discuss the news, our recent holiday in Chile and Argentina and M&B's holiday in Brazil. R. is off to Saudi Arabia next week on a work contract (management consultant) and we talk about working conditions abroad and what we miss away from Britain: mostly British newspapers, current affairs programmes, theatres and music, it seems.

8.15. We start eating smoked salmon with Chilean Blanc followed by Chilean red with the Cannelloni and salad.

9.00. Serve pudding and cheese.

9.40. Make coffee, tea and Ovaltine for me.

11.30. Guests leave. Stack dishwater and go to bed.

These activities were logged by hand on a sheet of paper throughout the day, and written up by word processor the following morning.

This was not a typical day for me, in that we have three cleaners and I seldom do any housework or laundry for the flats, but I help if no cleaner is available (perhaps twice a year). I make curtains and new chair covers, and do some decorating. We share manning the telephone and correspondence, but it is my husband's business. (We have been together five years.)

Usually I get up later, at 8.30 a.m. We have a leisurely breakfast, then handle any correspondence by post or fax, mainly enquiries about bookings.

Three mornings a week I go to a gym to exercise for 45 minutes. This is a recent undertaking, to combat weakness and weight gain. At 57 I must use it or lose it. I shop for food about three times a week, do most of the cooking, which I enjoy. We have a light breakfast (toast or muesli and fruit), bread, cheese and salad for lunch (or soup in the winter). We frequently entertain friends or go to them for dinner. We always have a bottle of wine with our evening meal. Food is one of our main pleasures.

I like to find time during the day to read (*The Independent* newspaper or my current novel). Sometimes I take a nap p.m. I usually watch the 6 or 7 o'clock news on TV. Sometimes we watch TV after supper, if there is a good programme.

I'm enjoying my new greenhouse which has been full of geraniums and fuchsias over the winter (I made 90 geranium cuttings in the autumn) and now includes seedlings of fruit and vegetables for the spring. I cut the lawns and tend the flower pots, but a friend grows the vegetables. We have a large walled garden behind our Victorian house, looking onto other large back gardens, so it is surprisingly peaceful and green for London.

Running the five flats with the help of three cleaners allows us to earn a living without too much effort. My husband developed this business over the past twenty years. We do this in partnership with a friend who has flats nearby, so we are able to relieve each other at holiday times. We have two or three holidays a year. In the past year we've been to East Coast North America (Rhode Island, New York, Washington DC), Yorkshire and South America (Chile and Argentina). I retired from running my business two and a half years ago when the recession diminished my level of activity dramatically. Although the export business has picked up I have no desire to resume taking companies to Spain, which was exhausting, and carried a lot of responsibility. Letting out my own property on short-hold lease provides me with sufficient income. I greatly enjoy retirement and still seem to be constantly occupied. It is wonderful having time and the means to do what I wish.

I'm looking forward to the birth of my first grandchild in June.

46 A COTTAGE IN FRANCE

Bill was eight and a half years older than me, but he had twice the energy. I began to think that retirement would be a better use of our time, now that he was 69. He wanted to go on forever, but I longed for a bit of peace from the constantly ringing telephone and the relentless flow of guests. To him they were a fresh supply of stimulus every week, because he loved to talk to strangers, but I longed for a quieter life. We either had to spell each other on the telephone, or if we were out together the mobile phone constantly interrupted us with enquiries about bookings. Sometimes Australians would telephone in the middle of the night, confused by the time change. People came and went in our apartment without knocking and I never felt private.

Justin's wife Liz was a school teacher. She was highly competent and stylish. She would make an excellent manager for the apartments. Gradually I persuaded Bill to think of buying a house in the country where we could spend time away from the pollution of London and the constant over-flights from Heathrow. He said all right, so long as it isn't more than fifty miles from London.

We drove out to the Chilterns to look at country houses. We only looked at one. It was prohibitively expensive. I would have had to sell my house to buy it. Then Justin said he'd seen an advert for a cottage in France for 20,000 pounds. It must be a misprint, said Bill, more likely 200,000. No, we found a variety of cheap properties advertised in rural France. Let's go and take a look, he suggested, and days later we boarded the ferry for France for a three day trip. Chris said 'Don't make any hasty decisions!' Of course not, we said, we'll take time to reflect, whatever we see.

In three days we looked at half a dozen properties. One of them, the cheapest, sparked our interest. It was a row of derelict cottages in a third of an acre garden in the centre of a village on a hill in Charente Maritime. They were asking 10,000 pounds. We could buy it between us for cash. We sat on a wall in the garden, looking at its situation, the outbuildings, and the massive potential which was obvious to both of us. We bought it the next day. The village of Le Retail (it means 'the clearing in the woods') was surrounded by forest where wild boars are hunted and edible fungi grow in abundance. It was March 1997. The weather was still dull and cold. The garden was overgrown. The house was uninhabitable. We couldn't wait to tackle it.

We'd bought a caravan a few months previously, and a piece of land in Gloucestershire. We'd been disappointed to discover that we couldn't put the caravan on the land, despite its access road. It didn't comply with building regulations. So we trailed the caravan to France and lived in the garden for six months until the house was habitable. There was no toilet, no kitchen or facilities whatever. At first we used the toilets behind the *mairie* (mayor's office). Our roof leaked, the wooden floors had rotted, it was full of spiders and years of dust. Before that it had suffered decades of neglect. We didn't hesitate for a moment. We both had vision and tackled it with gusto.

The neighbours seemed sorry for us. They must have thought, poor old people, how can they live in a dump like that? They must be hard up. But over the next couple of years as the house was transformed and Bill re-roofed it, concreted the floors, installed under-floor heating with ceramic floor tiles on top, made two beautiful kitchens, installed three bathrooms, built a garage and two patios, and added a bay window extension, they could only gaze in wonder at the transformation.

After he'd installed a bathroom and kitchen, the next thing I asked Bill to make was a pergola across the garden between the house and outbuildings, to drape an ancient Wisteria and form a bower in which to relax. He and Marcel our helper built it in November, in muddy conditions, on grey days. The following spring the wisteria brought forth huge pendulous purple blooms with heady perfume, followed by foliage affording summer shade. I planted three kinds of clematis and honeysuckle growing up the supporting beams, and aubrietia, verbena, lavender and tulips along its border. Honey bees flitted over its blooms. Gekkos, a praying mantis and stick insects appeared on the house walls, now painted magnolia. Bill installed new double glazed windows and I painted the entrance hall terracotta. I made patchwork curtains and upholstered old chairs with brocade. It was a work of unmitigated love.

Bill's attention to the job in hand was truly focused. He would not leave for anything, and sent me hunting in local towns for the building materials we needed. I explored Secondigny, Parthenay and Niort. I used Yellow Pages and a road map, driving and negotiating in French, expanding my vocabulary to include heating, plumbing, double glazing, gravel, pebbles, bricks, cement, pumps, ceramic and roof tiles, fountain and so on. His system was organic: he would knock a hole through a stone wall two feet wide and then say 'Go and find me a double glazed window to fit that.' His energy was prodigious. I asked him to make a gate and wall by the entrance, sketching a decorative gate I'd noticed in the Cotswolds years before and indicating the curved stone wall I envisaged. Within a week, with two helpers for the hard labour, it was done. Bill was every woman's dream when it came to home improvements.

For the first year I cooked on the metal plate of a wood burning stove. We had stacks of wood left by the former owner who died leaving a shed full of timber. Using a Dutch oven (cast iron casserole) this entirely changed my style of cooking. You have to smell lamb roasting in a little white wine with garlic and rosemary, to appreciate the experience. Every afternoon at six I put on the same Mozart record to signal 'Tools down and dinner's ready'. At that stage Ros's son Richard spent six weeks helping us. Peter came, did some stonework and installed a bedroom window.

I made flower beds bordered with stones I found in the garden. Our neighbour Madeleine sprinkled seeds from her garden on the bare earth, producing godetia in abundance. This showy flower seeded itself each year. We built patios and added a sun awning over the back door. Every time I looked out of the kitchen window at the outbuildings and patio opposite, the flower beds and the old village church beyond, whose bell tolled the hours, I appreciated our beautiful surroundings and said a prayer of thanks for this idyllic setting. We named the property *Beausejour,* which means a good place to stay (sojourn).

A few years earlier I had taken a course of six patchwork classes, and brought the samples with me to France, thinking to make something with them. A wall hanging emerged, which hangs today in my house in America, illustrating the patterns I'd learned. When the scrubbing and painting had been done, I started to sew, and for six years produced a flow of wall hangings, bed quilts, curtains, appliqued cushions and other projects which mostly hang today in my children's houses around the world. I made more than forty items. While Bill continued to build and develop, I sewed. I don't think I was ever happier.

Before we bought the cottage Bill and I had many good holidays together. Our first was a brief trip to the *Pas de Calais* in France, then we drove to Geneva in Switzerland and on to Vitry en Charolais where we stayed in a lovely farmhouse *gite* (guest cottage). We had a weekend in Madrid, and visited Granada and the Wetenhalls at their villa near Estivella, Valencia.

In 1991 we went to South America for three weeks, visiting *Santiago de Chile*, driving over the Andes by taxi to Mendoza in Argentina. We went to the Falls of Iguazú in the rainforest and to *Salta* and *Buenos Aires.*

The next year we went to Expo '92 in Seville and to La Gomera in the Canaries. At Easter 1993 we were in Venice for a week, followed by a week in Florence.

In '94 we went to East Coast United States (driving between Washington, New York and Rhode Island in minus 30 degrees snow), and to beautiful Madeira in the Atlantic for a holiday in sunshine.

In 1995 we went to Chile (visiting Jacqueline in Concepcion) flying short hops every three days all down the coast of Chile and up the coast of Argentina to the capital. The highlights of that holiday were being in the world's most southerly town of *Punta Arenas* where Darwin passed through the straights of Magellan on his momentous voyage in the 1830s, and seeing the ice blue glaciers crumbling into the water, from a tourist boat on Lake Argentina. That year we also went to the Edinburgh Science Festival, to Ireland for Patrick and Kate's wedding, to Devon and to Cyprus where we rented a villa in the northern, Turkish territory near Kyrenia.

In 1996 we went again to Ireland and Madeira.

In 1997 we bought the cottage in France and our holidays began to shrink. We were in Ireland in '98 for Emer's christening, and friends loaned us a villa in Estepona (when we called in on Richard and Carmella). In 1999 we visited Tenerife in a relaxing self-catering apartment. We drove from our cottage in *Charente Maritime* to the south of France to visit Chris and Ros who were holidaying there. In 2000 we were in Tenerife again, above Los Cristianos. In 2001 we went to friends Lucy and Bobby in Miami, John Paul and family in Arizona and La Jolla, Calilfornia (where we visited Toni Volcani) and in December we spent Christmas at Torrevieja in Alicante. We did not know that Alicante would be our last holiday together.

The Brits in our region of Charente Maritime had organized themselves into a social entity called the Get Together group. Bill dubbed it 'Ghetto Gether'. However, it was the source of most of our social life, the opportunity to meet others willing to invite each other for dinner and events that made our life more enjoyable. We would have loved to socialize more with the French, but the French in general were not so keen to socialize with foreigners. The best French friends we had were the two retired farmers who helped us with the heavy work in our projects, who had sociable wives willing to exchange invitations to dinner out of the goodness of their hearts. We truly valued Marcel and Joseph who took us into their homes, and they in turn were included in our barbecues and suppers.

What gentlemen they were. They arrived to work, always polite and friendly. They worked hard and produced solid results. They brought us produce from their vegetable patches. Marcel gave us a peach tree from his garden and an arum lily which I treasured, planting them kindly in our flower beds. They treated us with warmth, always ready with a smile and the French way of greeting, handshakes and two kisses. We felt privileged to be invited for meals and tolerated for our English strangeness. They remained courteous even when we were ragged. I loved them for their genuine humanity.

Another younger French couple, Sylvie and Jean-Claude, Anglophiles both, were popular with the Get Together group. Sylvie had elegance and style. Their house was beautiful. Sylvie had worked for Laura Ashley and their décor exemplified her style. Syvie was a fabulous cook and spoke excellent English. They were also warm and generous in their hospitality.

Our neighbours Simon and Madeleine, in their eighties, grew vegetables in a huge garden and shared them generously with us. One Autumn Simon gave us a wheelbarrow full of seventeen pumpkins he had grown, a fraction of his crop, which provided us with soup all winter. Another neighbour, Madeleine Genty, invited us for supper and took a keen interest in all our activities. Roger and Claudine nearby amused us with their anecdotes and vivacious Claudine and I talked recipes every time we met. Edmonde, an octogenarian dressmaker who had sewn for the stars in Paris, showed us the stacks of exquisite needlework she had accumulated, and the museum she was assembling in an ancient stone building in the centre of the village, next to our property.

There were retired English couples from a range of social backgrounds in the Get Together group. One of the most entertaining men was a former prison officer from the Isle of Wight, who had guarded the Kray twins among other notorious criminals. Bill and his wife Carole welcomed us with pleasant dinners and amusing anecdotes. They were involved in a local church, good Christians both. He was an assiduous gardener who planted an herbaceous border that would have graced a stately home. On retirement they had sold their house in England, bought a luxury caravan and spent years touring Europe in the way many dream of, but few accomplish. I admired their spirit. Passing through this area of France they had noticed a cottage for sale that they could not resist, and although they still spent the winters in Spain in their comfortable caravan, their summers were spent in France, cultivating their extensive cottage garden. I have seldom met a more contented couple. We are still in touch by frequent email.

A man whose hobby was painting had bought a house with a barn, and turned his barn into a beautiful art gallery where he offered his pictures for sale.

Another English couple were attractive, entertaining and enjoyable company. The husband was an accomplished raconteur and they were popular. I still chuckle at some of his remembered jokes. But I was taken aback when he announced suddenly to his wife that he was selling their French property to buy another, some miles away, without consulting her. I marvelled that his wife took it in her stride despite her obvious dismay. She had settled in their previous home after lengthy renovations and had no desire to move. But he was ready to start again with another property full of problems and challenges. My sympathies were entirely with her.

A Scottish couple bought a house in our village. Later I would discover through email that Sarah was an entertaining correspondent. I love the vignettes she sends me of village life and mutual friends, keenly and wittily observed. I'm only sorry that I didn't better appreciate her when we lived nearby, almost passing strangers. She's a keeper, as they say in America about a special person.

Another couple in the village bought and sold three properties while we knew them, exhibiting energy and flare for making beautiful homes out of modest cottages. They were a hub of the British community while also socialising with the French, continually developing their grasp of the language. Sheila and I shared a love of sewing.

Many of the wide range of couples we met were in second marriages. Perhaps such a jolt kick-starts the adventurous spirit, encouraging people to sample life in a new country. I felt that all of them, mostly retired, were enjoying this stage of their lives. Of course there were the odd irritating characteristics that Brits manage to exhibit everywhere, but on the whole they were good natured and very sociable. They joined in the French Bastille Day celebrations, attended the Apple Festivals and *vide greniers* (yard sales, literally translated 'empty the attic'). This was an apple growing area, with not a vineyard for miles. Often the British chose properties with large amounts of land, thinking it a bargain, before realizing that all those fields and hedges need mowing and maintenance. But there were few complaints and many accolades to the pleasures of living in France. The summers were lovely.

In 1999 after three years spending the major part of the year in France, when the house was largely finished, Bill decided to buy a second property in the village. It stood next to the church, visible from our back door. Painted a dusky pink many years before, we referred to it as 'The Pink House'. It was up for sale at 17,000 pounds and Bill wanted it. It was in terrible condition with 14 small rooms (which he later reduced to 8), with no proper kitchen or bathroom. Behind the house was an uninterrupted view over beautiful farmland and in the distance stood a small *château* in a wood. It would be an ideal holiday house, more bourgeois than our cottage, and Bill was itching for a new project.

I'd looked forward to the time when our own building work was more or less complete, and we could begin to explore France. We had seen little of it with our heavy work routine over the past three years, and would see nothing of it over the next three, while Bill worked compulsively, six days a week. Because he was determined to tackle it with or without my consent I reluctantly agreed to put in half the money to make it happen.

He knocked down the side extension, and all the interior walls, rearranging the space, put in a new kitchen and tiled floor, double glazed windows, a new front door, new staircases to the first floor and attic. A friend sketched a maintenance free garden plan for us; we put gravel around the sunken fuel tank, and built a patio and path, so weeding was minimal, no lawn to cut. He built a pergola outside the living room. I planted roses and clematis, honeysuckle and herbs. Marcel and Joseph helped us to work on this property also. Marcel repainted the whole house in a lighter pink so we could still call it *La Maison Rose*. I did less and less painting, and more sewing.

Bill concentrated so hard on this project that he became a toiler rather than a happy worker. He worked six days a week and would not leave it for more than an occasional half day to visit a nearby town. In the process, he wore himself out. He was thinner than ever and tired. He was now 74 and made no concessions to his age, running up stairs, working on ladders, sawing wood by hand a hundred strokes (he counted them). He took understandable pride in his fitness, but the pace was unrelenting. Uncharacteristically, he became frustrated. It's significant that we had no holiday in 2002. Suddenly, just before we were going home for Christmas in London, he announced after three years working on this project (with still some months' work to do), that he was selling up and moving back to London. This was entirely unexpected. Five months earlier I had bought a holiday apartment on the coast at La Rochelle, from the proceeds of the Chelmsford house. We had three properties in France, and Bill wanted to abandon them all.

I didn't want to move back to London, but there was no discussion about this, simply the announcement that Bill had made the decision. I recalled the disapproval I'd felt for the man who obliged his wife unwillingly to move. I'd moved most of my favourite furniture and treasures to France, filling the house with patchwork curtains and bedspreads. I intended to die there. All of it had to be left, because I had no room to store it in London. Until the last moment before we left for England, Bill was making shutters for the Pink House which I painted, installing them before the paint was dry. I'd spent the week since his announcement throwing out rubbish, packing and sorting what I could take, sadly saying goodbye to what had to be abandoned. My sewing room shelves were stacked with hundreds of pounds worth of material. I was heart-broken and stressed. I became agitated, and asked the local doctor for pills to calm me, recognizing a bipolar attack. We arrived back in England on Christmas Eve, to find Peter waiting for me, alerted by my telephone call that I was not feeling well. When Peter found in a medical directory that the French pills were designed for epileptics, he stopped me taking them and we sought frantically for an alternative prescription. It was Christmas Eve and the clinics were closed. In the absence of any pills or a doctor, I completely lost my mind. I didn't stop talking, I couldn't sleep, and finally Peter took me to the local hospital. I don't even remember being admitted. It was the most severe attack I ever suffered.

I give all credit to Peter for being my best carer in times of trouble. He understood my state of mind, providing stability and strength when I was haywire, was a calm presence when I needed quiet, listened when I talked too much, took better care of me than anyone else has done in my entire adult life, beyond my Mother. When I'm ill it's to Peter that I turn. His patience, steadiness and compassion are rock-like. Peter was like a father to me in that dark period.

As soon as I had medication, I was back to my own senses (within a couple of days). I stayed in the geriatric mental ward (geriatric, *moi?)* for about three weeks, then Peter and Andre came to seek my discharge, taking me home to Andre's house. I still needed peace and quiet and time to regain my composure. I didn't intend to leave Bill, but I couldn't go back to him while I was ill because he talked a lot, and exhausted me. I needed quiet and time to recover.

I stayed with Andre and Deanna in Norfolk for three weeks, then drove home to Ealing. I went to see Bill, hoping to find him friendly and kind. I said 'I have missed you,' and he said 'Oh, you can't come back now, I'm chasing someone else.' I was shocked. I know he found my illness upsetting. Perhaps he just wanted a change, or maybe he got his retaliation in first, thinking I was leaving him. He wasn't much committed to marriage anyway. A couple of months after we married he had said casually 'It's only a piece of paper, if we change our minds we can just tear it up.' To friends in Le Retail later he said, *'Je ne regrette rien.'* Bill never regrets; it would be an admission of error.

I moved into the ground floor flat in my own house.

I went to stay with Patrick in Ireland for two weeks. In his and Kate's loving care, I recovered. It takes a while for balance to be completely restored, so I was flat in those weeks, but entirely rational. When I got back to my house I was appalled how quiet it was. For the first time in my life I was living alone.

On a sunny day I sat on the bed just inside the patio doors to the garden. The warmth was comforting, but the silence was complete. I couldn't even hear a fly buzz. Dust motes floated in the sunbeams. The world seemed to have stalled. I thought, if I don't move, don't speak, or do something, nothing will ever happen to me again. I lost my appetite and 14 lbs. in the next month. What did I have to look forward to? How would I live in this vacuum? I was depressed and frightened.

Knowing I must find occupation I went to the volunteers' bureau. They made an appointment to interview me six weeks hence. Dear God, I thought, I could be dead in six weeks at this rate. I walked around the shops and offices of Ealing, looking for activity. I went to the YMCA, to the Polytechnic and University offering secretarial help or Spanish conversation classes to students for nothing. Absolutely nobody was interested. After a couple of weeks the Oxfam shop took me on as a volunteer two mornings a week, 10 – 2 pm. At last, I had a structure to my day.

I walked the mile to the shop from home, for exercise. I talked to shoppers and my fellow volunteers, worked the till, priced the books, culled the rubbish and made coffee. I felt totally flat the whole time, but the activity of getting ready for work, washing my hair, dressing, walking, working and putting my feet up afterwards, gave a shape to my week. When you are depressed and joyless you need an incentive to put one foot in front of the other. The worst you can do is sit home and do nothing.

Peter came with me on one last visit to Le Retail, to fill the car with all I could pack of my treasures. Bill loaned me his larger car for this trip. I gave all my sewing materials to my friend Sheila. It was painful leaving *Beausejour*. I would never see *La Maison Rose* completed. Both houses were subsequently sold by agents.

Many months later Peter also accompanied me by air to La Rochelle, where we could only pack what fitted in our suitcases. On that trip I was fortunate to sell the apartment to the Englishman on the floor below. We went to the notary's office and signed all the papers that week. I had to leave the entire contents, including the antique table I'd spent weeks restoring, and the flower print pictures and mirrors, the kitchen equipment, the bedding and all the furniture. There was no way I wanted to visit alone, where I had no friends.

That summer Mark emigrated to Australia and Andre to Virginia, within two weeks of each other. Patrick had gone to Ireland some years previously, and John Paul had moved to Arizona. Now all my grandchildren were abroad. I could feel the sense of deprivation in the pit of my stomach. After my boys, the grandchildren are the most precious people in my world. It was not until Andre was working in his new job in Virginia that my life began to go in a new direction: one that would offer opportunities and happiness that I could never have envisaged in those grey days.

I had asked Bill to let me buy his share of the Pink House so that I still had a foot in Le Retail. He refused. I asked why? He said 'I couldn't bear to think of you happy there with someone else.' In any case, it wasn't finished, and although he subsequently finished it, we made a loss on that project. Eventually all the French properties were sold.

For two years afterwards I had a mental block about sewing.

I say to my boys, 'I don't regret marrying Bill. I had a good time. We had twelve happy years. That's longer than the average marriage. He was fun. I loved living in France. I loved our lifestyle. And he helped me improve my finances so that I could be independent in retirement. It was generally a good experience. I learned a lot. He made me stronger. And the irksome bits, when he was controlling and my interests came second, are behind us. Now I'm strong enough to live life on my terms, and I wasn't before. So, although I still miss France, I've no regrets.' On that at least we agree.

To my deep sadness, Marcel died with colon cancer shortly after we left. Joseph's wife succumbed after a struggle to breast cancer. In my kitchen in America I have a good sharp knife for chopping vegetables that I bought in the *Supermarché* at Secondigny. I use it daily, it reminds me of France, and each time I replace it in its sheath I say, 'God rest their souls,' thinking of Thérèse and Marcel.

Since we left several of the elderly villagers of Le Retail have died. Sarah sent me photographs of the headstones of Madeleine and Simon, and

Madeleine Genty in the village cemetery. But they are still vivid in my memory.

VISITING FRIENDS

We enjoyed the company of many friends who came to visit us in France. The *gite* at the side of our house was ideal for visitors, with its own kitchen and bathroom, living room and bedroom. We had knocked a door through onto the patio beside our cottage, where we sat under a striped awning enjoying the sunshine, drinking coffee.

Bill's sister Jean and her husband Syd brought his brothers Ken and Desmond by car to stay. Justin and Liz and Liz's parents came twice; Claire and Julian with their two daughters Hattie and Rose; Paquita and Bill Wetenhall came with Paquita's sister Lucy; Chris and Ros and Ros's son Richard; Peter and Angela, David and Sean; Mark and Sam; Andre and Deanna. Sarah brought Ben, Leah and Charlie when Charlie was only two, just before Andre's wedding. Bernie and Molly, Maureen and Dave (whom we'd met while travelling in Chile), my old friend Lyn and her husband Dave came on a motor cycle, after touring Spain. Max from the printing software company brought his girlfriend, and David Dawson came with his wife and son William. Rita and Steve brought their two boys. Patrick and Kate brought Emer and Luke, and Kate's brother Luke brought his wife Nora and four daughters from Ireland. Dorothy Bell, Claire Bayliss and Pamela Wentworth came singly.

Most surprising of all, Hilton Mace and his wife Phyllis came from Australia, after Bill located their telephone number while surfing the net. Last seen with a petrol can in Peru, Hilton and Bill had a lot to talk about.

47 ON BEING BIPOLAR

It's not all bad. When on the upper or lower slopes of bipolarity, it can grant insight that eludes one in normal moods. It's the extremities of mood swing that are awful.

Being too high is as dangerous as being too low, although for a while it can be entertaining. The first time it happens you may feel you understand people and concepts on an unprecedented level, and you do. Your sense of humour can bubble up to the level of comedy script writers. Puns and comical interpretations occur to you at speed. I remember telling someone in that mood: 'My son is dating a girl who is epileptic. If she gets pregnant, will she have a fit?' In reality it wasn't funny. A lot of very funny and creative people are bipolar, for example Spike Milligan and Stephen Fry. But they have black days too.

There's a phase I call 'Eileen's Theory of Relativity', when everything in the world relates in circular fashion: you understand everybody's point of view. There's symmetry to the world. I have wondered if God sees the world like that. I think it's because you are thinking so fast, you can hold a great deal more in your brain than normally. Unfortunately, this stage doesn't last. In a day or two it escalates until you crash, or if you are lucky it recedes (usually with the help of medication and experience). Then you are just an ordinary person again with pedestrian views, and inspiration ebbs.

The manic phase of bipolarity is seductive, because the subject's really having fun as he or she mentally soars. It's dangerous however, because your sense of proportion, caution and common sense are lost to the winds. If you are driving, you may be weaving in and out of traffic and a danger to yourself and others. You feel in a sense omnipotent, but you aren't. If you are careless with money you can run up thousands of dollars in debt in a few days. That has never been a problem to me: my sense of fiscal responsibility has never been that impaired. I'm not a shopper. But some people will shop till they drop and then spend months or even years paying off their debts.

Don't make big decisions when you are high, because your judgement is seriously impaired. Don't buy a car or a house or propose marriage in that state.

I'm reluctant to write about the depressive polarity, because it's so black, it's unbearable. By definition, depression means without hope, and it's hard to live with that level of pessimism. I feel it physically as a weight on my chest. Despair aches in my chest at intervals throughout the day and night. You can't take a positive viewpoint on anything. You may even contemplate suicide as a much-to-be-desired relief. Resist that temptation at all costs, because the mood does not last. At such times I'm glad to be mortal. Immortality would be truly dreadful. This has at least given me a positive attitude to death.

Some people who are bipolar are on a constant see-saw of ups and downs that make a misery of their lives. I have been fortunate that I've only had six serious episodes in 70 years, starting with post natal depression. For some people the chemical imbalance is enough in itself to trigger the mood swing. In my case the onset of an episode is always triggered by stress. This does not mean that all stress unbalances me. I've had more than my share of stressful life situations, and most of the time I've coped with them, like most people do, and better than some. I have never gone too far up or down during a tranquil stage.

For a long time I refused to take Lithium, all that was on offer thirty years ago when this was first proposed. It was put to me by a psychiatrist in the 1970s that I should be 'on medication for life' which I greatly resented, as the stress that unhinged me in those days was largely the result of being in an unsatisfactory marriage from which I saw no way out, having five young children. How would medication help that? My husband said, 'I want you to take medication. If your Mother dies, or one of the children is involved in an accident, I don't want you flipping again.' I did not see why I should be taking drugs, when he was the primary source of my stress, so I refused. When I suggested that he was depressed, and that's why he was shouting at us, he said, 'There's nothing wrong with me. *You're* the one who has breakdowns.' We were both right, and both wrong.

The twins were fourteen when I finally made the leap to be independent. Immediately we all felt a great sense of relief, including Richard.

After I had the last serious episode when Bill decided to sell our home in France without consulting me, I took Lithium for two and a half years. I watched the pounds pile on as it lowers the metabolism. It is known to cause obesity and also leaves one so flat in mood that most of life's pleasures fail to lift the spirits. With the psychiatrist's permission I carefully weaned myself off Lithium over a period of twelve months, dropping one sixth of the dose every two months until I was off it. There followed eighteen months without medication or problem of any kind. This was a relief to my liver. But a small episode (limited now with insight and an immediate resort to medication) put me back on track. I accept that bipolarity is a lifetime condition that I must monitor with respect, and it doesn't frighten me as it used to, now that I have Depakote, and an understanding doctor.

On reflection, I would not have chosen to be bipolar, but feel that I would not have missed the experience either. The mind-expanding stage of mania and even depression to some extent, make one a more understanding person. In one 'up' stage Bill, laughing uproariously at my jokes over lunch in a restaurant, said 'You're wonderful! Why can't you always be like this? ' But only a few days later I crashed.

This is a controllable disease once it is diagnosed and treated. The biggest hazard is becoming overtired, and it's advisable not to drink much alcohol, or any at all when experiencing mood swings. I routinely drink two glasses of white wine most days. Being Bipolar is a lot more common than people realize. Currently Charlie Sheen is exhibiting classic signs, and Catherine Zeta Jones is thought to be suffering a bipolar episode as the result of Michael Douglas's cancer and the stress that caused.

If you are bipolar, read about it, face up to it. Seek advice and take medication if your doctor thinks you need it. It is not shameful to need a maintenance dose. In fact it's unwise to try to live without it. I do not expect it to be a problem in future, now I'm compliant with the medication.

If you are not bipolar, try to be supportive and sympathetic to someone you know who is, and don't let the perceived stigma of mental illness frighten you. Like Diabetes, it's not something to be ashamed of. Sometimes it's as much a blessing as an illness, when it lets you see over the mountains, into the wide and wonderful world beyond, unseen by others.

48 TALK RADIO

I came across Talk Radio in the mid-1990s, while searching for something to listen to one insomniac night in France, in our holiday cottage. Music is not my distraction of choice; I need speech to engage my interest.

Through tiny earplugs and a Walkman radio I could listen without disturbing Bill. He had no difficulty sleeping; from the minute his head hit the pillow until 7 the next morning, he was oblivious to my wakefulness.

There was a nightly four hour program in the early hours, hosted by a man who chatted with any and all who would call him on Talk Radio UK, about any subject of their choice. Sometimes it was disjointed but often a debate would develop between the presenter and his callers. Mike Dickin, a broadcaster for over twenty years, was better educated, sharper, and more tuned into current events than the handful of other hosts who presided over the small hours. He was likeable and entertaining.

His flaws were that he was homophobic and vociferous with it, and his politics were way to the right, but otherwise he was intelligent and had a good deal of common sense. His first love was Formula 1 car racing and to my dismay at every opportunity he would revert to that topic. But he could respond to practically any theme raised by his callers.

Recently I read on the internet: 'People enjoyed Mike Dickin's crusade and tirades against political correctness, quangos and general waste & corruption, inept government, the feckless, the hoodies, yobs, thugs and scum that infect our world, lawlessness, lack of discipline, the ineptitude of the criminal justice system and general lack of respect and decency.'

It was Mike Dickin who broke the news while I was listening in the early hours of the morning in July 1997 that Princess Diana had died in a car crash in Paris. Everyone was shocked by this event. Her death became the sole topic of conversation on Talk Radio for the next two or three weeks. The outpouring of grief in Britain was unprecedented. The death of a beautiful young woman in her late thirties, leaving two adolescent sons and a very large gap in the nation's consciousness, was poignant. But there was an element of social hysteria as people wept openly on the streets and strangers embraced each other. A carpet of flower tributes on the pavement near her home became a mountain. It seemed that the population took this loss personally and wanted to talk about it. Mike Dickin coped admirably with this distressing topic.

But after a while Talk Radio reverted to its usual paltry level and I decided it could not go unchallenged. I wrote a letter to the program's producer. I said that one of the hosts in particular was not fit to take out the garbage, and I suspected that this had been his role until a distracted producer shoved a microphone in his hand one uneventful evening and invited him to have a go. I wrote that it was inexplicable how these broadcasters, with the exception of Mike Dickin whom I dubbed 'a consummate professional', had been allowed to host a show at all, given their low level of intelligence or skill. I wrote 'Much of what they say is drivel, but Talk Radio is redeemed simply because you sometimes take the nation's pulse.'

I received no answer to this letter, but about two weeks later as I lay there in France, listening in the dark, I heard Mike Dickin say 'I have a new phrase for you, it's the sort of phrase that advertising executives get paid huge sums to think up, that our producers would pay a million pounds for. "Talk Radio sometimes takes the nation's pulse".' He didn't give me credit for this phrase, or even admit that it was not his own, but I lay there in the dark, smiling.

The next morning over breakfast I mentioned this to Bill who immediately protested that my idea had been stolen, and the presenter should be exposed. I said 'I don't need to get the credit for this. I'm happy just to know that my idea was aired for millions to mull over. That's enough for me.'

The best nocturnal talk radio I can find in Virginia is a national broadcaster who gives advice to under 30s about issues that are troubling them. Dawson McAllister is not a psychologist or even a counsellor, but he gives a lot of sound and sympathetic advice and he's worth listening to. He's only on the air on Sunday nights, for a couple of hours, and the rest of the week I am hard put to find anything worth tuning into at night, apart of course from the BBC World Service.

There is a huge, gaping hole in the market in America for good middle of the road night time talk radio. There are a couple of right wing ranters with their own daytime talk shows, and appalling religious broadcasts, but they are too aggravating to listen to. The number of listeners in the small hours astonished me in Europe, just when I thought the world was asleep.

And for every person who calls the program there must be hundreds of thousands simply listening.

There's a postscript to this. Sadly, in 2006 Mike Dickin crashed in his car and died, driving home from work in the early morning. We know he left three beautiful teenage daughters and a wife he loved, because he often referred to them fondly. I wonder how they coped with the loss of such a big personality, and who filled his shoes at Talk Radio? Without him, perhaps there was no one left to feel the nation's pulse.

49 FAMILY FAVOURITES: EILEEN'S 30 YEARS RECIPE BOOK

When John Paul got married he said 'Mum, could you write out half a dozen of your recipes for Sarah? You know, family favourites?' The boys started to cook at age two. Peter was rolling out play pastry (flour, water and salt) before he could talk. It was easier to include them in cooking than to play games with them. Mark was three and the twins were only two before they all started cooking. Andre's specialty was rock cakes and Patrick's was pastry. Today they are all accomplished cooks.

Peter and Patrick are more imaginative cooks than I am (at one time Peter worked as a chef). Mark and Andre make better curries. I catered for John and Sarah's wedding and planned the food for Andre and Deanna's, except on the day I was not strong enough to cook for fifty so Peter and Patrick stepped into the breach at the last moment. I said 'Just bone and stuff the turkey, roast the rib of beef, make this list of salads and prepare Lasagne for fifty.' I didn't even need to give them a recipe. I did the desserts.

Patrick impressed his future in-laws in Ireland by cooking lunch for 24 on his first visit. Now he regularly cooks for his extended family of eleven in-laws and their wives, and forty cousins.

From John Paul's prompt a book was born. I had been collecting recipes for thirty years in a publisher's dummy. I typed out the lot, put the result on a disk and handed it to Patrick. He formatted, got a friend to index, and ran off nine copies. They were hard bound in the same red cover as the original; it made a good Christmas present. Everybody in the family (and the indexer) has one. A second edition of one copy was produced and bound for Rupert's thirtieth birthday present. He's the twins' school friend and honorary Dight. There were tears in Rupert's eyes as he received this at their thirtieth birthday dinner in Dublin.

'Cooking is a loving experience, but we mustn't love each other to death,' I wrote in the Dedication to My Boys. 'Wherever you can use a lighter ingredient (yoghurt for cream, fruit juice for syrup, sunflower and olive oil for dripping), do your arteries a favour.' I counselled, 'Never make a child eat what he doesn't like: it infringes his autonomy and you may win the battle but provoke a war. Should he become a starving refugee he will no doubt eat what he is given. Meanwhile, try a boiled egg.'

When I married I could cook three dishes. I ran out of ideas by the Wednesday. I made something new and recorded it, every day for three months. Then I felt I could cook. Our annual production of 90 pounds of marmalade is mentioned, as is the twins' disgust when cooking lessons in school started with toast and instant coffee. At home they were making pizza and apple strudel. They took to school the ingredients to make a scotch egg. We weighed two sets of tiny amounts of sausage meat, flour and salt and made breadcrumbs in the liquidizer, toasted in the oven. Next day they came home saying, 'Mum, we were the only people there with homemade breadcrumbs. Didn't you know you can buy them in a packet?' Well, no, I didn't.

There are menus from great family occasions, our philosophy on food, conversion tables, and around five hundred recipes. The recipe for fruit cake my Mother made for my wedding was used for every wedding and Christmas in our family. The chutneys we made from donated vegetables and fruit are recorded in the Preserving section. There's a section on Jams and tips on how to get it right. All our favourite desserts are there, together with fond reminiscences like the way Patrick always ate too much at Christmas when he was little, causing him to crawl to the sofa in agony after dinner.

All our social activities revolve around food and cooking for friends. In their teens the boys would invite a girlfriend to supper in Girton, and the rest of us would go upstairs to watch TV in my bedroom, leaving the kitchen and dining room free for them to entertain.

You can get most recipes these days on the internet, but it takes thirty years to collect your family favourites.

50 IRELAND THEN AND NOW

When Bill and I started visiting Ireland in the early 90's after an absence of ten years in my case, thirty in his, he said as we packed for our journey, 'We must take wine, olives, that sort of thing. Ireland has nothing like that.' I was surprised, but as usual listened to him. I packed olives, hummus, a jar of anchovies, a few life-savers. In 1982 I had driven four of my children and Nana camping all over Ireland but at that stage restaurants were beyond my budget so I was no judge of Irish culinary standards.

We disembarked from the French Channel Ferry at Cork in the early morning and half an hour later were sitting in a bright restaurant on the main street. 'Do you have whole-meal bread?' Bill asked the smiling woman behind the counter. 'We do,' she said, and he ordered toast. I asked Egg and bacon? 'Sure now, take a seat,' she said and brought us superb fresh coffee in a cafetière. That made Bill's eyebrows rise. Mine shot up minutes later when she placed before me a plate of eggs, bacon, black pudding, sausages, mushrooms and grilled tomatoes. Things were looking up.

Next we strolled around the town and stumbled upon Cork's modern covered market. Smartly decorated in turquoise corporate colours, its stalls were laden with fresh vegetables, meat, fish and seafood reminiscent of a French market. There were locally baked breads, fresh meat, salamis, pâtés, European delicacies of every kind and a whole stand heaped with olives. If it had been in his temperament Bill would have eaten his words at that point, but characteristically he chuckled, beamed at the assistant and bought a wide selection.

The need of a map was our first priority. We were on our way to the wedding of my son Patrick to his Irish bride Kate O'Connor at Killeedy, County Limerick, a village so small it would not appear on signposts until a mile or two from home. We searched Cork shops in vain for a map of Ireland, not even knowing in which direction to leave the city. We found a map for sale at the third filling station. 'Sure, what would we need a map for?' was the imagined response, 'We all know where we're going.'

Leaving Cork we began to appreciate the new roads that embodied the European Community's grants to Irish infrastructure. When Ireland joined the European Community in 1973 it was the poorest country in the Union. All EC member countries contribute to a central pot according to their wealth, which is shared amongst its members, according to their need. This explains the eagerness of countries like Poland and Turkey to join the Union, and the ambivalence of richer countries like Britain. Many Brits have been sitting on the European fence for years, arguing that they are worse off for the association. But exclusion from the Union would deprive the UK of easy access to this important international market of 495 million citizens. There has also been peace in Europe which eluded us for centuries, since our economic interests are in the same basket.

In the nineties, thanks in no small part to 32 billion pounds in Euro grants, Ireland was the second richest European country per capita (after Luxembourg). The Irish embraced the Euro and its many opportunities, while rejoicing in their independence from the British who had historically oppressed them. When I admired the many ancient castles that I assumed had been defence against the English, Patrick said 'It was the English who built them to oppress the Irish.'

A few hours later we arrived at Kate's family home where her parents raised twelve children on a farm. Her father Joe had been manager of a creamery as well as a small farmer, now retired, but still tending his chicken unit behind the house. Bill and Joe fell into easy conversation in which Bill quizzed him about his chickens, volunteering that Bill's father had kept chickens during the war. After they'd swapped chicken know-how for a few minutes Joe O'Connor asked 'and how many chickens had you?' 'Thirty six' said Bill, 'how many have you?' 'Oh, around four thousand,' said Joe.

During that first week in Ireland we met the impressive O'Connor family in which Kate is number ten in birth order. She and her sister arrived after eight sons, followed by two more boys. All of them are musical, good looking with sunny natures, warm personalities and attractive partners. Most of them are teachers: Kate and her sister are nurses. One is a priest and the oldest, Tim, a diplomat. He was involved in the Peace Process negotiations in Northern Ireland that brought to an end more than thirty years of modern Irish troubles. More recently he was in New York as Irish Consul, then Chief of Staff to the Irish President in Dublin.

As we drove up to the house Kate came out to tell me that Ben had just been born in England. John Paul and Sarah had to miss the wedding for this important event. I was overwhelmed at the news of my first grandchild's birth and the tears flowed. Kate's mother Kathleen hugged me with understanding.

All twelve O'Connor siblings play guitars, keyboard, flute and so on, and they formed a melodious choir at the wedding, entertaining us with folk songs while the band was taking a break. If you haven't danced and sang at an Irish wedding, you've missed a singular treat. It was the most enjoyable wedding I've ever attended, that went on all day and past four o'clock in the morning, long after Bill and I retired, exhausted.

In the following days we toured Killarney, Galway and Northern Ireland. We ate at restaurants all over Ireland and the quality of food was outstanding. Their clam chowder is every bit as good as New England's. I've eaten some of the most memorable meals of my life in Irish restaurants, most notably at a remote hotel restaurant in Galway with a picture window overlooking a salty inlet with wildfowl wading. We started with one slice of tender beef fillet as a taster, followed by five delicious courses of quality, all served with pride by the young French trained owners.

In Dublin, where Kate and Patrick lived for the first nine years of their marriage, there is a wealth of expensive restaurants. On one occasion Patrick, Kate and I went to one with starkly simple decor, where each table had a single bloom in an elegant fluted vase. We ordered one main course each, nouvelle cuisine on a plate so elegantly garnished it called for a camera as much as a set of teeth. That and a bottle of wine cost Patrick 150 pounds. When he got home he made himself a plate of buttered toast, saying he was still hungry. It's hard to connect this gourmet environment with the fate of the four million population, only a hundred and fifty years ago, being halved by potato famine, death and emigration. The population has lately returned to pre-famine numbers again, thanks to large families, prosperity and European immigration. Irish people who had left in search of jobs had returned to Ireland with job opportunities and its enviable lifestyle.

Everywhere looks prosperous, from restored thatched cottages and well maintained old houses to modern villas, luxury hotels and golf courses. The price of property is astronomical compared to America or even Britain; there is a palpable sense of prosperity. Country roads are still narrow and the parking spaces would defeat most American drivers. Green countryside stretches between old towns. The precipitation of Irish rain from clouds that have crossed the Atlantic above the Gulf Stream, ensures Ireland's emerald reputation, and air is fresh in the absence of industry. Modern Irish industry concerns intellectual property, not manufacturing.

In 2008 I flew from America to attend my nine year old grandson Luke's first communion. Carmella had arrived a day or two before from Spain and we were catching up on news. In their usual manner Patrick and Kate were relaxed and sociable. Apart from two hams and a turkey in the fridge, there was no sign of preparation for the morrow. They both make light of any effort. I asked Kate how many of her family were coming next day. 'I've no idea' said Kate. 'I texted all of them but nobody answered.' She seemed unfazed.

In the morning a neighbour arrived with a couple of pot luck dishes and a few more appeared casually. Patrick filled a tub with ice in the garden and topped it with soft drinks and beers, put a few bottles of wine in the fridge, but still all seemed low key.

A van arrived with an inflatable bouncy castle and ten foot slide, and erected it on the front lawn while we were at Mass. Luke wore his school uniform with burgundy sweater, a white ribbon and a wide smile. After photographs in the churchyard, we drove home. The bouncy castle was higher than the house roof. Of the forty cousins, twenty eight of them were at the party, swarming up inflatable ladder rungs on the left and down the precipitate slide on the right, from midday to nine at night. As the day wore on they became bolder and more adventurous, doing handstands and mid-air flips that suggested to me broken necks and hospitals, so I had to sit where I couldn't see them. 'Sure, they'll come to no harm,' said their Nana Kathleen with equanimity; she who raised twelve has more confidence than I, who only managed five.

All the family but one turned up for the meal and the craic that accompanies every Irish gathering. There was food aplenty that took two days to finish. The wine did not run out, but in every Irish party they soon resort to large pots of tea. The children only left the bouncy entertainment briefly to eat chips, cakes and sausages, then energy replenished, they were back to work. There was never a moment when they bothered the adults - they had better things to do. By nightfall they were all exhausted and went home to sleep it off. The next day our four were physically wrecked. They couldn't even feel their feet. Draped over sofas, they only raised their heads to watch TV or play Nintendo. Nobody bothered with swings or trampoline that day.

I complimented Kate on the fabulous organization and delicious food: smoked salmon pate, cured ham and turkey, salads, desserts and cakes. I said how remarkable that there was enough for everybody, how did she know how many to cater for, since nobody had responded to her invitations? 'I know my brothers,' she said, 'they never miss if they can make it.' Only Tim was absent, commanded by the President.

Two days later Harry and Sam were playing on the trampoline. By now I was beginning to feel blasé about the risks as they flipped and cannoned into each other. So when six year old Harry came in crying, it took a moment to realize that his hand was at an unnatural angle. 'He's broken his arm!' said Kate, leading Harry towards the fridge for a cooling packet of frozen peas. It was obvious that he had broken both his radius and ulna, the two main bones in his left forearm. He cried noisily while 4 year old Sam continued to jump, giggling, on the trampoline with his tee shirt pulled over his face, which is how Harry had misjudged his landing.

Kate rushed Harry off to hospital where he was detained overnight for an operation to reset his bones. Either the morphine or some happiness drug helped him sail through the ordeal with smiles and equanimity. He was soon back on the climbing frame, despite his plaster cast.

At home we shared every step of his adventure by cell phone, text messages and even a photograph of him sitting in his hospital bed, smiling, emailed by Kate. Did I mention that today Ireland is the IT capital of Europe, never mind the olives?

[Post script 2011: Following the global economic collapse in 2009 Patrick comments that Ireland is now 200 billion Euros in debt.]

51 INHERITANCE AND ABORTION

In 1980 in an Economic History seminar at university, we learned that after the First World War in France all the young men who had been killed left a huge gap in farming and industry. Because they were 'only sons', France's economy was difficult to re-establish for lack of labour.

Because French law stipulates that family property (including farms) has to be divided equally between the children, families were kept small. They had families of one or two children at a time when the English typically had six. (My father was one of six, my mother one of nine.) I asked the lecturer, 'How did they manage to limit their families when there were no birth control pills?' and he had no idea. We speculated that people either practised abstinence, inserted a vinegar sponge, or resorted to infanticide. 'No evidence exists in the history books as to their methods,' he told us.

I was fascinated by this subject. When we went to live in a small French village in rural south west France in the nineties I seized the opportunity to ask the old women I met about it. They all looked slightly uncomfortable, shrugged and said they had no idea. From this I suspect that infanticide was indeed involved, to preserve the farm as inheritance.

If it was abstinence that kept the families to one or two in 19th century France, does that explain why French men so often had mistresses? Economic history is fascinating.

French law remains rigid about property being divided equally between the existing children, which is why Bill was worried that his one son Justin might have to share the French properties equally with my five boys if we still owned them when we died. I promised him I would see to it that Justin would get a half share and my sons would get the other half, but Bill would not have it. The two properties we owned jointly in France were only worth about 130,000 pounds altogether. This is one reason he suddenly decided to sell up and move back to England. The other was that his first grandchild was about to be born in London.

52 VISITING VIRGINIA

In 2004 Andre and Deanna settled near Harrisonburg, Virginia. It had taken Andre several months to find a job in America. He was taken on as a technician by the Turkey Growers in the Shenandoah Valley associated with Pilgrims' Pride, a poultry meat processing company. It was way lower than his previous status and salary, but he was happy to get a foot in the door. Managing Bernard Matthews' combined poultry farms in England and Hungary, he had overseen the annual production of millions of turkeys and his expertise was established in that field. He knew he'd soon prove his worth.

'Come and stay with us for a holiday' they said and I didn't need prompting. They had emigrated the year before with Connor who was then a little over a year old. The flight takes eight hours from Heathrow to Dulles International Airport in Washington DC. Andre met me and drove 120 miles to their rented home at Massanutten Mountain. I came for six weeks on a visitor's visa.

Having sold his house in England Andre brought 60,000 pounds of equity with him to America. Because it took some months to find a job (while they stayed with Deanna's father and then her aunt), their savings were soon depleted. Andre was so anxious to preserve what he had left that he bought a plot of land near Harrisonburg, intending to build when their finances and credit rating improved.

The Shenandoah Valley is beautiful, renowned for its mountains on both sides, the Alleghenies and the Blue Ridge, both part of the Appalachian mountain range. The famous Skyline Drive along the ridge which stretches for a thousand miles from Georgia to Connecticut passes near Harrisonburg. The Shenandoah River flows through this agricultural valley. There are rolling green hills, white farm houses and barns, and small towns. The Civil War was fought largely on this territory. The prosperous farms constituted the Confederacy's 'bread basket' which the Yankees destroyed by fire. They torched the barns and crops and slaughtered the cattle to curtail the war. Custer (later General Custer of Indian war fame) burned down the Mill at Dayton, ten miles south of Harrisonburg. The whole of Dayton would have been burned if it had not been for the good relations forged between the townspeople and some of the military whom they treated courteously. An officer galloped into town to ask the military commander to rescind the order. Thanks to that speedy horse and the officer's initiative, the town of Dayton still stands today with its quaint houses and pretty village stream. Ducks waddle on the banks, and cars slow to let them cross the road. The Mill has been rebuilt, housing a handsome gift shop for tourists. An excellent museum stuffed with artefacts and civil war relics, enables visitors to slip back into that era, only 150 years ago, when Americans fought Americans over political power to unite the States and to abolish slavery. It seems only yesterday as resentment against the north still sometimes smoulders, just below the surface. We are very much in the south, here.

I had a lovely holiday. Andre took me to look at the plot where he intended to build the following year. It was on a housing development in a secluded valley. 'We want you to look at another plot just down the road,' he said. 'We considered it, but decided to take the plot at the top of the hill instead.' Only ten houses away from his choice was another bare space between established houses. It was on a very steep slope, too steep to step onto, too rough to walk on. It was full of small trees, apart from a space that had been cleared to build on. 'We'd like you to buy it, Mother' he said. 'We would so love to have you living near, where we could walk down to you for Sunday lunch, and home again. I said 'I couldn't live there, it's steep and I don't like heights!' I dismissed it totally, but they took me back at least four times to look at it in the following month.

In France Bill and I were in the process of selling *Beausejour*, and the Pink House would soon come on the market too. I also had an apartment in La Rochelle, bought the year before, which now was useless to me. I didn't want to go there alone where I knew nobody, and it was difficult to let from a distance. I had let it that summer, with my friend Jennifer's help, but it had been a constant worry. I would have money in France (after tax deducted by the French on point of sale) and thought it might be a good move to invest in the American plot. It seemed to have potential to go up in value. So I agreed to buy the plot in Dixie Ridge Run at $39,000 dollars. (A year later it would be valued at $100,000.) I signed a contract to buy the land.

One morning Deanna and I took Connor in his pushchair to walk around Charlottesville, a pretty town 50 miles away on the other side of the mountain. It has a beautiful university campus and pedestrianized shopping. We had lunch out. We planned to return with Andre at the weekend to see Monticello, the stately home and gardens of Thomas Jefferson. However, it would be two years before this happened.

When we got home, Andre was sitting in his car on the drive in front of the house. He was locked out and had waited two hours for us to come home. He looked anxious. That morning he'd been to see a doctor, who diagnosed testicular cancer for which he needed an operation, the following week.

The very next day he received the news that his job was ending. Pilgrims' Pride had decided to let go of the turkey farms, leaving over a hundred farmers to fend for them-selves. Within a few hours Andre was faced with cancer and unemployment.

On his return from hospital his colleagues came with covered dishes to express their support. This is cheering and a common practice in America. They were all facing redundancy and uncertainty for the future.

Before long the turkey growers and their advisers formed a plan to promote a Turkey Growers Cooperative and Andre was taken on to manage the turkey production. This was more the level at which he had worked for Bernard Matthews. For six weeks Andre worked for them without pay, organizing with others the set-up of the new company. His recovery from his cancer operation was mercifully smooth.

At the end of my holiday I went home with plans to downsize from London to a house in Cambridgeshire near Peter. I envisaged staying three months at least once a year in my American house, on a visitor's visa. I had no idea of moving to America permanently.

I sold the house in London near the top of the market. I bought a smaller one (a three bedroom semi with garage) in the next village to Peter's. Peter helped me enormously with the move and I soon settled in. It was a comfortable little house with a conservatory behind, and a small garden I could manage myself. I bought an electric mower with hopper. I had a little Daihatsu Charade car that John Paul had sourced for me when he worked for the company. I soon remodelled my curtains for the new windows and made myself comfortable.

But it was terribly lonely. Sometimes I went days without hearing a human voice, and would drive to the supermarket just to speak to the woman on the check-out. I walked around St. Ives, explored Huntingdon, joined the library, and the local University of the Third Age where nobody talked to me. I joined the Quaker group at Huntingdon where there were only a dozen members. I went with some of them on an outing one day to Wisley Horticultural Gardens, and to my dismay all the people in the coach walked off in groups and left me to walk around alone for three hours with no one to share the lovely plants, or to eat lunch with. I have seldom felt more alone than on that day. I seemed to be the only person among thousands who was unaccompanied. Eventually I went into the library and did some research about plants that would do well on east coast America.

I tried the Women's Institute and nobody there was interested to talk either. They had all been born in and around the village, and had no curiosity about a newcomer. But determinedly I enjoyed the comfortable home I made for myself, and busied myself with reading, sewing and gardening. I was contented but socially deprived. Peter and Angela, both working full time, would sometimes drop by to see me or invite me to their place. Peter often mowed the lawn for me and gave me hugs, but I felt spare in Earith. All my grandchildren, to whom I'd been looking forward for years, were abroad.

The next time I went to visit Andre and Deanna, Andre's job at the Cooperative was well established. I commissioned a local company to build me a house, choosing the design from a blueprint. I wanted a bungalow with three bedrooms so my family could visit me. The first design I chose was just too small by a couple of feet to be acceptable to the people who administered Battlefield Estates. So I chose the next size up, with a double garage, two bathrooms, open plan living room/diner/kitchen and a small laundry. There were ample closets and patio doors leading onto an open deck. I chose all standard fittings for the lights, kitchen and bathroom ceramics, adding a bidet to my en suite bathroom. The fittings were good enough quality for me to feel no upgrade was necessary. There was a large basement and I ordered windows to be installed so that it could later be developed. I paid the first quarter payment down and went home to England for the second time. Andre would oversee it in my absence. Next spring I would return to see the new house. It was an exciting prospect.

53 MOVING TO VIRGINIA

On 18 May 2005 I arrived in Virginia on a visitor's visa. The next day Andre and Deanna took me to see my just completed new house. The last time I'd seen it I'd stood on the garage floor, looking down on the shutters ready for concrete to form the basement walls. Now I planned to spend three months deciding how much of my time to commit to America.

Walking through the front door I was amazed at the light streaming through the back windows, by the generous floor-plan and cathedral ceiling, the patio door onto the deck and the beautiful view below. I was astonished by the elevation. Immediately I thought, 'I'm not going anywhere.' In that moment I mentally moved to America.

Andre took me to buy a Ford Focus and on 21 May I moved into my house with a borrowed bed, mug and teaspoon. The house was equipped with a microwave, electric cooker and dishwasher. I'd arrived with one suitcase of clothes. I spent the summer shopping.

I had not furnished a house from scratch since 1962, when we were grateful for any old bits of furniture our family and friends threw at us, renovating old chairs and tables. Now I had enough money to buy everything new. Furniture and most other things are much cheaper in America than in Britain. I had a good time selecting the best designs at reasonable prices. I stacked the kitchen cupboards with plain white plates and mugs, stainless steel saucepans, coffee filter machine etc. I made curtains for the sitting room and bedroom. I had not yet decided to sell my house in England, simply to move my centre of gravity to Virginia.

The most striking and attractive feature about my house in its third acre garden was the height it had been given to fit on the sloping plot, with a basement 12 ft. tall, giving the main floor a commanding view of the valley. I'd had windows built into the basement with the intention of developing a letting unit, but discovered that subletting is not permitted on this development. It will be a terrific selling point one day, because the size of the house could be doubled with modest investment.

No one overlooked me. The houses either side were distant. The estate was set in a valley with many trees and hills on the skyline. Three years later I would enlarge the deck, screened in with sloping roof, adding a room to the house, a compelling fresh air feature.

There was a drought when I arrived, and months of high temperatures (in the nineties) but it is a condition of the development that within two weeks of occupation a lawn must be laid. All that summer, sprinklers encouraged the seeds to grow.

Two neighbours in Battlefield Estate, Mimi and Karen, came to call on me. They welcomed me to the neighbourhood, telling me about Valley Greeters, an organization run for and by women to help newcomers find their feet socially. It's a spin-off from Welcome Wagon. They invited me to a monthly Valley Greeters' lunch where around a hundred women chatted and listened to a speaker. I found they had a Book Club, and a Film Goers luncheon group. I was delighted to join and immediately felt included. What a contrast to my experience in Earith.

Another excellent organization was the Lifelong Learners' Institute, where I enrolled in a five weeks course on Writing Your Memoirs. It was the best class I ever attended. This book owes its existence to the class tutor, Judith Stough, who told us to write about any incident in our past that we felt moved to describe that day and to forget about writing memoirs in sequence. 'Put them in a concertina file and rearrange them later,' she advised us. Hey presto, the mental log jam in the river dispersed. I learned recently that this technique was first proposed by Mark Twain.

I found my first friends in the Book Group: ten women who met monthly in each other's houses to discuss a book we'd read. Next I joined the Quaker Meeting at Dayton, ten miles away. I'd already met them during earlier visits and found them to be interesting people who made me feel welcome. Right from the start I had a sense of being welcome in the Valley.

It was a happy day when I discovered I did not have to return to England to start the laborious process of applying for a Green Card. I could apply now and be given temporary permission to stay, on the strength of John Paul's sponsorship (already a citizen). I engaged a lawyer to handle my application and ten months later I had an official Residence permit for ten years, renewable. During that year Peter had overseen the rental of my house in England. Now he undertook its sale and shipment of my goods to America. I am profoundly grateful for his capable efforts and support by his power of attorney.

I joined the Free Clinic that autumn, once the house was set up, and in the ensuing six years have spent Tuesday mornings helping medical staff and patients to communicate. It's rewarding work and has kept my Spanish fresh.

When my goods were shipped over I was delighted to receive the antique bookcase and all my treasures. It cost more than the furniture was worth, but familiar pieces are a great comfort to a woman.

In March 2006 Jake was born, the greatest possible boost to a woman who loves grandchildren. That's only five years ago now, but so much has happened in those years, it seems twice as long. We just celebrated Jake's fifth birthday.

54 THE FREE CLINIC

There is a major shortfall in this country for people on limited incomes with no health insurance from employers. Health care in America can be unaffordable. I didn't realize when I came to live here from England that medical insurance and prescriptions would cost me over $10,000 a year for routine care. Imagine the financial strain on a family with children. Millions of Americans have no recourse to doctors without paying fees that are beyond them. I broke a tooth on an olive stone; it cost over a thousand dollars upfront to cap it.

I meet people with few teeth, diabetes, high blood pressure and other chronic conditions who have never had medication. Their cholesterol levels are unchecked, no blood pressure or routine cancer prevention tests for them. If they collapse they are asked for their credit card number on arrival in hospital, and if necessary given a payment plan which may take them years to repay. It is not only the under-privileged that suffer. Unexpected health problems can make a family bankrupt. On TV I saw a documentary about children with cancer. One affluent white collar family had an eight year old daughter who had been fighting cancer for three years. She was losing the battle. Their medical debts exceeded two million dollars but they were about to try a new treatment. How will you pay? asked the presenter. 'If necessary I'll rob a bank' said her father and I'm sure he meant it.

When I first came to Virginia on holiday I contacted the Quakers. One of them picked me up to take me to a meeting. As well as being a farmer he is a pharmacist, who volunteers at the Free Clinic. He told me about the people they help with volunteer medical and administrative staff, raising funds to provide free medication. The patient's misfortune is to be poor. He said that illegal immigrants also fall outside the system. Without papers they cannot register for social security or work benefits.

'Do you have any call for a Spanish interpreter?' I asked. 'Oh my goodness, yes, they would welcome you with open arms.' And they did. Once established in my new house I went to the Clinic to volunteer. On Tuesday mornings I help immigrants from Mexico and South America who cannot speak English, communicate with doctors and nurses who cannot speak Spanish. It's rewarding. Both sides are relieved to understand each other. The staff comprises people who volunteer because they care; they are cheerful and friendly by definition. All devote one or two half days a week in their busy lives to support the service. The mood is caring, sympathetic and practical.

We cater for patients with chronic conditions like asthma, diabetes and hypertension. We arrange mammograms and smear tests, X-rays and surgery if necessary. They are often troubled by adversity and sickness. Patients are asked to pay $3 for their medication which might cost hundreds of dollars to buy at a pharmacy, but only if they can afford it. They have to answer searching questions about their income and expenses, living arrangements and responsibilities to be sure the system is not abused by people looking for a freebie. Staff are respectful and pleasant and I often tuck an apology into the explanation, about why we must ask intrusive questions.

Teeth are only treated by extraction; there is no time for fillings. Some people endure toothache on a waiting list for weeks. They telephone weekly in the hope of a cancelled appointment. The wonder is that more people do not rob banks.

I was touched by one young family from Uruguay. They had two children: a boy of 7 suffering from asthma who needed inhalers and a girl of 3 months. In Spanish the Mother and I were chatting while waiting for the doctor. I said how lucky she is to have a son and daughter. 'Yes, my family is complete now.' The little boy (a lovely child) said 'Mama, I want a little brother!' and we exchanged glances. Then in came the father who kissed his wife and then his little boy, murmuring to him *'Hola mi vida, te quiero con todo mi alma'* (Hallo my life, I love you with all my soul.) I was moved. What a close unit. The parents looked attractive, intelligent and well turned out. The father is working as an odd job man. They are recently arrived. I felt sure they would soon be established when he learns English. It is hard for beginners. Immigrants are often paid low wages for menial jobs. Many of them lack any education and some never learn English even after decades, living and working in a Hispanic environment.

Sometimes I meet women who never went to school, and sign their names with a cross. Some mothers have been abandoned by their husbands with several children. They exist on food stamps and subsidized rent. Many live co-operatively with two or more families in one unit. Some parents have left older children with grandparents in Mexico, Peru, El Salvador, Honduras, Dominica, Venezuela, Cuba, and so on, and send what they can to support them. I met a woman from Guatemala who has not seen her children in ten years, but they keep in regular touch.

Many Americans resent the immigrants who send their hard earned money abroad, not appreciating that their alternative is to stay at home and starve together. Immigrants without English, visibly identifiable as foreign, without legal status or resources, sometimes on the receiving end of exploitation and hostility, missing their own music and communities, are not here for the fun of it. They are the more enterprising ones, the brave or the desperate. The established community are unable to imagine being born in a society without education or work opportunities, driven to find income abroad at the expense of abandoning their own culture and relatives, sometimes fleeing from political pressures, even though that is why many Americans first came to these shores. Only Native Americans originated here.

Immigrants typically work in the poultry plants, gutting chickens on a production line. They are the lucky ones with regular income of around $300 a week. But their rent can be $500 a month, sometimes living in trailers. They live on beans and walk everywhere. Their children speak English learnt in school and one is more hopeful for their future. But how must life look to men and women at this level who cannot even read their own language? They may not be stupid or lazy; they drew a low card in their origins. The path before them must seem like a mountain. Yet they love their children and sometimes open their hearts to me in conversation.

It is fascinating work and a privilege to be an interpreter.

55 THE DIGHT TIMES

In April 2006 I started a family newsletter to keep us all in touch. The first issue of the *Dight Times* had four pages. It was the first time I used two columns. I discovered how to change the font colour. As yet there were no pictures. In the second issue I used three columns, added a few pictures and experimented with the heading. Issue number 3 had pictures of all the children, and particularly welcome were the children's contributions. I included their spelling mistakes, for their charm and being representative of their current tender years. It's already amusing to look back on their first writings and see how far their skills have developed. In 2006 it came out in April, June, August, October and November. From 2007 on, *Dight Times* became a monthly publication. I soon invested in Publisher software and a digital camera and taught myself desk top publishing.

The newsletter naturally attracted emails and photographs from the family, as a convenient depository. From the start there was a recipe page (we are all keen cooks), and always a sprinkle of jokes. I select the best 'forwarded jokes' for publication. Any news of house moves, new jobs, new babies, is recorded. Issue number 4 is all about my visit to Australia. Issue No. 8 had a feature about Andre's growing hobby: Epiphyllums, and the first Family Horticultural Competition was launched. The differences in climate between our various locations were highlighted, from UK to Ireland, Spain, Virginia, Arizona and Australia. Richard wrote: 'Everyone will have to plant when Spring begins in their area. I will get to work on finding everyone's Climate Zone.'

Ben and his friend Alex recorded an Epic Ride on their mountain bikes in the desert near their homes.

In April 2007 Patrick and family came to Virginia on holiday. It never occurred to me that they had come to mark my 70th birthday. On the day, we all went to breakfast at Bob Evans restaurant. 'A table for eleven, please' I said proudly, as we were welcomed. We ordered our breakfasts and a short while later, in came a line of waiters with our orders. I looked up, and the lead waiter was John Paul. I couldn't believe it! What a thrill, that he had come to join us! A few minutes later the coffee arrived. When

I looked up, the coffee was served by Peter! At this point I dissolved into tears of joy, overwhelmed by the presence of my sons. At that moment there was not a happier woman in the United States, never mind Virginia. The following weekend they organized a party with my friends from Quakers and the book group.

Issue 11 in May 2007 front-paged Frodo's miraculous return: Sarah and Mark's Burmese cat had walked out one day and didn't come home. After much weeping and posting of lost cats, they accepted that Frodo was no more. But months later they had a call from a vet in New South Wales who had scanned the cat's microchip after she was found begging food from customers at a café, two and a half hours drive from home. Mark went to collect her and the story hit the newspapers in Australia, as well as the *Dight Times.*

There are pictures of our gardens, our homes, children and celebrations; articles about hobbies, especially by Peter who is a keen beekeeper, fisherman, gardener and metal detector. Peter has found Roman coins and artefacts around the area where he lives in Cambridgeshire, and a diamond ring which became Angela's belated engagement ring.

Peter and Angela were married in Australia and Angela kept a record of their trip to share with us. Angela runs for charity (and to keep fit), Andre gardens and keeps pets; he designed and built a patio and pool for his garden at New York Avenue, completed just before he moved house again, back to Confederacy Drive. Mark started a poetry page which recurs sporadically, and established his new law practice. Ben took up photography during his solo visit to Virginia aged 12. We had a wonderful time visiting local sights, and making Ben's first video on his new camera. Ben has become a skilled photographer. John Paul reported on micro-lighting and mountain biking, kayaking and his kids' Karate moves. Charlie featured playing in a soccer team, Connor plays basketball and Clay plays the piano.

Andre and Gianna's wedding at New York Avenue had an entire issue to itself, as did my lovely holiday in Ireland in 2010, on the Dingle Peninsula, with Patrick and family, Peter and Angela.

In Arizona Ben formed a band, The Point Blank, with his friends Alex and Will, and performs at parties at home and for local events. John Paul and family went skiing in Arizona. Andre and Peter both kept bees and chickens for a while. In March 2008 the Second Horticultural Competition was announced, to grow the tallest Sunflowers, won by Jake who was only 2, too small to hold the biggest flower standing up. He's pictured with it on his lap as he sits on the grass. The following year Emer grew the best Peppers.

And so it goes on. In the summer of 2010 I assembled the first fifty issues of the *Dight Times* on a CD, circulated to all the family.

On New Year's Eve 2010 *The Daily Telegraph* published an article I wrote in response to their request for ways in which ex-pats could benefit from modern technology. They published it on their website under the title: Family History Recorded as it Happens.

Throughout the month I gather interesting pictures and articles from the web, in particular the *Telegraph* website, seeking to expand the children's horizons and spark their interest in Nature, Space and environmental issues. The best editions contain articles by other voices. The family in general is so busy, only I have time to concentrate on producing the *Dight Times*. Most of all we like to hear from the children.

I hope one day one of the children will take up the challenge and keep recording family history on behalf of the Dights, when I am past it.

[In *The Telegraph* on line a British expat wrote about *Expat Technology* and the Telegraph invited readers to comment. The following was published Dec 31 2010]

HOW EXPATS CAN STAY IN TOUCH

An expat's first concern is often staying in touch with family. If six out of seven members of a family are expats, as in our case, in five different time zones, something has to be done about it.

I came from London to live in Virginia USA in 2005. Of my five sons, four had emigrated, taking all my grandchildren abroad. We had moved house every five years or so throughout their lives, for their father's work as a scientific civil servant, so we had no geographic base. Their father, after our divorce, had already retired and moved to Spain with his second wife.

Now the family was scattered around the world in UK, Ireland, Spain, Virginia, Arizona and Australia. It's wonderful to have ten grandchildren, but better if you see them. I moved to Virginia so I could at least be near one young family.

I started a family newsletter, the *Dight Times*, and each month I assembled news, photographs, features, articles, recipes and jokes. From four pages without pictures in the first issue, it soon grew to a dozen or more pages illustrated in full colour. I taught myself desk top publishing. During my career I'd designed a newsletter for a charity, so it was only a step further to do it myself on the computer. With a digital camera and Publisher software anyone can do it.

In 2005 all the children were under ten and few of them could write, but even as three year olds they could dictate comments and stories to their fathers, who emailed them to me. Digital pictures were mailed from phones and cameras to my computer. We're all keen cooks, so sharing recipes was an established interest. I gathered a page full in each issue of the best jokes forwarded by friends. We had themes like a Family Horticultural Competition where all the children were encouraged to grow sunflowers, and measure them, the tallest winning. We featured pictures of our gardens in one issue, sitting down to Christmas lunch in another, pictures of our houses, local scenes (the Arizona desert, the Shenandoah Valley, Australia's spectacular beaches, the Dingle Peninsula). Two new babies made the front page. The UK couple's holiday in Australia was documented for all to enjoy. We became familiar with each other's climates. While we shivered in the snow, our Australia based family frolicked on the beach on Queensland's Gold Coast. In Arizona they were still air conditioned when we in Virginia needed central heating. Hobbies were shared: fishing, beekeeping and metal detecting in Cambridgeshire, gardening, mountain biking and kayaking in Arizona, fencing and horse riding in Ireland, and so on.

The *Dight Times,* originally printed and posted, grew in size and popularity, becoming prohibitively expensive in printer cartridges and global postage. So it became electronic, delivered in .pdf form to the families and others who took an interest.

The children's entries were delightful. 5 yr old Sam's father gave him a mini tool set he'd had since small. Sam dictated: Dad's tools – by Sam 'He gave his tools to me. And they are blue. They are not dangerous. I can play with them and fix stuff. I have a hammer and a screw driver and I have nails and they come in a square box and I like them. And I have a measuring tape I can measure stuff like a leg, a head, a glass house. I used the hammer for hammering things. My favourite food is stuffing and ice creams but not together. The end.'

His four year old cousin in Australia dictated a story. An extract: 'The fairies went back home and bought a puff ball creature and fed the puff ball some biscuits. The fairies bought a wand and put some batteries in it. They chopped up some onion and put it in some soil and then added soup around it. Then it was all cooked up in the oven and put in a lunch box.'

There are pictures of the boys selling lemonade and jellybeans in their garden to the neighbourhood (an American tradition). There are

Halloween costumes from every country, reports of school concerts and sports: soccer teams, athletics, Aikido, dancing. The adults' job changes and house moves are recorded. Family Birthdays are listed for reference. A check list of holiday packing items has been repeatedly used.

In Virginia my sons live either three hours behind me, five or fourteen hours ahead. It's tricky keeping in touch at convenient times. But the *Dight Times* is available 24/7 by email. We watch the children growing up although we haven't seen some of them for years, and the two year old in Australia we've never seen, except on Skype. Looking back over three large ring binders, we can see how the oldest now fifteen, was a boy only three years ago and now he's a young man of 6ft 2", playing guitar in a band: family history recorded as it happens.

The newsletter, now in its 56th issue, around 16 pages a month, is a labour of love for me, and a permanent record of the family developing, better than an album, which my grandchildren can look back on and share with their children long after I'm gone. The first fifty issues are on CD, and the next one is always on the stocks.

When I was young it cost a week's wages to phone a relative in Australia for three minutes at Christmas. Now we can talk for 2 cents a minute, anywhere in the world, on the computer. The world has definitely shrunk. Although I miss my precious grandchildren, it's not nearly so hard as it would have been, without the *Dight Times.*

56 ANIMAL LOVER

I have loved two animals in my life: a duck and a dog. The duck was a day old and I was seven. I was his imprinted mother and my heart was full of love. He slept in a box beside my bed, skidded and shat on the lino. I recall the gentle nibble of his rounded beak on my hand, the softness of his yellow feathers, the pleasant smell of his little body. Donald followed me chirping when I went for a walk (the quack develops later). When he got tired he stood still and chirped forlornly, as if to say 'I can't go any further'; then I would pick him up and carry him in my palms. Neighbours stopped to admire him. After some weeks he became too dirty in the house for my tolerant Mother, and my Father built a pen parallel to the chicken run so Donald would not be lonely. At this point we introduced Donald to water, in the form of an enamelled washing up bowl sunk into the earth. Alarmed at the water, Donald would not go in, but my Father put his foot in it, when shutting up the poultry after dark. I cannot recall his exact words, but he was obviously not pleased. After that we stopped trying to teach Donald to swim. Donald wasn't very bright, but he was sociable. He formed a friendship with a particular chicken, and they were so desperate to be together, they ran up and down in parallel on each side of the chicken wire. So we let Donald into the chicken coop, but he was a messy eater. He messed in the chicken's food and water, so we decided to put Donald and his friend together in the duck coop. By this time his feathers were white, his bill bright yellow and his eye less trusting than when he slept in my bedroom, but I still loved him.

One day I came home from school and found that my Mother had taken Donald to the doctor. She said he was not well. Doctor Power, who was Irish, had a collection of poultry behind a large walled garden in the village. About a week later, waiting anxiously for his recovery, I recognized Donald's quack behind the wall and ran home in excitement to say 'Donald is better, can he come home now?' But I never saw him again. He had been banished for his table manners. There is a twist to this tale: a month after moving to the doctor's house, Donald laid an egg. I could never get my head around his sex change.

The other animal I loved was called Bullet. He was a mongrel and lived in the villa in Mallorca where I spent 1958-9, with the Fieldings. Bullet had intelligence, dignity, empathy and a sense of humour. Martin the butler used to tease him in the kitchen, saying (in Mallorquin, which I could barely understand) 'Bullet, there is a rabbit outside' in a confidential voice full of promise. It sounded like *'Hay un conejo de forra'*. Bullet's ears would prick up, but he didn't go look because he'd heard this before, and knew Martin was joking. Bullet loved to run through the pine trees and down to the beach with Dodge Fielding who was thirteen. Bullet was the sort of dog that every boy should have, and hardly ever does. He was intelligent, playful, enthusiastic, co-operative and fun, but he could also sit quietly in the sun on his own. I do appreciate dignity in a dog.

One day I was feeling down. I was twenty one years old, living in isolation without transport, and the only other accessible building in that stunningly beautiful bay, big enough to house the Sixth Fleet, was the Hotel Formentor, frequented by rich people on holiday who had nothing to do with me. At mealtimes I ate alone in the dining area. I was desperate for company my own age.

I was sitting in my bedroom, having a little weep in my loneliness, when Bullet walked in. He walked slowly up to me, laid his head on my lap and looked at me with an expression I would be thrilled to see in a person. It said 'I feel your sadness, I'm your friend and I'd like to help'. I loved that dog.

But I don't care for animals in my house. People say that a dog or cat would keep me company, but they wouldn't. Of animals in general I like horses and birds best. Horses are graceful, powerful to watch and useful. Birds are like tiny dinosaurs, little flying miracles. They are musical, decorative, and lift my spirits, especially in spring. I put out food for them and watch them with delight, but I don't want to touch them, or horses.

Andre is passionate about animals. He always yearned for pets. I'm sorry now that I was not more understanding, when he was small. I felt that five little boys in the house made enough mess without introducing animals, so I only allowed pets that would be no problem. Goldfish were good, they don't make a noise or bring in muddy footprints, but you can't pet a goldfish. Stick insects were my favourites - they didn't move for days on end and stayed silent in their jar. We once looked after six snails for a school friend while he was on holiday and one got out. We replaced it with another from the garden and he didn't notice, but the original snail turned up three months later, on the back of my bed-head. What on earth had sustained it?

I once bought a rabbit for John Paul but it escaped so many times from any sort of pen we could make, eventually I took it back to the market where I had bought it. He was sad. The hassle of running after it through neighbours' gardens got me down. But how could I have been so heartless?

The tortoise the boys found in Aberystwyth only stayed a day. They had built it a pen but he escaped, with other plans. Their disappointment was tangible.

Sometime later we bought two gerbils (sisters, I was into birth control). They were fine until the day one escaped while being petted and went down a tiny hole in the sitting room floorboard. It was a Victorian house and the sitting room 24 ft by 12. They could see the gerbil with their flashlight, in the foot deep gap below the boards, but it took hours to rescue her. I had visions of taking up the floorboards but eventually they trapped her in a biscuit tin.

At long last I agreed that Andre could get a dog. His need had become more pressing than my antipathy. We went to the RSPCA to offer our loving home, and were given a Welsh sheep dog with a sweet face, about a year old. Andre named her Gemma. Whenever I picked up a broom she cowered and we realized she'd been maltreated. We were all kind and encouraging, but she preferred to sit alone behind the sofa. She never recovered from her early trauma and resisted every attempt by Andre to train or play with her. When taken for a walk she pulled neurotically on her leash to go home, and peed on the carpet for years, ignoring our rural garden. I routinely blotted kitchen roll under my shoe. Luckily the carpet was old, the house was huge, and her favourite spot was an upstairs corridor. Later Andre as an adult had proper dogs, Pip and Sydney, cocker spaniels, and trained them most effectively. Now he has a black standard poodle, brave Olive.

Canaries were perhaps the most successful pets. Andre bred them in a cage in his bedroom in Cambridge. Sadly he left the cage door open one day, and they all escaped through the open window. An aviary of Roller canaries was his next hobby, as a student. He wrote a dissertation at university about the way they learn to sing, which earned him the title Student of the Year in a national competition. Later he looked after turkeys by the million. The vet described him as the best stockman he has ever met.

Julian (aged 11) asked if he could bring a rat home from school because they had a surplus in the laboratory. I said No, I couldn't bear a rat. A day or two later he asked if I would accept a mouse? Well, all right, I said reluctantly, realizing that my selfishness was unfair to them. Julian lived in an attic bedroom at the top of our three storey house. I had long ago bought duvets for all the boys so I wouldn't have to make beds, and at the time was fully occupied as a mature student in university, so I didn't go up to his room for weeks. My Mother used to change their bed linen. One evening I said 'Julian, your mouse is getting very big.' 'Well actually Mum, it's a rat.' I was shocked. 'You didn't let me have a rat so I said it was a mouse.' Well, what can you do after the event? The rat lived with us for three years. It moved house with us twice. It lived in a cage in our Girton sitting room (I became more liberal as time went by). One day I noticed there were holes in my curtains, which the rat had nibbled through the bars. I managed to mend them invisibly. A friend, Tina, came for a drink after work one day, and as she left said 'Well, I'll come again someday, when you get rid of the rat.' To my relief the rat was taken back from Cambridge to Aberystwyth, a day long journey by train, and left with a former school friend.

I watch documentaries about wildlife with fascination and I'd enjoy a photo-safari.

I like to see images of animals; I've sewn several wall hangings with animal themes for my grandchildren. I'm always impressed by the dignity of animals' faces, especially the large cats, like cheetahs and tigers. But I never want to touch animals. If I pat a dog I wash my hands immediately. It revolts me to see people kissing dogs and being licked on their faces. Have they seen where those tongues have been? I positively dislike cats, a phobia picked up from my mother. I like their appearance but can't stand the way you can feel their bones move around inside their fur, and their vicious claws emerge like Madam Krebb's toecap dagger. I respect the dignity of cats and their wonderful independence. Cats don't need people. They know that if we forget to feed them they can find another sucker.

In England people generally have more time for animals than children. The opposite is true of Spain. I love everything about human babies, but don't want to touch animal flesh, fur or feathers. I'm pleased that my children's interest today ranges from Aviaries to Zebras, through bees, cats, dogs and guinea pigs, but I am still not an animal lover.

57 SERENDIPITY

One sunny weekend I drove to Williamsburg in southern Virginia, a round trip of 400 miles. On the return I decided to follow scenic Route 5, and a couple I asked for directions drove out of their way to put me on the right road.

Reminiscent of the verdant tree-lined byways of France, the route was lined not with chateaux, but plantations. The sun was shining and I admired the beautiful scenery and lack of traffic. At intervals I passed small churches, and as it was Sunday morning, decided to stop.

In the car park of a modest white clapboard church I saw two women. I asked 'Is there a service I can join in?' First to arrive, they took me in with a friendly welcome. 'Momma Merle' as she introduced herself was a retired teacher, who had taught many of the congregation; she gave me brief biographies. I soon realized this was a black gospel-singing Baptist church. Mine was the only white face, but people stopped to shake my hand and chat. Most there were born in the vicinity and knew each other, in contrast to my own state of rootlessness, unable to call anywhere in the world 'home'.

A choir of ten men, with varying soloists, sang in harmony accompanied by a jazz pianist and an electric bass guitarist of considerable talent. It was like Blues Brothers music, swinging hymns interspersed with scripture, the congregation clapping hands and singing along. Irresistibly, my body language rocked too. Although mostly unfamiliar, the hymns were melodious and easy to follow, I joined in every one. The preacher spoke of a changing world, a culture subject to innovation and stress, people being less concerned with others than themselves. There was humour and humanity in his message. He spoke his love for Jesus and the people encouraged with constant interjections, 'Yeah, Hallelujah, Amen!'

One chorister, a strikingly handsome guy, thanked friends for the support he'd received after his recent operation. He said, 'the good news is, I'm declared fit again, and the bad news is, the pastor will now stop mowing my grass.' The preacher welcomed all, including 'the visitor sitting by Ms. Merle'. The service lasted two hours and I was sorry when it ended.

Dozens shook my hand, many hugged me and everybody smiled. They must be descendants of slaves from the old plantations. I've seldom felt more welcome. It was an unforgettable experience.

58 LOOSE ENDS

Peter sent an email to me in America about cancelling my Automobile Association membership in UK. They were about to help themselves to another year's subscription, which I should have cancelled over a year ago. He gave me a number in France through which I could access the UK membership department.

A competent bilingual woman answered with a slight French accent but protested that this was the European Emergency Breakdown Service, implying that I was wasting her time and should phone the UK on an 0800 number. I pointed out that this is impossible from abroad and reluctantly she found me another number. Options came and went as I pressed relevant buttons, and finally a guy called Chris introduced himself. 'Oh, I'm so pleased to meet you,' I said, and described my desire to cancel my subscription. 'What is your post code?' he asked and my mind went blank. I had only lived six months in that house over a year ago. I offered my membership number and policy, my name, age and date of birth, but he said 'We don't work on that system, I need your post code.' Through gritted teeth I said 'You are able to access my money, so if you can't access my membership details I am going to be seriously pissed off.' (Yes, I did.) Fortunately I located the postcode in my Filofax.

Chris cancelled my membership, saying 'You're still covered until 7 July.' 'Please don't bother' I said, I gave the car to my son in Ireland months ago and last week it was stolen.'

Patrick had taken his children to the swimming pool and left the car in the car park. Then he found his keys were missing from his locker. Obviously someone had followed him in and taken the keys and the car. His heart sank.

A year or two previously his other car had been stolen in Dublin by joyriders, who crashed it and set fire to it on wasteland, reducing car, contents and the children's safety seats to ashes.

But this time it happened that the Irish police were manning check points on roads leaving town that day, and when they received notice of a stolen car they found it listed in their check point records. One of them remembered seeing a known criminal driving such a car. The police went to his house and there was the car parked outside.

Patrick was so happy to get it back. When I passed it to him it only had about 20,000 miles on the clock because I bought it in 1997 just before we went to live in France, and left it parked in London for the rare occasions when I needed it. In 2011 Patrick is still driving my old blue Daihatsu Charade.

59 THE HIGH PRICE OF EQUALITY

I was married a long time ago. I already had a baby before I heard of the Beatles in 1963. The swinging sixties happened after I'd settled down with a civil servant in a semi in the south of England. The nearest I came to swinging was dancing the twist in a sedate suburban party.

I was fourteen when a man in the church choir whom I admired said, 'Eileen, if your husband can count up to ten you only want to count up to eight,' and I thought 'How wise.'

Fearing that a degree might make me unattractive as a marriage prospect, and keen above all else to have children, I took a secretarial course and flitted around offices in London and Madrid until it was time to be married. I enjoyed it. I was conscious that nobody was more fortunate than a reasonably attractive young woman. Men of every age noticed and courted girls like me, particularly in Spain where to be young, blonde and without a chaperone was to be a winner.

In those days to be over 25 and unmarried was synonymous with being an old maid, a fate that terrified me. I really wanted babies. A week before I turned twenty five I married my current boyfriend. I embraced the joys of being married unreservedly, learning to cook being my first priority. In all things I compromised. If Richard wanted to stay home and read rather than go to the cinema, that was OK by me. When he put a strict limit on my housekeeping, I strained (literally) to live within it. I recall a week when the expense of visitors left me without money till the end of the month. We ate carrots and potatoes from the garden and little else. I had to wait for the next week's housekeeping money to replace a tin of shoe polish, despite the fact that we put away sixty pounds every month for the next car. His control of the budget was total. We didn't have a joint account. The two cars (eventually) were both in his name. If I needed a few extra pounds to buy a pair of shoes (a frequent need with five growing boys) I asked my Mother for it. Whenever his job required it, we moved. I never questioned whether this suited me, I just did it.

The dirty dishes always awaited me. He never did the washing all the time we were married, he only once changed a nappy when I was out working in the evening. He didn't bathe a child or even read to him. He liked to garden and he spent his weekends at it. He didn't cook, clean, shop, or make the bed. Eventually he even left the decorating to me. He once offered to teach me how to change the oil in the car, but I drew the line at that.

He wasn't lazy. He gardened assiduously. He worked hard on improving the property, painting the woodwork, servicing the car. He spent hours tying flies, not so much time fishing. He read half a dozen scientific books a month from the library. He was a man with hobbies, never in need of entertainment. Later he would spend twenty years happily gardening in retirement, transforming an acre of rough land in Malaga to a beautiful garden with orange and lemon trees, avocados and flowers. His gardens were always exemplary.

When our children were aged two to ten three of my women friends and I enrolled in an evening class entitled 'The changing role of women'. It was 1973. Between four of us we had twelve small children. We were amazed at the things we learned in this class. It was our first introduction to feminism.

The tutor was a former nun who had left the convent, taken a degree in Psychology, worked in industry for years and then became a lecturer at the University of Wales. Oonagh became a friend to all of us, but her appreciation of our situation was somewhat limited. Having told us of the age-old undermining of women by the patriarchal system, she said she would introduce us to a couple who had made a success of their egalitarian marriage. We were delighted. Perhaps this would point the way. The next week the couple turned up, both graduates, and proceeded to tell us how they took turns in moving for each other's work, sometimes to suit the husband, sometimes the wife. They shared the chores. They both cleaned the toilet. They had a joint bank account, and shopped together. We felt euphoric at the prospect. 'And who stays home if the children are sick?' I asked. 'Oh,' they said, 'We haven't got any children.' Our euphoria dissipated like a balloon pierced by a crossbow.

I came home with enlightened ideas and proceeded to share them with my family. The children were mostly too young to be interested, and Richard was put out. For years afterwards he would say 'You were a good wife till you went to that evening class,' and he wasn't joking. I tried in my head not to include him in the perception of men oppressing women, but gradually I failed to kid myself. It caused friction when I questioned whether it was fair that my say in the family budget was limited to my housekeeping allowance. It didn't cause any changes, just friction.

I struggled to accept my fate. I acknowledged that Richard was a reliable and conscientious provider and that I was lucky I could stay home to look after the children, but I was determined to raise my boys to examine the world from a woman's point of view too. I pointed out at every opportunity the short straw that girls drew. One day Andre came home saying 'Our teacher said that a woman's place is on her back, and even the girls laughed. When I protested, the girls laughed at me too.' We often talked about such issues. I didn't want them to be feminist, simply egalitarian. I felt quite proud of them until two of my daughters in law moaned about them failing to process their own washing. I hadn't done as well as I thought. But when they got married, in almost every case my boys could cook better than their wives. Perhaps their mothers had raised their daughters not to be too clever at the chores, and I can understand that.

In some churches in those days it was pointed out that women were created second, but were the first to sin. There were no women priests in the Catholic Church then or now. When my first baby was born my Mother went with me to be 'churched'. I didn't realize until I was going through the ritual with the priest that the purpose of this exercise was to cleanse me from the filthy effects of childbirth, so that I was fit to enter the church again. I felt disgusted about this, although I made no protest to the priest. I certainly protested to my Mother, and never went through that ceremony again. I don't think they do it now.

The Bible has a lot to answer for. Here's an example from 1Timothy written in the second century:

Let a woman learn in silence with all submissiveness. I permit no woman to teach or to have authority over men; she is to keep silent. For Adam was formed first, then Eve; and Adam was not deceived, but the woman was deceived and became a transgressor.

There are still churches where this edict is observed. When the Mennonites in Virginia described how their officials are chosen, I asked about a woman's role, and was told 'Their role is vital. It is to produce the children.' But not to hold authority, I notice.

I cannot name any society where the birth of girls is valued over the birth of boys. A family of all girls is seldom seen as an advantage, whereas a family of all boys is often admired. In China, where they adopted a one child only policy a few decades ago, the result was wholesale abortion or infanticide of females. Predictably there is now a serious shortage of wives for the men. Their solution is to import wives from other Asian countries, presumably exporting the problem. A Chinese woman I met explained that where a family is too poor to import a wife, one son's wife is also required to service his brothers. At the very least, many Chinese men will live and die as bachelors.

Surely in 2011 I don't have to give further examples to explain why a woman has a rude awakening when she learns about inequality of the sexes. In America women doing the same work as men often earn 75% of a man's wage; in Britain when I last heard the figure was 60%, although it may have improved since. The excuse was always that men had families to support, so they merited higher pay, but today there are more single mothers than single fathers coping with children, and still the women earn less.

There is a wide gap between the pensions received by men and women, yet their living costs are the same.

Our marriage ended after 24 years. I had to postpone divorce until I had only three in school, and could manage with my inferior salary and maintenance. Even with a degree my income was only a third of Richard's. I don't regret spending the years raising a family rather than developing a career. And I'm truly grateful to Richard that he made it possible by being the sole breadwinner for most of that time.

Although nervous at the prospect of being independent, I found I coped far better even with reduced income when the budget was entirely in my hands. We hardly noticed the deprivations, but we enjoyed the freedom.

The year we separated Richard had six holidays and the twins and I had three days bed and breakfast in Cornwall. I was not complaining. Every time I turned the key in my front door I opened it to a friendly reception. The boys never presented the trials many parents go through with their adolescents. Their support was wholehearted. Together we tackled shortages and problems, and together we solved them. I am certainly not a feminist that denigrates men. I would rather be called egalitarian. I have respect and affection for the other half of humanity. I greatly enjoy men's company, which is different in quality to women's.

The husband I chose second time around was cheerful and outgoing, and fully attuned to the feminist argument, so it was some time before I realized that, although egalitarian, when his own interests were under pressure he became assertive. He used to say 'all relationships are a power struggle', whereas for me a partnership is an attempt at cooperation. Despite a dozen largely enjoyable years with Bill, there were elements of relief when that marriage ended too in divorce.

Although I believe that marriage to a loving and cooperative companion is the ideal, I don't know many relationships I envy. I was married for 36 years, of which I would count twenty years as happy. Despite my pleasure in many positive aspects of being married, and aspirations to be a good wife, I share responsibility for the failure of two marriages. I should have been more assertive from the start.

I miss having a partner, I'm not a natural loner, but I relish the tranquillity and the autonomy of living alone. It's a high price to pay, but worth it.

60 GOOD VIBRATIONS

I wrote this in 2005: Two nights ago I had a strange and wonderful experience. I had woken at two in the morning and couldn't sleep, with a deep sense of unease. There are many changes going on in my life at present, which I endeavour to control but which need decisions. I'm also concerned about health problems which are minor at present but could escalate. At two in the morning one is at one's lowest ebb.

I read, to calm my mind. Eventually I felt ready to attempt sleep again. I glanced at the clock and it was about 3.30. As I composed myself to sleep I sighed and said aloud,' Oh Mum, Oh Mum.' My Mother died ten years ago and since she had dementia in her later years I had not seen her as a source of comfort for a very long time. Before she was ill she was a wonderful mother.

Sleep felt accessible and I was comfortable. Suddenly my whole body seemed to have a gentle weight resting on it, vibrating, as if I was being massaged all at once. It was the most wonderful sensation, a soft pummelling, unique in my experience. There was no sound, just this physical touching and reassurance. I thought, Oh this is wonderful. I was not frightened in any way. I felt it for my Mother's touch. Am I asleep or awake? I opened my eyes to verify that I was awake and saw the soft light from the bathroom nightlight illuminating the rectangle of the open door. I closed my eyes and luxuriated again in the physical touch, quite firm, pulsating all over. Then I fell asleep and awoke refreshed about 8.15. At first I was convinced it was a real experience; then as the day wore on I wondered if it could have been a dream. Yet the sense of reassurance was real. Perhaps it doesn't matter if it was just a dream: I felt connected with my Mother for the first time since she died. Her death was such a relief; I had lost her years before to dementia and welcomed her demise as a release from mental turmoil. Now I feel she is there and she is herself again. And she is still caring for me.

The implications are mind blowing.

61 SLOPPY VOCABULARY

When I first came to America it seemed that everything was either awesome or cool, unless of course it was gross. 'Awesome' to me suggests standing in a cathedral at the moment when sunlight hits the stained glass and the organist plays crescendo. In American 'awesome' can describe a chocolate cake, new curtains, a trip to Las Vegas or the view from space.

I cannot stretch my imagination to call an untidy room 'gross'. Gross to me is eating live maggots, or cleaning up someone else's vomit.

'Cool' is even more perplexing. I gather it means anything the speaker approves of, while giving no clue to its merits: amusing, handsome, useful, original, endearing, laid back, memorable or what? I asked my grandson what it meant and the unsatisfactory reply was 'It means something is hot.' I rest my case.

Some years ago a woman in Wales was telling a group of us about the clothes line she asked her husband to put up in the in garden. He made such heavy weather of this task, that although she assembled the post and the line, 'he didn't do it for yonks', she said in disgust. Oh dear. How long is yonks? Did she mean days or weeks or months or even seasons? Without judging the delay I cannot calculate the measure of her chagrin. Now I'll never know the answer.

How can we measure if we do not have reference points? A fellow mature student at university had a six year old son. She was fey in a way that disturbed me. Her son asked her, 'How old am I, Mummy?' and she answered 'Six'. 'How old are you, Mummy?' 'Seven.' She smiled at the recollection. I was concerned. 'How will he calculate things if you give him wrong information?' I asked. 'What?' 'If he thinks the difference between you is only one year, how will he calculate time?' She thought I was ridiculous. I thought she was making her son's life more difficult than she should. When I was thirty my four year old son said, You must remember, Mummy, you are old. He's forty eight now and I am really old, but not *that* old. Not so old that I can't still do somersaults in my mind. I remember doing handstands, cartwheels, back-bends and high jumps. The only thing stopping me now is my body.

SLOPPY VOCABULARY

Words are meant to communicate and clarify our thoughts. When I was young 'sloppy' was a euphemism for 'making out.' 'Was he sloppy?' we'd ask about a boy, meaning 'Did he try to kiss you?' We knew exactly what 'sloppy' meant, which is more than one can say about cool. Or awesome.

62 WHERE ARE YOU GOING?

None of the boys had any idea of where they were going in terms of careers. I wanted them to find their own way, and advised them to think in general terms about what appealed to them. Do you prefer to work in an office, or outside? Do you take an interest in building, selling, administration, medicine, law? And so on. They shook their heads at every suggestion. I said 'You need to find something you enjoy doing, and someone who will pay you to do it.'

One's choice of job colours one's whole existence. My Father hated his work as a boiler inspector but it was something he was qualified for, and it was well paid and reliable during the thirties when so many people were out of work. My own lack of ambition had channelled me into secretarial roles. I wanted something better for the boys.

I urged them to keep their options open and pursue studies that would help them achieve their aims. When you are in your mid-teens and don't know what your aims are, that's a tough assignment. They all did well at school. They had good brains and they worked adequately to pass exams. None of them was particularly academic but they could get the grades they wanted when they applied themselves.

Andre thought he would like to be a vet. I think he would have made an outstanding vet because he's so attuned to animals, but I knew that he would need four 'A's at A level, no small achievement, and he would have to spend six years at university. All we had to live on was my meagre income. The maintenance from Richard stopped when they left school. It did not seem achievable.

I always thought Mark would make a good lawyer because he was thoughtful, weighed pros and cons carefully, and he worked at a slower pace because he spent so long deliberating. He seemed to me naturally attuned to the law. But he really wanted to be an actor.

Patrick was keenly interested in his computer. Richard had bought him an Amstrad at age fourteen because he was so keen to develop this interest. The twins were the last class to receive no computer training at school. Today children learn to use the computer from the beginning of primary school. Jake (now 5) could play games on screen before he could speak. Pat spent the whole of his summer holidays engrossed in the computer, learning its capacities, producing drawings without specialised software. While studying Art at Hills Road Sixth Form College he produced the first computer generated pictures to be entered in an art exam. He drew an old boot, and a bicycle with all its spokes. His aim was to go to Art school. He wanted to make cartoon movies. (I enrolled him and Mark in a weekend course on film making.) However, during his first year at Hills Road he won the Business prize (he was also taking Business Studies) and his interest in business was kindled. One of the girls in his year had a father who urged her to go to UMIST (University of Manchester Institute of Science and Technology) to study Management Science. Patrick decided that was his choice too. He was so determined on this course, when I asked him 'What will you do if you don't get good enough grades to go to UMIST?' he answered 'I'll repeat the year until I do.' He passed first time

John Paul started a four year Business course at Leicester Polytechnic but dropped out after his first year, saying he was fed up with studying, he wanted to get on and 'do it'. He always had a drive to be active and engaged. As far as he was concerned, he'd had enough of formal education.

Peter had dropped out of school the Christmas before his 'A' levels. He was studying Geology and two other subjects. I could imagine him as a Geologist as he was always interested in the subject, thanks to Richard's enthusiasm for the study of rocks. But instead he became a chef, a builder, fork lift truck driver, double glazed windows installer, etc., a versatile and energetic worker. His range of skills and tools is impressive. He plumbed in the central heating in my Girton extension. He rebuilt the conservatory roof on my house in Earith, and decorated inside. He has always had plenty of interests to occupy him. He taught himself computer programming from a manual. He's a keen beekeeper, gardener, fisherman and now historian as he develops his interest in metal detecting which has led him to discover a Roman site near home in Cambridgeshire. Peter is a happy man.

I was gratified to have three sons in Hills Road Sixth Form College at the same time. There were teachers there who couldn't get their own children into the school, which was by competition. But during his first term, while I was in Spain on business, Andre quit school and found himself a job in a flour mill laboratory. He wanted to contribute to the household income, but the reality was that I lost the maintenance Richard paid for him, so we were no better off.

After a while he changed jobs to become a trainee at Lloyds Bank. He worked there for some years but was disappointed at the quality of training they gave him. He was not making progress or earning much money. Their training scheme was a sham.

Meanwhile, at twenty he had formed a friendship with a colleague in the bank, Julia, and together they bought a small modern one bedroom terrace house. But later, having seen his brothers graduate, he decided he wanted to go to college. He got a place at Writtle College to study Rural Resource Management, extending this to a degree in Agriculture. He thoroughly enjoyed this phase of his life and won the nationwide Student of the Year competition for all Land Based Industries, through his thesis on the breeding of Canaries.

When the boys graduated I was looking for job opportunities in the quality press. I think it was in the *Independent* or the *Guardian* that I saw an advert for sales in legal software. Mark took up software sales which gave him an immediate and generous salary with commission, enabling him to buy an apartment in west London. But after a couple of years he yearned to take up acting and succeeded in getting a place to do Drama at LAMDA (London Academy of Music and Drama). He loved this course and had high hopes of becoming an actor. He found that there were around ninety applicants for every audition, and although he acted in some fringe productions, he couldn't live on the income. He sold his apartment which funded him for a couple of years, but eventually he was forced by economics and the fact that he now wanted to get married, to go back to selling legal software. This was certainly lucrative and he and Sarah bought an apartment in London, and then a terrace house in Cambridge, from which he commuted.

Sarah had announced as soon as they got engaged that their plan was to have a baby in England, and then emigrate to Australia. In Australia Mark would finish his solicitors' finals and also be called to the Bar, so he achieved his goals and opened his own law office.

When Andre graduated with a degree in Agriculture, I looked again for job opportunities in the national press. I spotted one for a trainee manager in a turkey farm in Norfolk. Andre landed the job at Bernard Matthews, Europe's largest turkey production enterprise, and became the youngest poultry production manager ever in that huge operation, responsible for millions of turkeys per annum.

While on a trip to Canada for Rupert's wedding, Andre met Deanna, an American nurse from New Jersey, staying at the same hotel, who eventually became his wife.

Patrick had told me when he was about eight that he planned to grow grapefruit (he was picking seeds out of fruit at the time), establish a plantation, and sell the fruit at the gate. He was about ten when he announced his intention to make a million by the time he was thirty and retire to build a log cabin in Canada.

With his degree in Management Science Patrick found himself a job in a software company. He worked in Ealing and lived in my house in Queen Anne's Gardens. Kate rented a room there and they were naturally drawn together, one of those fortuitous connections that few of us experience. He was the first to emigrate when Pat and Kate moved to Dublin. I wept when I left them there after my first visit with Bill. Little did I realize that Dublin was but a skip and a jump from Ealing (I could take the tube to Heathrow and a bus from Dublin airport to the end of their road), and that I'd be grateful for that in future, when his three brothers changed continents.

John Paul was spreading his wings and off to the States at every opportunity. When he married Sarah they seemed to be settled in England. In Holt he told me they thought they would live in that house for the next twenty years or so. But he rang me one night to tell me that they would shortly leave for America to live in Phoenix, and that by the way, Sarah was four months pregnant with their third baby. My heart sank yet again at the prospect of losing my grandchildren to emigration. I visited them at Andre's house where they stayed just prior to their departure, and taking Ben and Leah for a walk with Leah in her buggy, Ben and I stopped to sketch leaves we saw on our walk, making a connection that wrenched my heart more than I can express. He was four and I fell in love with him right there and then. I had seen little of them while I was busy in France. After their departure I was bereft and tearful for days. Bill thought my reaction exaggerated. I thought it entirely in proportion to my sense of loss.

Shortly thereafter I spoke to Ben on the telephone. He said, 'Granny, could you come and visit with us this weekend?' I said 'Oh Ben, it is a long way. It's far across the sea. It's impossible.' Then Ben said, 'What's the name of the grandpa at your house?' and I said 'Bill.' 'Well, tell Bill to drive you round in the car.' We had a great visit in 2001 when Charlie was a year old.

In 2003 Mark and Sarah emigrated to Australia with Harvey (going east) and Andre and Deanna left for America with Connor (going west) within two weeks of each other. Now all my grandchildren lived abroad. Later I would realize that not one of them would have an English accent.

My marriage to Bill and idyllic sojourn in France ended at the end of 2002. I could not know then that the Dight Diaspora would lead me on to yet further adventures.

63 AUSTRALIA TRIP 2006

1. I'm in Hawaii

I'm on my way to Australia to visit my son and his family whom I haven't seen since they emigrated three years ago. I dread the journey but I have never seen their daughter who will be two next month, and their invitations have becoming pressing. I'm nervous, mindful of the threat of deep vein thrombosis, and because I routinely pick up a bug from the recycled air on long flights.

I'm sitting in a hotel bedroom in Hawaii, breaking the journey, and the forecast is: rain. On the weather channel the Hawaiian Islands are a string of modest specks surrounded by uninterrupted Pacific Ocean unto all horizons. It makes Aberystwyth in west Wales look like the cultural capital of Europe.

I wait outside the hotel for a bus to take me to Waikiki. This is the holiday spot in Honolulu, Oahu, famous for its magnificent beach and high rise buildings. I didn't know that last week. A man at the bus stop asks, 'Where are you from?' 'England.' (I can't explain about Virginia.) He has Polynesian features. 'What are you doing here?' 'I'm going to see my son in Australia' I answer, as simply as possible. He embarks on a rambling account of a film he saw on TV about 'an event in Australia' where some tourists camping under trees met attackers who cut their hands off 'and only one survived.' 'Stop it' I say, 'you'll make me sorry I left home.' I ask if there are any problems with violence here? He says 'Only problem is, people steal from you. You don't even know it is happening.' I manage not to check my body purse hidden inside my shirt. He says 'Here is the bus. You need $2, they don't give change.' 'Oh dear' I said, 'I haven't got change (looking in my wallet). 'I can change money for you' he says with alacrity. 'No thanks, I'll go back to the hotel for change' and I move away just as the bus stops. When I look back he is still sitting there and the bus has moved on.

I get change from the receptionist, explaining about the scruffy local. How much is a taxi? $35. Perhaps I couldn't trust a taxi driver either, who might spot a vulnerable old doll at twenty paces. The receptionist advises me to take the hotel shuttle to their sister hotel down the road, the Plaza, and take the bus from there. At that bus stop a man is sleeping on the bench. I keep my distance until the bus arrives.

To my dismay the original scruff is already on this bus. Where has he been for the 40 minutes that elapsed since our encounter? Was he waiting for me? I studiously avoid eye contact, like a London underground passenger.

A few stops down the road a slim, well-dressed woman gets on the bus shouting 'Fuck you! I fuck all of you!' to no one in particular. The bus driver warns her to be quiet on his bus, and for the most part she is, occasionally muttering at people and asking them to take her hand, which they decline in silence. Suddenly she moves to sit next to me. I grip my purse tighter and sit perched on the edge of my seat. The mentally ill woman gets up at the next stop, then sits down again opposite, staring at me. I begin to wonder if I am paranoid. I am mighty relieved when she and the scruff get off at Chinatown, which markets look inviting, but I have been warned about Chinatown by the hotel staff.

Another woman strikes up conversation on the bus. She is on her way to a dancing exercise class. She is 86! She tells me about the ethnic groups on the island and diverse languages (she is of Japanese descent and speaks Hawaiian), 'but everyone speaks American.' I ask her, 'Do you ever feel isolated from the rest of the world?' 'Oh goodness no,' laughing. She says she has travelled a lot and is always glad to come home, born and bred here. I enjoy this encounter and she wishes me a happy holiday.

I get off at Waikiki Beach and start to walk along the strand. It is beautiful. The sea is deep blue with gentle white surf, the elegant front is lined with trees in bloom and mature palms. I walk into a hotel to use their rest room and request a tariff. I'm looking for a better hotel to stay in on my return trip. The tariff is $260 per night. I'm paying $170 a night at the Airport Hotel which is scruffy and neglected with dirty walls, grubby carpets, cheap wrinkled wall paper and no restaurant. I will feel like a loser if I go there again.

In a smart china shop I get into conversation with the owner who recommends a restaurant nearby where I can find salad and fresh fish, my fancy for lunch today. He directs me to Duke's Canoe Club which is on the beach. It's elegant and full of happy diners. I try a delicious baked local fish called Opah, with a Caesar salad. The fish has only just finished swimming. With a Budweiser beer it's the perfect lunch. We are beside the white sandy beach with blue Pacific backdrop. The rain they forecast on TV has not materialized. It's 88 degrees with a welcome ocean breeze and clear blue sky. Surrounded by affluent young families enjoying their lunch, the paranoia on the bus disappears.

'Aloha' means 'love' and is not as I supposed an anagram of 'haloa'. Tomorrow I have a ten hour flight to Sydney, followed by two hours to Brisbane.

2. Gold Coast

I miss the connection at Sydney. Our plane was an hour late leaving Hawaii. Later I find that this was the day a plot was revealed in London to take bombs simultaneously onto several international flights. Mark has been waiting for me at Brisbane for two and a half hours when I arrive.

Next day I discover that I have arrived at a difficult time. Everybody has difficult phases in their lives and the timing of my visit is not good. There is physical chaos because four men are digging up the garden to replace a pebbled area with lawn, and a line of dark trees is giving way to graceful palms, thus opening the garden to sunlight and the vista to our view. This is a great improvement to the property. The landscaping is provided by Mark's next door neighbour, in a fit of gratitude to Mark for a favour. 'I'll do it at cost,' he had offered, but as the work progressed the costs escalated and suddenly there is a bill for $6,000. They do not have six thousand dollars, but luckily I do, and I lend it to them by credit card transfer.

We are in economic chaos because my son has just qualified as a barrister, and the process has denied them two months' salary while he does exams. His wife has had the strain of buying groceries without funds. He is exhausted from the exams he completed the day before. His status is now 'self- employed' which means that until he gets clients, he will earn nothing. His wife is working as a nurse, not easy with two young children. Sarah has lost her sense of security. They are tired and stretched to the limit of their endurance. Their son, aged four, is picking up every negative vibe in his stress. His small sister has a runny nose and fever which lands her in hospital the first weekend with 40 degrees temperature instead of 36. She has had convulsions before with an erratic body thermostat.

On the other hand they are living in a four bedroom detached bungalow with swimming pool in the choice suburb of Ashmore. As a defence lawyer Mark had a salary and the firm enjoyed the profits. Mark is in the process of improving his earning power. Once established his daily rate will be cheering, but at present, he is not established.

He sees the bigger picture. Although there will be rent to pay for his chambers whether he has clients or not, he knows he can re-mortgage their house (and proceeds to do so) to keep them going. I empathize with my daughter-in-law's stress. I comfort her as best I can, and try to sooth my grandson's unease. The only serene one is my granddaughter, nearly two and talking fluently, but still coughing.

I give up on my plan to fly to Perth to visit my much loved cousin Wendy, because the flight money would be better spent on groceries. Mark goes to work in Brisbane each day in pursuit of commissions. Sarah goes to work four days a week as a nurse in the hospital. The children go to Kindergarten from 7.30 till 3.30, except when they are ill. I spend a day with Harvey throwing up when he is brought home from Kindergarten with sickness and diarrhoea. This goes through the whole family except, happily, for me.

Without transport I can only go out alone by taxi. But I like cooking for a family and my daughter in law enjoys a break. In an effort to save electricity on the dryer, I drape the washing on a clothes horse, a ladder and various chairs in the sunshine, because the old washing line was thrown out when the garden was remodelled. The kitchen tap that had to be turned off with a wrench each time we used it, is finally replaced by a plumber who earns more than a lawyer. Sighs of relief all round, but the oven still does not work. Luckily we have a cast iron pot from France, which provides a series of pot-roasts that cheer. Soon after my visit they will have a new kitchen installed.

At this point I send off an email to a friend about the joys of Australia, with full credit to Bill Bryson's excellent book, *Down Under*. How grateful I am to him! Australia is obviously a fascinating country if you have time to explore it. She e-mails back: 'I enjoyed this account but would like to hear more of your impressions.'

From Bryson's book I learn that the population of Australia is 19 million. Its place in the world economy is equivalent to the state of Illinois, yet it is the world's sixth largest country. I am astonished to realize that Australia is similar in size to the United States of America. It's the home of vast natural wonders, like the Great Barrier Reef and Ayres Rock. It has more animals that will kill you than anywhere else on earth. The world's ten most poisonous snakes are Australian. Its funnel-web spider, box jellyfish, blue-ringed octopus, stonefish and paralysis tick, are the most lethal of their type in the world. If you are not stung or gored in some unexpected fashion you may be eaten by sharks or crocodiles, or sucked out to sea by irresistible currents. Most of Australia's wildlife is unique. Eighty per cent of all that lives in Australia exists nowhere else.

Bryson tells us there were Aboriginals in Australia (who probably arrived by raft from Indonesia around 60,000 years ago) before there were humans in America or Europe. Yet Captain Cook didn't discover Australia until 1770. When his men first encountered Aboriginals they were astonished to find that they could tie shoe laces European style, so it is possible these explorers were preceded.

To run out of petrol in the vast arid outback can be fatal. Australia's seasons are back to front, its constellations upside down – I saw a U shaped crescent moon for the first time.

Just before you arrive in Australia you lose a day. It's Wednesday instead of Tuesday, but fortunately you get it back on the way home. You can arrive in Los Angeles before you left Sydney, time wise. For us in America, it is always tomorrow in Australia.

Bryson relates anecdotes that illustrate the Australian culture. He tells of an American tourist at a rural Queensland hotel in the 1950s who was served a plate of cold meat and potatoes. He stared with disappointment for a moment, and asked whether he might have a little salad with it? The waitress looked at him with astonishment and disdain, and turning to the other guests, remarked 'The bastard thinks it's Christmas.' Now there is something endearing to me about a culture which speaks its mind so frankly and in language familiar to a Brit.

After the war Australia sought European immigrants to boost its meagre population. They brought with them the tradition of good food, olives, wine and culture. Today there are excellent restaurants with inviting menus that set the world a fine example, and the standard of coffee everywhere rivals the world's best anywhere.

I heartily recommend anyone visiting Australia to read Bill Bryson's book.

I'm a people watcher, and what I see around me is a great many British faces. The Brits are not the world's handsomest people, and neither are Australians. The majority have little sense of style when it comes to clothes. It must be purgatory for Italians. The people I watch in Brisbane where Mark takes me for the day while he's working look as if they have dressed in old clothes pulled from the back of a dusty cupboard, hoarded in the hope that fashions would come round again. Perhaps they have, and I'm old enough to have seen them the first time. Although it's officially winter on the Gold Coast, the temperature is in the seventies and everyone is dressed for summer. The city of Brisbane is handsome, with broad-walks on the banks of a wide river, the trees and plants are beautiful, the shops and restaurants inviting.

We enjoy days out as a family (a day in the rainforest 40 miles away and a trip to Byron Bay with magnificent views from the lighthouse). We see wallabies and bush turkeys in the wild. We enjoy several meals in restaurants and the children are so good. Sarah reads them the menu and they make their choices thoughtfully. We go out for breakfast on the Gold Coast, which is all high rise buildings and a magnificent white beach that stretches as far as you can see to north and south, along Australia's east coast.

Mark takes me to the top of the tallest building on the Gold Coast, a spectacular viewing platform on 73rd floor, taller than the Empire State building. From there we can see miles of Queensland's sandy beaches and New South Wales. Sarah and I take the children to 'Dreamworld', a concoction of TV characters (Dora, The Wiggles) and exciting rides with a lot of animals on show. Sarah impresses me by taking the scariest rides, hanging upside down on one ride, plunging a hundred feet on another - as scary as a parachute jump - she loves them! The climate is lovely (in September it's almost spring), the air the cleanest you can find, thanks to the purifying Pacific Ocean. I see flowers and shrubs in vibrant bloom, beautiful trees, exotic birds too numerous to count - it's like living in an aviary. From their back garden I see lorikeets, kookaburras, herons, ibis and pelicans. The birdsong sounds like that in a rain forest.

Australia is wonderful.

3. Sydney

To begin with I feel my presence is helpful. After three weeks I decide to visit Sydney for five days, to get back into my own head. I fly to Sydney with four nights booked in a central hotel. I don't know a soul, but Sydney is exciting, full of glittering buildings, botanical gardens and other attractions. My visit to the tourist office the first evening proposes art galleries, museums, the harbour, Opera House, ferries and restaurants galore. I spend four full days visiting as many of these as I can. I ride the monorail. The setting of Sydney Harbour is breath-taking. It's not one harbour, but many. The Opera House was built on the site of an old fort, a stunning location. Its sail-like roofs are visible from every direction, apparently floating on the ocean. The project was designed to impress and delight the world, and it works. I take the tour around the concert hall and the opera stage, but sadly, tickets for performances are all sold out.

I take a ferry up river for ten miles or so, then back to Circular Quay. I visit Darling Harbour, a pedestrianized zone full of beautiful restaurants, exhibitions and a conference centre. I tour three art galleries, two museums, the Aquarium, the Imax cinema and the Rocks area which was first developed in nineteenth century. Its old buildings have been restored as charming shops and galleries. The Queen Victoria building in Sydney's centre was restored in the 1980's, with elaborate and colourful period detail, housing boutiques like Dolce & Gabbana, Prada, Louis Vuitton: the sort of shops that Princess Diana and her friends frequented. I don't go in: I peer through the glass, humbly, and entirely without envy. I see so much, the only thing that stops me seeing more is my aching joints from so much walking. I pick up my email in internet cafes and joyfully dispatch messages of praise for Sydney.

On my last day in Sydney it rains: the wettest September day for 123 years. I can pick 'em. In the rain I take taxis instead of buses to the art galleries.

4. The grandchildren

Imogen turned two while I was there. She is a sweet child. Her smile of pure goodness melts my heart. She has a loving and undemanding nature. She's also extremely bright and articulate enough for a four year old. She speaks in grammatically correct sentences. She's cooperative and kind to her brother, the cat and her parents.

Harvey is four. He's bright too and articulate. He's dramatic. When he loses his toy car (he has a couple of dozen) he laments, 'I'll never see it again!' but he finds it next day, under the car seat. He's tremendous fun to play with. And he loves stories.

These two delightful children astonish me with their personalities, intelligence, humour and imagination. I'm proud to be their Granny Eileen. Imogen finds 'Granny Eileen' a mouthful, so she dubs me 'Green', the nicest nickname I've ever had. 'Green, Green, tell us a story,' and they both sit and listen intently.

I've never had a better audience. We start with 'Jack and the Beanstalk', the fairy story I remember best. When we get to where the giant approaches the castle kitchen, stomp, stomp, stomp, and Jack is hiding in the oven, then in the pantry, then under the table, and the giant booms 'Fee, Fi, Fo, Fum, I smell the blood of an Englishman,' Harvey's eyes are about to pop. (I now know how Laurence Olivier felt before audiences at the National Theatre. It's heady stuff.) 'Tell us another story, Granny Eileen,' he says, until I have told him all the stories I know. I'm not good at thinking up stories, although with practice I later learn that putting a character into everyday situations is a good starting point: 'Chicken Licken learns to drive,' for example. Harvey and Imogen sit in front of me on the stool where I rest my legs. I have a camera on my lap and take snaps of their sweet faces. A listening child is nourishing. Two listening children are a feast.

They want to act out the story. Harvey is the giant and Imogen is Jack; he stomps and she squeals, as they run back to my seat. Then they are both Jack, climbing the beanstalk, eyes wide with anticipation at what they'll find at the top. The kindly maid welcomes Jack each time, feeding him a portion of dinner on a plate. Later the giant will sit and eat the whole pig, and buckets of roasted vegetables with it. Jack returns home three nights running, forgetting to take his mother food, who is predictably put out. In fact she's starving. But at last Jack tumbles down the beanstalk with the giant climbing clumsily down behind him. Jack seizes the axe and chops the stalk and the giant falls down ...*dead*. Oh, those beautiful children, eyes fixed on mine. I have never enjoyed myself so much with a fairy tale, and I've told a few in my time.

Next, Harvey teaches me for the first time in my life (I'm ashamed to admit it after raising five boys), How to Play with Cars. Every boy knows this but I'm a girl, and never before grasped what fun you can have with a couple of dinky cars. Harvey has loads of them and is deeply attached to each one. I think his favourite was a battered red truck. He has seen the movie 'Cars' and he's wild about Lightning McQueen, the red racer.

On the dining table I have a blue sedan and Harvey has his red truck. We're going camping. We push our cars around the table and enact pitching our tents beside the river, beneath the trees. 'I've brought the frying pan,' I tell Harvey, 'and the sausages. Did you bring the matches?' 'Yes!'... 'Oh, that's good. Let's build our camp fire here. We need big stones to support the pan so it doesn't fall in the fire.' Our fingers arrange everything.

The sausages and eggs taste delicious in the fresh air. We fry sliced bread too – imaginary food is in no way fattening. Harvey and I have a great time. We realize we've forgotten to pack some things, so we improvise. You can improvise anything under the sun, with imagination.

Months before I had made them pillowcases (Harvey's has dinosaurs appliquéd on it, and Imogen has a log cabin patchwork in vibrant pinks and blues) and I see them lying on the floor to watch their favourite videos, like Cinderella. They are Dora the Explorer fans too. Every night Harvey listens to a talking book of fairy stories as he goes to sleep.

Imogen sleeps in her cot and Sarah pats her shoulder gently until she goes to sleep. They are adorable and I'm so happy to know them. It's a terrible wrench to leave them, knowing I might not see them again for years. (It will be nearly five.)

5. Journey home

During my last week in Australia I catch Imogen's persistent cold. By the time I get to Hawaii (after a 5 hour stopover in Fiji's cheerless transit lounge with nothing to eat or drink and a second overnight flight of nearly seven hours), I am ready to die.

I go to bed for the entire two days and one night I am in Hawaii. This time I'm in a good 4 star hotel in central Waikiki, but the only thing of interest to me is a supermarket in the block where I buy yoghurt and fruit salad to eat in my room. I cough. And cough. I feel profoundly sorry for the passengers sitting next to me on the flights; I hate sitting next to passengers like me.

In Phoenix I pause to spend five enjoyable days with my three extrovert American grandchildren, but I'm still feeling ill. Eventually I arrive home in Virginia, seriously jet-lagged, despite two stopovers. The next day I visit the doctor, who sends me for a chest X-ray. 'Is that really necessary?' I ask. 'It is,' he said, 'You may have walking pneumonia.' In the event, I haven't, but I still feel lousy. It takes two courses of antibiotics over six weeks before I stop coughing. My muscles are sore in every rib.

Australia was an unforgettable delight and being with my family after a long break, like a thirsty traveller visiting an oasis, but I was 43 hours in flight and spent thousands of dollars. It was so exhausting. I don't think I could do it again. I would not have missed it for the world. But if anyone else says, 'How lucky you are, having sons who live in such exotic holiday spots,' I shall spit.

64 MARIA'S DAY IN COURT

I taught English for two years to a Columbian woman in her forties, through the Literacy Council in Harrisonburg, which matches volunteer tutors and pupils. Maria had been in the States four years, but working with Spanish immigrants in a factory, she had small opportunity to learn English. She had been a competent office manager in an architectural firm in Bogota, but here she was working twelve hour shifts overnight, packing plastic bottles into boxes. Her lack of English was holding her back.

One day Maria was approached by a policeman who was following her on her way to work over the railway crossing. She was driving slowly, and recognizing a police car with flashing light behind her, supposed that he wanted to pass in a hurry, so pulled over. He stopped behind her, checked her licence, asked where she was going, where she worked, what hours and so on. She asked him four times why he was questioning her, before he said 'You were doing 54 miles an hour in a 25 mph zone.' She denied this fiercely, but he handed her a yellow slip with a fine to pay. He advised her to pay up without going to court. Maria is about 4ft 10, slight and feminine. However, she has a feisty spirit and was outraged by the unjust fine.

I emailed my lawyer son. I said she was definitely not speeding. The policeman was lying and she was going to challenge it in court. Did he have any advice for her?

He said that unless she engaged a lawyer, she hadn't a chance of winning the case; it was her word against a policeman, and the world is full of corrupt policemen. He said it would be cheaper to pay the fine. Maria's husband agreed (the same thing had happened to him, and he capitulated) but she decided to fight.

I turned up at the court where Maria and her husband were waiting to be summoned. I said 'Ask them if you can have an interpreter, and tell them you've brought your own.' I was invited from the back of the court to join them at the bench.

Maria and I had prepared one sheet of a statement in large font so the judge could skim it quickly, stating that she was on her way to work, a journey she takes daily, on a street near home, with plenty of time to get there, when the policeman stopped and questioned her about her immigrant status, before giving her a speeding ticket which she refuted. The judge ran his eye down the sheet and then consulted the policeman, who repeated his testimony. To Maria he said 'Do you plead guilty or not guilty?' Searching for the world *'culpable'* (only remembering it seconds later) I said in Spanish, 'Did you do it or not?' and she said vehemently, 'No!' To the judge I reiterated the points we had placed before him. He turned to us and said, 'Case dismissed.' Maria's husband and I led her away from the bench without a word. Only when we got outside did she realize she had won a dismissal.

My opinion of American justice went up a notch.

There is a sequel to Maria's story. When a friend was looking for an office receptionist four years ago I mentioned Maria. I said, 'Her English is patchy but she's smart and understands a lot. She's educated, competent and hard working. She ran an office in Bogota, did the accounts, booked the architects' travel tickets, organized the filing system, and generally kept them happy for twelve years before coming to the States. She's a warm, positive woman and I trust her.'

My friend came to meet Maria casually at our next English lesson in my house, and offered her a month's trial. Maria blossomed in her employ, worked willingly and took every opportunity to demonstrate her commitment. I stopped teaching Maria as soon as she was in an English speaking environment and she has taken off, like a bird tossed into the wind flaps its wings and soars.

65 POLITICAL PERSPECTIVE

Here's my routine: get up, put on bathrobe and slippers, switch on computer and start a pot of Columbian coffee. While it's brewing I check who's emailing me. The *Telegraph* informs me of the global situation. The BBC sends me breaking news. I like to check nothing awful has happened overnight.

This morning something awful has happened. Benazir Bhutto has been assassinated in Pakistan. I remember clearly when her father was hanged by the administration on controversial charges, almost thirty years ago. We were appalled in anticipation and in retrospect. The name Bhutto is synonymous with democracy. Even though Benazir had been accused of corruption, which may or may not be true, she was Pakistan's best hope of a democratic government. It's a sad day indeed: sad for Pakistan, sad for the world, and especially so for her children and husband.

I reflect that for all the political passions I've witnessed in a lifetime, I was seldom at risk, and my admiration for people who put their lives in danger for the sake of politics is immense. The nearest I've been to political uproar was the protest in Whitehall against the Suez invasion when I was 19. I stood still with my back to a government building, while the crowd's passions vented alarmingly.

I firmly believe in peaceful demonstration, but Tony Blair ignored a million marchers in London urging him to stay out of the war in Iraq.

I've sat at the table in a Madrid restaurant where two politicians were shot to death while dining the previous year, by Basque separatists from ETA. A few years after the event, all that lingers is the story: except of course, for those victims' families. Their loss of life had no impact whatever on the political situation.

In Central London during the dark days of the IRA who never gave sufficient time or accurate information before exploding bombs to express their grievances, I've waited for trains in trepidation. It was like Russian roulette, living in London then. One of the last London bombs, in Ealing, exploded in a shopping centre in the nineties, destroying buildings a mile from my home.

For thirty years we watched as bombing campaigns came and went while Catholic Irish terrorists battled Protestant bigots. People relaxing in restaurants with their friends had their legs blown off by exploding parcel bombs. Children watching the Remembrance Day service in Omagh became instant objects of remembrance to their devastated parents. Two off-duty British soldiers taking a wrong turning in their car found themselves at an IRA funeral, and were butchered on the spot. Litter bins were removed from London streets, too hazardous to use, potential bomb depositories. It went on and on. We watched in disbelief the financial and moral support the IRA gathered in America, spent largely on munitions. Thousands on both sides of the conflict suffered as their loved ones died in front of them, often on their doorstep. It was impossible to understand the logic.

America woke up to the reality on 9/11.

While Hitler's Fascism churned up Europe, then the world, with its vicious determination to dominate and exploit humanity, I walked to infant school in suburban London through an air raid, running the last few hundred yards before the bombs started dropping. For six years we lived with strictly-imposed blackout. I saw the first unmanned rocket with its tail ablaze, flying over my village. Nightly we lay under the steel shelter in our living room, listening to overhead planes and exploding bombs.

But we in Britain were the lucky ones, once removed from the havoc, over-flown but never occupied, unlike millions of Europeans who became unwilling refugees. After the war, eight million people were forcibly redistributed in central Europe as boundaries were redrawn. There are refugee camps to this day in Palestine, inhabited by people who were born there. Political bitterness prevents them choosing another way of life.

Man's inhumanity to man flourishes, seemingly unchecked.

How fortunate I felt this morning that my brushes with politics have been so slight. Kneading dough to make a loaf, I felt peaceful and protected. As far as I knew, at that moment, all my family were safe and well, far from the ravages inflicted on people like the Bhutto family. But such violence diminishes all of us. This is a sad day indeed.

66 WORLD VIEW

Looking after small children is like taking up *petit point* embroidery or microsurgery, or pinpoint observation by satellite: one's attention is focused on a very small world, rich in detail and delight.

Caring for my two small grandchildren this week I felt this shift in perspective. Feeding and changing a month old baby requires intense attention to his comfort and safety. Watching Jake's face as he feeds, I see many expressions fleet over it. I watch for signs of discomfort, and change his position. I notice his eyes watching me, his breathing, swallowing, squirming. His need to expel wind finds me burping in sympathy. He has neat features and gazes intensely as I talk to him: 'He's a beautiful boy and his Granny loves him,' I say, paraphrasing my eulogies to my sons, engaging his full attention. I swear he smiled at me yesterday.

His brother Connor (3 next month) is good at imaginary games. Friends sent a large envelope with an outfit for the baby. I picked up the empty envelope and said to Connor, Shall we see if there are any more presents? I put in my hand and pulled out an imaginary present, put it on my palm, closed it over and said 'Open it'. He opened it with alacrity and we both gasped at the beautiful present. Then we discussed who it was for, and what it was, and this went on for some time. Everybody got presents. He opened his palms just like I did and looked amazed every time. Then I said 'Would you like to go fishing?' (I sat with babe in my lap, burping him). Connor nodded and I said 'Here is a rod for you, and here is one for Granny.' I cast it over the water. He did the same. I lifted my wrist a couple of times, but Connor reeled in with his right hand as he held the rod with his left, round and round, as he must have watched his father doing months ago. We both caught fish. Then I gave him the keys of the car and invited him to drive. 'Careful!' I said, to start with, then 'Here is a straight road, you can go fast!' and he did, stopping at red traffic lights. He joins in all this with concentration and enjoyment and never says 'Oh, I want a real present'. He gets the idea immediately.

After some hours of this it is a kind of relief to zoom out again at my house, to the wider world: pick up a newspaper, turn on TV, watch the news where a crazy world is obsessed with the latest homicides, and threatening Iran.

At home I can put down a hot cup of coffee without fearing a spill, check my email, cook a meal and relax. It's a privilege as a grandparent, to switch between these two enjoyable worlds.

67 THE JUGGLER

Patrick sent me a video of Chris Bliss, juggler extraordinaire, juggling to a Beatles song, 'Once there was a way to get back homeward'. I hadn't heard it before. He started juggling conventionally with two hands, three balls, in an even pattern. Then he started to throw the balls at odd angles, asymmetrically. He threw first one ball underarm and behind his back, then two, constantly varying the rhythm and curve of his arcs in a routine of skill, speed and artistry that took my breath away. I was struck by the impossibility of what he was doing. He might be the only juggler in the world who can make these moves. Despite grey hair, his routine, smooth and sophisticated, was energetic and athletic. I marvelled at his brain patterns. He encompassed aerobic exercise as he worked. An ergonomic worker par excellence, his entire outlay in equipment was three balls; he carried his skills and income in his pocket. He needs no qualifications, no infrastructure: his intellectual property is inimitable artistry. But his investment in training must have taken years. John Paul told me later that he had seen this man live, doing a comedy routine and almost as an afterthought, he'd started to juggle. The audience expected to laugh at his ineptitude. Instead, his act ended in a standing ovation.

On the video as the Beatles' song changed pace, his moves became short, staccato and on the beat. Spontaneous applause rippled from his audience as his juggling evolved, becoming more complex and unbelievable, a crescendo rising to a roar. I recognized an emotion: felt tension rising in my body. I was moved, then tearful, then sobbing. I felt myself, in my thirties and forties, juggling priorities, children, husband, mother, chores, economics, strains, illness, aspirations, breakdowns, loss of trust, fear, rigid endeavour....afraid to let a ball drop, exerting myself physically and mentally to balance and sustain a large family of tender egos. In those days I saw myself often as a juggler or plate spinner, rushing to spin the slowest plate before it fell off the pole, keeping them all up, never daring to drop my vigilance. I was sobbing at the remembrance of it. I had forgotten the superhuman efforts I used to make to keep my family and its diverse interests in motion.

From the perspective of a tranquil life in retirement, having gradually over years relinquished responsibility and control to newly competent adults, the routine I had sustained, exemplified by the juggler, was *unbearable*. Out poured all the tensions I couldn't afford to express before. Then I had pictured myself as a pressure cooker with the 15 lb. valve in place on my head. I felt if I tried to let out the tensions, the valve would blow and I would explode, so I kept them in, lid on tight, at the expense of physical and mental turmoil.

No other work of art or artistry has evoked this response in me. This juggler seems superhuman. I am not. People often ask when I mention that my last three babies were born within sixteen months, However did you cope? I didn't always. I dropped some dreadful clangers. I ended up in hospital three times. Major disruption, a sense of failure....then gradual recovery, struggling to cope anew with the complicated routine, flexing muscles as the pace picked up again, endeavouring to get back in the swing.

Later Andre arrived and I showed him the video, without comment. Over his shoulder I watched the routine again, deeply moved. I managed to keep calm, but when he said 'Amazing!' I answered quietly 'Isn't it,' gulped and retreated to my room to calm my breathing and dry my eyes in private.

68 MY PERCEPTION OF TIME

During the Social Science classes I took in Cardiff in 1974-6, I was introduced to Studs Terkel's book Working. He interviewed dozens of people about their work, their lives and their philosophies; the book is subtitled 'The Autobiography of America'. He brought his subjects vividly to life on the page. I commend this book (and others by Studs Terkel) to anyone who is interested in people.

It occurred to me that people's attitude to Time and how they spend it, would also reveal much about their characters. I wrote an article in 1981, published in the National Housewives' Register Newsletter (circulation 25,000), inviting people to write about their experience of Time. This resulted in around 15 contributions. It was apparent from the variety of these answers that if I gathered them in sufficient number I could produce a book. Over the next thirty years I kept prompting people individually to contribute their thoughts on Time, but it was a slow business. Even those interested enough to promise a piece, seldom produced it.

In the nineties The Mass Observation Archives asked people to describe their attitude to Time: at last that seemed a good source of material. I went to Brighton with Bill one day to meet the curators of the collection, and to read some of the responses they had archived. I was fully engaged by the contributions, but not allowed to photocopy. Only written notes could be taken. I didn't have a laptop (then costing around a thousand pounds) and I didn't have several weeks (or even days) to devote to the research. I was helping Bill to run Ealing Tourist Flats at the time and it wasn't possible to fit in a prolonged stay in a hotel, even if I had a laptop.

One contribution in particular struck me forcibly: a young man with AIDS wrote poignantly about his truncated prospect of life.

With the advent of the internet it occurred to me in 2006 that I could speed up the process with a website. Perhaps by Christmas I'd have enough to fill a book, I thought. I put together a page of ideas which Patrick uploaded to the internet for me on www.perceptionoftime.com

I posed the question 'How do you view Time? If you have waited an hour for a bus, a day for forgiveness, a week for a biopsy result, months for a baby's birth, years for a divorce, decades for vindication, you know that time is relative. Of all calculations, it's perhaps the most flexible, its measure the most subjective.

'What is your attitude to filling and using time? Do you cram as much as possible into the day? Do you spend it luxuriously, at your own pace, without pressure? Are you able to change gear? Does your perspective differ as you get older? In your thirties do you suddenly realize that twenty years have gone by in a flash? Is time the reason you fear to turn forty? In your seventies do you hope for another decade? How does it strike you at ninety?'

John Paul suggested the title 'Perception of Time'. It was a good choice. But several Christmases came and went. I've received around twenty contributions in the past five years. Getting people to write has been like pulling teeth. Studs Terkel was a remarkable interviewer who travelled around the country seeking material for his books, armed with a tape recorder and a publisher's commission. I simply wasn't in his league.

One of the bonuses of my website has been to make contact with three people who live far away whom I've never met, but with whom I'm often in correspondence. When they wrote and I answered, a chord was struck which developed into friendship. Two of them email me several times a week, one at intervals of weeks. I value them all as interesting and empathetic friends.

Paul (in his fifties, young enough to be my son), lives in Hove UK. He has been writing elegantly and interestingly to me about his life for three years. Alex (86) lives in a retirement community in Tennessee and belongs to a writers' group which chose 'Perception of Time' as a theme last year. Alex arrived in Panama as a refugee from Nazi Germany at age 14 and has a perspective seldom found in America; he is still culturally a European.

A journalist in Montana telephoned me one day, having researched 'Perception of Time' on the internet, to interview me for an article she was writing for a local newspaper. That article was read by Jude who emailed me to contribute to my collection, and keeps in touch sporadically. Jude (in her sixties) owns a health food store and has a daughter in her twenties. She writes about the freezing winters and deep snows of Bute, and the glory of spring when it arrives at last. Jude flees the harsh winter climate of Montana to visit her daughter in the California sunshine. It is extraordinary how richly one can relate to people through correspondence.

This has been a project so long in progress, it has seemed impossible to bring to fruition, but reviewing the material I've amassed so far (with many good quotations included), I think I have enough for a small book. That may be the one I'll work on next when my Memoirs are complete.

69 ANXIOUS MOTHER

When they were small Richard used to say 'With a mother like you, Columbus would never have discovered America.' I knew I was over anxious and didn't want to burden them with that. I couldn't disguise my anxiety when small boys walked along a pier by the sea peering down at fish, or stood on a cliff (I suffer from vertigo) but I could keep quiet about my night vigils.

In their late teens and early twenties, sometimes they came home intoxicated and I relied on the hangover to teach them a lesson. They were happy drunks, feeling mellow after a few beers. It's a rite of passage in Britain. Some of their friends were obstreperous in that state, but not my boys. They were more inclined to giggle.

I lay there last week remembering the first time one was not home until 2 in the morning. Richard and I lay awake feeling anxious. My imagination is vivid and I suffered the anxiety of any mother wondering how and where her chicks are. When they came in, treading softly on the stairs, Richard said 'Now don't let them know you were anxious.' So I didn't.

I found myself in a familiar and uncomfortable situation last week. Three of the boys decided to go out for their last evening in Virginia together. (Peter had a cold and went to bed early.) They were looking for a few beers and a game of pool. They borrowed my car and said they'd come back by taxi and collect the car in the morning. I went to bed and sleep around 10 pm but awoke at midnight. Everything was quiet. I supposed that John Paul had crept in and gone to bed, but when I looked, his bed was empty.

Well, they would surely come home soon. Harrisonburg must be quiet after midnight. I lay in bed remembering the hundreds of times I had waited for them to come home in the middle of the night in their youth. Five boys do a lot of socializing and they were never subject to curfew after the age of 18.

Once they walked across the River Cam on a weir, for a bet. Another day John Paul took Mark parachute jumping. Mark was under age and needed parental consent, so they exaggerated his age like his grandfather in 1915 when he volunteered to fight in France. They played me a video showing them as specks jumping out of a plane, floating down, then walking past with armfuls of parachute mouthing 'Sorry Mum' at the camera with wicked grins.

Years of listening for their advent followed. I trust my boys, but sometimes others are unreliable. Last week I pictured my three mature sons aged 36 (the twins) and 41 enjoying each other's company in a pool room, perhaps observed by one of the local gangs with knives in their pockets, recognizing an easy target in three benign Englishmen. There have been two murders in Water Street car park since I've lived here. Although tall and sturdy, my boys are no match for the vicious.

Or perhaps they were walking home, having failed to find a taxi service. I knew they would not drive after a drink. It's three miles from town and there are no sidewalks along route 33. I pictured one or more of them being run down by a careless driver as they walked back in the dark. Between them those three have nine offspring and all those fatherless children briefly flashed through my imagination. Get a grip, Eileen!

Yesterday I spoke to Sarah in Australia on the telephone. She remarked how Mark said recently 'We had so much freedom, my Mother never worried about us.' I laughed and said 'I worried all right. I just didn't let them know.' Let me tell you, nobody brings up five boys without some hairy moments.

Sometimes they took out canoes on choppy seas, and one of them has been in several car crashes. The police phoned me to say that John Paul at seventeen was in hospital after the car in which he was a passenger had rolled over. He broke his finger in his haste to extricate a girl who was hanging upside down by her seat belt, in case the fuel ignited. He had slight concussion and a few bruises, but after a night in hospital he came home safe. But two of his friends died as a result of car crashes in Aberystwyth.

At one o'clock in Virginia I heard the front door open softly and knew John Paul was home. 'Thank you, God' I said, for the several hundredth time, having consulted Him earlier. JP made himself a hot drink and it was 1.30 when he got to bed. He saw my bedroom door ajar and we spoke briefly. I said 'I'm glad you're home, I was worried in case you were run over, walking home, or fell foul to a local gang.' He said, 'That's funny, you never worried about us when we were young....'

Ha!

70 GAMES WE PLAY

Jake (aged 4) and I were playing with two tiny toy soldiers and a horse. The horse and one rider (Noble and Sir Peter) are mediaeval and the second soldier (Frank) wears modern garb, kneeling with a rifle. We are totally unfazed by anachronism. As usual we were playing on my knee which sometimes is a mountain, or a forest or a helicopter pad. On this occasion it was a castle.

I jiggled Frank and said 'Who goes there? What is the password?' (I had already told Jake the password was 'Apple'.) 'Apple!' he said (he only needs telling once). 'Right,' I said, 'come in, friend.' Then he brought the horse forward. 'Halt! Who goes there? What's the password?' and Jake as horse answered 'Apple'. 'That's right! Come on in!' I said.

Then Jake took the modern soldier, Frank. He asked Sir Peter 'Who goes there?' 'Strawberry' I said. 'No, no, it's Apple!' he said. I tried to explain to Jake that if the wrong password is given, you don't let them into the castle, and don't tell them the real password, but he hasn't quite got the gist of it yet.

We often play with Sir Peter and Noble. Sometimes we have to hunt high and low to retrieve them after his absence for a few days. They may end up in the box with all the other toys. Being small, they fall to the bottom, but we always find them. Jake likes to be Noble and I'm Sir Peter most of the time. He always starts, wiggling Noble on my knee, 'Good morning! What shall we do today?' I say 'I'd like to go for a ride in the forest' and he says 'Jump on my back,' and off we go to the other knee. Or I say 'Let's ride in the fields today,' or 'Let's visit the castle.' We have total freedom to go anywhere and do anything because we are limited only by our imaginations.

Another game Jake enjoys is 'Rescue'. I wiggle two fingers, pretending to be legs, saying 'Help, help! I'm stuck on the mountain and I've hurt my leg!' 'What do you need?' asks Jake, who has an impressive array of vehicles to come to my rescue. He lands on my knee and I jump in and he flies me off to hospital where he becomes the doctor. He speaks in a deep voice: 'I'm the doctor, tell me where you hurt,' and I say 'My leg is broken' (or whatever ails me) and he says 'Don't worry, I'll fix it,' and in a few seconds we are off to the next peril.

'Help, help! I'm on the roof of my house and the river is flooding!' Or 'Help! I'm lost in the forest and I can't find my way home!' or 'My cat is up a tree and he can't get down,' and along comes Jake in a helicopter or boat or fire engine or whatever we need, and he rescues me yet again. Sometimes he says 'Are there any alligators?' and he throws me a rope.

His vocabulary blossoms. His latest word is 'stretcher' to go with the ambulance. When I said, 'help! I've run out of petrol!' he looked perplexed until I said 'I mean gas.' So he is also going to be bilingual.

It's quite tiring, but I'm rewarded when he says 'That game was really fun.'

71 JOHN PAUL AND FAMILY ARRIVE IN VIRGINIA - 2010

I was so excited to see the family, anticipating their arrival around 1a.m. that I stayed up with soft lamps and candles lighted, making the house look so inviting, longing to hug them all. But at quarter to three I gave up and went to bed. I checked the news so I know the plane landed safely. I assumed there had been a delay in getting the hire car, or that they'd stopped en route for a meal. I fell asleep and when I woke at 6 a.m. could see they had arrived and installed themselves silently. So I'm still waiting for the hugs.

The morning is beautiful. I can only hear birds singing and a distant dog barking, the soft hum of the fridge in the kitchen, and the quiet click of my keyboard. Some of my favourite people are going to wake up soon and then we'll cook full English breakfast. This afternoon Gianna is cooking. Andre has been working on the patio he's been building all week, and by now he should have the fountain connected and flowing. He already has some tiny goldfish and pond lilies he transferred from the plastic tub. Jake (4) asked 'Have you got sharks in there?' I am keen to see them interacting with their cousins.

When we took Connor and Jake to see the film *Toy Story* they said the scariest part was where the toys were being tipped towards the fire at the dump. I said I liked the bit where Buzz Lightyear's switches got thrown and he spoke Spanish and danced flamenco. Gianna liked it when Ken tried on all his gay clothes to show Barbie. We agreed that the babies at the day centre who played roughly with the toys were too violent. I told JP on the phone, who had taken his family to see it for Leah's 12th birthday, 'I cried when Andy was leaving for college' and he said 'Oh, so did I! I was thinking about Ben!' 'I was thinking about you!' I said. There are tender hearts in our family. Imagine crying at a story about plastic toys and cartoon people, but the heartstrings they pull are not plastic.

After the film we went to the Steak House (I had ribs) and Connor boasted he had been there six times already, holding up six fingers. Jake looked at me across the table and confided quietly, 'He's lying,' and held up two, then on reflection three little fingers. The food is good but they give you a bucket of unshelled peanuts as you sit at your table, and encourage you to throw the shells on the floor. At intervals the waitresses (clones with long hair, cute figures, short shorts) do a happy- clappy sort-of-square dance together between the aisles. It amuses kids and childish adults. But the ribs are finger-lickin' go-od. And the glass of wine was too. Many restaurants here serve no alcohol.

My Arizona grandchildren are all interested in cooking. I've had good times making lemon meringue pie with Charlie, brownies with Ben and pies with Leah. They always want to cook with me, and are patient when I ask them to wait their turn because cooking with more than one at a time is overwhelming when you are getting old. They ask many questions, are eager to help, and interested to learn. They're a pleasure to cook for too, trying everything and being polite even if they aren't impressed. They are highly sociable and polished. Everyone remarked on Ben aged 7, handing drinks around at Andre's wedding in London. Leah could chat for America. She was barely two when I first visited Arizona with Bill, standing beside her Daddy at the computer, saying 'Oh, dot com, Daddy's got mail.' Leah is as sharp as can be, catches on effortlessly to any idea you run past her and picks you up if you make a mistake.

One day I said to them 'You kids are so good, trying new things, you never complain when I give you something strange. Tonight we're having something you haven't tried before: Porcupine!' Their social training showed when nobody cringed. They just looked wary but polite. A moment later John Paul brought in the dish he and I had been compiling: a mound of mashed potato with hot dogs sticking out all over like quills, with currants for eyes. They laughed with relief and when I go there, Charlie still asks 'Can we have porcupine?'

They are affectionate kids. Ben often gives me a hug in passing, 'love you Granny', casually, and Charlie is always ready for a cuddle. We like to watch movies together while Charlie snuggles under a blanket. He giggles easily. I go to watch him play soccer and he runs like the wind. He's kind to other kids, and popular. He's the tallest in his soccer team.

All the children swim well and are active. They ski, kayak and fish. They love to holiday in their camping trailer. Ben goes mountain biking in the desert with his friend Alex. They all studied Aikido for a while and Leah took dancing lessons. Recently Charlie and John Paul made a go-kart. They all work well at school.

I taught Leah to use a sewing machine one year when she was about ten. She made an apron, a cushion cover and a dress. She needs encouragement to tackle sewing on her own, but she's competent and knows how. I'm confident she'll tackle new projects when she's older.

I asked John Paul to buy Publisher software so I could teach the children how to do desk top publishing. He came home with it next day, we loaded it, I showed Leah and Charlie how to 'insert' a text box and get started. While I went to the bathroom Leah took it up and wrote half a fashion page, illustrated with a picture from Clipart, entitled 'Pink is the New Black'. They didn't need my input.

I gave Ben a camera for his twelfth birthday when he came to stay with me in Arizona, flying alone for the first time. He is artistic and has a natural eye for a picture and its frame. I was delighted when he took up photography with enthusiasm, and made his first one minute video, exploring my house while giving a commentary.

A couple of years ago his parents bought him a guitar and he started lessons with Alex and his mother Roxanne, who busked her way through college. The boys learned fast and practised frequently and soon they formed a band with their friend Will – three rock guitars. Last time I visited they had added a drummer and called the band 'The Point Blank'. They are just 16 and they're so good, they're playing for their friends and their parents' parties. We've had some wonderful evenings as they played on the patio. They are talented and focused. Ben and Will sing too. They are going to be popular when they are students.

Any minute now the family will be up and we'll start the day. I know that whatever we do, we'll enjoy it. They are all positive in outlook and a joy to be with. You can't do this on Skype.

72 FRIENDS

We left friends behind every time we moved house. I kept in touch with one or two all over England, Wales, and several in Spain and France too. It was particularly hard for the boys moving to Cambridge at an age when they had established friendships in secondary school.

Some friends thread throughout our lives, whether we see them or not. I met Klaus from Essen, Germany, when I was sixteen (he was training for the priesthood) and again at seventeen and forty. He had a profound impact on my life out of all proportion to our brief encounters.

At school I had a close circle of friends, three named Anne, and Pamela. I've only kept in touch with Pamela. I hear every year from Margaret in Adelaide, met in Earls Court when I was seventeen. I have very fond memories of John to whom I was engaged for four months at age 22. I had distant contact with Mariano until he died of cancer in 2000. A number of sweethearts still reside, forever youthful, in my memory.

Richard's friend Alec and his wife Jill were our best friends. Alec and Richard were at Wye College together. We went to their wedding soon after ours. They were the most enjoyable company we ever kept. They were also the most hospitable. Nobody else (even our relations) welcomed five boys to stay. It's a question of will, not bed space. The boys slept in a row on the floor of one room in sleeping bags, utterly content after the days spent playing on the farm and enjoying joint family meals. Jill and Alec had a beautiful Victorian farmhouse (shabby when they bought it, later looking like something out of *Homes and Gardens*). They kept a pig farm in Shropshire. Their two daughters and one son were similar in age to our boys. Eight children appeared only at meal times, eager to eat whatever we put before them. They played in harmony with hay bales in the barn, in acres of fields with a small stream at the bottom of the hill. Jill and Richard shared a passion for gardening and would roam around their extensive flower beds and glass houses, talking plants. I recall Richard laying a hosepipe on the lawn with Jill, mapping out a new herbaceous bed. Meanwhile Alec, who lectured on Food Science, chatted with me in the kitchen as we prepared the next meal for twelve. It was no strain. Alec had all the ingredients to hand and a head full of recipes, and we rinsed, peeled, chopped, fried, stewed, and composed delicious repasts together. Jill made exceptionally good puddings. Her Almond Tart is recorded idiosyncratically in my cook book under 'Jill's Scrumptious Almond and Mincemeat Tart', along with 'Jill's Fabulous Chocolate Pudding, Jill's Cherry Cake, Golden Tart, Chocolate, and Yum Yum Cakes' – all listed under 'J'. We sat down at a huge table in the farmhouse kitchen, the most convivial meals we remember.

Going to Shropshire was a treat of first dimension for all of us. One weekend I packed all our clothes, sleeping bags and gear into the car and was sitting on the swing in the garden ready for the off, when Richard came to tell me that Jill had phoned. Her Father had died suddenly, and the weekend was off. I wept for Jill, knowing how she loved her father and what a pivotal member of her family he was. And I wept for myself because my keen anticipation of their company was disappointed. Half an hour later the telephone rang again. Jill said, 'Come anyway. We need you. It'll help us all to get through this.' We piled into the car and left immediately. Despite the sorrow, perhaps even because of it, we enjoyed each other's company as much as ever, and felt privileged to share the family's grief.

Jill's family owned a remote cottage in mid Wales. They loaned it to us and our happiest holidays were spent in the cottage by the stream. The children ran around all day naked in the sunlight, playing in the stream, while Richard and I practised our treble recorder and guitar respectively. Neither of us played well, but it was a tranquil pastime. We collected firewood and in the evenings the children toasted bread over the fire. 'This is better than television,' they said, watching the flames. I read to them the stories of Narnia, one twin sitting on each arm of my chair and the others on the floor. Precious times.

When the children were all grown up and I had remarried, Bill and I went to stay with Jill and Alec for a weekend. I was concerned that being so different from Richard, and from our own backgrounds, Bill might not be so welcome there. But they embraced him, enjoyed his character and conversation, and left us both feeling the joy of their company as we drove away.

Their children grew up to study agriculture, astronomy and chiropody.

In Radyr I had some special friends: Joan and Lyn. Joan was married to a paediatrician and had three children in three years, similar in age to Mark and the twins. Her oldest was Chris, a shy boy, beautiful of face, with blonde hair, who hid behind his mother's skirts. I would never have believed he'd grow up to be a stand-up comedian. Joan mentioned this in her Christmas cards and one day, switching to a television comedy programme, one of them struck me as familiar in his speech pattern and gestures: they were Joan's. When the credits rolled I was delighted to read 'Chris Addison' in confirmation.

Lyn, a nurse and her husband Dave, a blood specialist, were a few years younger. They had two little boys and lived near my Mother's bungalow in Radyr. Dave's father was a mason and Dave inherited his skilled hands. They bought a big house in Cardiff which Dave rescued from neglect and rebuilt. Later they moved again, always in the same area. When Bill and I were living in Le Retail they arrived on a motorcycle on which they'd toured Spain. I was aghast at this adventure. Lyn said ' All you need is a pannier and a spare pair of knickers.' They were good fun. Today we forward funny emails and brief news. Dave has become a pastor.

In the sixties two women writing to the *Guardian* newspaper set up an organization to help people who moved frequently, to find friends in their new area. I joined the National Housewives' Register in the early 1970s in Cardiff. 'I'll join the Aberystwyth NHR group to find new friends', I thought, but when I got there, there wasn't one. Each time I met a new woman over the ensuing months I asked, if I organize a coffee evening at my house to set up an NHR group, will you come? I was given the telephone numbers of two women who 'might be interested', Claire Bayliss and Dorothy Bell. Dorothy said 'I'm too busy to join but I'll come along to support you the first evening.' Those two and eight other women turned up, and they all joined.

We met monthly with a year's topics mapped out in advance about themes to discuss or speakers to invite. It was the source of all my friendships. Dorothy and Claire in particular were mates. Dorothy was a Librarian working at the University and Claire was a Lecturer in Librarianship. Dorothy and I often met in the college dining hall for lunch when I was an undergraduate. She and Claire celebrated my fortieth birthday with me over a drink in a hotel bar on the front. Both of them visited me separately, in *Beausejour* in France. Claire died of cancer in her fifties, leaving Dorothy and me, bereft.

I left Aberystwyth in 1983 and Dorothy continues to be my closest friend, frequently in touch by letter, sometimes once in a month, sometimes three times in a week, depending on our needs. She is my confidante, my support, she knows me better than any friend alive. Dorothy is sensitive and caring, nurtures many people and empathizes. She ran the local Samaritan group for years. People turn to her for advice and comfort, and sometimes overwhelm her with their needs because she is so generous in her attentions.

Dorothy has rejoiced with me when I was buoyant, cheered my triumphs, soothed my anguish, listened to my worries, laughed at my jokes, wept with me, comforted, supported, understood and sustained me for thirty four years. Even when we are not in touch for a week or two, each knows the other is there and that we can count on her. Mostly this has been done by mail, only recently by email. In the years since I left Wales we've met less than half a dozen times, yet we are constant in each other's lives. Dorothy's middle son emigrated to America. We both understand the anguish of distant beloved sons. When I wrote that I was staying in America Dorothy answered, 'Oh dear, yet another person I love is moving to America,' and I wrote 'It doesn't matter where I am. We don't see each other anyway. But we are always there, always friends.'

I credit Dorothy with saving my sanity on many occasions. I shared with her the turmoil of my marriage and divorce. When she offered to counsel Richard and he gladly accepted, I felt jealous, not of my husband, but of my friend. I didn't want to share her. If Dorothy had not been my friend, I would have been impoverished and adrift.

Toni Volcani came into my life in 1971 and left it when she died in 2006 – 35 years as my friend and mentor. She dazzled, counselled and validated me. She didn't mother me. Had I been her daughter she might have been obliged to love me, but she loved me without obligation. When I felt undervalued or misunderstood, I thought of Toni's approval and was comforted. When I took problems to her she enlightened me with insight, wisdom, humour, derision, dismissal or her empathy. She put everything into perspective. She never failed to amaze me. She was original. She loved life. She reviled some politicians and approved of others. She was an example to me as a woman. I could only aspire to her courage and independence, but she showed me the direction in which to travel. She had no pretensions. She was authentic and genuine.

When Toni left me the first time, to return to America after 9 months in Radyr, I wished I was going with her. Each time she left after a visit I felt the loss keenly, but after I'd been to see her in La Jolla in 1979 it became easier, because I could picture her in her own surroundings (as later I would be able to picture Mark and his family in Australia).

When Toni expressed apprehension at having heart surgery I wrote to her that she was the most important person in my life outside my immediate family, that she had changed my life and taught me 'not to take crap from anyone'. She replied she was so touched, she wished she could take my letter into the operating room. She had lived bravely all her life but I had not. I drew what resolve I mustered from her example and encouragement.

Toni and I communicated with such enthusiasm and frankness, when she died I felt a sense of comfort that we had said it all.

73 BEING IN A MENTAL HOSPITAL

Not a lot of people are admitted to a mental hospital, and those that are don't generally talk about it. This can be because they are ashamed of the experience or because it's too painful to relate. Perhaps others are embarrassed to hear about it. After 48 years I feel I ought to make a stab at it.

1963

I can only speak from my experience of three short stays in 1963, 1978 and 2003. I was in Saxondale Hospital, Nottinghamshire, with post natal depression in 1963. Peter was three weeks old when I had an allergic reaction to the medication I was given by the GP. Although I was safe and being cared for well at home, and the baby was fine, they didn't know how to resolve the rash that covered my body from top to toe. Obviously they had to stop that medication (Largactil), but what should they put in its place?

I was 26 and had never felt like this before. All I knew about mental hospitals was that crazy people went there. That's a common misconception. In fact they are designed to provide treatment for people who are suffering mentally. One person in six in their lifetime is likely to become mentally ill.

In earlier days they were huge asylums with hundreds of unseen patients who had been institutionalized, sometimes twenty years before. One of the categories was single mothers originally committed by their shamed parents. That would not happen today.

Richard and his mother took me to the hospital, referred by the GP. They were deeply concerned and solicitous. It was a bright and airy building with polished floors, clean furniture and cheery pictures on the walls. Mop drew my attention to the fine surroundings.

The thirty or so women in my ward were mostly friendly but of course they were all suffering from depression and unease or loss of memory. Some didn't speak, but others reached out. Their remarks were upsetting: 'Oh you poor girl, I came in twenty years ago with post natal depression and I've been in and out of here ever since.' There was fellow feeling but a shocking range of human experiences which people shared freely. There was a woman whose husband had gone bankrupt and the strain of it had made her so ill, she could not remember simple things like how to dress herself. Every morning one or other of us would say 'Start with your underpants, now your blouse' and so on until she was dressed. She did as she was told but clearly none of it made sense to her.

Another woman, mother of three, was there because she had attempted suicide. She was educated and refined, but took an overdose when she discovered she was pregnant with a fourth child. In those days abortion was illegal. They patched her up and sent her home (still pregnant) and God knows how that turned out. I have been pro the right to choose ever since.

Yet another was sent there by the courts for child abuse. She had stood her children on the mantelpiece for hours to keep them under control. Even those who were critical of her cruelty were sympathetic to her misery.

Twice a week selected patients were subjected to shock therapy. Richard and I were asked to sign a paper giving them permission to give me this 'treatment' as it was dubbed. The word 'treatment' has had sinister connotations for me ever since. The patients were terrified of it. They were strapped to a bed, a rubber device put in their mouths to stop them biting their tongues, a metal device placed around their temples and electric shocks applied which made their bodies rigid, and left their minds in such a state of lost memory, they had to ask us the way to the bathroom, although many of them had been living there for months. We signed the papers because we were helpless in the face of this situation, formerly a closed book to us. ECT is still controversial and I am thankful I never had it, although some find it beneficial.

Twice a day as a means of occupying us, we were required to polish the floors of the hospital ward and corridors. We all had bumpers – a long wooden handled device with leather on the bottom block. We also laid the tables, cleared them and washed up. This was not voluntary, although the vacuum cleaning was. I was so glad to be occupied I volunteered to use the vacuum cleaner. But I dreaded washing the bathroom floors on my knees, as I was scheduled to do the day my Mother rescued me. Coupled with the brusqueness of some staff, this felt like punishment rather than patient care. It did nothing for our self-esteem, already sadly depleted as we perceived ourselves as 'mental patients'.

Some members of staff were kind, addressing us respectfully by our first names. Some were bossy, saying 'Dight, do this, Dight, do that'. One time we all had boiled eggs for breakfast and when we opened them with our teaspoons, discovered they were inadequately cooked. I would guess they had spent one minute in the boiling water, from their runny whites which had not had time to become opaque. We looked at each other in consternation and the braver souls said 'Nurse, I can't eat this, it isn't cooked'. Nonsense!' said the nurse, 'Get on with it and stop complaining!' One could sense the tension among as we glanced in silence at each other. Then another nurse came along, saw what was happening and said, 'Oh, you poor girls, you can't eat those! Take them back to the kitchen and ask them to cook some more, properly.' Picture our relief.

Every night we went to bed at 9 o'clock, endeavouring to sleep. One of my symptoms was a complete inability to sleep at all for three months after the birth, without a hefty dose of sleep medicine. The trauma of the birth drove through my head repeatedly. Today it would be recognized as PTSD. The young nurse who checked us all at midnight and gave pills to those who were not asleep, would say 'Stop considerin' ', in her West Indian accent, advice it was impossible to comply with. I would wake again before the birds whose dawn chorus started around 6 a.m. The hospital was set in beautiful gardens. We were allowed to walk around the gardens during the day, a great solace.

Some patients were given drugs to make them sleep for several days. I think this would have been preferable to the depression and terror I experienced in the eleven days I was there. The average stay was six weeks but after eleven days my Mother turned up at the hospital, having taken a train from London and then a taxi by herself, to take me home to Richard.

Peter was three months old before I was able to look after him by myself. Before that my Mother stayed a while with us. We took her back to London where I left Peter for a week with my parents and went home with Richard. One afternoon I went for a walk and talked to a woman in the village who had four children. On my way home along the farm roads I suddenly felt the depression lift, and a couple of days later we drove to London to pick up Peter. The trauma very slowly subsided but was still troubling me when I had John Paul two years later. His birth largely helped my recovery.

1978

The second time I was in mental hospital was in South Wales. Following John Paul's depression at age 13 when he cried for three hours a day for three months, I was unable to sleep with the strain of it and it took its toll. It was bank holiday weekend in August and the staff from the open ward had been slimmed down for the holiday. They put me in a lock-up ward. I was surrounded by severely sick people with delusions and erratic behaviour, a totally different level of sickness to that I had witnessed before. Some of these people really were mad. I sat down on a chair and the woman next to me shook her fist, shouting 'Get off my land! You've no right to be here! Get off!' until I moved. Others were too far gone even to talk.

The admitting doctor asked if I was allergic to anything and I said yes: Largactil. Minutes later she mistakenly injected me with 100 mg of Largactil which knocked me out immediately. Next morning I got up, fainted, and broke my leg. I was put in plaster from toes to hip and given crutches. After the weekend they moved me to the open ward where the worst that happened (apart from denying that I was allergic and that they were responsible), was an elderly patient who repeatedly stole my pretty dressing gown, and then urinated on my bedroom floor. Poor soul, she was demented.

We were not required to clean in this hospital and the staff were generally pleasant, but the mix-up with the pills alarmed me and I was fortunate to leave there after two weeks.

2003

My third brush with the mental health system occurred when I got high during my break up with Bill and we couldn't find a doctor to give me a prescription on Christmas Eve. I was so distressed Peter took me to Hanwell Hospital, where my Mother's sister Eileen had been a nurse eighty years before. With no medication I completely lost my reason and remember hardly anything about my admission. This was the worst episode of my life. It will never happen again because I now take medication to control my bipolar condition. This was the first time I heard the expression Bipolar, although manic depression had been mentioned on earlier occasions. During the 25 years since my previous breakdown the condition had become well researched and better understood, and suitable drugs been developed to correct the chemical imbalance that causes the illness. It need no longer be feared, if the patient is compliant with the medication.

Here the standard of care was excellent. The doctors and nurses were cheerful, empathetic and understanding. They removed my lifelong fear of mental hospitals. It was Christmas Day when I woke up, feeling rational after the drugs they had given me the night before. A patient the previous year had knocked over the Christmas tree, tangling all the Christmas lights. I volunteered to sort them out, thus endearing myself to the woman in charge of the ward, a wonderful nurse. (I wish I could recall her name. I wrote to the hospital later to express my appreciation of her care and professionalism.) It took me an hour to untangle the lights. The following week I carefully wound them around a cardboard spool to store them for the next Christmas.

I was fortunate to be given a single room and Mark gave me a pocket radio with ear phones which I still use today, eight years later. It was peaceful in my room and I was grateful for the repose. During the day I walked along the corridors for half an hour at a time to keep fit. I watered the plants that were withering in the hospital corridors. I drew cartoons and sketched ideas for a wall hanging. Peter, Mark and Andre came to visit me. Bill came a couple of times, clearly uncomfortable. Liz and Justin came and were very kind. I was there nearly three weeks when Peter and Andre came to take me back to Andre's home where he and Deanna helped me to get my life back on track. I stayed with Patrick and Kate in Dublin and that helped too. What you need when you've had a mental upset is a quiet haven with people who love you.

A stay in a mental hospital can leave vivid, disturbing memories, or prove a breathing space you badly needed. They are so much better organized and the treatment more effective than fifty years ago. An average stay used to be six weeks. Now it is seven days. The whole climate of mental health and medication has changed. I hope it doesn't happen to you, but if it does, remember you are not nuts, you are suffering from mental strain from which you need relief. You need special care and respite from the challenges you cannot handle alone.

74 PETER

Peter is my first born. I named him Peter because all my life I'd heard my Father speak fondly of his best friend, Peter Marsh, who was married to my Mother's sister Eileen and I liked the sound of 'Peter and Eileen'.

He had a most difficult start as a result of his traumatic birth. I didn't see him for 48 hours after he was born, not even a glimpse. They broke the bond that should have been established if they'd handed him to me immediately, but the staff, too busy, seemed indifferent to finer feelings. He had a hand tremor, the result I believe of the forceps delivery after he became distressed in the womb. As if this damaging delivery were not enough, his mother had a breakdown three weeks later, and failed to provide him proper care for the first three months of his life, despite her best intentions.

He was 21 inches long and 8lb 9ozs, strong and lusty. When they handed him to me to breast feed at two days old, my inability to breast feed compounded my massive feeling of failure. For two years after I was still talking about my depression and subsequent dismay. What a rotten start for Peter.

Peter was a challenge because he didn't really care if he was loved or not, he just did what he wanted. When a child is that reckless, a parent feels confused and helpless. Sitting in his high chair, I would put his favourite cereal on the tray with milk and he'd protest, he didn't want milk, so the next morning I'd serve it dry and he'd protest, he wanted milk! He was ingenious about inventing opportunities to rile me, and I was not clever enough to fence at his level. I started every day determined not to let him provoke me, but he always won.

Richard's interest in Peter was minimal. He still had not picked him up at six months old and I said 'If you don't play with him, he won't love you.' Richard answered 'He doesn't have to love me. He just has to do as he's told.' Between us we failed Peter dreadfully.

We thought that an interval of two years would be the best between siblings. Richard was two years younger than his brother John. We didn't know about the Terrible Twos. Now I think a three year interval would have been preferable, from Peter's point of view. He was 26 months old and still not talking when John Paul was born. Naturally he was jealous of the new baby and I couldn't leave them alone. Once I put John Paul on the sofa for a minute and when I turned around, Peter was sitting on his face. Luckily it was only for a matter of seconds.

He behaved well at school. He was slightly dyslexic and didn't read until he was eight, but there was no doubt about his intelligence. He was dexterous and inventive with Lego. He was only eight when I realized he was vastly more logical than I was. This was a painful realization because until then I had thought myself quite logical. He also astounded me with his spatial awareness. When we had a problem with a faulty car door handle, he worked out and mended it, slipping small intelligent fingers into the space and jiggling the mechanism which we had failed to correct. When I corrected his spelling of 'cheeze' he asked me 'Well, how do you spell breeze?' His take on things was always logical and entirely independent.

And he was always, always in charge of the extent to which he cooperated.

It was hard for Peter to watch four younger brothers arrive by the time he was 8. We were stressed and so was he. He fought to stay home when the twins were tiny. His knuckles were white as I prized them off the garage door to insist on him going to school. It was heart breaking. I took him to the doctor and said how disturbed he was. The doctor said 'Ask your husband to give him some individual attention, perhaps take him to a football match at the weekend.' When I mentioned this to Richard he said 'I can't afford to go to football matches.' He did take him swimming a year or two later. Peter became a strong swimmer thanks to regular lessons on a Sunday morning with Richard and John Paul.

Peter liked to fish and so did Richard. We went on beach holidays to Pembrokeshire in Wales several years running. As the oldest he was often helpful in looking after the younger ones, in particular spoon feeding the twins. He grew so fast, I was always making him new trousers. He was eleven before we bought his first proper shop pants. There was little spare cash for clothes or toys. He played rugby in second hand boots a size too small for him. It makes me wince with guilt, but I had no money to buy him new ones. He never complained.

He got a job washing up in the Bay Hotel in Aberystwyth when he was about thirteen. He worked there all one summer. He was not lazy. He also cooked with me a lot, and when he left school on his own initiative just before his 'A' level exams, he got a job in the Four Seasons hotel kitchen and was soon promoted to chef. He was always an inventive cook. The owner paid me to come in for a week to expand Peter's repertoire. I was apprehensive that Peter would not welcome my presence, but in the event we had a wonderful week working together. He was keen to learn all I could suggest. I was astonished at the skill he showed in this job. He was happy there until the owner bought a second, larger hotel and left managers running the Four Seasons with whom Peter clashed. He was not the only one. Several staff left in protest at their management style, and Peter eventually quit. I didn't blame him.

For a while Peter lived on the dole. The summer he was nineteen I got concerned about his drifting and at the same time, criticizing our lifestyle (I was at university and Richard was supporting all of us on his salary). I said 'If you don't like it, leave,' and he did. He just disappeared, and I didn't even notice because he often stayed out overnight, sometimes sleeping under a hedge, asserting his independence. If he didn't turn up for meals we assumed he was eating elsewhere. I was grateful when I received a nice note from him in the post, explaining that he was living in the Graig coffee bar and not to worry about him. I sent a note back saying I hoped he was enjoying himself, and any time he wanted to bring his washing home I'd be delighted to see him.

He invited me to the Graig one day, for coffee. There I met the woman with two daughters who owned the place. Peter introduced us and we chatted for a while. Later he told me she was interested to meet me and I wasn't as bad as she had expected. This still makes me laugh.

He rented a cottage with one of her daughters, in the country. It was a nice place and he invited Richard and me to tea. When we arrived, he asked us to take off our shoes at the door because he had vacuum cleaned the place thoroughly and he didn't want to have to do it twice. As his room at home generally looked like a war zone with bomb damage, we were surprised, but compliant. In fact Richard and I enjoyed the occasion immensely. It was so nice to meet Peter on his own territory and he was a gracious host.

Cosmopolitan Magazine ran a competition one time entitled 'The letters you always wanted to write.' I thought I'd have a go. Without hesitation my letter was addressed to Peter, whom I called James, his second name, to spare his blushes. It was published in the book *Cosmopolitan Letters* in 1986:

Dear James,

PETER

I was not pleased when you told me you planned to sell 'four dirty postcards for a pound' through an ad in Private Eye. It is not the sort of career a mother envisages for her son. However, when your brothers explained to me that you buy plain white postcards and dip them in a bucket of dirty water, I was mollified.

What career did I envisage for you when I changed your nappies, dressed you in your first school uniform, nagged you about 'O' levels? In my wildest dreams you were a lawyer, a pilot, an accountant. That shows the limitations of my middle-class imagination. As I bathed your cut knees, washed your rugby kit, shut the door on the tip that was your bedroom, I never foresaw that your first pay-cheque would be from the DHSS and you signing on every fortnight.

But you are tall and beautiful with your long hair and beard, and you look stately in your Oxfam suit. Your friends are weird and mostly incomprehensible to me, as I must be to them. I don't know how you fill your jobless hours, but you do.

Your brother Paul just came in after midnight. He and Charlie were out celebrating. Just as they were trying on a litter bin that looked like a space helmet, a policeman came along. 'Is that your bin?' Paul assumed his best Welsh accent and explained that Charlie was on leave from the navy, and he hadn't seen his best friend for six months. Fortunately that was an understanding cop. Paul's poly course starts in a fortnight. Four years of business studies – it's a race between finals and his surviving brain cells.

Mike and the twins are back at school. Mike is full of good intentions, like confining his hangovers to weekends. Rob is glad to be busy again, after the long holiday. Philip, the youngest of you by twenty minutes, is the only one who has his career planned, and with his goldfish, canaries and the dog we have half a zoo already.

We all went to see Mike in his play. Rob noticed a very pretty girl in the cast (blond, interesting face, neat figure) and said, 'Mum, I'm in love!' It gave him the necessary incentive to buy some new clothes, so the next day we bought an outfit for him in the sales – canvas trousers, olive sweatshirt, white shirt and trainers, yellow socks. He looks lovely! but the girl has gone back to Scotland.

Having five sons is more fun and less hassle than you would think. I've been looking after you for 85 years now, but fortunately your lives are concurrent. It has sometimes been hard to make the money go round, but love never needs to be rationed – it's the only thing that multiplies when it is shared out. When I look at you all, tall and handsome, fit and friendly, I can hardly believe my luck.

Sometimes I am in danger of taking your good health for granted. When you had your appendix out I was frantic to see you ill. You weren't allowed to drink for three days after the operation. You were so thirsty, you drank your mouthwash. 'Kill or cure,' you said.

Do you remember when you broke your arm at the age of six? We only noticed because you winced every time you hit Paul, who was two years younger. You enjoyed the X-ray and the plaster. You had to hit him left-handed after that.

The nicest compliment I've ever had was when a friend said, 'You give me hope, you're living proof that there is life after maternity.' It delights me to discover that too. I love my job. Every morning I get up and off to work with enthusiasm. I tell the boys, 'Find a job you like doing and get someone to pay you for it.' Writing the charity's newsletter and raising funds to help homeless children is an enjoyable challenge. But sometimes I get tired, working full time and having a houseful to feed every evening. By the time I cycle home from work I've run out of steam. When you were all in school and I was at university I must have been the only student who cooked for seven every night.

For recreation I've been constructing my own private heaven. In heaven there will be room service and good food. I'll take my turn at the cooking but someone else will always wash up. There will of course be something to drink. All my friends will be in heaven and nobody will be jealous. There will either be no aggravating characters or I shall have developed an indifference to them. There'll be a lot of laughter and friendship; plenty of work to do (I don't want to be idle) but I'll have ample energy and only feel tired at bedtime.

There will be books and music and trees, mountains, grassy slopes (and I will be young enough to roll down them) and rivers. There will be the scent of bonfires and roses and no petrol fumes. We'll be able to fly. There will be all the different nationalities and territories (without conflicts) because I shall want to travel, especially if I have wings.

Speaking of travel, I'm entering a competition in Cosmopolitan to win a 5,000 pounds holiday for two. I plan to set out for India on the Orient Express. I'll send you a postcard (a clean one).

Hasta la vista! - Mother.

I didn't win the competition.

PETER

Peter worked for some years for Geoff, a property wheeler dealer who kept his money in his wellington boot. I saw him fish out a bunch of fivers when he bought me a beer in the pub. His appearance belied his wealth. He owned a stately home as well as the former student accommodation block on the front. Peter worked with him, restoring first the sale rooms in town where he had a flat, and then the block on the front, which Peter managed. At this time he married Alison, a beautiful girl but the only person I've ever met who would look back at you when you smiled, without a hint of warmth. That marriage didn't last long.

After a spell in Taunton as a manager for McDonald's, and his divorce, Peter moved to Cambridge to live with us for a while. He took a series of temporary jobs, including driving a fork lift truck. He drove at speed and could turn it on a sixpence, which came in handy when he learned to drive a car. These days he's a warehouse manager.

Peter stayed in Cambridge when I moved to Ealing. He met Angela, another of our family's good strokes of fortune. He helped Angela raise her two boys who were 8 and 10 at the start and are now in their twenties. Angela is the wittiest person in our family. To my delight Pete and Angela got married when they were on holiday in Australia a couple of years ago, honeymooning in Tasmania, on the fishing trip of a lifetime. Peter collects fishing gear as well as tools, and has more productive hobbies than any man I know. He has twenty four beehives and an expertise in beekeeping gleaned from the hundreds of books he has collected and read on the subject. I've heard him give lectures in UK and America, and was hugely impressed by his knowledge, and his delivery. He gathers hundreds of pounds of honey each season.

He also gardens, growing flowers; on his allotment he grows vegetables and soft fruit. He makes jams and chutneys which he exhibits in local flower shows, often winning prizes. His latest hobby is metal detecting. He found a diamond ring in the orchard where some of his bees reside, which Angela wears. He found a cache of Roman coins, a Roman site and a Roman road in the vicinity of his home. He's now reading history and giving talks about his discoveries, being deeply involved in a metal detectors' club. He writes excellent articles about these activities for the *Dight Times*.

He also taught himself to write computer programmes, working his way through the manual and producing software solutions for local companies. He can do plumbing and woodwork and he invents ingenious contraptions to mystify Angela's workmates. He desk top publishes for his company's social club and enjoys digital photography. He's a man of many, many talents. At 6ft 4 inches he towers over his 6ft brothers as a first born should. You can tell I'm proud of him.

For Christmas Peter wrapped and presented Angela with the bathrobe she had left behind in Tasmania which he secretly retrieved. He's original. He has more integrity than anyone I know. He still has a problem with authority, but as I don't have any anyway, that's all right.

75 JOHN PAUL

John Paul was eighteen the summer we moved to Cambridge. He had just left school after 'A' levels. He joined us in Tenison Avenue. While waiting for his exam results he took various jobs in a bar, a shop etc.

There was a boy living near Nana in a terrace house with a tiny front garden, who mended bicycles. John Paul stopped to talk to him one day, and gave him a hand. JP was always dexterous. He had made tiled wooden coffee tables at twelve, and carved pine love spoons. Now he cleaned bicycle chains and reassembled them, mended punctures, replaced and polished parts. He liked to be busy. He did this for nothing.

When the 'A' level results came, they were good enough for a polytechnic. He applied, but was turned down. Later we would discover that his teacher at school had given him a poor reference in revenge for a prank when he and others advertised the teacher's car for sale in the local paper. I discovered this when I wrote from Cambridge, asking for a reference as a prospective employer, and received a copy of the same damning reference. This illustrates more about the teacher's petty attitude than John Paul's mischief. JP decided to spend another year at school taking an 'A' level in Law. The result came while he was flying back from Italy following six weeks working at the Charity's summer camp for children. I phoned a message to the airline and the air hostess told him as he landed in London, 'You got an A in Law!' This earned him a place at Leicester Poly with four years grant to read Business Studies.

In his first term he was elected chairman of the Rag, raising money for charity. He raised more money for his polytechnic than ever before with innovative schemes, and thinking his business skills were innate rather than learned, decided to leave his course at the end of the first year.

JP was back in Cambridge, looking for a job. A talent for business needs a business in which to operate. He had no money with which to start one. He worked briefly for an estate agent. He tried selling double glazing. He even borrowed my ladder and bucket and cleaned windows. He was trying to invent himself.

He worked hard adapting the derelict swimming pool on the back of my house in Girton to make a letting apartment. He acted as project manager and main contractor. Together we had estimated it would cost 6,000 pounds, and he brought it in exactly on budget. In return for his work on this over a couple of months I bought him his first car, a little clapped out Renault, for 350 pounds.

Meanwhile the bicycle repairer opened a shop called 'Mike's Bikes'. His father, a policeman, helped him establish this outlet. When he moved to a larger shop John Paul helped him to double the showroom size, extending the back yard behind this shop and the adjacent one. The two young men concreted the floor, erected a corrugated plastic roof with metal supports, and Mike bought more stock. John Paul became shop manager. Mike, whose business went from strength to strength, was practically illiterate. JP wrote the signs and kept the records, and bought his first mountain bike.

He could take a bicycle out of its flat pack and assemble it in four minutes. He developed a good sales patter. One day a man came into the shop and JP sold him a bike. The next day the man came back, saying a friend of his wanted to meet JP. He had a sports distributorship in Nottingham. JP took the train to see him. He was offered a job selling mountain bikes imported from America to dealers all over England.

At mountain bike conventions JP invented the 'Bunny-hop' competition. Cyclists competed to 'hop' their bikes over a low rope. He picked up the microphone to give articulate commentaries. He sought sponsorship from Daihatsu, who provided four cars for the company.

He wrote articles for sports magazines about mountain bikes in various settings, including skiing in *Val d'Isère* in France (expenses paid). He photographed a friend cycling into the mouth of a lengthy drain pipe, and 'emerging' at the other end (a spoof). He wrote about his fitness training for a bicycle race. He had a natural writing style. He also has a light heart.

Feeling adventurous, JP went to America on holiday on a visitor's visa. He stayed in Rhode Island where he had some friends. One day he went into a delicatessen to buy bagels and coffee. He met the Leonard family. Pat and Lyn were running the deli with help from their daughter Sarah. JP asked Pat if his daughter would show him around Rhode Island a little. And that's how JP met his wife Sarah over twenty years ago.

After his second trip to America Sarah came to England to stay with him in Kent on an extended holiday. At the end of six months (after Pat and

Lyn visited to check us out), JP and Sarah were married from my house in Queen Anne's Gardens, at Ealing Registry Office.

JP was invited by a former Daihatsu executive to work with him in Canterbury for Chrysler Jeep, training and motivating all the Chrysler dealership managers in Britain. He devised exciting trips to Denver for the top 20 salesmen, where they were met at the airport in a limo, taken to a five star hotel, feted, flattered and incentivized.

Later he moved to work for Landrover as manager of their Norwich dealership, with a staff of 36. He had never sold a car, but had good management skills.

Ben was born at Cowslips then three years later Leah was born in Holt, Norfolk. I looked after Ben while they went to the hospital to have Leah. What a joy, a girl in the family! Pat Leonard was living near them at this stage and we hugged with delight at the news.

Meanwhile I had married Bill and moved into Gordon Road. When Bill and I bought the cottage in France we saw little of the family as we were away for months at a time.

One night in London I got a telephone call from JP to say they were selling their house, moving to America, and by the way, Sarah was pregnant. Charlie was born in Arizona.

Getting established in America is not easy. Although they arrived with a substantial sum from the sale of their house, they needed to establish a year's history of earning and careful spending before they could get a credit card or a mortgage. John's first job was selling cars. He found it very different from managing staff. One day he sold a car to a man who worked in Information Technology, and asked him to let him know if he ever heard of a sales opportunity in his field. In this way he moved into the IT industry.

He gained experience through several jobs and today works as Sales Manager in a company providing software solutions for training certification. So he's still a Motivator to a sales team. At 46 he rides his mountain bike on nearby desert trails, and keeps fit kayaking. He keeps a beautiful garden too.

My brother used to say John Paul was the perfect example of doing whatever you do, to the best of your ability. He couldn't know when he mended his first puncture, that it was his first step to a successful career.

John Paul developed an ear for French during our summer holidays. For three years running during his teens we went to a campsite in Amboise in the Loire Valley, and each time he met the same French girl, Sophie, on holiday with her family. It was touching to see them meet up again by coincidence and as she didn't speak any English he was motivated to learn French.

During his two summers in Italy when he worked for SOS Children's Villages in their summer camp for European children, he learned German from Austrians. The German spoken in Austria is much softer than the German we more often hear. He became fluent enough to take a job on a farm in Germany, helping with the potato harvest for a few weeks.

John Paul is self-disciplined, energetic, focused, conscientious, reliable and honest. His special talent is understanding and good counselling. He is highly articulate. Whenever I have a dilemma, I call him. He listens. And then he gives good advice. Even as a child I leaned on him for moral support. He reasons well and encourages. His honest opinion is always worth seeking. He reminds me strongly of my Father.

76 MARK

Julian, who later chose to be called by his second name, was born at home, attended by a midwife. This was the only time Richard was present at a birth. I held Julian in my arms and said repeatedly 'Oh, he's *beautiful*.' His was the easiest of births. He was also the heaviest, at 8lb 13 oz. He arrived at 6 o'clock in the morning on November 10 1969, while Peter and John Paul were asleep. The boys soon heard the commotion and came to see him, still covered in the white film of a new baby. If it can be accomplished safely, a home birth is unquestionably preferable.

My Mother had bought the house next door less than a year earlier, and as usual she was there to help. She had gone to Australia on a world cruise while I was pregnant with Julian, and I was never more pleased to see her than when she came home early.

When Peter and John Paul were in bed in the evenings, I paid particular attention to Julian, giving him his bottle, then cuddling and talking to him. He was only three weeks old when I sat him on my knee, facing me, and talked to him thus: 'Oh you are a *beau*tiful boy, and your Mummy *loves* you,' as I have to all of them in turn. I used to murmur like this for a minute, then stop. He gazed at me intently, and when I paused, he said 'goo', as if in answer. It was enchanting. Yes, a three week old baby can speak.

He was only seven months old when I became pregnant with the twins. We moved house when he was thirteen months old. For the last three months of my pregnancy I couldn't walk further than from room to room, with my bad back. My Mother took total charge of him and when he started toddling. She looked after all of us while I was unable.

On his second birthday I wrote down all 250 words he knew. He was the most forward of the boys in speaking, but they have all been outshone by my granddaughters who could speak in fluent grammatical sentences at that age.

He started nursery school in the mornings at age three, but his teacher asked me to withdraw him after he stood behind the piano and howled one morning. I took him out for the rest of the year as he was obviously not ready until he was four.

He was a reflective child, day dreaming often. His school reports said he was intelligent but slow in his work. I think he was thinking far more than most people, to give that impression. He was gentle and sweet natured. In fact he was so gentle, at school he was teased quite a bit which toughened him and made him more resolved and cynical than seemed to be his nature.

HIs teacher asked me one day to help Julian with his three times table. 'He's the only one in the class who doesn't know it,' he said, 'and he's holding us back.' I went home and wrote 1 x 3 = 3, 2 x 3 = 6 etc. and fixed the page on the wall in the bathroom. Julian used to sit there enjoying the quiet at the back of the house. He tried, but he still couldn't learn the table. But the next evening, when he was given fifteen lines of prose to learn for the morning's assembly, I was thinking he'll never learn that, but he did so in about ten minutes. I was astonished then had a brain wave. I wrote the table in words, once three is three, two threes are six, etc. and stuck this up in the bathroom. He learned it immediately. By the end of that week he had learned all his tables from prose. I rushed to share this insight with his teacher Mr. L, who said dismissively, Very interesting Mrs. Dight, clearly without interest. A year or two later I saw an article about this phenomenon in the national press and wrote to the author, who agreed that this discovery had still not been recognized or acknowledged in education circles. That's over 30 years ago. I hope they've got the message now.

In Aberystwyth Julian loved to sit on the top lawn by himself and observe nature all around him. We had a field behind us, with horses. He liked to be quiet. He sometimes said he would have liked to be an only child. It must have been difficult to be the middle child between four other brothers. One evening he and I sat there at dusk and noticed a bat flying between the Scots pines, a rabbit in the grass and an owl sitting on top of the swing. It was a magical experience. I wish I had shared with him more quiet moments like that.

One day when he was about three I took Julian to Cardiff by train. As we sat on a station bench waiting, he was watching birds fly in the air when he sighed and said wistfully, 'I *wish* I could fly.' He was lovely company, articulate and willing to talk. At one stage he used to say with a Welsh accent, 'What are you doin', mammy?' He was a good, serene, gentle boy. His daughter Imogen reminds me of him now.

At primary school he entered an Eisteddfod competition, reciting in Welsh a poem about a postman. I watched in awe as he delivered it with convincing Welsh intonation. He joined the school orchestra, taking lessons on the oboe. He was a keen performer. When cuts were imposed on the school budget we were required to buy a musical instrument, and unfortunately we couldn't afford the four hundred pounds. At the time Richard's salary was 12.000 pounds p.a. to sustain 7 of us, so 400 pounds was a lot of money.

One day he constructed a sundial on the top lawn. He broke pieces of twigs off a hazelnut tree, to outline the hours. He sat with a watch all day, marking the shadow of the sun appropriately. I admired his enterprise and patience. When Richard came home he noticed only the twigs lying on the lawn and told him off for making a mess, ordering him crossly to clear it up, which he did in silence. I told Richard 'He has spent all day making a sundial. He doesn't deserve to be told off.' Richard's response was, 'He needs to learn not to vandalize trees.'

Julian settled well into Penglais secondary school but we had to move house at the end of his first year. He liked living there, and was dismayed to leave his established friends. But I knew that a move to Cambridge would eventually be to his advantage. It was at this stage he chose to use his second name, Mark. We refer to him as Julian until the move to Cambridge, and Mark thereafter. He did well in the new school too, and earned a place at Hills Road Sixth Form College where he chose to study English, Law and Drama. I saw him as a pirate captain in a Gilbert and Sullivan operetta. He erupted onto the stage with flashing eyes and tremendous presence. I had no idea it was Mark until a few minutes later. His ability to learn prose was astonishing. He took over the lead in a play at Penglais only two weeks before it opened, giving a great performance. He relished playing a character.

Mark studied Law at Sheffield at the same time Patrick was at UMIST in Manchester. I don't know how they managed on their student grants for living expenses (their fees were paid). I couldn't give them anything, being a single hard up parent, but Richard gave them an allowance of fifty pounds a month each while they were at university. I kept them in the holidays. One summer Mark and John Paul worked as chauffeur punters on the River Cam and went on holiday to Italy on the proceeds.

Mark got his Law degree and started work selling books and software for a legal publishing company. He bought a two bedroom apartment near Ealing where he lived for a couple of years before deciding to attend LAMDA, the London Academy of Music and Dramatic Arts. He wanted to be an actor. He certainly had the talent for it, and enjoyed his year there immensely. But competition for parts at auditions was fierce. There were perhaps ninety applicants for every part. He sold his flat to sustain him during this period, and appeared in London fringe theatre, but eventually the money was spent and he had to return to selling software to lawyers.

Mark met Sarah who had grown up in London, although her father came from California and her mother was Australian. Sarah was a student nurse at the time, and later graduated as a paediatric nurse. As soon as they got engaged Sarah informed me that their intention was to emigrate to Australia after their first baby was born. I was predictably dismayed, but said nothing so she didn't seem to notice.

They had a beautiful wedding in a stately home in a London park on 14 September 2001, three days after 9/11. Several of the American guests couldn't make it because of the attack on the World Trade Center and the Pentagon. All international flights were grounded for several days. John, Sarah and Charlie as a toddler, arrived on the last plane to land at Heathrow from America, and left on the first to fly out on the following Sunday. This was a traumatic background to our celebrations, but their wedding was still a lovely occasion, with parties in a marquee in Sarah's parents' garden at Belsize Park.

They took Harvey abroad at a year old and Imogen was born in Australia. Mark stopped work to study for his bar exams, while Sarah supported them by nursing. Mark qualified as a barrister and a solicitor. After a spell as a defence lawyer in Brisbane he moved to Melbourne to work as a prosecutor.

Mark opened his own law office a year ago in Queensland and is doing well, with Sarah's help in the office. We all met up in Arizona in April, coinciding with Sarah's parents' 40th wedding celebration in California. It was the first time I met my youngest grandson Benjamin who would be three in July, and the first time the children met their American cousins. Mark and Sarah's three children are all bright and beautiful.

77 PATRICK

When Peter and I went to a weekend course on Developing the Psychic Faculty, the woman who led the course was a psychic named Marie Cherry, and in the bar during the evening I showed her a picture of my three youngest boys, wondering if she would pick out the twins. It's the photo taken in front of the house in Radyr with Patrick, Julian and Andre aged about 3 and 4. I said 'What can you tell me about these boys?' She pointed at Julian and said 'You're going to have to give this one a lot of support', to Andre 'He is going to be exceptionally happy in his family life,' and to Patrick, 'This one is never going to give you any trouble. He will be successful and happy in everything he does.'

Patrick was certainly easy to raise. He was a self-contained little boy, always with a project on the go, or a prototype he was developing. He had great concentration and would follow through until he was satisfied with the result. He once spent two days (he was about 7) perfecting a parachute he made from a handkerchief, a weight and some string. He kept retying it, running up two flights of stairs to his room on the top floor in Glen Rosa, out onto the flat roof, dropping the parachute and watching it fall, then running down the stairs again to repeat the process. He was entirely absorbed in this, and bothering no one as he worked.

He had a deep voice, even as a small child. Nana called it 'his navy blue voice'. He was slight, several inches shorter and thinner than his twin. He didn't have an ounce of spare flesh on his body because he was always active. His knees had huge joints that stuck out of his little legs, showing beneath his shorts. He ran like the wind, and was capable. When he climbed on the railing by the beach I was confident he would never fall. When Andre did that I had my heart in my mouth, because he was likely to tumble. I discouraged Andre from going on the roof. They were so different in every way, that it was difficult to believe they were twins. I seldom referred to them as 'the twins' (having read Doctor Spock's *Baby and Child Care* in which he advised against treating them as a pair). They never wore matching clothes. I wanted them to function individually, unlike my twin cousins who were co-dependent.

As well as smart at school, Patrick was artistic. He drew wonderful pictures, one of which won a prize in the Eisteddfod in junior school. It was a colourful drawing of Jack and the Beanstalk, green leaves filling the page, Jack climbing the stalk. For years it hung on the kitchen wall with Blue-tack. Patrick knew how much I admired this picture. A couple of times when he was cross with me he took the picture off the wall and hid it in his bedroom to show his disapproval. He was not rebellious or naughty, but every mother needs correcting at times. It was a good safety valve. When he took it down I would say 'Oh please Patrick, don't take away your picture,' adding value to his gesture. He always brought it back when he'd forgiven me.

I can only remember one occasion on which I felt cross with Patrick. I don't remember what caused it, but I recall telling him off and he protested. I sent him upstairs to cool off. Crying noisily, he threw his bedding down the stairs, first the duvet then the pillow. I was alarmed because that was not like Patrick, but I was still cross. I ran up the stairs saying, 'You naughty boy! Take those back to your room immediately!' and he went and sat down on his bed, sobbing. I was so touched by his anguish, I sat down next to him and put my arms around him and kissed and hugged him, at which his anger dissolved and he relaxed in my arms. It was astonishing how fast the situation changed from confrontation to empathy. I wonder what on earth could have provoked this tension? I doubt if Patrick remembers either.

For the rest of his childhood he was a good boy. He responded to directions, was always helpful in the kitchen, liking nothing better than to prepare a meal from about the age of seven. On Mother's Day when he was about nine he prepared a whole dinner for the family with something cooked, salad and cheese, bread, I don't recall what else, and at the last minute he opened a tin of tuna to add to the feast. He was so willing. He loved to make bread rolls and could produce a bread basket full of handsome knots and twists, without supervision. His favourite pudding was Velvet Refrigerator Cake which he would make at the drop of a hat.

He and Andre loved to do the catering on camping holidays in France. Patrick was so small and nimble, he moved easily around the van, cooking on the stove. The twins laid the tables, served the food and were generally useful. That's the sort of company you want on a camping holiday.

He and Andre were good shoppers too. I took them to Tesco's when they were about fourteen and left them there with a hundred pounds to do a week's shopping. I must have been busy with something else to do that. When I picked them up they had a trolley full of all the right things, even without a list. They bought the right bread, sugar free cereal, fresh vegetables etc. that we favoured. I couldn't have done it better myself. They were assiduous label readers.

Patrick had a yearning to grow something in Radyr (which we left when they were five). Richard would not let them plant anything in the garden, so Uncle Ted who lived opposite made a seed box for Patrick in which he planted radishes, and I paid him a penny for each one he harvested. With a third acre garden at his disposal in Aberystwyth, it was sad that Richard still would not let them have even a yard of it. Patrick was confined to the seed box and pots. Today his garden flourishes in Ireland, where he grows vegetables and flowers.

He was the last to learn to swim. All the others were swimmers, Andre being exceptionally able in the water, but Patrick was nervous. He was eight when I taught him how to float on his back, and in the process, found I could float too. What a triumph, learning to swim at 41! I have Patrick to thank for that. Finding that I could relax on my back and move about in the water using my arms, I gained confidence and at last I could swim in the deep end, and so could he.

I was nervous nonetheless, especially when older boys jumped in the water around us and churned the water. Patrick and Andre swam like pilot fish beside me, saying 'Don't splash our mother,' to bemused strangers.

Patrick and Andre were compatible, while being totally different. I asked them in the second year at primary school if they would like to be in separate classes? Oh no, they said, without hesitation, we like being together. Yet their interests and friends were different and they seemed no more twin like than any other two brothers in the family. It was only in their teens and as they grew up that their bond was more in evidence. They seem closer as adults than they were as small children.

Despite the fact that Andre was about six inches taller than Patrick, there was no rivalry. Neither twin was dominant. Patrick didn't feel intimidated by Andre's height and Andre didn't feel put out by Patrick's quicksilver personality. They both did well in school, evenly matched in their results. They had different skills and interests. Patrick did not share Andre's passionate interest in animals. He spent the whole of the summer he turned fourteen learning to programme his Amstrad He produced pictures of a bicycle with all its spokes, without any software, a remarkable achievement. He became so engrossed in the computer that just before his 'O' levels his teacher asked me, 'Please Mrs Dight, don't let Patrick spend any more time on his computer or his exam results will suffer.' I went home from the PTA meeting and explained this to Patrick, who without demur said 'OK Mum,' and didn't switch it on again for weeks. I could always convince Patrick by discussion because he was open to reason. It was not in his nature to argue for nothing.

Patrick's hearing was slightly impaired by all the throat infections he had suffered. In addition to this, his attention was always focused on whatever he was thinking about at the time, which accounts for him often being the last to realize what was going on around him. He remembers remarkably little about his early life. Andre's recall is vivid, but Patrick's is minimal.

In sixth form college Patrick's heart was set on studying Art. As well as practical art he studied the history of art, and I thought 'Oh, he won't find that very interesting,' but I was entirely wrong. He absorbed everything they taught him about art history. He went on a trip to Paris to look at pictures with his art class. He produced a picture on his computer of an old boot, with lots of detail and character, and entered it successfully, the first pupil to contribute such an entry at 'A' level. His work was exhibited at school and I saw it all with pride.

At the same time he was doing Business Studies, and in his first year won the Business prize. This switched his focus from art to business. He decided he wanted to study Management Science at UMIST (University of Manchester Institute of Science and Technology). I drove him to Manchester with his possessions and saw him move into student accommodation at the University.

The following year he moved into a scruffy student house which he shared with friends. Naturally he did a lot of the cooking. I visited him there once, sleeping on the mattress on the floor in his bedroom while he shared his friend's room. During the night I heard a rustle of paper from the sandwich bag I'd brought. It was a mouse. I moved onto the sofa and went back to sleep. We went out to eat in an Indian curry house. We had such a good time.

Patrick suffered from a series of sore throats and his doctor in Manchester advised tonsillectomy. He had finished his exams but booked into the hospital in Manchester at the end of term for the operation. He came back afterwards on the train by himself, to Queen Anne's Gardens in Ealing. The next night his throat started to bleed. It was alarming. I took him in the middle of the night to Ealing Hospital where they kept him on a trolley for an hour until eventually the bleeding stopped, and I took him home again.

The next night the bleeding started again, worse than ever. Bill was staying with us that night and spent a couple of hours with Patrick, as he leaned over, spitting out blood in alarming quantity. I was frantic, terrified of losing him. The next morning Bill and I drove him to a different hospital where he was admitted, and immediately started bleeding again. He had to have an emergency operation to repair the cut that was too deep from the original tonsillectomy. He was put on a drip and stayed for two or three days before he was allowed home. I was mighty glad of Bill's support in that episode. This was the only occasion I can recall when Patrick caused me any worry.

Patrick took up fencing at about fourteen years of age while he was a pupil at Parkside Community College. He regularly played in tournaments and when he moved to Ireland he won the Irish Open one year. I proudly wear the silver brooch he won at that competition. I'm sad to say I only saw him fence once. All this he accomplished by himself.

When I started Export Connect, Patrick did my accounts. I paid for his driving lessons as a reward, knowing he needed a car to get to work when he left college; but he would have done it for nothing. He was wholly supportive.

Pat was the only one of my sons who knew what he wanted to study. When he graduated he found himself a job where his computer skills would be developed. When he moved with Kate to Dublin he became a highly paid contractor. He bought an end of terrace house in dire need of repair, and fixed it. He bought another house in Nenagh when he was thirty, letting out the one in Dublin. He developed his own business providing software for accountancy. He has been a key member of the team developing BHSL (Biomass Heating Solutions Ltd). Patrick is not a conspicuous consumer. He often makes and mends his own equipment, being competent at woodwork and electrical skills, which John Paul taught him in his teens. He installed three kitchens, put in double glazed windows in his Nenagh house with Peter's help, and plumbed in new bathrooms. He transformed the garden for the children to play in.

Pat and Kate have four children. Emer is the oldest; Patrick goes horse riding with her. The three boys, Luke, Harry and Sam, have varied interests and Patrick is an involved father. All the children play team games and are competitive at the same time as cooperative. He does puzzles with them, and board games. His energies are evenly divided between his work and his family. He and Kate are happy.

He formatted and printed the 200 pages plus of my Recipe Book. He's now formatting my Memoirs. He's my financial adviser. He is completely reliable.

True to Marie's psychic forecast, he's successful in his family and working life, and has never troubled me for anything.

78 ANDRE

When they were little I taught the boys to 'say their numbers', one to five, to check they were all present. Andre always ended on an up note, 'five!' and perhaps this contributed to his sense of being the youngest, albeit by only twenty minutes.

When I put them to bed in their cots Andre would look at a picture book when he was about a year old, turning the pages slowly. Patrick would invariably tear the pages, so I gave him old magazines to shred and picked up the pieces in the morning. When they moved to beds Andre would compose himself to sleep, pulling the blanket up to his ears and closing his eyes, but Patrick would get up and wander around the room. Sometimes I'd find Patrick asleep with his feet on the floor and his body sprawled on the bed, mid action, and I'd pick him up and tuck him in. I got up most nights when I heard (even in my sleep) a child turn over, to pull the blankets over him, returning to sleep almost without waking. As they grew older Andre waited for Patrick to fall asleep before he turned the light off, because Patrick didn't like the dark.

When I left them at primary school sometimes Patrick would cry and cling to me. Andre would say 'You go Mummy, I'll look after him.'

Andre and Patrick were quite different physically, in temperament, interests and growth rates. Patrick was 5 lb. 14 oz. and Andre was 5 lb. 8 oz., but Andre began to grow faster right from the start. By the time they were aged seven, Andre was around six inches taller than his twin. Today they are both about 6ft tall, muscular and strong. They both have plenty of energy and work hard.

They worked well at school, their results even, although their interests were so different. Patrick was absorbed in his computer and Andre said at fifteen that he had no intention ever of using one of those. Theirs was the last year at school to be deprived of computer lessons.

When Andre learned that we were divorcing, his first response was to get a paper round so he could earn his own pocket money.

Before he could speak Andre registered his intense interest in animals. From the back window of the car he would squeal with excitement if he saw horses in a field, and he always wanted pets. He would have liked to be a vet but the exams were onerous (four A results at 'A' level) and then six years at university. Although he could have achieved the exam results he wanted, I could not sustain the expense of such a lengthy education. The vet here in America who became his good friend, said that Andre is the best stockman he has known in his entire career.

He would have enjoyed working in a zoo, and whenever he had the opportunity to visit one, he would not leave until he had seen every animal. His bedtime reading was animal reference books, as a result of which he can name every species that appears on television, however obscure. I wish he could have landed a job with David Attenborough, making wildlife documentaries. His son Jake has all the same qualities.

His early interest in keeping canaries won him the title Student of the Year at University in a nationwide competition. He bred dozens of canaries every season, knowing every bird, by sight and personality.

Andre is also a plantsman, a passion he picked up from his father. After seeing Richard's epiphyllums in Spain, Andre ordered an envelope of cuttings by post, and today his porch is festooned in mature epiphyllums that bloom at long intervals for a couple of days, spectacular vivid flowers that are worth waiting for. His garden is full of decorative plants and he has a vegetable patch as well, growing tomatoes, lettuces, courgettes, onions, beans, beets and herbs.

He has also become an accomplished patio builder, having started in New York Avenue with a stone patio and pond, and in his present home a stone path, patio and pergola are planned.

He took up beekeeping but has had bad reactions to beestings which landed him in hospital a couple of times.

Andre told me years ago when I lived in Ealing that he looked forward to caring for me as I get older, if and when I need it. He encouraged me to move to America after my second divorce and has given me great support and love.

Andre suffered testicular cancer seven years ago, and at the same time job loss, when Pilgrims' Pride withdrew from raising turkeys in the Valley. While recovering from his operation which fortunately cured the cancer, he helped to set up the Virginia Turkey Growers' Cooperative, working six weeks without pay at the beginning. After a couple of years successfully establishing good practice and management systems in the Turkey Cooperative, he lost his job to a local man through office politics.

He retrained as a science teacher as Deanna did not want to move from Harrisonburg and nothing else at his level in the poultry industry was available in the district. He taught Biology for a year at Turner Ashby High School but his position was lost in the budget cuts, despite a petition by his pupils to retain him as their teacher.

Andre's first marriage ended abruptly and painfully. He suffered from depression for a while. But his great capacity for love is evident in his second marriage, and the way he raises his boys, Connor and Jake, with whom he is deeply engaged. He's an understanding, loving father and stepfather to Gianna's son Clay.

Andre established my American garden and cut the lawn for five years until he became so busy, I found a boy to cut it. He helps me with jobs around the house, and on the computer. He and Gianna often cook and entertain, and include me. He has transformed his garden and continues to enhance it. They fixed up the house in New York Avenue and improved its condition. He and Gianna always make me welcome and give me a sense of comfort and security to live near them.

After a career in turkey rearing Andre now works for Biomass, where he advises on poultry ventilation in the new system using Biomass' combustion engine which burns chicken litter to heat the poultry house., He has developed into an accomplished negotiator with farmers, investors and environmental specialists. This entails a lot of travelling to Europe and beyond, but hopefully more of his work will be in the States once Biomass is established here. He is certainly in the right career to use and develop his skills and interests.

79 FAMILY SETBACK

During the past four years the family suffered a setback when Andre and Deanna's marriage fell apart. I won't write about the details – that is not my story – but simply record that their dispute was never about property or third parties. Andre was suffering from depression. Since coming to America he had cancer, he was made redundant, his father was dying in Spain and he was briefly hospitalized as the result of his depression. Deanna couldn't understand why he didn't just snap out of it, and sent him to stay with me. When he tried to go back, they argued bitterly. After three attempts he refused to go back again.

He was prepared to let his wife and children keep the family home and all their goods. His only claim was for joint custody of the children. I warned them both at the beginning that a legal battle would benefit only the lawyers. The children meant more than anything to Andre who could not let them go without a struggle. He is a deeply committed father. Andre had been fully involved in their care, especially with Jake for whom he was primary carer while Deanna worked after he lost his job and he was retraining to be a teacher. At the start Connor was three and Jake was a year old. We did not see them at one stage for six weeks, until in court the judge imposed Andre's visitation rights.

Andre stayed with me for a year. It was a time of turmoil and distress for all of us. In addition to our pain that access to the children was sporadic and unreliable, we were all distressed at the effect this had on the boys, who missed their father. Andre and Deanna were both broke from the costly custody dispute. Both our extended families suffered emotionally and financially from the fall-out.

Fortunately I had two spare bedrooms so the children were able to stay here overnight when we had them.

Gianna who was their neighbour, befriended Andre, counselling him about his troubles, and in the process they became close. This new relationship added to Deanna's distress. To ease the tension Gianna moved out of her house. When Gianna's lease on the temporary apartment ended she looked for a place to rent for herself and son. The rental properties she and Andre researched were either expensive or scruffy. I decided to buy a modest house in which Gianna could live and Andre could help her to improve it, still living with me while waiting for his divorce to become final. They showed me a 1942 fixer upper in New York Avenue which had plenty of potential but needed a lot of work to upgrade it. I put in an offer within half an hour of viewing it, and Gianna had only a month to wait to move in. I mortgaged my own house to buy it. The rent would cover the mortgage.

The following month the financial melt-down hit the market. Both houses lost value and like everybody else I lost 40% on the value of my investments, although much of this would be restored when the market recovered. My pension was miniscule. It was difficult to sleep in this perilous scenario. But we didn't regret buying the house, because it felt homely. Our first improvement was to put a high fence along the open side of the back garden, for the children's safety. Over the next couple of years they decorated the rooms, updated the bathrooms and installed a new kitchen. Andre extended the deck and transformed front and back gardens with flower beds. I remodelled my old curtains to fit their windows. (As a frequent mover I never throw away curtains.)

Once the judge awarded joint custody to Connor and Jake's parents we could see them regularly. The boys had known and trusted Gianna as long as they could remember. Gianna already loved them and Clay was their close friend. Connor in particular looked forward to playing with him on every visit. Gianna had given Andre all her support and kindness during the year he lived with me. Her warmth and love sustained him when he was at his lowest ebb. She also supported me in the roller coaster times. A further bout of depression unsettled Andre during the court proceedings, when he could see no end to the dispute. I don't know how we would have survived without Gianna.

Soon after the divorce was finalized Andre and Gianna were married in the back garden of the house in New York Avenue. It was a happy, sunny, informal day enjoyed by their friends and families. Gianna's sister Betsy catered superbly for the wedding and John Paul was best man. The three boys wore matching cricket shirts Andre had bought them in England, and proclaimed themselves Brothers. I looked on with more gratitude in my heart for Gianna, and Andre's recovery, than I can express.

Eventually Deanna found that the house, now in negative equity, was too big and costly for her. The judge ordered the house to be sold and they tried to sell it, but the housing market is dead. To avoid deeper financial hardship, Andre offered to move into the house to let Deanna find more affordable accommodation, and wrote off what she owed him. They were reluctant to leave New York Avenue, where Andre had just completed a stone patio with pond, and lavishly planted the garden, but it was the best solution for all of them. We re-let it.

Deanna and the boys found a nice modern house to rent near the hospital where she works, and Jake's nursery school. Deanna was a lot happier now that their disputes were settled and her home was more manageable. She made it very attractive. I was relieved that now I could have the boys at times even when it wasn't Andre's turn, and we found a happier way to relate. I was always conscious of the strain she suffered during this difficult time, and wanted to be mother in law as well as grandmother. I now take the boys out for meals with Deanna, and I care for them when the schools are closed by snow, or if they are unwell while she is working.

Throughout it all the boys have remained our main priority and our joy. They are well adjusted, loving and full of charm. They are both smart. Their characters are developing well, their interests widening and they are loved by everybody in both families. Deanna's Aunt Dee and Uncle Al in particular have been stalwart in their support of all concerned, kind and understanding towards Andre and me, and generous and loving towards Deanna and the boys. Theirs has been a healing influence throughout. They feel like grandparents to the boys, and the boys adore them.

Connor is an outstanding reader and this month got straight A's in his school report. He plays soccer and basketball and does karate. Jake is Daddy's little helper in the garden and with other hobbies. He now plays soccer too. He loves to watch Nature programmes with me and play games. He's surprisingly competent for a 5 year old. He likes to take Olive their poodle puppy for a walk with Andre, and is training her to 'sit' and 'lie down'. He and Connor are keen players of computer games.

Clay taught Jake when he was 4, to ride his two wheeler bicycle on the back lawn at NYA. Clay (9) is extremely bright and musical. His piano composition recently won an inter-schools talent competition and he's a gifted boy. He has started to play American Football, looking professional in his smart outfit. All three play energetically on their trampoline.

After retraining as a Science teacher, and working for a year at a local high school, jobs were being cut back in education. Andre became a poultry consultant and now works for BHSL, in the development and promotion of their chicken litter combustion system. This entails frequent trips to Europe and beyond. Throughout this time Gianna has continued to be Director of the Collins Center, and counsellor in the treatment of victims of sexual abuse. I will never forget that she took Andre on when he was broke, jobless and sad. Now he's well, happy and has a great job.

Gianna is a talented homemaker, parent, carer, cook, organizer, entertainer, decorator, counsellor and friend. She's professional and competent. I'm proud and grateful to have her in the family.

80 THE DINGLE PENINSULA

In June 2010 Patrick and Kate rented a holiday house on the Dingle Peninsula and invited Peter, Angela and me to join them and their children. Before we could leave there was a lot to do. Patrick was busy on the computer with Biomass until late on Friday night. Kate was packing two cars with all we would need for our self-catering holiday and the amusement of four children. My contribution was merely to list essential holiday items, and buy a case of wine.

On the Saturday morning before we left Patrick trimmed the hedge, treated the new wooden gates he'd just installed and built a frame for the peas he was growing to climb up; they were knee high and threatening to collapse. Kate's brother Luke promised to water the garden and Sam was a great help, watering the window boxes and vegetables before we left.

With forethought Patrick had made and frozen a turkey and ham pie the previous Christmas especially for this occasion. It defrosted nicely on the journey. Into two cars Kate packed clothes, food, books, games and seven people.

On the way we stopped at Killeedy to visit Kate's mother Kathleen, who welcomed us with a cake she'd baked that morning. Jack and Cushla (who look after 15 thousand free range chickens nearby as well as Jack being the inventor/developer of the Biomass litter combustion boiler), greeted us warmly. They have four children.

All over Ireland the fuchsia hedges were in bloom. On our way to the house above Ventry, west of Dingle, we saw yellow irises, purple foxgloves, pink roses and blue cornflowers growing wild in the countryside. We found our rented house with all mod. cons. on a flint track up a mountainside overlooking the Bay of Dingle. Surrounded by small green fields divided by grey dry stone walls, with a breeze blowing off the sea, the only sounds were of birds singing, sheep bleating and a few cattle lowing.

We arrived at 5 o'clock and Patrick said that Peter and Angela would be there by 7 in their rented car from Kerry Airport. 'How on earth will they find us in the absence of road names or signs?' I asked. The lane ended among fields soon after passing us. 'I emailed Peter a map reference,' said Pat with some glee, knowing Peter would be challenged but confident he'd handle it, and to my relief they drove up on time after only one wrong turning in a farmyard. Don't ask me how they did it, but I suspect Google Earth helped, and the fact that Angela has a degree in Geography.

An old donkey was tethered in the nearby farmyard and a roaming goose and chickens scratched about behind the fence bridged by rusty old bedsprings. Behind us blue mountain tops sloped down over green hills and sparkling rivers to the sea below. Irish skies are rarely so cloudless and blue as they were that week.

On the first evening we feasted on the turkey and ham pie prepared earlier. It filled a huge rectangular baking dish with a porcelain blackbird supporting the crust. It was delicious and more than enough for the nine of us. Our spirits were lifted by the company and good food. We settled to watch World Cup Soccer on TV, cheering and jeering in unison. The children loved playing with Peter who teased and tickled and excited them with his challenging games. We played Scattergories, Go Fish, Dungeons and Dragons, and they learned new card tricks. All enjoyed reading. I had not laughed so much in all the previous year as I did that week. Angela's wit delighted us all, and we shared the cooking.

I have never known children so enterprising in play. They handle board games and puzzles with competitive intelligence, being sharp as a tack, but also amuse themselves with improvised games, jumping over sticks, racing, digging without spades and arranging shells. They play cooperatively, in exemplary fashion. The TV 'Supernanny' series should make a documentary about them as an example and antidote to dysfunctional families.

They hired two motor boats for a fishing trip, and Peter supplied rods. He'd brought hundreds of pounds worth of fishing equipment, it being one of his pet hobbies, and bought simple frames with lures for the children. Luke caught the most fish. Harry caught the largest (4lb 10 ounces), pulling up 3 pollock at once. Kate landed her first fish ever. They came home with more fish than the nine of us could eat. Patrick and Peter gutted the catch and fried it with boiled new potatoes and mange-tout peas, and we froze the surplus.

Another day we spent on the sandy beach, with a windbreaker, a camping stove and a pan full of sausages. The highlight of my holiday was sitting in a beach chair with a windshield arranged around me by Patrick, and a towel on top for shade; five star treatment fit for a queen. When a

Naval ship anchored in Dingle Bay I said, 'I didn't know Ireland had a Navy.' Patrick said 'Yes, and that's probably it.'

We explored Gallarus Oratory, a stone building raised 1300 years ago by early Christians, still waterproof and in good repair after centuries of buffeting Atlantic gales. One evening Kate's brother Jim and his friend played their guitars and sang at Paddy O'Shea's pub nearby while I seized this rare opportunity to 'babysit' my grandchildren. How I wish that was a frequent activity rather than a rare privilege. One evening Kate bought two tickets for a Folk Concert and took me to see the Staves sisters from England, who sang like angels, and a Dutch busker with two guitarists and a drummer, a memorable musical treat.

On the way home we stopped again at Killeedy, where Jack played in the hayfield with the kids, smothering them with hay. It was hard saying goodbye to Kathleen, she and I both sensing it might be our last meeting. We hugged and I fought tears. Kathleen always made me feel so welcome, and she has been wonderful to Patrick.

Luke and Nora invited us all for tea in their garden. We ate French cheeses, scones and clotted cream in the sunshine. The vegetables Luke had watered in our absence seemed to have doubled in size. Courgettes, potatoes and peas were rioting. The garden never looked better. The fruit trees had all set fruit and in the corner of the garden beside a purple clematis, an elderflower bush was in bloom. Kate and I made elderflower champagne, and rhubarb compote. Harry (8), who at first wrinkled his nose at rhubarb, changed his mind and ate three helpings. On Father's Day Harry cooked scrambled eggs and toast for Patrick's breakfast and took it up to him just as he was waking. Every time I look Harry in the eyes, I see my Father looking back at me.

It was a wonderful holiday. Sharing it with Pete and Angela made it even more special. Patrick and Kate made us feel entirely welcome. I observed the children's latest stages of development and went home feeling refreshed, rejuvenated and replenished by my wonderful family.

81 KATHLEEN O'CONNOR

Kathleen died in November 2010, the day after her 81st birthday. Because of her birthday all her children were there to say goodbye. She had ten sons, two daughters, forty one grandchildren and a great grandchild, all of whose birthdays she remembered. She was a constant and loving presence in all their lives. I shared four grandchildren with her.

Kathleen was tireless in her love of family and always in good spirits. She was the only person in my world who felt to me like a motherly presence. She was a wonderful second mother to Patrick who loved her dearly.

The O'Connors are a remarkable family. Her two daughters are nurses, most of the sons are teachers, one is a priest and one a diplomat who worked with the Irish president during the resolution of the conflict in Northern Ireland. We were at Declan's wedding and later in the pub I sat next to Kathleen, surrounded by her family playing keyboard, guitars and singing. Kathleen beamed at me and taught me the chorus of an Irish song. At the end of it she squeezed my hand and chuckled, 'There now, you just sang an IRA song.'

She was born only 500 yards from the Church where she was buried. Most of her life she lived within a two mile radius of the Church. 'Her travelling was inward,' wrote her son Luke. At her funeral Luke gave a moving Eulogy which is published in full in Issue 56 of the *Dight Times*. He described his mother as 'A woman whose life was built around core values such as a profound and utter commitment to family, a deep sense of God working with and watching over all their lives, a kind and generous heart, a genuine interest in people and a special compassion for those burdened by life's crosses, a capacity to live fully in the present moment, a passionate commitment to the duty of hope, an unfailingly positive outlook, an ability to see around corners, a modesty coupled with quiet steeliness, an instinctive willingness to work hard, a flexibility that allowed her to adapt and change to the various stages of life, a selflessness that meant she put others first and was always last to sit down at the table, a wisdom that was the fruit of years of genuine engagement with people enriched by moments of quiet reflection.'

Luke described her hospitality: 'The table became a powerful metaphor for who she was. It was a place of failte, of hospitality, of conversation and debate about life's challenges and issues, all guided by her unique moral compass and her grounded sense of perspective of life. You got up from her table feeling renewed, affirmed, empowered, and above all with a sense that things would work out and that you would be able to cope.

'The dinner might have been prepared for 10 but when 15 sat at the table she had this amazing ability to ensure that everybody had enough. She often made the miracle of the loaves and fishes look quite ordinary.

'Mam had a deep faith in God and this was a very important part of her life. She wasn't pious in the traditional sense but she prayed every day and had a very real sense of God's presence and protection. A kind neighbour commented the other evening that her death was well planned by God around her birthday celebrations. Because of the planned birthday party we were all around... Her timing was impeccable.'

It is an enormous blessing to have known and loved, and been loved by Kathleen. I'm profoundly grateful to her in particular for the love with which she embraced my sons who knew her best, Patrick, Andre and Peter.

82 VISIT TO IKEA

It has been gratifying to discover that all my boys write well. Peter has written many good articles for the *Dight Times* about his hobbies, and I've heard him lecture on Beekeeping in England and in America. He has inherited his Father's lecturing skills. Mark writes legal arguments, absorbing letters and poetry, Patrick writes good business plans but would like to try his hand at science fiction when he has time. Andre has published articles about Canaries and written a company newsletter, and John Paul sold several articles to sports magazines. It's good to know they all have the writing gene.

John Paul wrote the following in 2006:

I told this story to a lady on the plane to Orlando. We were swapping kid stories. She suggested I write it down. You might enjoy it.

Ten days before Christmas in 1998 we had been staying at Tom's house for the weekend. I have been allergic to cats since I was a teenager and didn't realize that Tom had one until it was too late. I took an antihistamine and toughed it out. We hadn't seen each other for a long time and enjoyed a big feast and went to bed late Saturday night. By Sunday morning I was exhausted from lack of sleep, hung over from too much red wine and puffy eyed from the cat. I was glad to pack up our Landrover Discovery and head for home with my wife Sarah, who was pregnant, and our four year old son Ben.

A three hour drive in prospect, we would be home and I could relax for the afternoon, maybe even watch some Formula One racing on TV, and doze on the sofa. The M25 was busy but by eleven o'clock we were approaching Dartford and the new bridge over the Thames. My eyes were still puffy but the hangover was subsiding. Things were improving. Then Sarah spotted IKEA. Now most men I know hate shopping and I'm no exception. Shopping the week before Christmas just compounds the problem. I put my foot down and said no way were we stopping.

My wife's logic when it comes to shopping cannot be faulted. Like most families we lived on a budget and apparently IKEA had Christmas gifts like picture frames, wooden toys, kitchen gadgets and the like that could not be purchased for twice the price in Norwich. How was she to stick to the budget if I didn't let her shop at IKEA? Besides, there is a Crèche we can put Ben into, a restaurant where we can get a cheap lunch and it will be just the two of us shopping together. If we are quick we can still make it back for the racing and not need to stop for lunch on the way. She had me. Though not pleased, I resigned myself to be patient and pleasant, after all Sarah puts great emphasis on quality time together and we could do with saving some money on Christmas presents.

I knew I should have stuck to my guns when we couldn't find a parking space. IKEA has perhaps the largest car park of any store in the South of England. I suggested turning around but I had apparently 'promised' so it was no use. We went in the store and lined up for twenty minutes to put Ben in the Crèche. This at least would give us a break. He was ornery and tired and dealing with him in my state was compounding a tedious experience. We got to the front of the line before it really registered with Ben what was going on. When the penny dropped that he was going to be separated from us he had a fit, started bawling and despite all bribery and promises of good and bad things happening to him, he refused to be left in the Crèche.

Miserable, with head throbbing and thoroughly defeated we headed into the crowd. We moved slowly through the store, which is built in such a way that you have to go through every single aisle to get to the check out at the other end. I had been conned as usual. OK, we saved some money on some cheap Christmas presents, but there was no sign of the things we desperately needed for our house. The cart filled up with non-essential items that were sure to break the budget yet again. Ben was constantly in danger of getting lost in the crowd and wouldn't listen. Why had I not stuck to my guns?

The line to the restaurant was so long that even Sarah was convinced we'd be wasting our time trying to eat there. Sometimes emotions pile on top of each other: frustration, anger and despair combined into a new feeling never experienced before. The checkout lines created such a moment. 'An hour at least' was the best estimate one of the store employees could give. Great. Now on top of exhaustion, hangover, a busted budget, an upset four-year-old, hunger and a fight with my wife, we have to wait in line and miss the Grand Prix. Of course I tried to ditch the trolley and head for home but it was useless; we had got this far and there was no way we were turning back.

When we finally got out of the check-out area I went ahead and fetched the car and brought it back to the loading dock. We had a lot of boxes and struggled to fit them in on top of the luggage in the back. Not a pleasant task when you are not speaking to each other. It took several attempts at stacking, this way and that, to get it all in and still see out the back window.

The car loaded, we were about to leave when Ben decided he needed to go to the bathroom. 'You take him' said Sarah, and I was in no position to argue. She was as tired and frustrated as I was but she was pregnant to boot. We walked together back to the front of the store, but Ben refused to hold my hand.

At the front of IKEA is a large rotating door. I walked through expecting Ben to follow by my side. Instead he stayed outside and froze, staring at the big scary rotating entryway. I headed back to fetch him only to discover that by this point he had peed in his pants. Both of us somewhat embarrassed, we headed for the bathroom and made a futile attempt at getting him to pee again, but it was too late. I took off his pants and tried to dry them under the hand drier. Take it from me, it doesn't work. So with paper towels shoved down his pants and a lot of crying we headed back to the car. It is hard to get really mad at your own children, but I couldn't help thinking that he had done this to punish us for dragging him around the store and threatening to leave him in the Crèche. We had no choice but to find him some pants before we could go any further.

Unfortunately the pants were in a suitcase underneath all the IKEA stuff. I had no patience left. My anger bubbled over and I lost it. Sarah pulled Ben aside and I threw the IKEA stuff out of the car onto a pile. I opened the suitcase that had been buried underneath, grabbed Ben, stood him up in the suitcase and dropped his pants. Just as I was beginning to pull his new pants up, the heavens opened. The rain came down hard and started soaking the pile of boxes by the car. Sarah and I looked at each other in disbelief and then turned to Ben. He turned his head sideways, rolled his eyes, put his hands up and said "Oh fuck!" He hasn't to my knowledge said it since and certainly had never been heard to say it before that day. Sarah and I looked at each other and burst out laughing. We cried with laughter for a good five minutes.

We packed up the soggy boxes, jumped in the car and headed for home. The tension had been broken and we were a happy little family again on our way home from IKEA, all thanks to Ben.

83 ARIZONA REUNION APRIL 2011

When Sarah's parents Trisha and Paul celebrated their 40th wedding anniversary in April 2011 with a family get together in California, we seized the chance to meet up with Mark, Sarah and their three children in Arizona, the next state. John and Sarah were their hosts and I rented a house a mile away as second base for Andre, Gianna, Connor, Jake, Patrick and me. We were missing Kate and the children and Peter and Angela, but this was a significant occasion because Mark's and Andre's children were meeting for the first time. I hadn't seen Mark's family for nearly five years, during which Benjamin had been born and was now three months short of his third birthday.

We spent a happy week just watching the cousins getting to know each other. There was so little friction they were all busy enjoying themselves. It reminded me of an O'Connor gathering. If you put enough children together and leave them to it, they sort themselves into compatible groups. They played hard all day and at night, hit the sack gratefully.

John Paul and Sarah had assembled a great stock of hospitality and dispensed it generously. We were glad to be able to entertain them sometimes too, and the younger children played in our small swimming pool, fondly watched by the adults. Connor (he had a stitched knee) drifted on a blow-up bed, pulled around the pool by Harvey, both giggling happily. Those two hit it off especially. Jake demonstrated his ability to submerge his head (triggering Granny's water phobia) and little Benjamin skimmed around the pool, held up by a noodle. The Australia and Arizona Dights are all professionals in water, anyway.

The children ranged in age from 2 to 15 and integrated remarkably. Ben, Leah and Charlie related to their cousins with patience and understanding, playing with each at his or her own level. They organized a three legged race with no thought for winning or matching sizes, simply intent on having fun, teaching the little ones technique. Charlie and Leah, being practised, athletic and matched, would have won every race of course, but it was not competitive. Similarly they had egg and spoon races where the little ones simply held the egg in the bowl of the spoon and ran like mad. 'It's impossible, otherwise,' explained 5 year old Jake.

Charlie, Harvey, Connor and Jake organized a four strong synchronized DS game, in a line on the sofa. They built Lego vehicles and at one stage played poker like pros. Harvey, Charlie and Connor played an imaginative game about dinosaurs.

On the Saturday night John and Sarah threw a grand party for around a hundred guests, catered by a Mexican family who set up, cooked, manned the bar and cleaned up afterwards, organized by friend Kishore. The food was delicious with plenty left over.

The garden was decorated with paper lanterns hung from a tree and table lights; yellow tablecloths added colour. The highlight of the party was *The Point Blank*, Ben's rock band, sounding better than ever. Ben's singing has developed noticeably. They're getting plenty of practice, playing for friends' parties.

The hibiscus bloomed. Palm trees and flowering shrubs added glamour to the scene. I noticed Nana's papyrus standing proudly in a pot and sent her a thought.

Leah spent the evening applying glittering tattoos to willing subjects, up to half a dozen each, which will need a lot of soaking in the bath. Jake proudly showed off his parrot, a soccer ball, rock guitar etc. and Imogen had cherries, butterflies and flowers on her arms. Leah and Imogen added grace to the party.

On Easter Sunday the little kids hunted buckets of chocolate eggs hidden all over the garden by the older ones.

The children visited the Zoo in Phoenix with their Dads and a gold mine where they panned for gold. John took the older ones kayaking and fishing on the river. Gianna took Patrick for some shopping therapy to buy surprises for his much-missed family.

I feasted my eyes every day on eight beautiful grandchildren enjoying themselves together. They were instant friends and so compatible. It was balm to my soul, being with so many of my family. Knowing our time together was short made it poignant and special.

The weather was perfect all week, with temperatures in the eighties. The children were reluctant to part. Connor said 'I'm sad to leave my family,' with tears in his eyes. At the airport Jake said he was missing his cousins already. I felt important bonds had been formed for the future. They now recognize their cousins in photographs.

We all missed Kate and the children, and Peter and Angela. When our ship comes home I hope we'll do it all again, all together.

84 POST SCRIPT

I can't head this 'Epilogue' because it isn't over yet.

As a child, every night before I went to bed, I opened my bedroom bay window and breathed in the night air. Its fragrance varied with the season and the weather, ranging from balmy summer nights to foggy autumn evenings when acrid air caught in one's throat; or it was so cold it hurt to breathe. The perfume of the blossom on the ancient lime trees in the adjacent wild garden in summer was unforgettable. I inhaled deeply and wished they would bottle essence of lime. The trees have since been felled, cleared to accommodate a housing development.

My window opened onto Mottingham Lane, the road gently rising, tree lined and bordered by handsome houses with gardens. Old fashioned gas lamps (long ago replaced) lined the street. At the top of the lane where W. G. Grace the cricketer once lived, there was a farm that became riding stables. When I was small the old woman living there used to drive her horse and trap along the lane, holding an upright slender whip, the horses' shoes briskly trotting on the tarmac road. Even then it was a singular sight. It was my home, and I was fully grounded.

Leaning out of the window at night I always said aloud, softly, 'Thank you God for this beautiful world.' It *was* beautiful, and I knew I was fortunate to live in a loving family.

Now I say 'Thank you for my beautiful, loving family, and my interesting life.' Five sons and their wives and a dozen healthy grandchildren have enriched my existence beyond telling.

Virginia 2011.

10970119R00213

Made in the USA
Charleston, SC
20 January 2012